THEIR LAST
FULL MEASURE

ALSO BY JOSEPH WHEELAN

*Bloody Spring: Forty Days That Sealed
the Confederacy's Fate*

*Terrible Swift Sword:
The Life of General Philip H. Sheridan*

*Libby Prison Breakout:
The Daring Escape from the Notorious Civil War Prison*

*Mr. Adams's Last Crusade: John Quincy Adams's
Extraordinary Post-Presidential Life in Congress*

*Invading Mexico: America's Continental Dream
and the Mexican War, 1846–1848*

*Jefferson's Vendetta:
The Pursuit of Aaron Burr and the Judiciary*

*Jefferson's War:
America's First War on Terror, 1801–1805*

THEIR LAST FULL MEASURE

THE FINAL DAYS OF THE CIVIL WAR

JOSEPH WHEELAN

Da Capo Press

A Member of the Perseus Books Group

Published by Da Capo Press
A Member of the Perseus Books Group
www.dacapopress.com

First Da Capo Press edition 2015

Library of Congress Cataloging-in-Publication Data is available for this book.
ISBN 978-0-306-82360-2 (hardcover)
ISBN 978-0-306-82361-9 (e-book)

Da Capo Press books are available at special discounts for bulk purchases in the
U.S. by corporations, institutions, and other organizations. For more information,
please contact the Special Markets Department at the Perseus Books Group,
2300 Chestnut Street, Suite 200, Philadelphia, PA 19103, or call (800) 810-4145,
ext. 5000, or e-mail special.markets@perseusbooks.com.

DESIGN BY JANE RAESE
Set in 12-point Bulmer

3 5 7 9 10 8 6 4 2

TO PAT, SARAH, AND ANN,

whose intelligence, drive, and sense of humor
continue to inspire me

CONTENTS

LIST OF MAPS

ACKNOWLEDGMENTS

I am indebted to the University of North Carolina's libraries, where I received help, guidance, and excellent suggestions as I was researching this book.

My hunt for source material led to the thousands of volumes of published journals, diaries, letters, and unit histories that fill several aisles of Davis Library and UNC's Wilson Library. Three of Wilson's special collections, a jackpot of Civil War primary source material, were particularly useful: the North Carolina Collection, Southern Historical Collection, and Rare Book Collection.

I am grateful to the full-time and student librarians and to the archivists at those Chapel Hill venues for their patience with a researcher's endless questions, and for their eagerness to assist.

The Library of Congress provided photographs and illustrations for this book, as well as good background information. My thanks go out to the librarians who aided my search for this material.

I am grateful to the Library of Virginia and its staff for pointing me to sources that helped me to write this book.

I thank Bob Pigeon, executive editor of Da Capo Press, for his support over the years. Few editors anywhere are as knowledgeable as Bob about American history.

My agent, Roger Williams of New England Publishing Associates, has been a steady source of encouragement and advice, for which I am appreciative.

Finally, my wife Pat has been an anchor as always.

PROLOGUE

Had the army made a show of surrounding [Fort Fisher], it would have been ours, but nothing of the kind was done. . . . There never was a fort that invited soldiers to walk in and take possession more plainly than Fort Fisher.

—ADMIRAL DAVID PORTER,
AFTER FAILED FIRST ATTEMPT TO CAPTURE FORT FISHER[1]

January 12, 1865
FORT FISHER, NORTH CAROLINA

The Yankee squadron had returned. As dread tidings do, the news swept through the Confederate garrison until everyone, from its twenty-nine-year-old commander, Colonel William Lamb, to the lowliest private, was scanning the Atlantic waters for enemy ships.

Before long the Union armada could be seen hovering off Cape Fear; it was the same fleet that had tried, without success, to capture Fort Fisher on Christmas Day. About sixty steam-propelled and sailing ships covered the blue waters to the eastern horizon—frigates, sloops, gunboats, tugs, troop transports, brigs, and barks.

The enemy's reappearance was not a surprise; Lamb had learned on January 8 that Union troop transports were rendezvousing near Beaufort, North Carolina, with Admiral David Porter's North Atlantic Blockading Squadron.

When the Yankee armada glided into position in the waters opposite his fort, Lamb requested reinforcements for his eight hundred men from the departmental commander, General Braxton Bragg. Bragg recognized that the enemy fleet's return meant that it had "the means and the will for a desperate effort."

Confederate President Jefferson Davis had sent Bragg to the Carolinas the previous fall as a troubleshooter. In November Bragg took charge in Wilmington when an attack on Fort Fisher began to appear imminent. He was a native North Carolinian and West Point graduate who had risen to prominence as commander of the Army of Tennessee following General Albert Sidney Johnston's death at Shiloh. Bragg's subsequent battle record was spotty: defeats at Perryville and Stones River followed by success at Chickamauga. After that battle Bragg failed to press his advantage and drive the Union Army out of Tennessee and instead laid siege to Chattanooga. A frustrated General Nathan Bedford Forrest grumbled to his fellow officers, "What does he fight battles for?" Grant drove Bragg from Tennessee in November 1863, and his subordinates clamored for his removal. Davis, who thought highly of Bragg, reluctantly transferred him from Tennessee to Richmond to become Davis's top military adviser.

The day after the appearance of Porter's armada, small boats began landing Union infantrymen from the Army of the James a few miles north of the fort. By 3 p.m. eight thousand bluecoats were ashore, foreclosing the possibility of Rebel reinforcements from Sugar Loaf, a Rebel position seven miles from the fort. At Sugar Loaf was General Robert Hoke's infantry division from the Army of Northern Virginia, sent by Robert E. Lee in December to North Carolina to help keep open the Confederacy's last major port, Wilmington.[2]

๑๏๑

The fort that William Lamb built was essential to both Wilmington's and the Confederacy's survival. Lee had told Lamb that Fort Fisher must absolutely be held or else he would be unable to feed and provision his army. For six months Lee's men had successfully defended Petersburg and Richmond against the powerful Army of the Potomac. But without supplies Lee's men could not hold Virginia's last two strongholds, and the Confederacy's downfall would be inevitable.[3]

As it was, the Union Army's stranglehold on Virginia had steadily tightened throughout 1864, while the effectiveness of Lee's army had just as steadily declined due to inadequate food and clothing. In August 1864 Admiral David Farragut had seized control of Mobile Bay, eliminating the port of Mobile as a destination for blockade-runners. That fall the destruction inflicted by General William Sherman on Georgia's farms and by General Phil Sheridan on Virginia's breadbasket, the Shenandoah Valley, had virtually halted food shipments from those areas. The Confederacy now more than ever depended for its sustenance on the supplies leaking through the Union naval blockade outside Charleston, South Carolina, and the richer stream entering the Cape Fear River under Fort Fisher's forty-eight guns.

During the last nine weeks of 1864 8.5 million pounds of meat, 1.5 million pounds of lead, 1.9 million pounds of saltpeter, 546,000 pairs of shoes, 69,000 rifles, 316,000 pairs of blankets, 520,000 pounds of coffee, forty-three cannons, ninety-seven packages of revolvers, and thousands of units of medicine reached Wilmington and Charleston on blockade-runners. Most of it came through Wilmington because the Union blockade was more porous there; the Union steamships were slow, and the island-dotted Cape Fear River estuary favored concealment. Once ashore, the precious cargo proceeded to Lee's army in Petersburg and Richmond over the Confederacy's ramshackle railroad system and roads.[4]

"Something must be done to close the entrance to Cape Fear River and port of Wilmington," Navy Secretary Gideon Welles wrote in 1864. "There seems some defect in the blockade which makes Wilmington appear an almost open port. . . . Could we seize the forts at the entrance of Cape Fear and close the illicit traffic, it would be almost as important as the capture of Richmond on the fate of the Rebels."[5]

❧

The keystone of Wilmington's unique status as the last fully operational Rebel port was Fort Fisher, the "Gibraltar of the South." Located at the tip of Confederate Point, the fifteen-mile peninsula that descended like a funnel from Wilmington was bordered on the east by the Cape Fear River, on the west by the Atlantic Ocean, and on the south by New Inlet. More than a half-dozen smaller forts and batteries guarded the river between Fort Fisher and Wilmington.

Construction of Fisher began in 1861, but it was Lamb, when he took command of the fort in July 1862, who pushed the project through to completion. Although lacking military experience when he entered the Confederate Army, Lamb was a student of military history, particularly the recent Crimean War; he reportedly designed his fort to resemble the Russian fortifications at Sebastopol. With five hundred black freedmen and slaves, Lamb constructed the Confederacy's largest earthwork of sand, soil, and a mat of saw grass covering the outer walls. The building material was exceptionally effective at absorbing cannon fire.

The fort was made in the shape of the letter "L," with the long side extending southward a little over a mile along the Atlantic beach to Mound Battery at Confederate Point. The fort's right angle pointed northeastward, and its short side, protected by a minefield, a wooden palisade, and a ditch, stretched a third of a mile east to west across the peninsula, blocking a landward approach.[6]

Weeks earlier the same Union flotilla—it too commanded by David Porter—had appeared off Confederate Point, bearing many of the soldiers who were now throwing up northward-facing fieldworks two miles from the fort.

Fifty-one years old and in continuous naval service since he was a ten-year-old midshipman under his commodore father and namesake, David Porter was the unflattering fifth choice of Welles and General Ulysses Grant when they were picking an admiral for the operation in the fall. Grant eliminated Admiral Samuel Lee from consideration because he was not aggressive enough. Welles favored Admiral Farragut, whose exhortation to "Damn the torpedoes, full speed ahead!" at Mobile Bay demonstrated that he was a fighting admiral. But Farragut was in poor health. Then Admirals S. F. DuPont and John Dahlgren were considered and rejected. The honor went to Porter, energetic, ambitious, and self-promoting. He had participated in the capture of New Orleans and led naval forces on the Mississippi River during the siege of Vicksburg.[7]

On December 7 General Benjamin Butler, who commanded the Army of the James and had been a millstone around the neck of Grant throughout 1864, began boarding sixty-five hundred troops onto transports at Bermuda Hundred, Virginia. They sailed down the James River and out of Chesapeake Bay, reaching the rendezvous point twenty miles off New Inlet on December 15. Porter arrived three days later—and so did an Atlantic storm, forcing the armada to put in at Beaufort, North Carolina.

Butler's assault plan depended upon the presumption that exploding a powder ship beside the fort would inflict such catastrophic damage on the enemy that Union troops could easily seize the fort. Butler had come up with the unorthodox plan after reading a newspaper story about the accidental explosion of two powder barges in the British port of Erith and the massive destruction that resulted. A similar explosion at Fort Fisher, Butler believed, could shatter the massive earthwork, disable the fort's guns, and strike terror into its garrison.

A prominent Massachusetts politician and a polished lobbyist, Butler laid out his plan to President Abraham Lincoln and his advisers. It aroused little enthusiasm: Lincoln was noncommittal, and Navy Secretary Welles flatly opposed it. But Porter thought it was worth trying; such an explosion, he believed, would stupefy Fort Fisher's garrison and cause homes in Wilmington "to tumble to the ground and much demoralize the people." Ignored was the opinion of the Union Army's chief engineer, General Richard Delafield, an expert on explosives and their destructive power: "I can find no reason to believe that these solid masses or sand hills and massive walls, distant more than 450 yards from the site of the powder explosion, are to be removed or destroyed in any way," Delafield concluded.[8]

About midnight on December 23 Commander Alexander Rhind and his crew guided the *Louisiana,* an aged, flat-bottomed warship, to within three hundred yards of the beach alongside the fort and dropped anchor. They switched on timers and slow fuses and lit a fire in the stern as a backup in case the fuses and timers failed to detonate the 185 tons of powder on board. Piling into a small boat, Rhind and his men rowed away to a nearby Union warship.

Thousands of men anxiously watched from the armada as the scheduled time of the explosion, 1:18 a.m., passed in silence. Then, at 1:46 a.m. on December 24, there were four loud explosions. The timers had evidently failed, and the fuses had detonated the powder in the separate compartments where it had been stored. Further muting the impact, the powder ship had drifted farther from shore with the outgoing tide. So little damage was done to the fort that Confederate troops believed that a ship's boiler might have exploded. Colonel Lamb wrote in his diary later that day, "A blockader got aground near fort; set fire to herself and blew up."[9]

On the 24th Porter's fleet drew within a half-mile of the fort and furiously shelled it for five hours. Although the bombardment destroyed half of the Confederates' quarters, Lamb reported only slight damage to the parapets, earthwork, and guns, with just four gun carriages sustaining damage.[10]

On Christmas Day the fleet resumed its shelling, and Butler's sixty-five hundred troops landed north of Fort Fisher. While half of them prepared to advance on Fort Fisher, the rest moved northward to repel any attempts to reinforce the fort from Wilmington; they captured two batteries and more than two hundred prisoners. A Rebel prisoner reported that General Robert E. Lee, concerned about Fort Fisher's fate, had dispatched Hoke's division from his army in Virginia. It had recently arrived in Wilmington, he said.

This was enough to alarm Butler, who, from the battles around Richmond, had firsthand knowledge of the fighting ability of Hoke's men.

While Butler fretted, General Godfrey Weitzel, Butler's infantry commander, continued to push his three thousand men toward Fort Fisher. Yankee skirmishers reached the fort under an umbrella of naval gunfire. Then, at twilight, the bombardment ceased and the Confederates emerged from their bombproof shelters and began shooting at Weitzel's men.

Butler called off the attack. "The place could not be carried by assault," he informed Porter, "as it was left substantially uninjured as a defensive work by the navy fire." Fort Fisher's defenses could be overcome by "nothing but the operations of a regular siege," he wrote.

The troops were re-embarked on their transports and returned to Hampton Roads—so hastily that seven hundred were left ashore and, because of storms, could not be evacuated for two days.[11]

Grant telegraphed Lincoln the night of December 28: "The Wilmington expedition has proven a gross and culpable failure." Welles wrote in his diary, "It was a mistake that General Butler, a civilian without military knowledge or experience in matters of this kind, should have been selected for this command."[12]

"To show that the rebels have no force here, these men [those left behind on the beach] have been on shore two days without being molested," a seething Porter wrote Welles on December 27 from his flagship *Malvern*. "Had the army made a show of surrounding [Fort Fisher], it would have been ours, but nothing of the kind was done. . . . There never was a fort that invited soldiers to walk in and take possession more plainly than Fort Fisher. . . . If General [Winfield Scott] Hancock, with 10,000 men, was sent down here, we could walk right into the fort." Porter all but begged to be allowed to try again.[13]

Grant had long wanted to be rid of Butler. Throughout the Overland Campaign of May and June 1864, Butler, at the head of the Army of the James, had been Grant's weakest link. A timid general like Bragg, Butler had failed to seize opportunities that a competent commander might have exploited to capture Richmond or Petersburg. Butler had done neither. Yet his political connections in Massachusetts were so important to Lincoln's 1864 presidential campaign that Grant was handcuffed in his attempts to remove Butler. With Lincoln's reelection in November, there was now nothing to prevent Butler from being relieved of command.

"I am constrained to request the removal of Maj. Gen. B. F. Butler from the command of the Department of N.C. & Va.," Grant wrote War Secretary Edwin Stanton and Lincoln. "In my absence Gen. Butler necessarily commands, and there is a lack of confidence felt in his Military ability, making him an unsafe commander for a large army." On January 7 Lincoln relieved Butler as commander of the Department of North Carolina and Virginia and sent him to Lowell, Massachusetts, to await orders.

Before General Edward Ord was even appointed Butler's successor, a second expedition to Fort Fisher was being mounted from Hampton Roads. This time eight thousand troops, instead of the sixty-five hundred dispatched in December, sailed as a Provisional Corps under the command of General Alfred Terry.

A division commander in the Army of the James, before the war Terry was clerk of the Superior Court in New Haven, Connecticut. The thirty-seven-year-old Terry had participated in amphibious operations at Port Royal and Charleston, South Carolina. He and his division were on the Fort Fisher beach in December when Butler elected to withdraw.

To conceal the strike force's mission, its posted orders said that it was going to join General Sherman's army in Savannah. The sealed orders that Terry opened after the armada cast off revealed that its actual objective was a second attempt to capture Fort Fisher.[14]

JANUARY 1865

The deep waters [are] closing over us. And we are—in this house—like the outsiders at the time of the Flood. We care for none of these things. We eat, drink, laugh, dance, in lightness of heart!!!

—DIARIST MARY CHESNUT[1]

The truth is the whole army is burning with an insatiable desire to wreak vengeance upon South Carolina. I almost tremble at her fate, but feel that she deserves all that seems in store for her.

—GENERAL WILLIAM SHERMAN[2]

This amendment is a King's cure for all the evils. It winds the whole thing up.

—PRESIDENT ABRAHAM LINCOLN,
UPON THE PASSAGE OF THE THIRTEENTH AMENDMENT
ABOLISHING SLAVERY[3]

January 1, 1865
PETERSBURG, VIRGINIA

On New Year's Day it was quiet along the thirty-five miles of trenches and fortifications that stitched the barren countryside from Bermuda Hundred to the lines south of Petersburg. There was no shooting because the Yankees knew that the women of Richmond and Petersburg planned to bring the Confederate enlisted men in the trenches a home-cooked New Year's feast.

The Rebels had reminded the bluecoats that they had not fired on them when they celebrated Thanksgiving, and so General Ulysses S. Grant announced an informal truce; there would be no firing during the holiday except in response to Confederate gunfire. "We are not to be outdone, either in fighting or magnanimity," Grant's chief of staff, General John Rawlins, wrote to his wife.[4]

The Southern women had held fund-raisers before undertaking the massive job of buying and preparing food for fifty thousand enlisted men. This would have been daunting enough in normal times, but during a time of food shortages in Richmond and Petersburg it was extraordinarily challenging. The half-starved Confederate defenders looked forward to their feast with keen appetites.[5]

Menaced on three sides by Grant's army, Richmond and Petersburg were the castle keep of the South's dream of sovereignty, now receding with the Confederacy's boundaries. Tennessee and Georgia had fallen out of its orbit at the end of 1864; what remained east of the Mississippi River were the Carolinas, Alabama, and parts of Virginia and Mississippi. To seize or defend these last remnants of the proud Confederacy, the soldiers in blue and gray were prepared to give "the last full measure of devotion" that President Abraham Lincoln had spoken of when he honored the dead at Gettysburg.

※

For nearly two hundred days, since June 1864, when Grant's armies had crossed the James River and attempted to seize Virginia's second-largest city, the enemies had been stalemated outside the "Cockade City." Like troglodytes, they had dug in, and the fortifications had multiplied like rabbit warrens and were defended in heat, rain, cold, and snow. The massive armies—124,000 Yankees in the armies of the James and the Potomac facing about 57,000 Rebels in Robert E. Lee's Army of Northern Virginia—were in ceaseless contact, and every day sharpshooters and sporadic mortar fire carried off a few combatants. Sometimes there were feints and flanking movements, sharp skirmishes, and full-throated battles.[6]

Major John Esten Cooke, a Confederate staff officer, wrote of the months-long stalemate, "At Petersburg, the fighting seemed to decide little, and the bloody collisions had no names. . . . It was one long battle, day and night, week after week, and month after month—during the heat of summer, the sad hours of autumn, and the cold days and nights of winter."[7]

On the first day of 1865 the battlefield was muddy, shorn of every scrap of wood, carved by dense networks of labyrinthine defensive works, and pitted by artillery fire. Between the lines, sometimes just a few hundred yards apart, were abatis and wire entanglements and chevaux-de-frise—timbers bored with holes through which sharpened stakes menaced attackers. Like birds of prey, sharpshooters and mortarmen on both sides kept a keen watch for the chance to pick off a careless soldier or to drop a round in a group of enemy troops.[8]

The seven-month stalemate had begun in June 1864, when Lee's men stopped Grant's army within sight of Petersburg's church spires after it had marched one hundred miles through Virginia from the Rapidan River—the most successful Union penetration into Virginia of the war. It was also the war's costliest campaign: sixty-six thousand Union casualties and thirty-three thousand Confederate losses in just six weeks. Grant had little trouble replacing his losses, but the replacements were not of the quality of the volunteers they succeeded; many were draftees, "bounty men," or substitutes paid to serve in someone's place. Lee's losses were fewer, but he had been unable to entirely make them up. Although Grant had failed in his object of destroying Lee's Army of Northern Virginia, he had succeeded in tethering Lee to Richmond and Petersburg, preempting any major Rebel offenses in the North like those in 1862 and 1863.

Lee had warned his generals that if his army were forced back into Richmond's defenses, it would become a siege, with defeat inevitable. Lee had been right about the siege but so far had thwarted the Union attacks to break or flank the Confederate lines or to cut the two railroads that still supplied Petersburg and Richmond.

Since June both sides had improved their fieldworks until they had become permanent fortifications and, in the process, had revived the arcane lexicon of siege warfare. Besides the usual entanglements and obstacles, the battlefield featured outlying lunettes—small earth-and-timber field forts—to stop or slow attackers before they reached the massive earthworks and forts. The main fortifications had walls dozens of feet thick at their bases and were defended by ditches eight feet wide and six feet deep. The walls were reinforced by thick bundles of sticks and twigs—fascines— and gabions, which were tall, cylindrical wicker baskets filled with dirt. There were parapets for infantrymen, loopholes for sharpshooters, firing platforms for artillery, and "splinter proofs"—thick shelters reinforced by railroad iron where artillerists could hide from enemy counterfire. The earthworks' walls were tall enough to conceal soldiers walking and standing upright in the wide trenches behind them. There were traverses to deflect flank attacks and a honeycomb of rifle pits, secondary ditches and embankments, and "bomb proofs," where soldiers could hide during enemy bombardments. Beyond that, the engineers had dammed creeks to create water barriers up to thirty feet deep, and they were constantly boring tunnels, either in the hope of exploding or thwarting another massive mine like the one that Union engineers had detonated beneath an enemy salient east of Petersburg on July 30. It obliterated the salient, killed three hundred Confederates outright, and created a thirty-feet-deep crater into which the badly led Union troops swarmed—and where they were slaughtered by Rebel reinforcements. These mines, countermines, and "listening galleries" for detecting enemy digging snaked for miles beneath the wasteland. The tortuous defensive complexes eerily adumbrated the Great War trench systems of fifty years hence.

It all required constant upkeep, with work parties, mainly from the combat units, performing maintenance duties and building new fortifications. The work was assigned to units by rotation. The 13th South Carolina detailed two to three hundred men to dig defensive works eight hours a day, six days a week, for two months. Lee requested five thousand black laborers to work on the Rebel defenses for sixty days but got just two thousand men because some slave owners claimed the soldiers abused their men.[9]

By turn too, regiments also manned the earthworks and rifle pits for days at a time. When a unit completed its shift on the line and another took its place, it retired to the surprisingly roomy bombproofs, dug deep behind the trenches and lined with timber and sheet iron. Some of them had fireplaces. When there was wood and fire, the living accommodations were almost comfortable, and the soldiers entertained themselves with fiddle and banjo music and stage plays limned by torchlight. They provided protection from artillery and mortar attacks, and the men often slept there too. Farther to the rear, units not on the line lived almost like townspeople in wood-and-mud huts built along streets. The soldiers dreaded leaving their firesides to stand picket duty in the muddy trenches in the cold and the rain and the snow. "It was endurance without relief; sleeplessness without exhilaration; inactivity without rest; constant apprehension requiring ceaseless watching," wrote a Confederate soldier.

Firewood was a priority. Union wood parties were able to fan out over a wide area to collect firewood, but the Confederates, having used the readily accessible wood within their circumscribed area, had a more difficult time. "We suffered for firewood," wrote Lieutenant J. F. J. Caldwell of the 1st South Carolina. "The growth about the camp, never heavy, was soon consumed by the troops . . . we were obliged to carry logs on our shoulders for the distance of a mile or more, in order to have any fire at all."[10]

The winter was an unusually cold one—so achingly cold on some mornings that the water began turning to ice in the soldiers' hands when they washed their faces; so cold that water froze in canteens; so cold that the streams the soldiers had dammed into lakes to thwart the enemy froze solid. In the North, where one could nearly forget that it was wartime, the thick ice covering the Potomac River attracted legions of skaters.[11]

The sufferings of Lee's troops far surpassed the discomforts of Grant's men. The Rebels shivered in thin blankets and ragged clothing; many of them had no shoes. Pneumonia and typhoid carved gaps in the ranks. Scurvy was commonplace because of the absence of fruit and vegetables. Subsisting mainly on half-rations of corn meal and bacon, the Confederates lost weight, strength, and stamina. At the same time, the Confederate currency was losing value so that a soldier's monthly pay—which came at intervals, if at all, these days—might buy a pair of socks.[12]

A Petersburg woman was appalled by a Florida soldier's appearance when he begged at her door for food. "His worn cotton clothes were hardly sufficient . . . to conceal his nakedness," Bessie Callender wrote. "When I handed him food his hands were filthy, his nails long like claws, and between his fingers were sores, which he said were itchy. I handed him some food on a plate, but he began at once to eat like a wild animal."[13]

But not all Confederates endured the same privations. Officers attended social affairs hosted by wealthy Petersburg families who provided music, dancing with eligible young women, and ample food. The Third Corps officers sponsored a "tournament" just before Christmas 1864 that was modeled upon the tradition of the English elite. The highlight was a coronation ball at the Bollingbrook Hotel.

Moreover, while army chaplains near the lines met the spiritual needs of the enlisted men, the officers attended Episcopalian churches in town. After services Lee, described as "a great ladies man," often flirted with the young women outside church. "The old genl. goes smooching around among all the pretty girls," wrote Captain Charles Dimmock, a prominent Confederate engineer, "& joked them as if he were a boy of 18."[14]

❧

Across the lines the Yankees also suffered from the same rain, snow, and cold, but they at least were well clothed and shod, and they had plenty of food. The US Military Railroad, operating fifteen trains daily that ran behind the Union lines, kept the Yankees supplied with food and ammunition. Even so, trench life was no idyll for Grant's men. They, like the Rebels, were plagued by afflictions and dangers small and large, from lice and, in the summertime, fly swarms to shrieking mortars—"the most disgusting, low-lived things imaginable," in the opinion of an engineer—and the black-hearted sharpshooters who transformed a mundane chore such as fetching water into a terrifying footrace.

"We have an indefinable dread, our nerves subjected to a continued strain which we know cannot end till the war ends, or we are wiped out," wrote a Rhode Island officer. Soldiers who cracked under the tension were sent to quiet "convalescent camps."[15]

❧

Far from the fighting, Northern citizens were more optimistic about victory than they had ever been. "Much has been done toward destroying the rebellion in these last twelve months. It is far weaker tonight than it was a year ago," wrote the diarist George Templeton Strong on December 31. A prominent New York lawyer, Strong was one of the founders of the US Sanitary Commission, a private relief organization that aided wounded Union soldiers. "God aid our efforts to put it [the rebellion] down and establish unity and peace this coming year as the last!" he wrote.[16]

Life in the North went on much as before, suggesting that the Union was not putting everything it had into the war. College rowing and baseball teams competed as always, and many new colleges had been established since the war began: among them MIT, Cornell, Boston College, and Vassar. People attended the theater, the opera, and the racetrack, oblivious to the desperate fighting and dying that was occurring a few hundred miles away.

Northern businesses reaped enormous profits after the financial panic attending the war's outbreak subsided. In Chicago seven thousand new structures went up in 1863 alone. Farmers enjoyed barn-bursting harvests of wheat and corn and surpluses of pork and wool. Thirty-eight arms factories produced five thousand rifles each day, compared with one hundred rifles made in the South. The US government, which would spend $3.4 billion during the war—two-thirds of it on goods and services for the soldiers—became a behemoth. The Quartermaster Department, with one hundred thousand employees, was larger than any private US business. Financial houses flourished. "It was distinctly a money-making age," wrote Emerson Fite of the North during the Civil War.[17]

The New Year's Day feast proved to be a terrible disappointment for the Confederate soldiers. Each member of a North Carolina regiment received "a few mouthfuls" of food and a teaspoon of apple butter. Another soldier reported getting a few small pieces of meat and "about four good mouthfuls of light bread."[18]

The 18th Georgia waited and watched all day for the arrival of its holiday meal. "What a long day that seemed to be!" wrote John Coxe. "We whiled away the tedious hours by telling stories and cracking jokes. At midnight Coxe went to sleep after the men on night watch promised to summon their comrades when dinner arrived. About 3 a.m. the Georgians were awakened and told that a detail had gone out to meet the dinner wagon. "But O what a disappointment when the squad returned and issued to each man only one small sandwich made up of two tiny slices of bread and a thin piece of ham!" After they ate it a middle-aged corporal lit his pipe and said, "God bless our noble women! It was all they could do; it was all they had." The veteran soldiers broke down and wept.[19]

The corporal was right; the women had tried their best to serve a holiday feast. The problem was that there was too little food in Petersburg and Richmond, and what was available was prohibitively expensive because of speculation and profiteering.

∂ℭ

The North's "total war" strategy of destroying the South's war-making resources was working; it was squeezing the life out of the Confederacy. The previous year had seen General William Sherman's army march three hundred miles through Georgia, destroying barns, fields, railroads, and livestock along a sixty-mile-wide swath. General Phil Sheridan's army burned Virginia's Shenandoah Valley, devastating Virginia's breadbasket and smashing Confederate General Jubal Early's army. Sheridan now controlled the valley from the Potomac River to Staunton. These destructive campaigns deprived Richmond and Petersburg of food from Georgia and the Shenandoah.

In 1864, too, Admiral David Farragut's squadron had fought its way into Mobile Bay. Although the city of Mobile remained in Rebel hands, Farragut's sailors had eliminated the port as a destination of blockade-runners. The increasingly efficient Union blockade had virtually closed Charleston too. That left just Wilmington, North Carolina, as the only viable Confederate port. Consequently, fewer imports were reaching the South, and fewer exports—cotton and tobacco, mainly—were leaving the Confederacy for sale abroad.

As a result of these developments, the South was now growing too much cotton for export and too little food for local consumption. The supply-demand imbalance and inflation had driven prices through the roof in Richmond and Petersburg, where most of the food came from the Carolinas and other Rebel-controlled parts of the South over two dilapidated railroads: the Richmond & Danville and the Southside Railroad, which ran from Petersburg to Lynchburg in southwestern Virginia.

The Confederacy was also grappling with a currency crisis, with $600 million in circulation in 1864. Before the war just $70 million circulated in the same eleven states. The Confederate Congress adopted emergency measures: encouraging the exchange of bills over $5 for 4 percent government bonds, with lower-denomination notes exchangeable for new notes at a three-to-two rate. After January 1 the old notes were subject to a 100 percent tax. The vigorous measures halved the amount of circulating currency but took longer to take effect than expected. Before they did, the value of the Confederate dollar in relation to the Union greenback fell from twenty-to-one to sixty-to-one, and some food suppliers stopped accepting Confederate scrip altogether.

The hyperinflated state of the Confederate currency was best described by the popular adage, "You take your money to market in the market basket and bring home what you buy in your pocketbook." In January flour cost $1,250 per barrel, and wood $100 per load; two months later wood would sell for $5 per stick. An apple cost $2, a pair of boots $250. "Second-hand shirts" were going for $40 apiece. A bed that once cost $10 now sold for $700. "What I fear is *starvation*," wrote the War Department clerk John B. Jones. Burglary was the great fear of the fortunate ones who still possessed a well-stocked larder and fuel. Fields, barns, and smokehouses were stripped of cows, pigs, flour, and bacon. By March a restaurant dinner and a night's lodging in Richmond cost more than $2,000.

The pinch of hunger and want worsened during the unusually cold winter. "None but the rich speculators and quartermasters and commissary speculators have a supply of food and fuel," wrote Jones, adding, "Much suffering exists in the city; and prices are indeed fabulous." He blamed speculators, bitterly observing that there would be enough food and clothing for everyone "if we had a Roman dictator to order an equitable distribution."

"Many people have no meat on their tables for months at a time," wrote diarist Judith McGuire. A friend who wanted something hot to drink at night and could not afford coffee, tea, sugar, or milk had to settle for hot water.[20]

Captain Charles Blackford, a military judge in Richmond, lived with his family "very hardly, and counted many meals as sumptuous over which now the most patient would grumble." They did without butter, coffee, tea, or sugar. "We had flour and meal, and the flour was made into very fair biscuits, and we had fat middling and sometimes a potato or cabbage." The Blackfords sometimes attended parties hosted by an upper-class friend and were surprised that the wealthy still lived in the grand old style. "The viands were very abundant, consisting of oysters, turkeys, game, and everything usual on such occasions, including champagne and other wines. The constant wonder was where they all came from."[21]

Living under an edged sword that might flash down upon them at any time, young upper-class men and women affected an almost frenzied gaiety. They attended parties where there was music and dancing but no food—"starvation parties," where only water was served.

There was also a "perfect mania" for matrimony. "Some of the churches may be seen open and lighted almost every night for bridals, and wherever I turn I hear of marriages in prospect," wrote McGuire. Sallie Putnam wrote that the patriotic young bride of a Confederate soldier remarked, "I had rather be the widow of a brave man than the wife of a coward," something that a Spartan wife might have said two millennia earlier. T. C. DeLeon, a protégé of Jefferson Davis, said the vivacity was "merely superficial, and under it was a fixed and impenetrable gloom . . . and over all brooded the dread cloud of a speedy evacuation of the city."[22]

By early 1865 Richmond had a "wretched" appearance: dilapidated homes and businesses, citizens in threadbare clothing, mud everywhere, even in the corridors of hotels, whose carpets had long ago been ripped out and sent to the military stores to be cut up for blankets. Many shops had nothing in them except broken packing cases and straw.

John B. Jones estimated that the city's population exceeded one hundred thousand, but the produce markets could not subsist seventy thousand. "Then there is the army in the vicinity, which *must* be fed," he wrote. City officials discussed the possibility of sending away "some thousands of useless consumers," but they never made a plan or chose a place to send them.

With rumors of evacuation growing by the day, however, a voluntary exodus had begun. Along Richmond's residential streets red flags fluttered, each signaling an auction of household goods, prefatory to a family's departure from the capital for Charlotte or Salisbury, North Carolina; Milledgeville, Georgia; or any safe place to the south.[23]

Lee asked his wife, Mary, whether she would leave their home on East Franklin Street in Richmond if his army had to abandon the capital. "You must consider the question & make up your mind," he wrote. "You will be able to retain nothing in the house, & I do not see how you can live or where go." She said that she would stay.[24]

Like the Confederate soldiers in the trenches, the civilians prayed daily for God's deliverance. "The Union Prayer-Meetings are great comforts to us," wrote McGuire. "They are attended by crowds; ministers of all denominations officiate at them" to lead prayers for the Confederacy and hymns of praise. "I am constantly expecting the blessing of God in a way that we know not," she wrote. One Communion Sunday at St. Paul's "not a sound was heard" when Lee, Jefferson Davis, and Confederate Treasury Secretary George Trenholm came forward and knelt before the sacramental table. At that moment the choir and organ began "Gloria in Excelsis," and to McGuire "it seemed indeed as if that house of God was the very gate of Heaven."[25]

Christmas had been an especially somber time in Richmond and across the South, where "the dire evils . . . had shrouded our land in sorrow and misery," wrote Sallie Putnam. "Praise and thanksgiving were blended with fasting and prayer, with deep humiliation and earnest contrition." At Christmas dinner "we sat down to the poverty-stricken board. We counted again the vacant chairs and glanced with eyes blinded by tears, upon the somber living of woe."[26]

For months John B. Jones had remarked that "my ribs stick out, being covered by skin only, for the want of sufficient food." But by January he was writing that his greatest fear now was "*starvation*; and I sincerely wish my family were on the old farm on the Eastern Shore of Virginia until the next campaign is over."[27]

Private Spencer Barnes of the 30th North Carolina, a three-year veteran of Lee's army, wrote to his sister on January 1, "Every thing looks quite gloomy at the present & prospects don't seam [*sic*] to get no brighter I hav [*sic*] hoped for peace and I fear that peace is never for me to see again I hav [*sic*] become disheartened like a great many others that is I don't care which away the war goes." "A mans life," he said, "has become so here it is not vallied [valued] no more than we woud [*sic*] a dog there."[28]

At the same time twenty-eight women from the Shenandoah Valley were petitioning the Confederate government to permit them and other Southern females to become soldiers. Outraged by Sheridan's destruction of the Shenandoah's farms and fields, the women vowed "to endure any sacrifice—any privation for the ultimate success of our Holy Cause." The women's offer was not accepted.[29]

Mary Chesnut, the diarist and social maven, had recently left Richmond for her home in South Carolina, where her husband, General James Chesnut, was now recruiting troops. She brooded in her journal, "The deep waters [are] closing over us. And we are—in this house—like the outsiders at the time of the Flood. We care for none of these things. We eat, drink, laugh, dance, in lightness of heart!!!" At social gatherings the many wounded officers "seem as utterly oblivious of the volcano we stand upon as our girls themselves." Oblivious Chesnut was not; she said Southerners were "living a Greek tragedy" in which the outcome was foreordained. "Here we stand—despair in our hearts . . . and our houses burnt, or about to be, over our heads."[30]

When John B. Jones went to the War Department on the morning of January 2 he found War Secretary James Seddon sitting before the fire with his head between his knees, bowed down by the enormity of the problems he faced. "Affairs are gloomy enough," wrote Jones, "and the question is how Richmond and Virginia will be saved. Gen. Lee is despondent."[31]

∂∿

Lee's pessimism was understandable after the slew of bad news he had received during the last weeks of 1864. On November 30 General John Bell Hood, who had abandoned Georgia to march into Tennessee with thirty-five thousand troops, suffered heavy losses at Franklin, Tennessee, while attacking General John Schofield's Union corps. Schofield, with Hood in pursuit, withdrew to Nashville to join the rest of General George Thomas's army. Then, on December 15 and 16, Thomas emerged from Nashville—just as Grant was poised to relieve him for not attacking Hood—and destroyed Hood's army. The remnants retreated across the Tennessee River and into Mississippi. Hood marched into Tupelo with just seventeen thousand men. "It was no longer an army," wrote General P. G. T. Beauregard when he saw what was left of it. At his own request, Hood was relieved of command.[32]

On December 17 General William Sherman's army of sixty thousand rugged Western troops reached the outskirts of Savannah, and Sherman demanded the city's surrender. Rather than lose his army, General William Hardee and his Confederate corps abandoned the city. Civil authorities surrendered Savannah on December 21.

Then, on Christmas Day, General Benjamin Butler's troop transports and Union Admiral David Porter's squadron had launched their amphibious attack on Fort Fisher. Only Butler's timidity had prevented the fort's capture.

Lee had warned Jefferson Davis two months earlier, after part of his army was driven back by Union forces at Burgess Mill south of Petersburg, that "I fear a great calamity will befall us" unless the army received an infusion of manpower. "On last Thursday at Burgess's Mill we had three brigades to oppose six divisions. On our left [were just] two divisions to oppose two corps. The inequality is too great."[33]

But at a time when Lee desperately needed more men, low morale, desertions, and hunger were steadily siphoning off troops and eroding the combat capability of those who remained—"Lee's Miserables" they sometimes called themselves.

"Truly deplorable" conditions throughout the South were another factor, observed Colonel Walter Taylor, Lee's adjutant-general. Mothers, wives, and sisters beseeched the soldiers "in the name of all that was dear" to come home. The army tried to intercept letters containing such pleadings, but Lee's army continued to shrink; only ample food for the soldiers and their relatives back home could stop the desertions steadily draining essential manpower.[34]

On the first of January 125,994 Confederates were counted "present for duty" in units east of the Mississippi River, while 198,494 were reported absent from the ranks. Between October 1 and February 4 nearly 72,000 men deserted, with their numbers increasing daily after mid-January. Private John N. Adams of the 37th North Carolina said that he "at last . . . got so hungry that the site [sic] of a well fed Yankee troop was too much. Taking a flag of truce, [I] crossed to the other side."[35]

"The insufficiency of food and non-payment of the troops have more to do with the dissatisfaction among the troops than anything else," Lee told War Secretary Seddon. "I have no doubt that there is suffering for want of food. The ration is too small for men who have to undergo so much exposure and labor as ours." He admonished Seddon to demand from the Commissary Department "increased effort, greater experience in business, and intelligent management. It may be that all is done that can be, but I am not satisfied that we cannot do more."[36]

Although rations and soldiers' pay were the chief reasons for the increasing desertions, they were not the only ones. Lee's army, at its best when maneuvering or on the march, had been penned up in the damp Petersburg trenches for six months. The Army of Northern Virginia, which excelled in the flash of battle, was instead forced to endure the steady attrition exacted by sharpshooters and enemy artillery, like the dripping of a faucet.[37]

Moreover, Abraham Lincoln's reelection and Sherman's march to the sea had been demoralizing as well. Walter Lee of the 4th North Carolina Infantry wrote in January, "The great part of the soldiers seem to be in low spirits and a good many say the Confederacy has 'gone up' . . . and that we are whipped. I have never seen the men so discouraged before." An Alabama soldier, R. P. Scarborough, believed that the men's spirits were at their lowest point since the war began.[38]

Sherman had punctuated his epic march from Atlanta to the sea with the exclamation point of Savannah's bloodless capture. Major Thomas Osborn of the 1st New York Light Artillery wrote to his brother from Savannah that it was "practically one of the easiest campaigns we have had" yet "one of the really historical campaigns of the war, much more so than some where vastly more fighting was done."

The red-haired, hyperkinetic Sherman celebrated the victory by writing to President Abraham Lincoln, "I beg to present you as a Christmas-gift the city of Savannah, with one hundred and fifty heavy guns and plenty of ammunition, also about twenty-five thousand bales of cotton."[39]

Lincoln responded with heartfelt gratitude: "Many, many, thanks for your Christmas-gift—the capture of Savannah. When you were leaving Atlanta for the Atlantic coast, I was anxious, if not fearful; but feeling that you were the better judge, and remembering that 'nothing risked, nothing gained' I did not interfere. Now, the undertaking being a success, the honor is all yours. . . . But what next? I suppose it will be safer if I leave Gen. Grant and yourself to decide."[40]

Sherman's march and Savannah's capitulation convinced many Southerners that the Rebellion was now doomed, and they held the Rebel government responsible. Sherman saw the change in the ebbing of "the terrible energy" displayed by the Confederates early in the war and in Southerners' growing fear of the Union's Western soldiers. Sherman's men too were beginning to believe themselves invincible. "It is simply and physically impossible for them [the Confederates] to defeat this army," wrote Major Henry Hitchcock of Sherman's staff to his wife, Mary. When among Southerners, one often heard the fervent hope expressed for a swift ending rather than a long, agonized one.[41] "The Rebellion is drawing to a close," wrote Navy Secretary Gideon Welles. "These operations in the heart of the Rebel region are destroying their self-confidence, and there are symptoms of extreme dissatisfaction among them."[42]

Others in Washington thought that Sherman's march was overrated—"illusory"—because so little fighting was done. War Secretary Edwin Stanton even criticized Sherman for letting Hardee escape from Savannah. "It is a sore disappointment that Hardee was able to get off his 15,000 from Sherman's 60,000," he grumbled. "It looks like protracting the war while their armies continue to escape"—alluding to Hood's flight from Tennessee after George Thomas's army defeated the Rebels at Nashville. But this viewpoint ignored the corrosive effect of these losses on Southern morale and the Southern armies' formerly "terrible energy."[43]

And now there was the question that Lincoln had asked Sherman—what next? Grant and Sherman had been exchanging views on this topic. On December 6 Grant had told Sherman that he wanted him to secure a base in Savannah and then sail with the rest of his army to Virginia "to close out Lee and his Army."

❧

At his City Point headquarters Grant, imperturbable as always, was busy planning his 1865 campaign, his second as the Union Army's general-in-chief. The major accomplishments of his 1864 campaign—the Army of the Potomac's march to Petersburg, Sherman's Georgia campaign, and Sheridan's Shenandoah Valley triumphs—had thrown the Confederacy irrevocably on the defensive. The days were now gone when Lee's armies would stream across the Potomac River into Maryland and spread panic throughout the North.

Grant was determined to end the war now, and he made his plans with confidence. Lieutenant Colonel Horace Porter, Grant's aide-de-camp, described the general-in-chief as being at the peak of his powers. "He was at this period indefatigable in his labors." Grant "never appeared to better advantage than in directing these masterly movements, which covered a theater of war greater than that of any campaigns in modern history," Porter wrote.

The forty-two-year-old Grant was a nondescript-looking man of average height and weight who preferred to wear a private's uniform, with his three stars sewn onto the shoulders, to the gold braid and epaulets most generals wore. Nine months as the Union Army's highest-ranking officer had neither changed Grant's appearance nor made him less modest or laconic. Lincoln had appointed the victor of Vicksburg and Chattanooga to command all of the Union armies in March 1864 after three years of failure by Eastern generals.

Lincoln hoped an aggressive Western general might at last crush the Rebellion, and he knew that without victories it was unlikely that he would be reelected. Even worse, his successor would almost surely give in to the South's demand for sovereignty rather than continue the war. Grant's strategy had produced victories, rescuing Lincoln's campaign, but they had not come from the Army of the Potomac in Virginia. Grant, who had become that army's de facto commander, had shifted the battleground from northern Virginia to Petersburg and Richmond, but without defeating Lee's army.

Grant's new plan reprised his 1864 strategy of putting several armies in motion at once, thereby preventing the Confederates from transferring men from quiet sectors to threatened ones. Besides giving Sherman a large role in the campaign, Grant planned to strip Thomas's triumphant army in Tennessee of more than fifty thousand troops and use them to help launch four smaller campaigns:

- General John Schofield's XXIII Corps would join General Alfred Terry's expeditionary corps in Wilmington after Terry captured Fort Fisher, and together they would march to Goldsboro.
- General A. J. Smith would reinforce General Edward Canby's Gulf Coast forces with sixteen thousand infantrymen, capture Mobile, and march north through Alabama.

- At the same time, General James Wilson and twelve thousand cavalrymen would enter northern Alabama and capture Selma and Montgomery.
- General John Stoneman would lead four thousand cavalrymen from eastern Tennessee into North Carolina.

While these armies were on the march, Grant, joined by Sherman in Virginia, would crush Lee's Virginia army. If Lee attempted to escape into southwestern Virginia, Thomas, with the remainder of his army from Nashville, would block Lee's path.[44]

⁂

Sherman disagreed with Grant over the role his army should play. "I had expected, upon reducing Savannah, instantly to march to Columbia, S.C., thence to Raleigh, and thence to report to you," he told the general-in-chief, although he conceded that traveling by ship would be quicker; he could reach Grant by mid-January. By land it would take at least six weeks after Savannah's capitulation for his army to join Grant.

Three days after writing that letter Sherman sent another one to Grant, expanding on his argument for marching rather than sailing to Virginia. "We can punish South Carolina as she deserves, and as thousands of people in Georgia hoped we would do," Sherman wrote. "I do sincerely believe that the whole United States, North and South, would rejoice to have this Army turned loose in South Carolina, to devastate that State in the manner we have done in Georgia."[45]

Thomas's victory over Hood in Tennessee, replied Grant, "has shaken me" in his determination to bring Sherman to Virginia by ship to "wipe out Lee." "I doubt whether you may not accomplish more toward that result where you are than if brought here," especially because Grant had been informed it would take two months to transport Sherman's army to Virginia by ship, "with all the other calls there is for ocean transportation." Grant withdrew his insistence that Sherman sail to Virginia.

It was becoming a Grant signature to yield to his two favorite field generals, Sherman and Phil Sheridan, whenever they disagreed with his orders on the grounds of wanting to pursue a more aggressive strategy. Grant continually encouraged aggressiveness in his top generals wherever he found it.[46]

Sherman was "gratified that you have modified your former orders," he told Grant on December 24. He proceeded to describe what he intended to do in South Carolina. He had deliberately left Augusta alone during his Georgia campaign, he wrote, so that when he crossed the Savannah River the Confederates would believe he was going either to Augusta or Charleston—and the enemy would divide his forces. In fact, he planned to march on Columbia, the state capital, and Camden.

General Henry Halleck, the Union Army's chief of staff, weighed in to interject his preference: Charleston. "Should you capture Charleston, I hope that by some accident the place may be destroyed, and if a little salt should be sown upon the site it may prevent the growth of future crops of nullification and secession."[47]

Sherman proceeded to describe for Halleck the South Carolina campaign that he envisioned. After his army reached Camden it would turn on either Wilmington or Charleston. "I take it for granted the present movement on Wilmington will fail," he said, referring to the anticipated December attack by Butler's expeditionary force, "because I know that gun-boats cannot take a fort, and Butler has not the force or the ability to take it." He would capture Wilmington after Butler failed, Sherman said. "I rather prefer Wilmington, as a live place, over Charleston, which is dead and unimportant when its railroad communications are broken." Columbia, he said, was "quite as bad as Charleston, and I doubt if we shall spare the public buildings there as we did at Milledgeville [Georgia]."

In South Carolina, Sherman told Halleck, he intended to "attempt the boldest moves" and to "make old and young, rich and poor, feel the hard hand of war, as well as their organized armies."

This war, he said, differed from previous European wars. "We are not only fighting hostile armies, but a hostile people." His army was eager to punish the place where the rebellion began. "The truth is the whole army is burning with an insatiable desire to wreak vengeance upon South Carolina. I almost tremble at her fate, but feel that she deserves all that seems in store for her."[48]

After the Union victory at Shiloh in 1862—the battle that marked his rehabilitation after his nervous breakdown in Kentucky—Sherman still held the conventional view that war was between armies and did not involve civilians. Partisan attacks around Memphis, however, and the populace's belligerence toward the Yankees made him see that "when one nation is at war with another all the people of one are enemies of the other." As commander of the District of Western Tennessee, Sherman ordered the destruction of communities that harbored guerrillas to discourage support for partisans. "We are not going to chase through the canebrakes and swamps the individuals who did the deeds, but will visit punishment upon the adherents of that cause which employs such agents," Sherman said. In October 1862 he told Grant, "They cannot be made to love us, but may be made to fear us."[49]

In February 1864 Sherman put into action his philosophy of "total war" on a larger stage, leading twenty thousand men on a punitive expedition across Mississippi. The Union Army destroyed or damaged barns, fields, and homes and seized thousands of head of livestock. Reaching Meridian, the Yankees methodically wrecked and burned everything that might serve the Confederacy. The campaign was no less than a rehearsal for Sherman's burning of Atlanta that fall and his march through Georgia to the sea.[50]

Some members of Congress, heartened by Sherman's Georgia campaign and frustrated by Grant's failure to destroy Lee at Petersburg, were now talking about making Sherman a lieutenant general like Grant, the lone three-star general. When Sherman learned about the embryonic movement, he urged his brother, Senator John Sherman of Ohio, to stop any attempt to elevate him to Grant's rank.

In a letter to Grant in January Sherman denounced the "mischievous" talk of "rascals who would try to sow differences between us, whereas you and I now are in perfect understanding." He went on to describe his great respect for Grant in words bordering on obsequiousness. "I would rather have you in command than anybody else; for you are fair, honest, and have at heart the same purpose that should animate all. I should emphatically decline any commission calculated to bring us into rivalry."

Touched by Sherman's expression of fealty, Grant replied that "no one would be more pleased at your advancement than I, and if you should be placed in my position and I put subordinate it would not change our relations in the least."

Sherman had the last word in this affectionate exchange. "I am fully aware of your friendly feeling toward me, and you may always depend on me as your steadfast supporter," he wrote. "Your wish is law and gospel to me, and such is the feeling that pervades my army."[51]

The men's failures in civilian life and during the war's early days had forged a rare bond between them. During the 1850s Grant, an unlucky farmer in Missouri, was struggling to feed his family by selling firewood on a St. Louis street corner when he encountered Sherman, a West Point acquaintance who had neither thrived as a banker nor as a businessman. That day they spoke briefly and parted. Afterward Sherman recalled thinking "that West Point and the regular army were not good schools for farmers [and] bankers."

Years later at Shiloh, fierce Confederate attacks on the battle's first day, April 6, 1862, nearly forced Grant's army to retreat over the Tennessee River. It was a bad day for both Grant and Sherman, who commanded a division that had suffered heavy losses. Three horses were shot from under Sherman, and he was wounded in the hand.

After the pounding the army had sustained, Sherman and Grant's other generals were stunned when orders arrived from Grant late in the day to be ready to attack at dawn. It was inconceivable to them that he would consider anything except a rapid withdrawal to interpose the river between them and the Confederates.

When he went looking for Grant that rainy night to urge retreat, Sherman found him standing alone beneath a tree, holding a lantern and smoking a cigar. Grant had entered a nearby log house to get out of the rain but discovered that it had been converted into a field hospital; surgeons were busily amputating wounded soldiers' arms and legs and the floor was covered in blood. One of the small ironies of the war was that Grant, who was often denounced as a "butcher," could not abide the sight of blood.

When Sherman saw Grant smoking his cigar in the rain, something made him hold his tongue. Instead of advising retreat, as he had intended to do, Sherman simply said, "Well, Grant, we've had the devil's own day, haven't we?" Parsimonious with words as always, Grant replied, "Yes, lick 'em tomorrow, though." His counterattack the next morning broke the Rebel lines.[52]

Grant was sharply criticized—and even accused of drunkenness—for the close call at Shiloh. Halleck reorganized the Army of the Tennessee and assumed personal command, making Grant his second-in-command.

Stung by the rebuke, Grant was poised to resign his commission when Sherman, noticing Grant's packed bags outside his tent, talked him out of it.

They fought together at Vicksburg and Chattanooga, and when Grant was promoted to general-in-chief he appointed Sherman commander of the Union forces west of the Appalachian Mountains. Grant's elevation elicited a touching tribute from Sherman: "I believe you are as brave, patriotic, and just, as the great phototype [sic] Washington—as unselfish, kindhearted and honest, as a man should be, but the chief characteristic in your nature is the simple faith in success you have always manifested, which I can liken to nothing else than the faith a Christian has in his Saviour. . . . I knew wherever I was that you thought of me, and if I got in a tight place you would come, if alive."

Later, Sherman, with his knack for pithiness, alluded to the nadir of his own early Civil War career, the nervous breakdown in 1861 that resulted in him being relieved of command in Kentucky amid blaring headlines that he was "crazy." Sherman said, "Grant stood by me when I was crazy, and I stood by him when he was drunk."[53]

About the time that Sherman's army was settling in at Savannah, Grant was helping to launch the Sherman Testimonial Fund of Ohio. Its purpose was to raise money from businessmen so Sherman and his family could buy a home. Grant donated $500 of his own money to the fund and wrote to the committee, "I can not say a word too highly in praise of General Sherman's services from the beginning of the rebellion to the present day." Sherman, he wrote, had "few equals" throughout history.[54]

☙❧

Sherman had accepted emancipation with reluctance, and during the last stage of his march to Savannah an ugly incident occurred that focused national attention on his opinions on slavery and blacks, whom he, as did many Union Army officers, referred to as "Sambos." Like many Northerners when the war began, Sherman had accepted the institution of slavery, and he was slow to change. His foster father and father-in-law, Thomas Ewing, the powerful former Ohio congressman and treasury secretary whom Sherman practically worshiped, had been aligned more with slave owners than abolitionists. Another influence was Sherman's antebellum Army service in the South and his two years as superintendent of the

Louisiana State Seminary of Learning and Military Academy, a position that he resigned in 1861. In 1862 he wrote that if blacks were liberated, it would be impossible for them to coexist with their former masters. "Either they or [their] masters must perish. They cannot exist together except in their present relation," said Sherman.[55]

Newly liberated slaves had followed Sherman's army on its march through Georgia. When the army reached Savannah's outskirts it was trailed by tens of thousands of former slaves, who regarded Sherman as their savior and whose appearance ignited spontaneous demonstrations of adulation. Sherman patiently answered their questions, mindful that they were his allies and that they provided his army with accurate intelligence. But Sherman and his staff were concerned that there was not enough food for both the blacks and the army.

Slowed by mud and harried by General Joseph Wheeler's Confederate cavalry, General Jefferson C. Davis, who commanded the Right Wing's rearguard, XIV Corps, decided on December 9 to rid his column of the hundreds of black refugees shadowing it. About twenty miles from Savannah, Davis ordered his men to bar the blacks from using the army's pontoon bridge over Ebenezer Creek. After the troops had crossed, the engineers took up the pontoons, stranding the refugees on the other side of the creek, which was swollen by floodwaters to a breadth of 165 feet. Major James Connolly of the 123rd Illinois protested strenuously. "I told his [Davis's] staff officers what I thought of such an inhuman, barbarous proceeding," he wrote. It did no good.

Pressed from behind by Wheeler's cavalrymen, the freedmen panicked when they heard shots fired. As Colonel Charles Kerr of the 16th Illinois Cavalry watched, the refugees rushed to the creek bank, "raised their hands and implored from their corps commander the protection they had been promised. . . . The prayer was in vain, and with cries of anguish and despair, men, women and children rushed by hundreds into the turgid stream, and many were drowned before our eyes."

Connolly later wrote a congressman a letter describing the incident, and it was leaked to the newspapers. In Congress a resolution was proposed to have the Committee on the Conduct of the War investigate the incident, although nothing came of it.[56]

The incident outraged abolitionists and Lincoln administration opponents alike, and when Sherman defended Davis, some of these critics also turned on Sherman, spreading rumors that he supported slavery and believed the institution would survive the war.[57]

Coincidentally, War Secretary Edwin Stanton was just then urging Grant to persuade Sherman to set up depots for recruiting black soldiers. "He does not seem to appreciate the importance of this measure and appears indifferent if not hostile," grumbled Stanton.[58]

Sherman dragged his feet because he believed that blacks made poor soldiers and that they should be used as laborers only. "It is an insult to our Race to count them as part of the [draft] quota," he wrote. He was just as annoyed by the recruiters from the North who descended on Georgia to help Northern states fulfill their draft quotas by enlisting the former slaves. They distracted the army from its mission of defeating the enemy, Sherman complained, and some of them reportedly even locked up the prospective recruits until they enlisted. Sherman threatened to arrest the agents, and he told the blacks that they were free and could not be compelled to enlist.[59]

In a private letter on December 30 Halleck warned Sherman about the growing firestorm. His alleged attitude regarding the "Inevitable Sambo" had aroused a faction "who are decidedly disposed to make a point against you. . . . They say that you have manifested an almost criminal dislike of the negro, and that you are not willing to carry out the wishes of the Government in regard to him, but repulse him with contempt." They accused Sherman of doing nothing to aid the tens of thousands of slaves that had followed his army through Georgia, wrote Halleck, and claimed that he had even driven them away. "Would it not be possible for you to reopen these avenues of escape for the negroes without interfering with your military operations?" Halleck asked. He urged Sherman to help them obtain food and work. "A manifestation on your part of a desire to bring the slaves within our lines will do much to silence your opponents."[60]

It was a "cock-and-bull story" about General Davis abandoning the blacks on the riverbank, and so was the massacre report, Sherman replied to Halleck. Davis removed the pontoon bridges, said Sherman, because they were needed to cross the next stream, not to obstruct the black camp followers. "Thank God, I am not running for an office, and am not concerned because the rising generation will believe that I burned 500 n—rs at one pop in Atlanta, or any such nonsense. I profess to be the best kind of friend to Sambo, and think that on such a question Sambo should be consulted. . . . The South deserves all she has got for her injustice to the negro, but that is no reason why we should go to the other extreme."[61]

Dissatisfied with Sherman's explanations, Stanton sailed to Savannah to personally appraise the situation. He arrived unannounced on January 11. Grant had suggested the visit, hoping that Stanton could persuade Sherman to at least enlist the new freedmen as garrison troops, thereby freeing white troops for combat.

Sherman initially assumed that Stanton had come to discuss his plans for the approaching campaign. But it quickly became apparent that the war secretary's chief concern was the plight of the freed slaves and their treatment by Sherman and his generals. Stanton grilled General Davis about the incident at Ebenezer Creek, and when he was finished he asked Sherman to summon Savannah's black leaders to a meeting.

Stanton questioned the twenty preachers and lay leaders who gathered at Sherman's quarters about the Emancipation Proclamation and what it meant to them. How would emancipated slaves support themselves, and would they live apart from whites or among them? "By ourselves," replied their spokesman, Garrison Frazier, a Baptist minister.

An hour into the meeting Stanton asked Sherman to leave the room and then solicited Frazier's candid opinion of Sherman. Blacks believed that Sherman was "a friend and a gentleman," Frazier told Stanton, and they wanted no one else over them.[62]

Before Stanton left Savannah he wanted to do something tangible for the freedmen. With Sherman's help, he outlined a plan to give black families lands abandoned by plantation owners along the coastal rivers and on the sea islands of South Carolina and Georgia. When three families submitted an application and the government approved it, they would receive property that could be divided into forty acres for each family. Whites were forbidden to live in the settlements, whose day-to-day management would be the responsibility of the freedmen.

The details were elucidated in Sherman's remarkable Special Field Orders No. 15 of January 16, 1865. Besides establishing the black settlements, it exempted the freedmen from conscription while offering incentives for able-bodied black men to enlist in the Union Army: bounties and the opportunity to live on the island or river settlement of their choosing.[63]

By the time Stanton returned to Washington, Sherman believed he had dissuaded the war secretary from forcing him to raise black regiments. "Mr. Stanton . . . is cured of that Negro nonsense which arises not from a love of the negro but a desire to dodge Service [forced substitutes]," he wrote to his wife, Ellen. "I want soldiers made of the best bone & muscle in the land and wont attempt military feats with doubtful materials. I have said that Slavery is dead and the Negro free and want him treated as free & not hunted & badgered to make a soldier of when his family is left back on the Plantations. I am right & wont Change."[64]

Racial attitudes were rapidly changing in the North and South. Amazingly, Jefferson Davis was openly advocating arming slaves to fight for the Confederacy and possibly rewarding them with emancipation. This would subvert one of the Confederacy's two cornerstones, slavery, leaving just the prospect of sovereignty to inspire Southerners to fight on. The controversial proposal provoked rage and despair—despair that military matters had reached such a desperate pass that the Confederacy was having to turn to the South's slaves to fill the army's ranks.

When US Attorney General James Speed predicted at a cabinet meeting on January 6 that the Confederacy would bring blacks into the army, Lincoln said, "When they reached that stage, the cause of war would cease and hostilities cease with it. The evil would cure itself." But in Richmond in January the idea appeared to be going nowhere in the Confederate Congress. That would change.[65]

In Washington Lincoln was pulling out all the stops to codify emancipation as the Thirteenth Amendment to the Constitution; if approved, it would be the first constitutional amendment since 1804, when the Twelfth Amendment clarified the procedure for electing the vice president. Lincoln didn't have to spend his political capital on such a politically risky objective; he had won re-election in November, and a new US House of Representatives would be sworn in March 4 that, if called into special session, would easily pass the amendment.

In 1864 the Thirteenth Amendment had cleared the Senate with the required two-thirds vote. But the amendment failed in the House, ninety-three to sixty-five, with Republicans supporting it and most

Democrats voting no. Lincoln decided to try once more to push the amendment through the House before the new Congress was seated.

In his Annual Message to Congress on December 6 Lincoln urged the amendment's reconsideration. "An intervening election shows, almost certainly, that the next Congress will pass the measure if this does not. Hence there is only a question of time as to when the proposed amendment will go to the States for their action. And as it is to so go, at all events, may we not agree that the sooner the better?" During the election "the will of the majority" had spoken for maintaining the Union, he said, "and, among the means to secure that end" was passage of the Thirteenth Amendment. The amendment stated, "Neither slavery nor involuntary servitude, except as a punishment for crime whereof the party shall have been duly convicted, shall exist within the United States, or any place subject to their jurisdiction."[66]

Congressman James Ashley of Ohio introduced the amendment in the House on January 6. Lincoln lobbied House members more aggressively than he had since pushing border-state congressmen to support gradual emancipation back in 1862. He especially targeted lame-duck congressmen—Democrats, mostly—who had lost their seats in the November election, dangling prospective government jobs and favors before them.

To Senator Edwin Morgan of New York, the outgoing chairman of the Republican National Committee, Lincoln said, "We are like whalers who have been long on a chase: we have at last got the harpoon into the monster, but we must now look how we steer, or with one 'flop' of his tail he will send us all into eternity." The president told Congressman James Rollins of Missouri that passage of the amendment "will clinch the whole subject. It will bring the war, I have no doubt, rapidly to a close."[67]

The congressional debate during January showed that Lincoln had been right to believe the amendment might pass before March 4. Politically active blacks in the North were lobbying for voting rights, the repeal of the infamous "black laws" aimed at their suppression, and integration of street cars in Washington and Philadelphia. Just before debate began in the House the border states of Maryland and Missouri approved constitutions that, among other things, abolished slavery. Lincoln believed that border-state congressmen, such as Representative George Yeaman of Kentucky, defeated in the November election, could be courted and won over. Yeaman soon conceded, "Seeing the people have determined to do it, it becomes the part of wisdom to let it be done as quickly as convenient and with no unnecessary opposition. Let the agony be over and the rubbish cleared away."

A defeated Democrat from New York, Representative Anson Herrick, voted against the amendment in 1864 but intended to vote for it now for the sake of the Democratic Party's future. "Every year and every day we are growing weaker and weaker in popular favor, while our opponents are strengthening, because we will not venture to cut loose from the dead carcass of negro slavery. . . . It is plain enough to my mind that if the Democratic Party would regain its supremacy in the Government of the nation it must now let slavery 'slide.'"

Congressman Chilton White of Ohio, another lame-duck Democrat, refused to change his opinion that slaves were property that could only be taken away by "due process of law"—a trial court—or by the states, not by a constitutional amendment. "Why, sir, the right to possess and enjoy property is essential to the very existence of man," he said. "It is guaranteed by the Constitution."

"If slavery is not wrong, what is wrong?" asked another border-state congressman, Representative Green Smith of Kentucky. "Go ask the South why they seceded, and the answer will be, to establish slavery. Go travel over this vast country and witness the thousands and thousands of new-made graves, and ask what caused them, and the answer will be slavery."[68]

As January's chilly days followed one upon the other, Lincoln pressed hard for the last votes to achieve the number needed for passage. To the two allies he had entrusted with procuring the final votes Lincoln said, "The abolition of slavery by Constitutional provision settles the fate, for all coming time, not only of the millions now in bondage, but of unborn millions to come—a measure of such importance that *those two votes must be procured*. I leave it to you to determine how it shall be done." Lincoln drew himself up to his full six-feet-four inches of height and added, "but remember that I am President of the United States, clothed with immense power, and I expect you to procure those votes."[69]

Lincoln's log rolling and arm twisting paid off. On January 31, before packed galleries and corridors and with the House floor crowded with senators, Congress voted on the Thirteenth Amendment. Every Democratic "aye" brought cheers from the spectators. Then House Speaker

Schuyler Colfax rose and, in a trembling voice, announced the final tally: 119 in favor, 56 opposed. The Thirteenth Amendment had passed with two votes to spare. Of the House's 80 Democrats, 16 had voted for it—14 of them lame ducks.

Noah Brooks, the correspondent for the *Sacramento Daily Union*, described what happened next. "For a moment there was a pause of utter silence as if the voices of the dense mass of spectators were choked by strong emotion. Then there was an explosion, a storm of cheers, the like of which probably no Congress of the United States ever heard before. Strong men embraced each other with tears. The air was stirred with a cloud of women's handkerchiefs waving and floating." Ten minutes passed before the cheering ended. The House then adjourned.

A hundred-gun salute roared from Capitol Hill, announcing the amendment's passage. Congressman Cornelius Cole of California wrote to his wife, "The one question of the age is *settled*. Glory enough for one session, yes, even for a life." To his friend Francis Lieber, famed for writing the code governing soldiers' conduct in wartime, Congressman Martin Russell Thayer of Pennsylvania wrote, "We have wiped away the black spot from our bright shield and surely God will bless us for it." Observed the New York diarist George Templeton Strong, "Who thought four years ago that John Brown would march so fast."

Lincoln savored what he called "a great moral victory." Gesturing toward the Potomac River, he said, "If the people over the river had behaved themselves, I could not have done what I have."[70]

The next day, February 1, the amendment was sent to the state legislatures; three-fourths of them had to ratify the Thirteenth Amendment for it to become part of the Constitution. Illinois ratified it that day, the first state to do so. On that day, too, John Rock of Boston became the first black lawyer admitted to the bar of the US Supreme Court.[71]

The day after the momentous vote the president told a crowd gathered outside a window of the White House that the Emancipation Proclamation had begun the task of eradicating slavery, and the Thirteenth Amendment had completed it. "This amendment is a King's cure for all the evils. It winds the whole thing up."[72]

Without opposition, General Alfred Terry's Provisional Corps of the Army of the James landed on the North Carolina beach above Fort Fisher on January 13. General Robert Hoke's division from Robert E. Lee's Virginia army, four miles to the north at Sugar Loaf, did not interfere.

The Yankees dug entrenchments to fend off attacks from that direction while conducting reconnaissance for the assault on the fort. "You must attack them at once," General William Whiting wrote to Braxton Bragg from Fort Fisher when he saw that Hoke was not reacting. Bragg had superseded Whiting as departmental commander upon his arrival in Wilmington; with no command or specific duties, Whiting had joined Colonel William Lamb at Fort Fisher.

Hours later Whiting asked, "Why are they not attacked?" Bragg surveyed the Union lines with Hoke from Sugar Loaf. Outnumbered four-to-one, Hoke concluded "it too hazardous to assault with such an inferior force," adding, "Fisher has been re-enforced with sufficient veterans to make it safe." In fact, just seven hundred reinforcements had reached the fort, bringing its strength to fifteen hundred, while facing eight thousand infantry and sixty warships. Another thousand men were coming down-river from Fort Anderson, but had not arrived. To Whiting, Bragg wrote, "The reinforcements being sent you . . . will render you impregnable against assault."

On January 14 Porter's ironclads, armed with heavy guns, sailed close to the fort and began shelling it. Confederate gunners returned fire, but the ironclads' hulls deflected it. Spotters in Porter's wooden fleet pinpointed the Rebel gun flashes, and the warships' gunners began systematically targeting the Confederate guns, concentrating on those defending the fort's land side, near the Cape Fear River—the objective of Terry's planned assault.[73]

The iron onslaught resumed at daylight January 15, and at 10 a.m. the entire squadron, including five former Confederate blockade-runners, moved within range and joined the bombardment. By noon all but one of the twenty Rebel guns on the targeted land face had been shattered or dismounted.[74]

Since December 25 Porter and his officers had quietly implemented fire control measures that markedly improved the fleet's gunnery, although Porter continued to insist that his Christmas Day bombardment had "completely silenced" the fort's guns. Porter's claim notwithstanding,

Lamb wrote that the Union gunfire on that day was "so wild that at least one-third of the missiles fell in the river beyond the fort or in the bordering marshes."[75]

The Union Navy's fire-control improvements made this bombardment a nightmare for the Confederates; at one point up to one hundred shells landed every minute. "No language can describe that bombardment," a Rebel garrison member later remarked. A Union observer said the shells came from every side except the west, "and they were falling and bursting faster than the ticking of a watch. The Confederate artillerists tried in vain to stand their guns. One by one, they were broken or dismounted, and the garrison driven to its bombproofs."[76]

In addition to Terry's attack on the fort's west side, Porter, at the last minute, decided to land a scratch force of sixteen hundred sailors, armed with cutlasses and pistols, and four hundred Marines with repeating rifles. The all-volunteer force had never operated together, and the admiral had virtually no experience in commanding troops on land.

Porter's two thousand men would attack the fort's northeast corner, near the sea. Because Porter's gunners had not seriously targeted the Rebel guns in this area but had instead concentrated on Fort Fisher's west side, nearly all of the enemy's twenty-four seaward-facing guns were intact. Terry's and Porter's two shock forces would attack the fort at 3 p.m. at a signal from the fleet.[77]

❧

General William Whiting had come to Fort Fisher to voluntarily serve under Colonel Lamb's command, a rare, humble gesture in an organization in which the prerogatives of rank were cherished and fiercely defended. Whiting had been a general in the Confederate Army since First Manassas in 1861. He led troops in Virginia during the Seven Days, was a commander in North Carolina, and served briefly at Petersburg before returning to Wilmington.

When Whiting last met with Bragg in Wilmington, Bragg had indicated a line on a map and said that he intended to fall back to it if Fort Fisher fell. Whiting interpreted this to mean that Bragg had already given up on Fort Fisher. When he arrived at the fort, Whiting said to Lamb, "Lamb, my boy, I have come to share your fate. You and your garrison are to be sacrificed."[78]

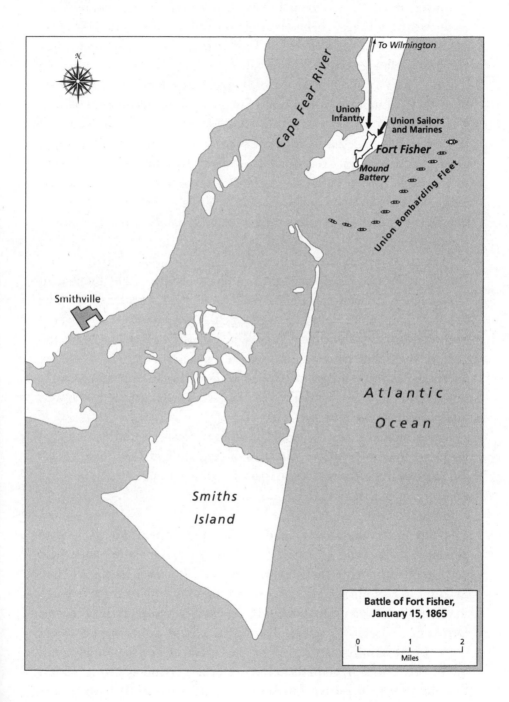

N

To Wilmington

Cape Fear River

Union
Infantry

Union Sailors
and Marines

Fort Fisher

Mound
Battery

Union Bombarding Fleet

Smithville

Atlantic

Ocean

Smiths

Island

Battle of Fort Fisher,
January 15, 1865

0   1   2

Miles

Indeed, that appeared to be the case. Lamb and Whiting had received no answer from Bragg when they telegraphed him the previous day, urging a simultaneous night attack on Terry's forces by troops from the fort and from Wilmington and Sugar Loaf.

On January 15 Whiting wrote to Bragg, "The enemy are about to assault; they outnumber us heavily. . . . Enemy on the beach in front of us in very heavy force, not more than seven hundred yards from us. Nearly all land guns disabled. Attack! Attack! It is all I can say and all you can do."[79]

Whiting's appeal moved Bragg to send reinforcements by steamship to Fort Fisher, but he did not order Hoke's division at Sugar Loaf to dislodge the Union amphibious force—as Whiting and General Robert E. Lee, in telegraphic contact with Bragg, that day had urged him to do.[80]

Dozens of boats shuttled the potpourri US naval force, led by Lieutenant Commander K. Randolph Breese, to the beach a little after noon. The two thousand sailors and Marines dug fieldworks several hundred yards from Fort Fisher's northeast corner. When the signal to attack came, the Marines, with their repeating rifles, were supposed to pin down the defenders while the sailors stormed the fort. Porter's men were not to begin their assault, however, until Terry's infantrymen reached the fort's walls one-half mile to the west.

In the interim the scene might have been idyllic, with the sound of waves lapping on the shore, the cries of seagulls, and a light breeze ruffling the sea oats—except for the roar of naval gunfire.[81]

At 3 p.m. sharp the naval bombardment abruptly ceased and every steam whistle in the squadron shrieked, "a soul-stirring signal both to besiegers and besieged." Terry's four-thousand-man assault force began the half-mile trek to Fort Fisher. But rather than wait for the infantrymen to reach the walls, Breese's sailors at once rose to their feet and advanced on the fort.

When the bombardment stopped, hundreds of Rebels poured out of the bombproofs and ran to the fort's northeast corner, believing this was the attack's main objective. Musket volleys and cannon fire flashed from the parapets into the ranks of the sailors as they struggled to cross twelve hundred yards of loose sand. Many of the Marines who were supposed to lay down suppressing fire on the parapet became caught up in the excitement of the moment and attacked with the sailors.

Admiral Porter's son, Lieutenant Carlisle Porter, and Lieutenant Samuel Preston were killed while leading their men through the Rebel fire. Fifty yards from the fort "the column suddenly stopped, and, as if by magic, the whole mass of men went down like a row of falling bricks," wrote Robley Evans, an officer from the *USS Powhatan* who volunteered for the mission. There they lay, "packed like sheep in a pen," while the Rebels lined the parapets with impunity and fired into the sailors as fast as they could reload, with "nothing to reply with but *pistols*," wrote Captain Thomas Selfridge.

The naval assault force disintegrated. The rear broke for cover, and then the rest of the attackers pelted back too. "It was certainly mortifying, after charging for a mile, under the most galling fire, to the very foot of the fort," wrote Selfridge.[82]

The Rebels celebrated their repulse of the sailors and Marines. "With small loss to ourselves we witnessed what had never been seen before, a disorderly rout of American sailors and marines," wrote Colonel Lamb.

But then four thousand bluecoat infantrymen emerged from the scrubby woods north of the fort. They were seasoned veterans of the fighting around Petersburg and Richmond. The three brigades of General Adelbert Ames's Second Division advanced toward the western walls. "Rough-looking, with frowsy clothing and disheveled hair and beards, after long and hard experience on the transports"—but carrying "clean and bright" arms—they dressed their battle line without bugles or verbal commands. The Union line suddenly swept over the sandy open ground toward the western side of the fort. Pioneers wielding axes led the charge, and they hacked pathways through the fort palisade for the troops following them.

The Confederate defenders frantically tried to detonate the torpedoes, connected by wires to galvanic batteries, that they had buried beneath the open approaches to the fort. But Porter's bombardment had severed the wires, neutralizing the land mines.

Ames's three brigades swarmed into the fort through breaches in the earthwork made by the massive naval bombardment. The Confederates fought hand-to-hand, muzzle-to-muzzle, but were driven back. The

Yankees captured two Rebel batteries, and the parapets suddenly blossomed with Union regimental colors.

A fourth brigade, under Colonel Joseph Abbott, entered the fort by a side gate as daylight began to fade, and the troops blazed away with their Spencer repeaters at the Rebels who rushed to meet them, cutting them down. The Yankees drove the survivors from traverse to traverse.[83]

As Lamb and his men celebrated their repulse of what Lamb believed had been the Union's main assault on the fort, he was astonished when he saw three Union battle flags suddenly appear on the fort's western ramparts. He rushed men from the fort's northeast corner to the west side to hurl back the assault.

General Whiting saw the flags too, and he quickly organized a counterattack. The Rebels drove Ames's men from one of the gun chambers, which echoed with deafening gunfire as the enemies shot one another at pointblank range. "As a man would fall, another sprang to take his place, our officers loading and firing with us," wrote a Rebel soldier.

Whiting was shot twice while attempting to remove one of the Union flags from the exposed western parapet. Then Lamb was wounded in the hip while leading a second counterattack. Whiting wrote to Bragg, "The enemy are assaulting us by land and sea. Their infantry outnumber us. Can't you help us? I am slightly wounded."

Porter's ironclads began firing on the traverses occupied by the Rebels and, "with deadly precision . . . drove in our Napoleons," wrote a defender. The monitors swept the western walls of defenders.

Lying beside each other in a field hospital, Whiting said to Lamb over the rumble of gunfire, "Lamb, when you die, I will assume command, and I will not surrender the fort."

Bragg sent General Alfred H. Colquitt of Hoke's division to take command and to order Whiting to report to Bragg at Sugar Loaf.

Colquitt arrived as Union troops were overrunning the fort. Lamb briefed him on the apparently hopeless situation, but said that if Bragg could attack the Union rear from Sugar Loaf, the day might be retrieved. Evidently believing this to be magical thinking, Colquitt left without issuing a single command or even attempting to evacuate Lamb or Whiting.[84]

With the arrival of darkness, Ames's and Abbott's brigades methodically suppressed Rebel resistance inside the fort, at times in ferocious close-quarters fighting amid "great heaps of human beings laying just as they fell, one upon the other."

About four hundred of Bragg's reinforcements reached the fort; the rest were driven off by enemy fire. Finding the situation beyond retrieval, the new arrivals hid in the bombproofs.[85]

About 10 p.m. Confederate resistance ended, although the hospitalized commanders, Lamb and Whiting, refused to surrender and were taken prisoner.

The signal beacon atop Fort Fisher's walls announced to the fleet that the fort was in Union hands. The Confederate flag came down; the Stars and Stripes took its place. Porter's fleet erupted in cheers, steam whistle blasts, clanging bells, and skyrockets.[86]

That night Porter telegraphed Navy Secretary Welles, "Fort Fisher is ours. . . . General Terry is entitled to the highest praise. . . . He is my beau ideal of a soldier."

Terry reported 955 soldiers killed or wounded, while Porter's botched land assault cost 393 sailors and Marines. Of the Confederate garrison an estimated 500 were killed or wounded, and more than 1,000 Rebels were captured. Those that escaped made their way upriver to Fort Anderson, Bragg's designated fallback position. Under his orders the Rebels abandoned and destroyed the works at Forts Caswell, Johnson, and Lamb.[87]

Sergeant Christian Fleetwood of the 4th US Colored Troops was aghast at the destruction and carnage he saw inside the fort after the shooting stopped: "Heavy guns bursted [sic], others knocked to pieces as though made of pipe clay, heavy gun carriages knocked to splinters and dead bodies of rebels lying as they fell with wounds horrible enough to sicken the beholder."[88]

Overnight, tragedy marred the triumph. Hunting for loot, some of the victors carried lighted torches into a large underground powder magazine containing tons of gunpowder. The tremendous explosion killed or injured up to two hundred Union soldiers, sailors, Marines, and Confederate prisoners. A board of inquiry that convened a week later at Fort Fisher concluded that the explosion was due to soldiers, sailors, and Marines "running about with lights in the fort, entering bombproofs with these lights, intoxicated and discharging fire-arms."[89]

Porter's personal examination of the Confederate bastion left him highly impressed by the defensive works' strength. He observed that General Whiting—although it was Lamb, not Whiting, who devoted two years to building the fort—"must have had an abiding faith in the durability of the Confederacy when he expended so many years of labor on them."[90]

War Secretary Edwin Stanton, returning from his surprise visit to Sherman's army in Savannah, stopped at Fort Fisher during his return trip. Stanton bestowed promotions on many of the higher-ranking officers who had led the assault; Terry became a major general.[91]

In Washington, Navy Secretary Welles wrote in his diary, "The glorious news of the capture of Fort Fisher came this morning." There were broad smiles in the White House and at City Point, where Grant was reportedly in better spirits than he had been in many days.

Ironically, Fort Fisher was captured just as Benjamin Butler was telling the Congressional Committee on the Conduct of the War that the fort could now only be taken by siege since his powder boat scheme had failed. "This will be severe for Butler," Welles drily observed.[92]

In fact, it was deeply embarrassing for Butler. He was before the committee defending his decision to call off the Fort Fisher attack because of the fort's supposed impregnability when revelry on the streets distracted him and the committee members. The people were celebrating Fort Fisher's capture.

"Impossible!" cried Butler. The committee erupted in laughter. "It's a mistake, sir," Butler insisted, but then, when the laugher increased, Butler joined in. The committee adjourned. As the members were filing out, Butler raised his hand and said, "Thank God for victory." The committee absolved Butler of wrongdoing.[93]

"The news of the fall of Wilmington, and the cessation of importations at that port, falls upon the ears of the community with stunning effect," Confederate War Department clerk John B. Jones wrote in his diary on January 17, correctly presuming that Fort Fisher's loss doomed Wilmington as well.[94]

So important was Fort Fisher to the Confederacy that Jefferson Davis telegraphed Bragg on the day of Porter's and Terry's final attacks: "We are trustfully looking to your operations; may Divine favor crown your efforts." When he learned of the fort's capture, he asked Bragg whether it could be retaken.[95]

Never sanguine about the Confederacy's long odds, Lee did not dwell on Fort Fisher's loss but instead suggested to Jefferson Davis that the Confederacy step up its illicit commerce with Northern merchants: Southern cotton, tobacco, tar, and turpentine for Northern clothing, food, and shoes. "The loss of the port of Wilmington, cutting us off in a great measure from access to the world by sea," required these steps, wrote Lee.

He recommended that the government begin to "impress cotton to- bacco & naval stores, especially where they are found in localities ex- posed to the enemy." The government should also find credible middle- men, compensating them with cotton and "the privilege of removing it from the country." Instead of competing with the government, as they now did, the contractors would serve it, Lee said.[96]

❧

Fort Fisher's fall sent fresh waves of despair crashing through the Confed- eracy just two months after Lincoln's reelection had served notice that the Union was not going to let the South go. The fort's loss abruptly halted the flow of supplies from Wilmington that had helped sustain Lee's army and the people of Richmond and Petersburg. Neither a starving army nor a starving people could endure indefinitely. With the "Gibraltar of the South" now a supply depot for the Union troops who would soon march on Wilmington and inland North Carolina, Southerners increas- ingly sensed that the Rebellion was doomed.

"The fall of this Fort was one of the greatest disasters which had be- fallen our Cause from the beginning of the war—not excepting the loss of Vicksburg or Atlanta," wrote Confederate Vice President Alexander Stephens, a small, frail man of large intellect known as "the little pale star from Georgia." Through the Union blockade of Wilmington had come "a considerable number of arms and various munitions of war, as well as large supplies of subsistence." Wilmington, "choked to wheezing as it was, by a cordon of armed ships, drawn around its neck," nonetheless performed the "respiratory functions of External Trade . . . for the whole Confederacy." Now it no longer could.[97]

The capture of Fort Fisher unified Confederate congressmen who had long been dissatisfied with the management of their government. On January 16 the Senate approved a resolution, fourteen-to-two, calling for Lee to be made commander-in-chief; for General Joseph Johnston, whom Davis had relieved of command in Georgia the previous fall, to be restored as commander of the Army of Tennessee; and for General P. G. T. Beauregard to oversee military operations in South Carolina, Georgia, and Florida. Davis had already appointed Beauregard to the Southeastern position, but he balked at giving Johnston a field command, pronouncing him unsuitable. On the 17th the Virginia legislature added its recommendation that Davis place Lee in command of all Confederate armies, writing that it would "operate powerfully to reanimate the spirits of the Armies, as well as the people of the several States."

Indeed, the spirit of Southern nationalism was flagging. Some states were invoking their sovereignty in defiance of the national government. Georgia Governor Joseph Brown flatly refused to send the old men and boys now in the state militia to the Confederate Army, condemning the government's conscription as "usurping" and "despotic." About the same time, Virginia Governor "Extra Billy" Smith withdrew two Virginia militia units from Confederate service.[98]

Confederate congressmen, led by Louis Wigfall of Texas, demanded that Davis purge his Cabinet of everyone except Treasury Secretary George Trenholm. But the Cabinet wasn't so much the problem as was Davis, who practically ran the government himself and did not brook disagreement. Unsurprisingly, the president, unyielding as usual, rejected the demand. Only War Secretary James Seddon resigned, disgusted with his fellow Virginians for supporting the demand and thereby removing the last Virginian from Davis's Cabinet. Seddon's successor was General John C. Breckinridge, a popular, respected Confederate Army general and a former US vice president. He had led divisions or corps in three different field armies and had served at Shiloh, Vicksburg, Chickamauga, and Cold Harbor. The Kentuckian's appointment was welcomed. "If I had an army I would at once put it under his command," Lee said. Breckinridge accepted the position on the condition that Davis remove the commissary general, General Lucius Northrup. Regarded as a Davis "pet," Northrup was universally blamed for the army's food and supply problems—although he was not entirely at fault—and he had few supporters in the army. Davis reluctantly eased out Northrup.

This wasn't nearly enough for the hard-core dissenters, who, besides Wigfall, included Stephens, Robert Toombs of Georgia, and Robert Barnwell Rhett of South Carolina. Some of them wanted to force out Davis and replace him with Lee. Stephens returned to Richmond from his Georgia home to preside over the Senate, rebuke the government for its failures, and call for Davis's dismissal. He also proposed immediate peace negotiations with the Union, believing that a quick settlement might preserve the Confederacy's sovereignty before another military disaster robbed the government of all of its bargaining power.[99]

"Are the people of this country fighting for the glory of Mr. Davis from Mississippi, or defending their liberty, lives and property?" wrote the *Richmond Examiner* on January 17, railing against a government run at "the unlimited, uncontrolled and uncontested discretion of persons who daily furnish new proofs of unskilfullness, and bad judgment, and defective character. In the next few weeks affairs must be definitely arranged."

Southerners had soured on Davis as the war progressed, and their disenchantment reached an apotheosis with the loss of Georgia, Tennessee, and, now, Fort Fisher. Davis's early states' rights supporters had turned on him for instituting national conscription, and the rift between the Confederate states and Richmond had steadily widened. Although Davis's character was never in question and his chiseled features, gray eyes, and aquiline nose radiated dignity and grace, the fifty-six-year-old Mississippian had fallen far in the public's estimation since 1861—and many quietly disparaged his wife, Varina, as a harridan. Southerners had once believed that the Mississippi senator, former US war secretary, and hero of Buena Vista would personally lead the Confederate Army to victory, with Johnston, Lee, and Beauregard acting as his lieutenants. "With him, the victory would be certain, and chance become certainty," wrote the *Richmond Semi-weekly Examiner*. In those days the *Richmond Dispatch* described Davis as "a tower of strength, with the iron will, the nerve, the energy and decision of Andrew Jackson and more than Jackson's knowledge and general education."

Four years later many Southerners believed that Davis had to go. "He is probably not equal to the role he is now called upon to play," wrote

John Jones of the War Department, who, compared with others, was mild in his criticism. "He has not the broad intellect requisite for the gigantic measures needed in such a crisis, nor the health and physique for the labors devolving on him."

Many Confederate leaders wanted Lee to take Davis's place. The fifty-eight-year-old Lee was the Confederate Army's matchless leader. Revered above any other public figure in the Confederacy, Lee was the son of "Light Horse Harry" Lee of Revolutionary War fame, and he was married to an authentic Virginia blueblood, Martha Randolph Custis, whose ancestors included George Washington's wife, Martha. A career Army officer since graduating second in his class of 1829 without a single demerit, he was highly decorated in the Mexican War and in 1861 declared his loyalty to Virginia over his country. Lee had taken command of the Army of Northern Virginia in 1862 when Joseph Johnston was wounded and, in a series of rapid movements, had wrecked George McClellan's Peninsular Campaign. A brilliant strategist, Lee was widely regarded as the Confederate Army's "most belligerent man" but also a pious man who believed that the South would triumph if it scrupulously obeyed God's laws. After the defeat at Gettysburg, Lee told his army, "We have sinned against Almighty God. We have forgotten his signal mercies, and have cultivated a revengeful, haughty, and boastful spirit." A relic of a bygone chivalric era, Lee had been thrust into a new age of industrial warfare.[100]

Congressman William Rives, chairman of the Committee on Foreign Relations, broached the subject with Lee of becoming the Confederacy's president—with dictatorial powers. The idea shocked Lee, who replied, "If the president could not save the country, no one could."

Lee did not even want the added responsibility that came with becoming the Confederacy's general-in-chief—duties that Davis had willingly ceded to him—although he professed to be "greatly gratified by the expression of your confidence in offering me" the position.

"I do not think that while charged with my present command embracing Virginia & NC & the immediate controul [sic] of the army I could direct the operations of the armies in the S. Atlantic States," Lee told Davis. "If I had the ability I would not have the time." Yet Lee said he would undertake the additional duties if Davis wanted him to, "but I do not wish you to be misled as to the extent of my capacity." A little later, in a letter to General Samuel Cooper, the army's adjutant general and inspector,

Lee wrote that although he was grateful for the appointment, "As I have received no instructions as to my duties, I do not know what he [Davis] desires me to undertake."[101]

Francis Preston Blair Sr., the illustrious former newspaper editor and one-time member of Andrew Jackson's "Kitchen Cabinet," remained an influential political figure at age seventy-three. In 1860 Blair had switched parties to support Lincoln, and now he and Horace Greeley, editor of the *New York Tribune*, decided to approach Lincoln about opening peace negotiations with the South. During a meeting with Blair in December, Lincoln carefully explained that although he would not sanction an official peace overture, he would permit Blair to conduct an unofficial mission of his own. He wrote a pass so Blair could travel through the lines to Richmond and meet with Jefferson Davis.

On January 12 Blair and Davis, two old friends from antebellum days, met once more in Richmond. Davis's wife, Varina, happily embraced Blair, reportedly saying to him, "Oh you Rascal, I am overjoyed to see you."[102]

When they got down to business, Davis told Blair that he would consider any plan that would bring "peace to the two countries," and he addressed a letter to Blair asserting his openness to negotiations. Blair then brought up a highly quixotic notion that he cherished—that Davis might lead a joint Union-Confederate expedition against Mexico to uphold the Monroe Doctrine, which France had violated by interfering in Mexican affairs.

The Mexican crisis had erupted when Mexico suspended interest payments to its European creditors. Encouraged by Mexican monarchists, French troops invaded the country and took over the government. Napoleon III of France named Ferdinand Maximilian, brother of the Austrian Emperor Franz Joseph, as Mexico's emperor in the fall of 1863.

Blair believed if the North and South waged war against a third party, it would reunite the enemies. Clearly the Lincoln administration would never support such a cockeyed plan as Blair's, and Davis evinced only polite interest in his friend's proposal. There would first need to be a cease-fire in the present war before he could consider Blair's scheme, Davis said.

Blair returned to Washington. As he related what was said during his meeting with Davis to the president, Lincoln, seizing upon Davis's allusion to bringing "peace to the two countries," said he favored peace too, but for "our one common country." The two leaders clearly were in disharmony over the Confederacy's postwar status—sovereign nation or part of the Union once again. Lincoln also rejected Blair's plan for a joint war on French-occupied Mexico.[103]

On January 18 Lincoln wrote Blair a note acknowledging that he had read Davis's letter to Blair, adding, "You may say to him that I have constantly been, am now, and shall continue, ready to receive any agent whom he, or any other influential person now resisting the national authority may informally send to me, with a view of securing peace to the people of our *one common country*." Blair returned to Richmond on January 23 with Lincoln's message.[104]

Davis raised the issue with his Cabinet on January 27. Skeptical Confederate leaders agreed to send a peace commission to Washington—doomed though the mission appeared to be, given Lincoln and Davis's discordant views on the bedrock issue of Southern sovereignty. The commissioners would be Vice President Stephens, a leader of the nascent peace movement and once a friend of Lincoln's; Senate Pro Tem Robert Hunter, a former US senator; and former US Supreme Court Justice John A. Campbell, now assistant Confederate war secretary.[105]

FEBRUARY 1865

My faith in the old army is unshaken. Like a brave old lion brought to bay at last, it is determined to resist to the death and, if die it must, to die game.

—A CONFEDERATE STAFF COLONEL[1]

The people of South Carolina should be made to feel the war, for they brought it on and are responsible more than anybody else for our presence here. Now is the time to punish them.

—GENERAL WILLIAM SHERMAN[2]

It seemed as though the gates of Hell had opened upon us.

—THE REVEREND ANTHONY STOKES,
AN EPISCOPAL PRIEST, DESCRIBING THE BURNING
OF COLUMBIA, SOUTH CAROLINA[3]

1

January 31, 1865
PETERSBURG, VIRGINIA

"Peace! Peace!" roared Rebels and Yankees alike as the small procession of carriages stopped behind the Confederate lines on the Jerusalem Plank Road. When three men in civilian clothing emerged, the soldiers swung their hats and repeated the words, as though shouting them enough times would make it so.

Before thousands of spectators, including well-dressed Southern ladies watching from Petersburg's parapets, the Confederacy's three peace commissioners crossed the no man's land between the enemy lines. Vice President Alexander Stephens, Senate President Pro Tem Robert Hunter, and Assistant War Secretary John Campbell climbed into ambulances sent by General Ulysses Grant—with Union soldiers assisting the frail Stephens into his conveyance—and rode away. Overjoyed by even the slim possibility of peace, the Rebel soldiers gave three cheers for the Union Army, and the Yankees reciprocated.[4]

The ambulances carried the three dignitaries to Grant's headquarters at City Point, where the Appomattox and James Rivers joined east of Petersburg.

Grant was there to welcome them. Stephens was impressed by the "great simplicity and perfect naturalness of his manners, and the entire absence of everything like affectation, show, or even the usual military air or mien of men in his position." Grant spoke with his usual concision "and covered the whole matter in a few words. . . . The more I became acquainted with him, the more I became thoroughly impressed with the very extraordinary combination of rare elements of character which he exhibited." Grant gave the men comfortable quarters on his steamer, *Mary Martin*, and awaited instructions from Washington.[5]

The next day a boat arrived at City Point with President Abraham Lincoln's trusted emissary, Major Thomas T. Eckert, superintendent of military telegraph service. Lincoln had sent Eckert to determine whether the commissioners represented a legitimate chance for a peace agreement.

If so, he would permit them to continue to Fortress Monroe, where an administration official would meet with them to discuss terms.

After questioning Stephens, Campbell, and Hunter, Eckert foresaw no reasonable hope for agreement. The commissioners would not consent to the Union's three inviolable conditions—disbandment of Rebel armies, restoration of the union, and acceptance of the North's new antislavery laws. Eckert denied them permission to proceed to Fortress Monroe, and he departed on the next boat going downriver.[6]

Dismayed by Eckert's peremptory foreclosure of the peace talks, Grant telegraphed War Secretary Edwin Stanton at 10 p.m. on February 1. "I am convinced, upon conversation with Messrs Stevens & Hunter that their intentions are good and their desire sincere to restore peace and Union. . . . I fear now their going back without any expression from any one in authority will have a bad influence." Grant then added, "I am sorry however that Mr. Lincoln can not have an interview with the two named in this dispatch if not all three now within our lines."

Grant's telegram struck a nerve. At nine o'clock the next morning, February 2, Lincoln responded, "Say to the gentlemen I will meet them personally at Fortress-Monroe, as soon as I can get there."[7]

Lincoln had already secretly dispatched Secretary of State William Seward to Fortress Monroe on the presidential steamer, *River Queen*, as rumors swirled that Rebel peace commissioners were already in Washington. Lincoln quietly boarded a train to Annapolis, and from there the steamer *Thomas Collyer* carried the president to Hampton Roads, the James River estuarial harbor adjoining Fortress Monroe.[8]

The president joined Seward and the Confederate commissioners on the *River Queen*. Lincoln and Stephens renewed their friendly acquaintance from more than a decade earlier, when they were congressional colleagues. They got down to business after agreeing not to keep official minutes. No clerks or secretaries were present in the steamboat's saloon—just the five men and a steward who brought them cigars and refreshments. "The conversation, although earnest and free, was calm, courteous, and kind on both sides," wrote Seward.[9]

Stephens wore a bulky gray woolen overcoat that padded his diminutive, ninety-four-pound body, and he was also swaddled in several scarves and a wool muffler. As Stephens shed his outer clothing, Lincoln's eyes glinted with amusement. "Never have I seen so small a nubbin come out of so much husk," Lincoln later said.[10]

Lincoln bluntly told the Confederate officials that the way to restore harmony was "for those who were resisting the laws of the Union to cease that resistance." Restoration of the Union was "a sine qua non with me," he said. The Rebel commissioners made neither demands nor "categorical refusals" but instead discussed all the issues raised "fully, intelligently, and in an amicable spirit."

Stephens suggested an armistice so the enemies might march together to Mexico, throw out the French, and uphold the Monroe Doctrine—Francis Blair's serendipitous proposal to Jefferson Davis. After that was accomplished they could negotiate an end to the war. Lincoln said there could be no armistice or peace treaty until the Confederacy agreed to reestablish the "National Authority." Lacking that, any treaty would be tantamount to de facto recognition of the Confederacy as a sovereign nation—to which he could never consent, Lincoln said.[11]

Hunter said Charles I of England had entered agreements with rebels without requiring these conditions. Lincoln said that he did not pretend to expertise in European history. "All I distinctly recollect about the case of Charles I, is, that he lost his head in the end," he said.[12]

The president also said he would not rescind the Emancipation Proclamation or send back into slavery anyone freed by the Proclamation. Seward then informed the commissioners of Congress's passage of the Thirteenth Amendment, abolishing slavery throughout the United States.

When Stephens asked whether the amendment's implementation might be delayed, Lincoln said that if he were Stephens, he would go home to Georgia, persuade the governor and legislature to recall Georgia's troops from the Confederate Army, rejoin the Union, and ratify the Thirteenth Amendment "prospectively"—meaning that it would take effect in five years. The president believed this would be acceptable.[13]

Lincoln said that he would favor "a fair indemnity" to the Southern people for their more than 3 million slaves—as much as $400 million—if the South disbanded its armies and returned to the Union, but Congress would need to approve it. The slaves were probably worth far more $400 million; modern historians believe that the asset value of slaves in 1860 equaled or surpassed the US productive capacity at that time.[14]

Four hours of talking moved the two sides no closer to peace, but the commissioners did tentatively agree to resume prisoner exchanges. Citing the South's refusal to trade black Union prisoners, Grant had suspended the exchanges in April 1864, although his real reason was to deny the Confederate Army veteran combat troops. Lincoln referred this question to Grant, who later agreed to resume the exchanges but without insisting that black prisoners be included.

The conference's other tangible result was the release of Stephens's nephew from a Northern prisoner-of-war camp. As the meeting broke up, Lincoln asked Stephens whether he could do anything personally for him. Release my nephew, Stephens said. Lincoln jotted the man's name in a notebook, and later in February Lieutenant John A. Stephens, who had been captured at Vicksburg, was released from the Union prison at Johnson's Island in Lake Erie. Summoned to Washington, the young officer met with Lincoln, who gave him a pass so he could return to the South as well as a letter for his uncle, requesting the release of a captive Union officer. A Lieutenant Murray of the 13th New Hampshire was freed and sent to the North.[15]

❧

Lincoln's impulsive decision to travel to Hampton Roads rankled with his Cabinet advisors, who did not think he should have gone at all, much less without informing them, although they granted that his motives sprang "from honest sincerity and without pretension." But even less welcome was his proposal, raised at an evening Cabinet meeting on February 5, to pay $400 million to emancipate Southern slaves.

Lincoln had already prepared a message to Congress requesting permission to issue 6 percent government bonds to raise the money. At the Cabinet meeting he said that as the government was spending $3 million a day on the war, which, he presumed, would last at least another one hundred days, his proposal's cost would be roughly comparable, while preserving the lives that would be lost if the fighting continued. When he had concluded his argument there was little discussion, yet Lincoln could sense the silent, implacable hostility toward the plan. He sighed and said, "But you are all opposed to me, and I will not send the message." The matter was dropped. Navy Secretary Gideon Welles wrote that Lincoln's well-meaning desire to negotiate peace was apparent, "but there may be such a thing as so overdoing as to cause a distrust or adverse feeling."[16]

❧❧

War hawks from both the North and South welcomed the peace conference's failure. "I hope all the croakers are satisfied and will hereafter keep silent," wrote Colonel Walter Taylor, Robert E. Lee's adjutant general. "Our people now know what they have to expect & unless we are a craven hearted spiritless people, the result will surely prove beneficial & cause every man & woman to be doubly determined to fight to the last." Confederate War Department clerk John B. Jones wrote, "There is a more cheerful aspect on the countenances of the people in the streets. All hope of peace with independence is extinct—and valor alone is relied upon now for our salvation. Every one thinks the Confederacy will at once gather up its military strength and strike such blows as will astonish the world. There will be desperate conflicts!"

"There is nothing left but to fight it out," wrote New York diarist George Templeton Strong. His thoughts reflected the sentiment expressed in Northern newspapers. "Let the people of the loyal States rally with enthusiastic energy to the support of their Government," said the *Boston Evening Transcript* with ill-concealed delight. "Let the thinned ranks of our gallant armies be promptly filled, not by bounty-jumping thieves and perjurers, but by men who love and would gladly serve their country."[17]

The peace conference's failure produced a "spasmodic enthusiasm" in Virginia for continued fighting, Richmond diarist Sallie Putnam wrote, but she believed that "despondency rested too heavily on the hearts" for the fervor to last. She hoped the spring campaign would "retrieve the reverses of the last few months."[18]

Lincoln's and Seward's refusal to release details about the meeting fueled a spectrum of opinions and conjecture in the North, with some people even speculating that Lincoln might be willing to negotiate away emancipation. Radical Republicans, who wanted a punitive peace, feared that Lincoln would be too easy on the South. There were murmurings of impeachment in the House of Representatives. But most people agreed that the war must continue until the Confederacy was crushed.[19]

Jefferson Davis appeared to be more disappointed than his advisers when the commissioners reported the conference's failure to the

Confederate Cabinet. "He thought Mr. Lincoln had acted in bad faith in the matter, and attributed this change in his policy to the fall of Fort Fisher," Stephens wrote. The Confederate president said it was clear that there would be no peace short of the South's unconditional surrender, followed by a complete change of the "social fabric throughout the South."

Davis proposed a publicity campaign to arouse the Southern people "to the full consciousness of the necessity of renewed and more desperate efforts, for the preservation of themselves and their Institutions," wrote Stephens. "He himself seemed more determined than ever to fight it out on this line, and to risk all upon the issue."[20]

More than twenty government speakers addressed crowds in Richmond to whip up support for the war. Even the usually reticent Davis mounted a speaker's platform on February 6 to make an extemporaneous address. His surprise appearance occurred at a rally at Richmond's African Baptist Church, the largest auditorium in Richmond. Up to ten thousand people heard Davis declare that the South should "teach the insolent enemy who had treated our propositions with contumely [sic] that in that conference in which he had so plumed himself with arrogance, he was, indeed, talking to his masters." He exhorted Southerners to recommit themselves and to never give in. "All must now be laid on the altar of country," he said. Even the Richmond *Examiner*, a frequent critic of Davis, said it was "a powerful and eloquent address" although at times "bombastic," betraying "that boastfulness characteristic of almost all of his oral utterances in the war."[21]

At a second rally in Capitol Square three days later Davis again electrified his listeners by boldly declaring that the war was still winnable. Vice President Stephens pronounced Davis's speech "brilliant, but little short of demented." Stephens declined to address the rally and, in fact, left Richmond that night for his Georgia home, where he intended to remain until the war ended. He "considered the Cause as utterly hopeless," but he did not want to interfere with the government's attempts to salvage a victory.[22]

The *Examiner* wrote that Seward had invited the commissioners to meet him "in order that all the world might see him administering to them a kick" and that now, "if the whole country do not rise as one man to sweep its invaders from the soil with a perfect tempest of vengeance, it will be because we do not wish and do not deserve to be free." In that spirit the Confederate House of Representatives passed a resolution during a secret session pledging its "unalterable determination to prosecute the war with the United States until that power shall desist from its efforts to subjugate them, and the independence of the Confederate States shall have been established." Officially anyway, the Confederacy was resolved to fight to the death while expecting to receive no quarter.[23]

On January 2, 1864, General Patrick Cleburne, backed by thirteen general officers in the Army of Tennessee, had proposed a solution to the manpower disparity between the Confederacy and Union: "that we immediately commence training a large reserve of the most courageous of our slaves, and further that we guarantee freedom within a reasonable time to every slave in the South who shall remain true to the Confederacy in this war." Cleburne said that arming the slaves would remove England's and France's objections to recognizing the Confederacy and would result in "both moral support and material aid." The proposal so alarmed Jefferson Davis that he suppressed it and ordered Cleburne and his commanders not to discuss the subject again, although the Alabama legislature had previously made the same recommendation.[24]

But in November 1864 it was Davis, in a message to the Confederate Congress, who cracked the door to arming the slaves, urging the government to purchase forty thousand slaves to work as laborers—with the promise of eventual freedom. Of course, there was more to it than that. Slaves already dug trenches, erected barricades, and served in the army as teamsters and cooks, but more of them were needed, Davis said. The South's black population represented a huge potential resource: 3.5 million people, about one-third of the South's inhabitants. But just a fraction of them aided the military effort.

Although Davis did not openly advocate arming slaves to fight beside white Confederate soldiers, he said, "Should the alternative ever be presented of subjugation or of the employment of the slave as a soldier, there seems no reason to doubt what should then be our decision." The forty thousand laborer slaves, he said, "would form a more valuable reserve force in case of urgency than threefold their number suddenly called from field labor."[25]

Safeguarding slavery was the primary reason the Confederate states had seceded from the United States and gone into rebellion. A corollary justification was the wish to create a sovereign nation, under the rubric of preserving "Southern culture"—a euphemism for a culture founded on black slavery. Thus, there was an instant backlash against what Davis was proposing. "Even victory itself would be robbed of its glory if shared with slaves," said Congressman Henry Chambers of Mississippi, who spoke for many of his colleagues. "God grant that our noble army of martyrs may never have to drink of this cup!" He said the black man, "whether slave or free, cannot be made a good soldier. The law of his race forbids it."[26]

The *North Carolina Standard* spoke for the majority of Southern newspapers when it wrote that arming the slaves "will proclaim by such an act that the white men of the Confederate states are not able to achieve their own liberties." A *Richmond Enquirer* column published the day after Davis's message to Congress said, "The existence of a negro soldier is totally inconsistent with our political aim and with our social as well as political system. We surrender our position whenever we introduce the negro to arms." Howell Cobb, one of the Confederacy's founders and a former US treasury secretary, said the day blacks become soldiers "is the beginning of the end of the revolution. If slaves will make good soldiers our whole theory of slavery is wrong." The *Richmond Whig* reminded its readers on November 9 "that servitude is a divinely appointed condition for the highest good of the slave." "Falter and hack at the root of the Confederacy—our institutions, our civilization," wrote the *Charleston Mercury*, "and you kill the cause as dead as a boiled crab."[27]

The repudiation of Davis's trial balloon in November did not end the debate. The Confederacy's losses in November, December, and January of Georgia, Tennessee, and Fort Fisher—and Lincoln's insistence at Hampton Roads on the South's unconditional surrender—kept the idea alive, and it began to win reluctant converts.

On February 10 a test vote in both houses on a measure authorizing the enlistment of two hundred thousand slaves was rejected by more than two-to-one. But two weeks later the Senate barely defeated a bill to arm slaves, with Senate President Pro Tem Robert Hunter casting the deciding "no" vote. The next day the *Richmond Examiner* reversed its position and endorsed bringing blacks into the Confederate Army. "The principle of slavery is a sound one; but is it so dear to us that rather than give it up we would be slaves ourselves?" the newspaper wrote.[28]

But the fulminations against the proposal by politicians and newspaper editors, noisy as they were, did not carry the same weight as the opinions of Southern fighting men—and they overwhelmingly supported the enlistment of black soldiers. "Few have been found to oppose it," wrote General John Gordon, commander of the Second Corps of the Army of Northern Virginia, on February 18. Lee's adjutant general, Colonel Taylor, had evidently asked Gordon to poll his men on the subject. Gordon's findings were not especially surprising, considering that just 37 percent of Lee's men owned slaves, compared with 63 percent who did not. Although many soldiers had slaveholder friends and relatives who regarded the "peculiar institution" as a pillar of Southern culture, most Confederate fighting men in Virginia had no direct economic interest in it.

That same day Lee told Congressman Ethelbert Barksdale of Mississippi that he supported Barksdale's bill to arm blacks without offering to emancipate them. "I think the measure not only expedient but necessary," Lee wrote. "In my opinion, the negroes, under proper circumstances, will make efficient soldiers."[29]

Lee in fact supported more liberal terms than Barksdale proposed for slaves who enlisted in the Confederate Army. In a letter on January 7 Lee fully explained his views on arming slaves to Virginia state legislator Andrew Hunter. The slaves were probably going to be emancipated anyway, either by the North or the South, Lee told Hunter. "We must decide whether slavery shall be extinguished by our enemies and the slaves be used against us, or use them ourselves at the risk of the effects which may be produced upon our social institutions," Lee wrote. "If it end in subverting slavery it will be accomplished by ourselves, and we can devise the means of alleviating the evil consequences to both races." Besides favoring the immediate emancipation of black enlistees and possibly paying a bounty for "faithful service," Lee also advocated freeing black soldiers' families at the end of the war. "Our chief aim should be to secure their fidelity," he wrote, adding that if the government intended to adopt this plan, it must not delay.[30]

In Europe, diplomats James Mason in Britain and John Slidell in France tried once more to obtain support for the Confederacy, suggesting that the South might emancipate its slaves in exchange for recognition by France and England.

French emperor Napoleon III deferred to Britain, which feared that recognizing the Confederacy could lead to an unwanted war with the United States. But Mason and Slidell presented their proposal anyway to Lord Palmerston, the United Kingdom's prime minister.

The timing was bad. Britain's secretary of state for foreign affairs, Lord John Russell, had just sent a letter deploring the Confederacy's secret shipbuilding program in England and Canada. Lord Russell said it was "manifestly offensive to the British Crown" and must stop.

After an amicable one-hour interview Lord Palmerston told Mason and Slidell that Britain would not recognize the Confederacy. "As affairs now stand, our seaports given up, the comparatively unobstructed march of Sherman, etc., rather increased than diminished previous objections," wrote Mason. The hope of European support was dead. "Great Britain gives us a kick while the Federal generals are pounding us," wrote John B. Jones, the War Department clerk.[31]

☙❧

The Confederate House of Representatives passed Barksdale's bill to arm slaves in February, but the Senate balked because of the stubborn opposition of the planter class and senators representing the regions not occupied by Union troops. Legislators whose districts were menaced by Union armies supported the bill, aware that the enemy was recruiting ex-slaves from newly occupied areas. Indeed, counted among the "aggregate present" in the Union ranks on January 1 were 180,000 blacks, 134,111 of them from ostensibly Confederate states.

Weeks went by without Senate action. A frustrated Davis told a senator, "If the Confederacy falls, there should be written on its tombstone, 'Died of a theory.'"[32]

In March, Barksdale's bill finally passed the Senate, nine-to-eight, after it was amended to cap enlistments in each state at 25 percent of the black male slave population eligible for service. It did not guarantee emancipation for enlistees, but Davis signed it into law anyway on March 13. Ten days later he corrected the omission with General Orders No. 14, issued through the War Department. It conferred "the rights of a freedman" on slaves accepted as recruits.[33]

Recruitment and training began immediately and was most visible in Richmond, where posters urged slave owners to volunteer their servants to "aid in bringing this fearful war to a speedy and glorious termination." Scores of slave owners did so, and the recruits could be seen drilling near Libby Prison. It was a momentous step for the Confederacy, but it came too late. "The passage of the act had been so long delayed that the opportunity was lost," Davis later wrote in his history of the war, *The Rise and Fall of the Confederate Government*.[34]

In the North, George Templeton Strong wrote, "So much for the visions of glory the South saw in 1860. The sacrifice of the first principles of the Southern social system is a confession of utter exhaustion."[35]

At a flag presentation ceremony at the National Hotel in Washington, Abraham Lincoln said the Confederate Congress's action was proof that "they have drawn upon their last branch of resources. And we can now see the bottom. I am glad to see the end so near at hand."[36]

❧

This was where things stood when General John C. Breckinridge assumed the duties of Confederate secretary of war. The former US vice president and seasoned combat leader succeeded James Seddon. In poor health and accused of erratic performance, Seddon had resigned during Congress's furious assault on the Davis administration following Fort Fisher's capture.

Breckinridge's first act was to meet with Assistant War Secretary John Campbell, just returned from the Hampton Roads Conference. Campbell told Breckinridge that the Confederacy's situation was hopeless; there was not enough money or resources to continue the war much longer. The new war secretary requested status reports from all of his department managers and asked them to also assess their future ability to meet the army's demands. Without exception, their responses described decay and dwindling resources.

Meeting with Lee only deepened Breckinridge's pessimism. The new Confederate general-in-chief was beset by innumerable problems—from increasing desertions and decreasing manpower to inadequate food and clothing for his troops. More clearly than anyone Lee perceived the outlines of imminent defeat.

Lee shared his increasingly glum insights with Davis, but Davis refused to accept the inevitability of evacuating Richmond and Petersburg—something that Lee already foresaw. "I fear Wilmington will have to be evacuated & Bragg fall back in the same direction, nor unless the enemy can be beaten, can Richmond be held," Lee told Davis. He recommended preparing for these contingencies and removing unneeded cotton and tobacco warehoused in Richmond and Petersburg. Davis bridled at removing or destroying the warehoused goods because these actions would "create concern and obstruct necessary legislation."[37]

In early February, when heavy rains and flooding disrupted Petersburg's food lifelines to the western Carolinas and the upper James River Valley, Lee's men were down to two days' rations. Lee appealed to the people to donate food to the army. "If some change is not made and the commissary department reorganized, I apprehend dire results," Lee wrote to the War Department. "The physical strength of the men, if their courage survives, must fail under this treatment. Our cavalry has to be dispersed for want of forage . . . you must not be surprised if calamity befalls us."

Breckinridge forwarded Lee's letter to Davis, who wrote on it, "This is too sad to be patiently considered, and cannot have occurred without criminal neglect or gross incapacity. Let supplies be had by purchase, or borrowing, or other possible mode." Ironically, while troops went hungry in the trenches outside Petersburg, rations that could have fed them sat on army warehouse shelves in Richmond.[38]

A few days later the unpopular General Lucius Northrup was relieved as commissary general, and General Isaac St. John, who had ably managed the Mining and Nitre Bureau, succeeded Northrup. St. John rapidly imposed his efficient management style on the commissary department, and more rations began to flow to the men on the lines, although not enough to satisfy their craving for food. On good days each soldier received a pint of cornmeal and one-third pound of bacon, but the ration fell below that most days. Typically the rations of six Confederates equaled that of one Yankee. Meanwhile the Rebels' clothing and blankets were in tatters, and they had no soap.[39]

With the food crisis being addressed, Lee turned to the manpower crisis, mainly due to an epidemic of desertions by soldiers to their homes and to the enemy. He proposed to Davis—and Davis agreed—that soldiers who returned to their units within thirty days should be pardoned because "it is necessary to bring every man back to the ranks that we can." Lee's thirty-day amnesty diverged from the army's usual practice of hanging or shooting deserters when caught, as their comrades watched. Desertions plagued the Union army too during the winter, but the runaways were mostly "bounty jumpers"—those who enlisted to obtain bounties ranging from $300 to $2,000 and who disappeared after they were paid.[40]

Deserters to the enemy left the picket lines after dark; soldiers who went home slipped away from their camps. "So common is the crime," wrote Assistant War Secretary Campbell, "it has in popular estimation lost the stigma which justly pertains to it, and therefore the criminals are everywhere shielded by their families and by the sympathies of many communities."[41]

During ten days in February, four hundred men deserted Henry Heth's and Cadmus Wilcox's Third Corps divisions. That period saw a total of nearly eleven hundred desertions from Lee's army. In just one night one hundred men disappeared from General Bryan Grimes's Second Corps division. Three of Grimes's five brigades were composed of regiments from North Carolina—the destination of many of the deserters.[42]

General D. H. Hill blamed the mass desertions to North Carolina on "a powerful faction in the state poisoning public sentiment and looking to a reconstruction." About twenty-four thousand North Carolina troops deserted their units during the war, twice as many as the next highest states, Tennessee and Virginia.[43]

Lee told Breckinridge that troops from western North Carolina were most likely to desert—and to take their weapons with them—because of "the representations of their friends at home, who appear to have become very despondent as to our success." Although western North Carolina had contributed more than its share to Lee's ranks, this region, like eastern Tennessee, had always been lukewarm toward the Confederacy, and it had a large Unionist population. Lee suggested that Breckinridge convince prominent North Carolinians to "do something to cheer and stimulate the people. These desertions have a very bad effect upon the troops who remain and give rise to painful apprehension." Lee sent a detachment to western North Carolina to round up deserters and a brigade to guard the Roanoke River crossings in southern Virginia.[44]

Lee wrote directly to North Carolina Governor Zebulon Vance, urging him to coax influential citizens "to explain to the people that the cause is not hopeless; that the situation of affairs, though critical, is critical to the enemy as well as ourselves." If this were done, Lee wrote, "I think our sorely tried people would be induced to make one more effort to bear their sufferings a little longer, and regain some of the spirit that marked the first two years of the war."[45]

A less visible problem confronting the Army of Northern Virginia—but just as serious as the desertions and chronic ration shortages—was the severe attrition of combat officers. The best field officers exposed themselves to enemy gunfire in order to inspire their men, and their valor exacted a high price in blood and leadership: since 1862 nearly nine of every ten officers had been killed, wounded, or captured. Their replacements were younger and less experienced and faced the challenge of winning their men's respect. The new commanders were also less effective in enforcing discipline and maintaining morale.[46]

Despite everything, grim perseverance kept most of the surviving Rebel veterans at their posts. "Those who remain have been held by a sentiment of honor only," a Confederate sergeant said. "They did not wish to disgrace themselves by deserting their flag." In the ranks fatalism reigned. A favorite song included this verse:

> Stand to your glasses steady,
> 'Tis all we've left to prize;
> Here's to the dead already,
> Hurray for the next man who dies![47]

A Confederate staff colonel told his sweetheart that he was resigned to death if that was to be his fate: "My faith in the old army is unshaken. Like a brave old lion brought to bay at last, it is determined to resist to the death and, if die it must, to die game."[48]

Lee would have agreed. "I intend to die sword in hand," he told a Confederate congressman. He pledged to his wife, Mary, "to do my duty & fight to the last." Lee placed his trust in "a Merciful God, who does not always give the battle to the strong. I pray we may not be overwhelmed."[49]

Although Lee the devout Christian might have prayed for the divine deliverance of his army from its seemingly hopeless predicament at Petersburg, Lee the pragmatist had a last-ditch plan to salvage his army's fortunes. In a letter to Davis, Lee predicted that part of Union General George Thomas's army in Nashville would be detached and sent to either Sherman or Grant now that it had driven General John Bell Hood's shattered army from Tennessee. If Thomas's troops joined Grant, "I do not see how in our present position he can be prevented from enveloping Richmond," he wrote.

The next day, confirmation came that fifteen thousand of Thomas's troops were on the march west of Winchester, Virginia. They belonged to General John Schofield's Army of the Ohio, and their numbers were actually closer to twenty-one thousand. But they were not on their way to Petersburg; they were headed to the North Carolina coast, via the Potomac River, to join General Alfred Terry's Provisional Corps near Fort Fisher.

Schofield's march, although not aimed at Petersburg and Richmond, lent urgency to Lee's contingency planning. If necessary—and it appeared that it was becoming so—Lee intended to break out of Petersburg, march southwest to Danville, Virginia, and unite with the under-strength divisions facing Sherman in the Carolinas. After dispatching Sherman, the combined Rebel forces would return to fight the Yankees outside Petersburg and Richmond.[50]

Although Lee, as befitted the Confederacy's "most belligerent man," dreamed of prosecuting such a grand offensive, the gritty facts dictated otherwise. Lee's army had not mounted a major campaign since 1863. At the beginning of February 1865, with Rebel strength steadily ebbing with each passing week, a Confederate offensive seemed less likely than ever. Moreover, Sherman and Grant, who operated on their own timetable, would not passively wait for the Rebels to take the initiative.

Sherman puffed meditatively on his cigar and gazed outside at the rain, which was finally relenting after drenching the countryside along the Georgia-South Carolina border for ten days straight, the region's heaviest rainfall in twenty years. Sherman's headquarters were in a one-story plantation home belonging to a Dr. Ficklin. Shaded by rows of seventy-year-old live oaks, the house had four large rooms and two smaller rooms added onto the rear corners. Sherman's staff officers stripped the Spanish moss from the oaks to pad their bedding on the floor. As February 1 neared—the new date that Sherman had established for launching his campaign—bluecoats began moving into coastal South Carolina.[51]

Sherman had hoped to begin his offensive in mid-January, but the epic downpours had disrupted his plans. Many officers now believed that the swollen rivers, endless swamps, and monumental mud left in the rain's wake demonstrated the folly of conducting a winter campaign in the soggy low country.

But the tall, lean, peripatetic redhead and his staff were undaunted; they had taken into account the rains and viscous terrain, never doubting that it could be done. "We must all turn amphibious, for the country is half under water," Sherman cheerfully wrote.

Sherman had good reason to be optimistic; his army had met every challenge it had faced. In 1863 it was victorious at Vicksburg and Chattanooga, and in September Sherman's men captured Atlanta, in the process destroying anything that might serve the Confederacy. It had then scorched a sixty-mile-wide swath from Atlanta to Savannah, three hundred miles away, astonishing the North and mortifying the South.

Sherman's sixty-thousand-man army was now poised to again go conquering. It was generously equipped with the bridging materials it would need to cross the innumerable rivers and swamps that lay in its path. Companies of ax-wielding pioneers would reduce the dense woods along the way to logs to corduroy the roads for the supply wagons. The army would carry provisions for twenty days and forage for seven, and thereafter live wholly off the land. Sherman's four army corps had done it before in Georgia, and they would do it again in South Carolina.[52]

The destination was Goldsboro, North Carolina—425 miles to the north. Sherman, who had a gift for logistics, perceived that Goldsboro, an important rail center, would make an excellent supply depot for his army. Railroads from the North Carolina ports of Wilmington and Morehead City could bring Sherman's army food, clothing, and ammunition shipped from the North.[53]

Theodore Upson, a soldier in General John Logan's XV Corps, had entered South Carolina from Savannah in mid-January aboard a transport ship with the 100th Indiana. The soldiers landed without opposition at Beaufort, a town situated on a maze of waterways and barrier islands fifty miles south of Charleston. The trip was somewhat of a lark, with the men enjoying the novelty of being at sea and practicing their marksmanship on the sea life. "The boys are amusing themselves shooting at the porpoises," he wrote in his diary. "The waves run pretty high and very few are able to hit them."[54]

Generals Oliver Howard and Henry Slocum commanded the two wings of Sherman's army. Howard's Right Wing, the Army of the Tennessee,* was made up of Logan's XV Corps and Francis Preston Blair Jr.'s XVII Corps—Blair being the son of the would-be peacemaker, Francis Blair. Howard's army entered South Carolina through Beaufort to mislead Confederate generals into believing that Sherman intended to march on Charleston.

Slocum's Left Wing, the Army of Georgia, consisted of XIV Corps under General Jefferson C. Davis, and General Alpheus Williams's XX Corps. After crossing the Savannah River northwest of Savannah, it would feint in the direction of Augusta before marching on Columbia, South Carolina's capital, also the destination of Howard's two corps.

Sherman repeatedly told his staff officers that "if Lee is a soldier of genius, he will seek to transfer his army from Richmond to Raleigh or Columbia. If he is a man simply of detail, he will remain where he is, and his speedy defeat is sure. But I have little fear that he will be able to move; Grant will hold him as in a vice [*sic*] of iron."[55]

"This is a great game that is being played and great men are playing it," Major Thomas Osborn of the 1st New York Light Artillery wrote to one of his brothers. "And the end is not far off."[56]

⁂

After days of downpours southern South Carolina was a vast quagmire of endless swamps, flooded rivers, and overflowing streams. The mud ostensibly passed for solid ground, and the mud was biblical, unlike anything that Chaplain John Hight had ever seen in his native Indiana. Here, he wrote, "the bottom falls out. Nearly every mule and horse stumbled at least once, usually throwing its rider head long into the mud." When

---

*The Union force was known as the "Army of the Tennessee," named after the river; the Confederate force was the "Army of Tennessee," named after the state.

the army began moving, the rain continued falling two days out of every three.[57]

Confederate General William Hardee, commander of the 13,700 Rebel troops in South Carolina, couldn't believe Sherman was going to attempt to march across lower South Carolina in the wintertime; most Confederates assumed it was impossible.

Sherman's men would prove them all wrong, inspiring Confederate General Joseph Johnston to later write, "I made up my mind there had been no such army since the days of Julius Caesar."[58]

General Jacob Cox described the obstacles facing Sherman's army as "bridging chaos for hundreds of miles." There were five large rivers to be crossed, along with flooded lowlands and swamps. The region was poorly mapped. Floodwaters covered parts of the existing causeways, which in places spanned long expanses of water, mud, swamp, and dense vegetation. The Yankees often discovered that enemy troops were dug in on the other side of the causeways, ready to shoot anyone attempting to cross.[59]

Forced to either improvise or bear heavy losses by bulling their way over each river, stream, and swamp, Sherman's men adopted a method of knocking out the Rebel strongpoints. At a three-quarter-mile causeway blocked by entrenched Rebels, two XVII Corps divisions, under Giles Smith and Joseph Mower, waded the swamp above and below the enemy position. Major Henry Hitchcock of Sherman's staff watched as Mower's men "waded through the swamp, the water up to waist and armpits, cartridge boxes around necks or held above their heads—and so the astonished rebs were *flanked again*." Laborious and exhausting, the technique worked every time.[60]

By February 1 two divisions of Slocum's Left Wing XX Corps were across the Savannah River and marching north toward the Coosewhatchee and Salkehatchie Rivers.[61]

"You will hear of me only through Richmond for two months," Sherman wrote to his wife, Ellen, who had been through this before during her husband's march through Georgia. "You have got used to it now, and will not be concerned though I think the chances of getting killed on this trip about even."[62]

The South Carolinians cringed before the storm that was about to burst upon them. They and Georgia citizens petitioned the Confederate war secretary to send an army corps from Virginia to defend their states. "We are sensible of the pressure upon Richmond, and the importance of saving the capital, but it is manifest that its defense must at this moment be made here," their letter said. Jefferson Davis forwarded the letter to Lee, who, believed Davis, "can best judge." Lee, who had already sent Robert Hoke's division to Wilmington, could spare no more infantry from Petersburg or Richmond.[63]

Instead, he sent General Calbraith Butler's cavalry division by train—it left its horses in Virginia—to reinforce Hardee's men and obtain fresh mounts. The division's departure drew down Lee's cavalry force by one-third, and Lee asked that it be returned to him in Virginia before the opening of the spring campaign. Lee also sent General Wade Hampton, commander of Lee's cavalry corps since Jeb Stuart's death the previous May. Reputedly South Carolina's wealthiest landowner, Hampton was ordered to help Butler procure horses, lead the defense of his home state, and rally its people.

In October, Hampton's cavalry corps, aided by two infantry divisions, had driven off two Union infantry corps attacking at Burgess Mill outside Petersburg. But it had cost him dearly: his son Frank was mortally wounded, and another son, Wade, was wounded while going to Frank's aid. The senior Hampton had time only to leap from his horse, kiss his dying son, and shout to his men, "Look after Wade!" before riding off to lead his men.[64]

South Carolina Governor Andrew Gordon Magrath issued a proclamation announcing the invasion of his state and his intention to resist. "There is no room in the state but for one class of men; they are men who are willing to fight in a cause. . . . Remove all your property from reach of the enemy; carry what you can to a place of safety; then quickly return to the field. What you cannot carry, destroy."[65]

Magrath's bracing words notwithstanding, South Carolinians believed their doom was at hand: the desolation of their homes and, ultimately, the crushing of the Rebellion. "There is great alarm all through the country and a strong disposition to give up, among the old residents even, and with the females especially," Confederate General Lafayette McLaws wrote from South Carolina to his wife in Georgia.[66]

"The actual invasion of South Carolina has begun," wrote Major George Nichols, a Sherman aide. "The well-known sight of columns of black smoke meets our gaze again; this time houses are burning, and South Carolina has commenced to pay an instalment [sic], long overdue, on her debt to justice and humanity. With the help of God, we will have principal and interest before we leave her borders. There is a terrible gladness in the realization of so many hopes and wishes."[67]

The Union troops felt "extreme bitterness towards the people of the State of South Carolina" and freely expressed their feelings as they crossed the border into the state. "Threatening words were heard from soldiers who prided themselves on 'conservatism in house-burning' while in Georgia, and officers openly confessed their fears that the coming campaign would be a wicked one," wrote Captain David Conyngham, an aide to Sherman.[68]

Sherman's army believed that South Carolina richly deserved "the scourge of war in its worst form" because, Major Nichols wrote, "this cowardly traitor state, secure from harm, as she thought, in her central position, with hellish haste dragged her Southern sisters into the cauldron of secession." But now, he wrote, "the ground trembles beneath the tramp of thousands of brave Northmen."[69]

Significantly, Sherman did not issue a prohibition, as he had in Georgia, against wanton violence and destruction. "I saw and felt that we would not be able longer to restrain our men as we had done in Georgia," he wrote, adding that he decided not to, "lest its [the army's] vigor and energy should be impaired."[70]

This was more than disingenuous; not only did Sherman not discourage willful destruction; he actively encouraged it. To Slocum he wrote, "Don't forget that when you have crossed the Savannah River you will be in South Carolina. You need not be so careful there about private property as you have been. The more of it you destroy the better it will be. The people of South Carolina should be made to feel the war, for they brought it on and are responsible more than anybody else for our presence here. Now is the time to punish them."[71]

Some of Sherman's men called it the "Smoky March" because fires that they had set raged practically everywhere, destroying railroad depots,

VIRGINIA

Clarksville

Bennett's
Farmhouse *Surrender Apr 26*

Greensboro
Durham Station

NORTH CAROLINA
Raleigh *Enters Apr 13*
SHERMAN

JOHNSTON

Smithfield
Goldsboro
SCHOFIELD

Mar 19–21 Bentonville
Mar 16 Averasboro
BRAGG
Kinston
New Bern

Charlotte

Fayetteville
Mar 11

Morehead
City

Chester
SLOCUM

Cheraw *Mar 3*

Cape Fear R.

Terry

BRAGG

Cox

S O U T H

HOWARD

Columbia
Feb 17

Wilmington *Feb 22*
Ft. Fisher *Jan 15*

C A R O L I N A

Augusta
SOUTH CAROLINA
RAILROAD
Branchville

Santee R.

A t l a n t i c

Savannah R.

HARDEE

O c e a n

Feb 1

Feb 17
Charleston
Ft. Sumter

Beaufort

GEORGIA

**Carolinas Campaign
February–April 1865**

SHERMAN Savannah

0   50   100

Miles

cotton bales, pine trees, resin barrels, factories, rail fences, barns after they were plundered, and abandoned houses. "In Georgia few houses were burned, here few escaped," wrote Conyngham. "The middle of the finest day looked black and gloomy, dense smoke arose on all sides, clouding the very heavens. At night the tall pine trees seemed so many huge pillars of fire."[72]

In Georgia and South Carolina, Sherman later wrote, he wished "to whip the rebels, to humble their pride, to follow them to their innermost recesses, and make them fear and dread us. 'Fear of the Lord is the beginning of wisdom.'"[73]

General William Hardee had sent troops to the Salkehatchie River's north bank in the hope that this obstacle, along with the rain and the flooded streams and swamps, might stop the advance of Howard's Right Wing.

Hardee, known as "Old Reliable"—the appellation "old" seemingly attached to any Rebel general over forty, and Hardee was forty-nine—was an able corps commander. Before the Rebellion he had fought in the Mexican War, was commandant at the US Military Academy, and wrote *Rifle and Light Infantry Tactics*, the standard textbook on the subject. After resigning his US Army lieutenant colonel's commission in 1861, he was appointed brigadier general in the Confederate Army. He commanded troops at Shiloh, Stones River, and Chattanooga as well as against Sherman during the Atlanta campaign. General John Bell Hood, who replaced Joseph Johnston in commanding the Confederate Army that failed to stop Sherman from capturing Atlanta, unfairly blamed Hardee when Atlanta fell, so as to deflect criticism from himself. Dismayed at being scapegoated and by Hood's reckless, costly assaults, Hardee requested a transfer from Hood's army in the fall of 1864, thereby missing its destruction at Franklin and Nashville. Hardee now commanded the Department of South Carolina, Georgia, and Florida.[74]

Hopelessly outnumbered, Hardee had made only token attempts to stop Sherman from marching through Georgia. When the Union Army appeared outside Savannah, Hardee withdrew his army to Charleston. Now Hardee believed he had a slim chance of stymieing Howard's Right Wing if he could use to his advantage the flooded Salkehatchie River and the adjacent submerged countryside, which offered no dry land for a mile or more. No army could cross the flooded low country in wintertime, he believed. The Rebels had destroyed the river bridges, leaving just the narrow causeways as potential crossing points, which the Confederates believed they could easily defend.[75]

Devoutly Christian and fearless under fire, General Howard, who had lost his right arm at Seven Pines in 1862, unhesitatingly sent his men plunging into the shallow waters. They waded through the flooded woods and densely vegetated swamps, where they stirred up snakes and hibernating alligators. Confederate artillerists tried to find the right range to stop the attackers, their rounds sending up geysers of brown water.

"The river was found to be a wide flat or marsh, one mile wide," wrote Major Osborn, "with the water running in 35 different streams." In places the water reached the men's armpits, compelling them to dangle their cartridge boxes, normally worn at the waist, from their musket muzzles.[76]

Howard employed what was becoming his standard method for flanking enemy defenders entrenched along waterways—deploying units above and below the main bridge, Rivers Bridge. With sharpshooter and enfilading fire, the flankers forced the Rebels to abandon their fortified positions. It was the Confederate Army's last determined attempt in South Carolina to stop Sherman's army.[77]

In two days Mower's division, its pioneers aided by privates who split wood and helped lay pontoons, built a mile and a half of bridges that spanned sixteen streams. At times they labored stoically for hours in icy, waist-deep water. They corduroyed so many miles of roads that a Confederate prisoner told his captors, "If your army goes to hell, it will corduroy the road."[78]

"I wouldn't have believed it if I hadn't seen it happen," Hardee wrote of the crossing of southern South Carolina by Sherman's army and its prodigious engineering feats.[79]

Sherman harbored "a species of contempt" for the scattered enemy forces facing him in South Carolina. Few Rebel units now dared to challenge the bluecoat army. Confederate General Joe Wheeler's cavalry felled trees in an attempt to block the roads, but Sherman's men merely picked them up, threw them aside, and marched on.

Sherman's men had a low opinion of most of the South Carolinian civilians that they encountered, disparaging them as "of the same 'cracker or sand hill' species we have found so plentiful everywhere we have been," wrote Major Osborn. "They are lower than the negro in every respect, not excepting general intelligence, culture and morality. . . . They are not fit to be kept in the same sty with a well-to-do farmer's hogs in New England." They lived in shanties with three or four half-naked children running around, "with an encrustation of dirt which entirely conceals the natural color." The children's mother, when asked where her husband was, typically replied, "in the Army" or "Ine haint never had no husband," said Osborn, adding that few men, except for Confederate soldiers, were seen anywhere, and there was a notable absence of bushwhacking.[80]

Even the upper-class inhabitants of the neglected-looking plantations failed to impress the invaders. "The people who remain at home seem an ignorant, forlorn set who don't care for their 'rights' or anything else," wrote Captain Charles Wills of the 103rd Illinois, part of XV Corps.[81]

Butler's and Hampton's two small cavalry divisions near Columbia, together with Hardee's corps, comprised a force of just fifteen thousand men, but Sherman knew that the remnants of Hood's army were coming by train from Mississippi. They were traveling over rail lines so dilapidated that the engineers did not dare exceed five miles per hour for long stretches. Walter Clark and his fellow Georgia "Oglethorpes" of General Alexander Stewart's decimated corps rode in unheated boxcars that were so cold that the soldiers were compelled to stand and move around frequently just to stay alive.

Sherman guessed that Hood's former army would add twenty-five thousand enemy troops to South Carolina's defenders, but his estimate was more than three times higher than the actual number. These men—allied with Hardee, Butler, and Hampton—Sherman believed, "if handled with spirit and energy, would constitute a formidable force" of forty thousand that might make the crossing of the Santee and Cape Fear Rivers "a difficult undertaking." But the Army of Tennessee, broken at Franklin and Nashville, was now little more than a phantom army. It reached the Carolinas piecemeal and in small numbers that posed no immediate threat.[82]

Sherman rode with General John Logan's XV Corps of the Right Wing and kept couriers shuttling orders between it and Slocum's Left Wing. He hurried the two wings north with the intention of uniting them at the South Carolina Railroad, which linked Charleston and Augusta, and then severing the rail line. Sherman expected the Confederates to fight for the critical rail connection.

Howard was positioning XVII Corps for what he expected to be a battle for the railroad in the endless rain when he saw a rider galloping toward him. Howard recognized him as one of his foragers. As the man neared Howard he shouted, "Hurry up, general; we have got the railroad!" The "bummers," as they were commonly called, had been ranging ahead of the main army as usual, looking for food and plunder. Seeing that the rail line was undefended, they had pounced on the prize before the army had gotten there.

With the railroad now in Union hands, Sherman put Howard's men to work tearing up and twisting the rails and then burning the ties. The soldiers had special tools, called "Poe's railroad hooks," for rendering the rails unusable. The devices made it easier for the men to bend the rails after they were heated. The resulting doughnut shape was called a "Lincoln's gimlet."[83]

Sherman discussed the march's next phase with Slocum and his cavalry chief, General Hugh Judson Kilpatrick, on February 10 at Blackville on the main road connecting Charleston and Augusta. Columbia, South Carolina's capital, was the new objective. Howard's Right Wing would march through Orangeburg, with Slocum behind it, while Kilpatrick demonstrated toward Aiken to sustain the illusion that Augusta was the army's destination.

When Francis Blair's XVII Corps of Howard's Right Wing reached the Edisto River south of Orangeburg, the bridge was gone. Confederate troops ranged along the opposite bank behind field fortifications. The river was deep and seemingly impassable, but Sherman's hardy men were now acclimated to the torrential rains, the mud, and the endless rivers, swamps, and streams. Their pickets were sometimes compelled to patrol the lines in canoes while the men slept in nearly knee-deep water. The officers, too, learned to take the waterlogged conditions in stride. General Alpheus Williams, commander of Howard's XX Corps, spent at least one night perched with his staff in a tree, serenely smoking his cigar and wrapped in a blanket. Despite the extreme discomfort of campaigning in South Carolina in the wintertime, the muddy legion's morale was as high as it had ever been. "I never saw the men in better spirits," wrote Major

Hitchcock. "I was struck with the spirit and gayety [*sic*] with which they stepped along through the mud and rain as if unconscious of both."[84]

Sherman sent a division to the Edisto to throw across a pontoon bridge. The bridge sank just short of the far bank, and the troops had to wade through freezing, waist-deep water. The result was the same as it had been at the Salkehatchie: the Rebels were flanked and abandoned their position. Captain Wills's brigade of XV Corps bagged fifty-four prisoners, and the rest ran, throwing away their weapons and knapsacks. "The men of this army surprise me every day with their endurance, spirit and recklessness," Wills wrote.[85]

The frustrated Rebels were growing used to this efficient procedure for dislodging them. "As usual with the enemy," disconsolately wrote Second Lieutenant J. C. Ellington of the 50th North Carolina, "with his overwhelming force of both infantry and cavalry, flanked our position, forcing us to retire."[86]

꘠

"Buildings by the dozen have been burned today, in fact, nearly every house in our line of march has been destroyed," wrote Captain Norris Crossman of the 56th New York as XV Corps pressed on beyond the Edisto. Crossman's observation was now a daily refrain. The previous day, at Adams Run, Crossman reported that Union troops burned the depot buildings and that "a great many houses have been burnt on our track today."[87]

Orangeburg was burning when XVII Corps marched into the city of eight hundred. Rebel troops had fired a merchant's cotton bales, and gusty winds had spread the flames. "If the town had been built on purpose for a bonfire it could not have been bettered," wrote Major Osborn of the 1st New York Light Artillery. "All that could be done was to watch it on the windward side and the outskirts of the town." Half the town was reduced to charred ruins.

The Confederates' insistence on burning cotton bales so Union troops could not have them perplexed Major Hitchcock. "The fools—why *they* should lose time in destroying it? What use could we make of it but to burn it? How could we use or remove it if we would?"[88]

Rebel cavalry General Wheeler offered to quit burning the cotton if Sherman would stop burning houses. Sherman replied, "I hope you will burn all the cotton and save us the trouble. We don't want it and it has proven a curse to our country. All you don't burn I will. As to private homes occupied by peaceful families, my orders are not to molest or disturb them."[89]

The Yankees assisted Orangeburg residents whose homes burned "with the same good will as they would have stolen everything in town under other circumstances," wrote Osborn. Guards were posted at an orphanage and outside intact homes that officers had selected for their quarters. As for the rest, "bummers" looted the stores and homes, dumping their contents in the street. The next day, Sherman's men destroyed the railroad depot, the tracks, and the cotton bales that the Rebels had not destroyed.[90]

The soldiers received permission to freely vent their destructive urges at Hardeeville, a town on the Charleston & Savannah Railroad. They gleefully tore down many of the town's buildings, including a large church. Stephen Fleharty of the 102nd Illinois of XX Corps described how several regiments from Slocum's Left Wing systematically tore out the seats and pulpit, then ripped off the blinds and siding. "Many axes were at work. The center posts were cut, the building tottered, the beautiful spire" began to lean. A tree that stood in the way was cut down. Then, with long poles, the men brought down the spire as someone shouted, "There goes your d—d old gospel shop." Fleharty concluded, "It was barbarous, yet it verified the words of the Bible: 'For they have sown the wind and they shall reap the whirlwind.'"[91]

South Carolinians often encountered Sherman's army for the first time when cavalrymen unexpectedly appeared at their doorstep. Mrs. Alfred P. Aldrich watched in horror as Kilpatrick's men reined up at her Three Oaks plantation, a half-mile outside Barnwell. "My heart sank within me, and I felt like falling," she wrote.

Cavalrymen burst into Mrs. Aldrich's home through every door and proceeded to smash all the locks in the house in their search for gold, silver, and jewels, which Mrs. Aldrich had sent away weeks earlier. "Finding nothing to satisfy their cupidity so far, they began turning over mattresses, tearing open feather-beds, and scattering the contents in the wildest confusion," she wrote.

Mrs. Aldrich happened to gaze out the window into her poultry yard to witness the bizarre sight of a soldier cutting off a turkey's head with a large pair of sewing shears. Inside the house "tables were knocked over, lamps with their contents thrown over carpets and mattings, furniture of all sorts broken, a guitar and violin smashed." Other soldiers tried to set fire to the house while Mrs. Aldrich and her terrified servants were still inside. They put out the fires before they spread. "The fire fiend spirit . . . possessed them," she wrote.

Before leaving Barnwell, until then a handsome little town of four hundred, the Yankees burned all of the public buildings. Somewhat surprisingly, Barnwell's Masonic Hall, along with its archives and sacred emblems, was burned to the ground; the fraternal spirit that had once united Masons, North and South, had become extinct. "Nothing in South Carolina was held sacred," wrote Mrs. Aldrich, surprised at the Yankees' casual destruction of the Masonic relics. Many residences were also fired; blackened chimneys marked where the incinerated homes had once stood. While the town burned, Kilpatrick presided over a ball in the hotel he had expropriated for his headquarters.

"We have changed the name of Barnwell to Burnwell," Kilpatrick proudly told Sherman after finishing his destructive work there. Other towns that went up in smoke at about the same time included McPherson-ville, Hickory Hill, Brighton, Hardeeville, Robertsville, and Perrysburg.

When Kilpatrick's men, followed by Slocum's bluecoats, had finished looting and vandalizing Three Oaks, the namesake trees had been reduced to stumps; the fences and the main gate had been cut down and burned. Also in ashes were the Aldriches' ginhouse, corn crib, stables, and two years' worth of cotton. The soldiers stole the horses, cattle, and sheep.[92]

Union cavalry were bad enough, but Confederate troopers sometimes also looted the homes of the people they had sworn to defend. A middle-aged woman living on a four-hundred-acre farm watched impassively as Union troops stole her corn and fodder; she had expected it, she told Major Henry Hitchcock. What she hadn't anticipated, she said, was being robbed by Wheeler's Rebel cavalrymen, who had passed through a day or two earlier and had taken whatever they wanted. "I didn't expect that of our own people," she told Hitchcock.[93]

Fires and dense smoke marked the track of Sherman's army, in places blotting out the sun and sky. "They looked like a dozen cities burning at the same time," wrote Major Osborn, who found a terrible "grandeur" in the spectacle. The fires singed the soldiers' hair and clothing and panicked the draft animals and horses, "who dashed hither and thither in an agony of fear," wrote Major George Nichols, a Sherman aide. "There was a terrible sublimity in this scene which I shall never forget."

Captain David Conyngham, another Sherman aide and newspaper correspondent, described the countryside as "one vast bonfire." On the blackest nights "the army might safely march . . . the crackling pine woods shooting up their columns of flame, and the burning houses along the way would light it on, while the dark clouds and pillars of smoke would safely cover its rear."[94]

Few Yankees felt any twinges of sympathy for the South Carolinians. "Pity for these inhabitants I have none," wrote Lieutenant Charles Mouse of the 2nd Massachusetts. "I believe that this terrible example is needed in this country as a warning to those men in all time to come who might cherish rebellious thoughts."

A Michigan lieutenant confessed that he was thankful the war was being fought in the South and not the North. "If such scenes should be enacted through Michigan, I would never live as long as one of the invading army did," wrote Lieutenant Charles Brown of the 21st Michigan. He said he would not blame Southerners if they chose to wage a guerrilla war against the Union Army.[95]

At her Low Country plantation home, Marion Porcher could only watch as the Yankees drove off horses and mules and slaughtered cattle, sheep, and hogs. "It was awful to hear the screams of cattle and hogs as they were chased and bayoneted." Union soldiers killed her pet calf and an old house cat, Aaron, "cruelly run through with a bayonet, right before my eyes, as he tried to escape under the house." Not far away the Reverend Paul Trapier, former rector of St. Andrew's Parish, wrote, "Every residence but one, on the west bank of the Ashley River, was burnt simultaneously."

Lieutenant J. C. Ellington of the 50th North Carolina seethed at the Yankees' wanton destruction of homes and at the impotence of Hardee's corps, to which he belonged, to stop it. "The history of this campaign, which ought to go down in history as a disgrace to the civilization of the American Nation, can be written in few words," he said. Every day "we could look back and see the homes of helpless women and children ascending in smoke, while they were turned out in the cold of mid-winter to starve and freeze."[96]

To uphold his pretense of targeting Augusta, Sherman sent Kilpatrick's cavalry on a raid in that direction while his infantry columns continued to march toward Columbia. The vanguard of Kilpatrick's five-thousand-man division rode into an ambush in the streets of Aiken. Two thousand of Wheeler's Confederate troopers suddenly struck both flanks, and a cavalry brawl exploded at close quarters, with the men fighting with pistols and swords.

The Yankee cavalrymen fled, with Kilpatrick at their head and Wheeler's men in hot pursuit. Five miles north of town along a stream the Union troopers regrouped and made a stand. Repulsed, the Rebel cavalry returned to Aiken and looted the town. The next day, Kilpatrick turned back with wagons overflowing with wounded men and missing at least thirty men, who had been captured.[97]

The Aiken fight attested to the abiding fighting spirit of the Rebel cavalry more than it revealed any congenital flaws in Kilpatrick's cavalry corps. Yet it did demonstrate that Kilpatrick, nicknamed "Kill Cavalry" for his reckless squandering of men, was not of the caliber of Phil Sheridan's Cavalry Corps generals; he was headstrong and often paid for his rashness with his men's blood.

The lack of serious resistance after passing over the Salkehatchie River puzzled Union soldiers. "If there is any place they ought to fight and fight hard it is right here where treason first was hatched," wrote Theodore Upson of the 100th Indiana, "but so far we have been able to brush them off our path like so many flies. Our boys are getting to have an utter contempt for them." Major Hitchcock described the South Carolinians as "whining" and "mean-spirited" and disparaged their propensity to blame their misfortunes on "'leaders who forced us into this war.' . . . Of all mean humbugs, 'South Carolina's chivalry' is the meanest," he wrote.[98]

If there was little fighting to test Sherman's hardy soldiers, his "bummers" faced the same challenge they had in Georgia: feeding sixty thousand men each day. They rose to the occasion by fanning out ahead of the army and cleaning out pantries, barns, fields, and feedlots of every particle of provender. Their foraging skills honed by weeks of living off the Georgia countryside, the bummers displayed a preternatural ability to sniff out the most cunning hiding places and find secreted food and valuables. A slave said of the foragers, "These Yankee soldiers have noses like hounds."

There were about five thousand of them. Although they might have looked like the army's flotsam, usually dressed in drab, filthy clothing but often clad in stolen hats and even women's raiment, the men were detailed to foraging duty. Besides breaking into and plundering houses and barns even before the cavalry got there—Kilpatrick grumblingly referred to them as "the infernal bummers"—they acted as long-range reconnaissance units, traveling far ahead of Sherman's marching columns and sending back valuable intelligence along with foraged food and supplies.[99]

"I doubt whether the history of war shows an organization equal to it in scientific and authorized stealing," wrote Major Osborn. Operating in twenty-man squads commanded by scout officers, the bummers foraged up to twenty miles in every direction, no detail escaping them. They "never hesitate to fight wherever the enemy can be found. . . . They invariably go to each other's assistance," frequently defeating larger Rebel forces, Osborn wrote. "We feel more safe with these men on every side of us than if we had ten times their number of organized cavalry."

The bummers also spared the army needless casualties, Sherman believed, by intimidating Confederate defenders into withdrawing. The bummers' confident bearing convinced the Rebels that the entire Union force was right behind them.[100]

But the foraging often exceeded the bummers' mission of supplying the army's needs and degenerated into robbery and vandalism. An eyewitness to the looting of Winnsboro, South Carolina, described the bummers as "truants out of school." They made bonfires of hams and bacon and created streams from dumped molasses and vinegar, into which they "set boxes and barrels of crackers afloat." They dragged the organ out of an Episcopal church and played tunes on it and then dug up a coffin, opened it, and stood it on end so that the deceased's remains could "watch" them burn down the church—and then the town. General John Geary, who commanded a division of XX Corps, stopped the destruction and sent the bummers back to their units. He ordered his men to extinguish the fires and guard the town against further depredations. But flames had already destroyed more than twenty buildings.[101]

Captain Wills was appalled when one of the army's inspectors found what Wills characterized as a "Golden Christ," either a statue or crucifix, in a department headquarters wagon. "Everything imaginable is found in the wagons," he wrote. "The stuff is given to civilians or destroyed."[102]

While they went to extremes to hide and withhold food from the Yankees, the people of South Carolina's northwest upcountry generously shared "the last mite" with the Confederate soldiers, wrote Lieutenant Ellington of the 50th North Carolina. "Whenever they were advised [of] our coming in time, the good women would have food in abundance prepared, and they would bring out large trays as we were passing, speaking words of comfort and cheer to us at the same time."[103]

2

February 16–18, 1865

COLUMBIA, SOUTH CAROLINA

South Carolina's capital city was the Carolinas' largest inland city and close to the state's geographical center. It was proud of its distinction as the "cradle of secession," but during the past two years it had been more sanctuary than rebellion epicenter. From all over South Carolina and beyond, people had converged on Columbia, believing safety lay there. The population had exploded from eight thousand in 1863 to twenty thousand, and there was a housing shortage. The refugees reasoned that if Columbia were attacked, it would undoubtedly be fiercely defended because of the government mint and the city's war manufactures. The refugees had brought with them their family silver, gold, and silver plate and placed them in bank vaults. The sudden demand overwhelmed the city's three banks, and soon Columbia had more than a dozen depositories.[104]

The Confederate Treasury Department had transferred some of its employees to Columbia because of Richmond's chronic food shortages. But in February, as Sherman's army marched north toward Columbia, the government transferred the employees back to Richmond.[105]

The people of Columbia neither heeded this warning sign nor paid were mindful of the deadly threat posed by the approaching Union Army until General P. G. T. Beauregard, the commander of Southeastern forces, shocked inhabitants by deciding to not defend Columbia. Sherman was moving too fast for him to bring Hardee's corps to Columbia from Charleston, he said, and he instead elected to make a stand with Hardee at Cheraw, eighty miles to the northeast, near the North Carolina border. The egotistical Louisiana Creole had been both lionized and scapegoated during his uneven military career, and this unpopular decision would be his last major one of the war.

As the long columns of Sherman's dreaded army approached Columbia's outskirts, Beauregard and Wade Hampton departed. Until this day, Columbia's residents had believed that their army would defend them and their homes; instead, their worst fears were becoming reality.

Pandemonium engulfed the city. Bowed down with luggage, people jammed the streets and the railroad depot, frantically trying to book passage to Charlotte, North Carolina. One of the last passenger trains to leave Columbia lumbered along with one thousand passengers, some clinging to the outside of the cars. Columbia was completely at the mercy of Sherman's army.[106]

On February 15 General John Logan's XV Corps of the Right Wing reached the Congaree River. Across the water lay South Carolina's capital. A Rebel battery on the opposite bank opened up on Logan's divisions and shelled them all night long, more nuisance than menace. Casualties were light, but by morning the Yankees were testy and longed to strike back. Major Thomas Osborn's battery from the 1st New York Light Artillery rolled up and began firing on cavalry and sharpshooters moving around the city streets, and on work parties building earthworks. After clearing them out—and interrupting the looting by Confederate cavalrymen, who had already sacked the South Carolina Railroad depot and reduced it to ashes—"we amused ourselves in shelling the town and seeing the people scatter." Sherman put a stop to this, but permitted the gunners to fire a few practice rounds at the new statehouse under construction a half-mile away. The shellfire pitted the building's granite walls.[107]

Sherman's General Order No. 26 directed General Howard's Right Wing to occupy Columbia and to "destroy the public buildings, railroad property, manufacturing and machine shops; but [to] spare libraries, asylums, and private dwellings." These instructions might have seemed harsh at the time, but later they would appear comparatively mild in light of what happened.[108]

On February 17, as Sherman and Howard sat on a log and watched, a brigade from Logan's XV Corps crossed the Broad River—it and the Saluda River form the Congaree in Columbia—and engineers began building a pontoon bridge to replace the one the Confederates burned. Mayor Thomas Goodwyn and three aldermen met the first Union troops when they entered the city, handing a surrender statement to Colonel George Stone, the brigade commander. Sherman remarked with satisfaction, "It's no small thing to march into the heart of an enemy's country and take his capital." He had done it once before, at Atlanta.

Stone's men and other brigades from General Charles Woods's First Division marched down Main Street to the state Capitol. "The negroes seemed crazy with joy," wrote Captain Charles Wills. Bales of cotton, the cornerstone of Columbia's financial success, had been laid in rows in some of the streets, and retreating Rebel cavalrymen had set fire to some of them and cut open others. As Sherman rode his horse on the sidewalk to skirt the burning bales, loose cotton was blowing around in the "high and boisterous wind," some catching in the trees, "reminding us of a Northern snow-storm," he wrote. Stone's brigade stacked arms and, aided by some citizens, used an old fire engine to put out the fires.[109]

Before Sherman's army reached Columbia it had entered Saluda, a small village on the river of the same name and the home of the largest factory in the South, Columbia Mills, which employed about four hundred women. Near the village was a recently abandoned prisoner-of-war camp, a place the half-starved Union captives had nicknamed "Camp Sorghum" because of their dietary staple, "poor and sickly sorghum molasses," accompanied by half-cooked corn. There, about a thousand men had survived in leaky dugouts and huts made from sticks and logs that the prisoners had gathered in the woods. Whenever it rained, the Yankees were soaked, and there were no fires to warm them. Chronic diarrhea compounded their misery. "Valley Forge was paradise compared to it," wrote one of the inmates, Adjutant Samuel Byers of the 5th Iowa.

However, Camp Sorghum was a relatively easy place from which to escape, and nighttime disappearances were so commonplace that the exasperated Confederates finally moved the captives to the "high-walled yard of the lunatic asylum" in Columbia, where the inmates built sheds in which to live. The memorable march through Columbia's streets to their new prison occurred just before Sherman's arrival. "A mob of people gathered around us, hooting and hissing their hatred at us," wrote Byers. "The mob, thirsting for our blood, did not dream what was about to happen."[110]

When Sherman's men departed Saluda to proceed to Columbia, they burned Columbia Mills. "It was sad to see in Saluda groups of female operatives weeping and wringing their hands in agony, as they saw the factory, their only means of support, in flames," wrote Captain Conyngham, the Sherman aide. "It is truly said, 'War is cruelty' . . . for the innocent suffer for the crimes of the guilty."[111]

☙❧

When Sherman entered Columbia two women with whom he had once been acquainted sought his protection. The mother superior of the Ursuline convent in Columbia, Sister Baptista Lynch, sent Sherman a penciled note reminding him that she had taught at the school that Sherman's daughter Minnie attended in Ohio. Sherman dispatched his inspector general and brother-in-law, Colonel Charles Ewing, to assure Sister Baptista "that we contemplated no destruction of any private property in Columbia at all."[112]

Sherman also visited the sister of a former hunting companion, James Poyas, from Sherman's posting at Fort Moultrie outside Charleston two decades earlier. The sister lived near the railroad depot, and her house, surprisingly, had not been looted. Even more amazingly, chickens and ducks roamed the premises, having somehow escaped the clutches of Sherman's bummers. She told Sherman she was indebted to him for protecting her home.

Puzzled, Sherman said he had issued no such order. "I did not know you were here till a few minutes ago," he said. She handed him Sherman's "protection"—a book he had inscribed in 1845 at the family plantation outside of Charleston. She said she had shown it to one of the soldiers who, after confirming that it was Sherman's handwriting, posted a guard, and she was then left in peace. Where was the guard? Sherman asked. The woman said the young man, who was from Iowa, was in another room minding the woman's baby. Sherman sent the woman rice and ham from his own mess stores.[113]

☙❧

As Sherman rode through Columbia's streets, with throngs of people pressing around him, two ragged men approached—escaped Union prisoners of war. Sherman dismounted to greet them. As he held his hands out to them, one of them gave him a piece of paper.

When the two were imprisoned in the Union camp on the Columbia asylum grounds Adjutant Byers, captured at Chattanooga in November 1863 while serving under Sherman, was inspired to write a poem extolling

Sherman's march through Georgia. The prisoners had read about the campaign in a Columbia newspaper they had found hidden in a loaf of bread that a slave delivered to them.[114]

Byers's poem, titled "When Sherman Marched to the Sea," begins,

> Our camp-fires shone bright on the mountains
> That frowned on the river below,
> While we stood by our guns in the morning,
> And eagerly watched for the foe;
> When a rider came out of the darkness
> That hung over mountain and tree,
> And shouted: "Boys, up and be ready!
> For Sherman will march to the sea!"

The prison glee club, which lived with its stringed instruments under the asylum hospital, put Byers's words to the tune of "Old Rosin the Beau" and played the song often. A prisoner who was being sent North hid a copy of the lyrics in his wooden leg and smuggled it through the lines. "When Sherman Marched to the Sea" quickly became a favorite among the Union troops and in the North. (Another song, "Marching Through Georgia" by Henry Clay Work, exceeded it in popularity when it was published months later. Sherman reportedly came to dislike Work's song.)[115]

When the Confederate jailers sent six hundred inmates to other prisons in cattle cars on February 15, Byers and his companion had hidden in the attic of the asylum hospital. They later slipped into the city, appearing when Sherman's men entered Columbia.

Later that day, Sheridan read the piece of paper given to him in the street—it was a copy of Byers's lyrics—and he summoned Byers to his headquarters. Sherman told him "how pleased he had been with my song," Byers wrote, and said that his army would sing it. On the spot Sherman gave Byers a place on his staff and assigned him a horse. Invited to dinner in Sherman's mess, Byers, still wearing rags, sat beside the general and answered the many questions asked by Sherman and his staff officers about the treatment of Union prisoners.[116]

As XV Corps marched into the city that day, February 17, citizens and blacks handed them buckets and bottles full of whiskey and wine. Besides being a repository for Southern refugees' silver, gold, and jewelry, the city had also become a storehouse for their vintage wines and whiskeys. General Beauregard and Mayor Goodwyn had pleaded with Hampton and the governor to destroy the liquor before Sherman's men arrived, but they had refused; it was private property, they said. Moreover, Hampton, before he abruptly abandoned Columbia, had vowed to defend the city "house to house."

Consequently, Union troops were now drinking heavily. "The men were very worn and tired and drank freely of it, and the entire brigade became drunk," wrote Major Osborn. Whiskey barrels and wine casks were rolled into the streets so that even more soldiers could banish their sobriety.[117]

They might have put out the fires started by the Confederates, but further arson was clearly contemplated, as evidenced by this bit of doggerel the troops were happily singing:

"Hail, Columbia, happy land
If I don't burn you, I'll be damned."[118]

Around dusk three signal rockets shot into the sky; they were red, white, and blue. Sarah Bryce asked a Union guard what this meant. He replied, "Don't ask me; you will know soon enough." Professor Joseph LeConte of South Carolina College also saw the skyrockets arching into the sky. "Instantly, fires burst out everywhere," he wrote.

Citizen firemen rolled out their fire engines and hoses, "but they were quickly rendered useless by the Federal soldiers," lamented Mrs. Bryce. "They destroyed the engines, pierced and cut the hose, destroyed the water-works and the gas-works."

Columbia became "a roaring, surging sea of flames," wrote LeConte. "The streets were filled with ten thousand yelling soldiers, running from house to house with flaming torches." The Reverend Anthony Porter, an Episcopal priest, wrote, "It seemed as though the gates of Hell had opened upon us."[119]

Drunken soldiers, joined by escaped Union prisoners, set fire to cotton bales and loose cotton, and new blazes sprang up in the brothel district and then in the eastern suburbs, where several large homes were fired, among them Confederate Treasury Secretary George Trenholm's and Hampton's. Flames leaped into the sky on Main Street and in the northern district.

"There were then some twenty fires in full blast, in as many different quarters," wrote popular novelist William Gilmore Simms, whose books celebrated the antebellum South and whose own country home, Woodlands, was pillaged and burned. Of the Columbia fires Simms wrote, "It was a scene for the painter of the horrible." The soldiers roaming Columbia "carried with them, from house to house, pots and vessels containing combustible liquids."[120]

Sherman had promised Mother Superior Baptista Lynch that her Ursuline convent and boarding school, located in the middle of Columbia, would be protected, and guards were posted there. The boarding school had become a refuge for the daughters of wealthy South Carolinians whose homes lay in the path of Sherman's army, and about forty girls and young women lived there, among them Mrs. Alfred Aldrich's three eldest daughters from Barnwell. As fires raged in the nearby business district, the sisters and the girls went to the chapel to pray. Then, they returned to the convent and began dragging their trunks into the yard as the guards taunted them with "You deserve it; you brought it on yourselves."

When soldiers began looting the convent, the nuns arranged the girls in ranks, and their priest, Father Jeremiah O'Connell, holding aloft a crucifix, led them in a procession down the street to the Catholic Church, which lay beyond where houses were collapsing in flames. The smaller girls were placed between the larger girls for protection. "We marched through the blazing streets with the precision of a military band," wrote Sara Aldrich. "It was our safety." The girls and nuns spent the hours until daybreak huddled outside the church doors and in the nearby cemetery. Back at the convent, soldiers with torches were seen on the roof. Fire soon consumed the building, and around 3 a.m. the cross on the convent cupola crashed down. Two frail nuns died from the shocks they received that night.[121]

Seventeen-year-old Emma LeConte, living with her family in a house on the South Carolina College campus, watched as "the drunken devils roamed about, setting fire to every house the flames seem likely to spare.

... They would enter houses and in the presence of helpless women and children, pour turpentine on the beds and set them on fire."[122]

Firemen responded with their engines and hoses, but the soldiers drove them off and hacked the hoses to pieces. "The firemen, dreading worse usage to themselves, left the field in despair," wrote Simms. At eleven o'clock Market Hall's clock announced the hour for the last time. Minutes later the clock tower crashed to the ground.[123]

"The wind blew a fearful gale," LeConte wrote, "wafting the flames from house to house with frightful rapidity." She and the other women barricaded themselves in the basement, but at 4 a.m. they went to the door of their home to see what was happening. "My God! What a scene! ... the State House [the old one, not the unfinished, granite building] was one grand conflagration." The fires transformed the night sky into "noonday ... a copper colored sky across which swept columns of black, rolling smoke glittering with sparks and flying embers." A "horrible roar" filled the air "while every instant came the crashing of timbers and the thunder of falling buildings."[124]

The streets teemed with dazed women and children, many still in their nightclothes, who had just witnessed the plundering and ruin of everything they possessed. Mothers madly rushed about trying to find their children. Invalids dragged from their beds lay coughing in the streets, exposed to the smoke and flames.[125]

While the fires raged their worst, Simms wrote, "groups [of soldiers] might be seen at the several corners of the streets, drinking, roaring, reveling—while the fiddle and accordeon [sic] were playing their popular airs among them."[126]

Sherman, fatigued after his afternoon ramble over much of Columbia, napped at the Blanton Duncan house. He awakened to see bright light dancing on the walls of the room. Sherman got up and sent an aide to find out what was happening. High winds, which continued to blow, had spread the flames beyond control, he was told. As his generals supervised efforts to extinguish the fires, drunken soldiers were busy setting fresh ones. Moreover, "the whole air was full of sparks and of flying masses of cotton, shingles, etc., some of which were carried four or five blocks and started new fires," Sherman wrote. The flames covered a square mile and "rolled and heaved like the waves of the ocean," wrote Major Osborn. "The scene was splendid—magnificently grand."

It wasn't until late that night, after the riotous soldiers had done their worst, that General John Oliver's brigade from XV Corps's Second Division was summoned into the city to clear the streets of troublemakers. The drunken soldiers refused to disperse, and Oliver's men had to arrest them all, often using lethal force. "Many men would not be arrested and were shot," Osborn wrote. Some were killed. Others died in the fires, too inebriated to escape the smoke and flames. Toward morning, order was restored, and the winds moderated. But half of the city lay in ashes, including the Capitol, Sister Baptista's convent school, and several churches as well as hotels, businesses, and private homes.[127]

The fires damaged or destroyed 84 of Columbia's 124 blocks, containing five hundred buildings. All that remained of many of them were smoking heaps of rubbish and bricks. "Everything combustible has burned and there remains on the site of the city only a forest of chimneys," wrote Major Osborn. "The destruction and desolation is complete." The rows of mature hardwoods that had shaded the streets "were blasted and withered by fire," wrote Conyngham. "The streets were full of rubbish, broken furniture, and groups of crouching, desponding, weeping, helpless women and children."[128]

The next morning, February 18, General Oliver Howard, the Right Wing commander, issued Special Field Orders No. 42 in reaction to reports that "certain evil and evil-disposed soldiers" intended to burn the rest of the city. Howard ordered all of his commanders to post guards, send out patrols, and take any steps necessary to prevent further arson, even "taking the life of any refractory soldier."[129]

❧

That morning Sherman and his staff appeared on horseback outside the Catholic church where the nuns and children had spent a harrowing night on the church steps and in the adjoining cemetery. Sherman dismounted and entered the cemetery to talk to Mother Superior Baptista. He pressed her hand and said cheerfully, "Ah! There are times when one must practice patience and Christian endurance." The sister replied, "You have prepared for us one of those moments, general." Sherman said he was sorry that her convent had burned.

Displeased by the criticism coming from a crowd of women who had come to see him in person, Sherman said loudly, "Ladies, it is all the fault of your negroes, who gave my soldiers liquor; it is the fault of your mayor, who ought to have sent off all the liquor before the army entered the town."

Turning back to the sisters, Sherman gave them their choice of any house in Columbia and promised to post a strong guard for their protection. They chose the home of General John S. Preston, which General John Logan was using as his headquarters and which he intended to burn down when he departed. Sherman countermanded Logan's burn order. When the sisters moved into the home they found combustibles still laid for its destruction.[130]

Major Osborn wryly observed, "One cannot conceive of anything which would or could make a grander fire than this one, excepting a larger city than Columbia. The city was built entirely of wood and was in most excellent condition to burn." Although the fire was an unequivocal catastrophe for Columbia's inhabitants, he wrote, "yet I believe the burning of the city is an advantage to the cause and a just retribution to the state of South Carolina."[131]

Sherman and his generals never intended to burn down Columbia. It "was not burned by orders, but expressly against orders and in spite of the utmost effort on our part to save it," Major Henry Hitchcock wrote to his wife. But he acknowledged that "everything seemed to conspire for its destruction," from the fires set by the Rebels to the freakish gale to "our drunken men" and escaped Union prisoners bent on retribution. "The citizens themselves—like idiots, madmen—brought out large quantities of liquor as soon as our troops entered and distributed it freely among them." The fire, "once started, with the furious wind blowing . . . was simply impossible to put out" despite the best efforts of the army's generals, their staffs, and hundreds of troops. "Our own officers shot our men down like dogs wherever they were found riotous or drunk—in short no effort was spared to stop it; and but for the liquor it might perhaps have been stopped."[132]

Fully aware of these facts, in his official report Sherman nonetheless placed the fire's blame squarely on Wade Hampton. "I disclaim on the part of my army any agency in this fire, but on the contrary, claim that we saved what of Columbia remains unconsumed. And without hesitation,

I charge General Wade Hampton with having burned his own city of Columbia . . . from folly and want of sense, in filling it with lint, cotton and tinder." Of course, Hampton hotly disputed Sherman's allegations. Years later in his *Memoirs*, Sherman admitted that he had prevaricated "pointedly, to shake the faith of his people in him, for he was in my opinion boastful, and professed to be the special champion of South Carolina."[133]

After a night of howling winds, roaring fires, wailing women and children, and collapsing buildings, Sherman's army had more destructive work to do. His men destroyed the Confederate mint and then marched to the State Arsenal, which they burned down after emptying it of weapons and ammunition and dumping them into the Saluda River. While the men were transporting artillery shells to the river a percussion shell exploded and ignited a trail of powder to a wagon laden with shot and shell. The ground-shaking explosion killed sixteen men.[134]

On February 20 Sherman's army marched out of what remained of South Carolina's proud capital city. Before leaving, Sherman gave Mayor Goodwyn five hundred head of cattle with which to feed his people and one hundred muskets to arm a security patrol. As the Yankees headed north the Columbia women who watched them go hissed and booed, and some of them spat on the soldiers and tried to assault them. A handful of Union loyalists left town with the army, including two striking beauties who attracted much attention: Mrs. Amelia Feaster and her eldest daughter, Marie Boozer, a blonde, blue-eyed teenager.[135]

Columbia burnished Sherman's notoriety throughout the South as a modern-day Attila and inspired a cottage industry of apocryphal stories. Diarist Mary Chesnut related one of them—that "Sherman marched off in solid column [from Columbia], leaving not so much as a blade of grass behind. A howling wilderness—land laid waste—dust and ashes."[136]

❧

It was inevitable, especially after the burning of Columbia, that Southerners' anger over the bummers' frequent wanton plundering would escalate to reprisal killings. Rebel cavalrymen murdered an infantry lieutenant and seven men—evidently part of a foraging party—after they surrendered. On their mutilated bodies were left papers reading, "Death to foragers," General Hugh Judson Kilpatrick reported. At the same time, Kilpatrick said eighteen of his own cavalrymen were killed the previous day; some of them had their throats cut. Kilpatrick informed General Joseph Wheeler that he intended to hang eighteen of Wheeler's men, "and if the cowardly act is repeated, will burn every house along my line of march." About the same time, thirteen bummers from Captain Charles Wills's division were found dead along a road. On the bodies was a card that read, "Fate of foragers." When four foragers from a sister division were killed, four Confederate prisoners were executed in retaliation.[137]

Sherman ordered Kilpatrick to "retaliate man for man and mark them in like manner. Let it be done at once. . . . You will, therefore, at once shoot and leave by the roadside an equal number of their prisoners, and append a label to their bodies stating that man for man shall be killed for every one of our men they kill." He insisted to General Howard, his Right Wing commander, that "it is clearly our war right to subsist our army on the enemy" and that foragers carrying out orders must be protected.

However, foragers who "commit wanton waste, [by stealing] such as woman's apparel, jewelry, and such things as are not needed by our army," were undeserving of protection, Sherman said. He declined to retaliate against civilians who resisted foragers while protecting their property but made the distinction that "the Confederate army must not be supposed the champion of any people."

Sherman's officers sometimes punished bummers who were caught abusing and robbing South Carolinians. Captain David Conyngham reported that two looters who were caught emerging from a house with armfuls of women's clothing, "leaving the family almost naked," were forced to put on the apparel and were tied to a wagon. For six days they marched behind it while wearing the women's clothing "amidst the scoffs and jeers of the men." A captain was also tethered to a wagon and marched behind it after he was seen robbing a house; he was also forced to relinquish his sword.[138]

Sherman protested the forager executions to Hampton and informed him of his intention to carry out retaliatory executions. "I hold about 1,000 prisoners captured in various ways, and can stand it as long as you," he warned Hampton. After opening the letter with that ultimatum, Sherman unaccountably shifted to a more conciliatory, chattier tone.

Hampton probably had not sanctioned the killings, Sherman said, but advised him to tell his men that Sherman would avenge each death.

Sherman believed that foraging "is a war right as old as history," yet he would stop it if the inhabitants would voluntarily supply his requisitions. "But I find no civil authorities who can respond to calls for forage or provisions, therefore must collect directly of the people." Although Sherman acknowledged that there had been "much misbehavior on the part of our men," he could not permit an enemy to "punish with wholesale murder."

"Personally," he continued, "I regret the bitter feelings engendered by this war, but they were to be expected, and I simply allege that those who struck the first blow and made war inevitable ought not, in fairness, to reproach us for the natural consequences."[139]

Hampton, however, had recently lost a son, his home, and, now, his state, and he was in no mood to be mollified. "For every soldier of mine 'murdered' by you, I shall have executed at once two of yours, giving in all cases preference to any officers who may be in my hands," he wrote. Fifty-six of Sherman's men would be held hostage for those Confederates ordered executed.

Hampton complained about the foragers' practice of burning private homes they had looted. "I have directed my men to shoot down all of your men who are caught burning houses," he said, bitterly adding, "I wish that every old man and boy in my country who can fire a gun would shoot down, as he would a wild beast, the men who are desolating their land, burning their houses, and insulting their women." He was particularly aggrieved by the latter. "The Indian scalped his victim regardless of age or sex, but with all his barbarity he always respected the persons of his female captives," Hampton wrote. "Your soldiers, more savage than the Indian, insult those whose natural protectors are absent."[140]

Hampton might have been alluding to a sad incident near Columbia. Confederate General James Chesnut, the husband of the prolific diarist, had stopped at a farmhouse where a woman and her beautiful teenage daughter were living alone. Chesnut warned them that Sherman's army was approaching and urged the mother to send the girl away. The girl stayed, seven Union raiders arrived, bound her hand and foot, and took turns raping her. When Wheeler's cavalrymen reached the farmhouse later that day, the mother was raving and her daughter was dead. The troopers rode after the Yankees, overtook them, and killed them all, leaving a sign near the dead men, whose throats had been slashed: "These are the seven."[141]

꒰ꙮ꒱

Hampton's and Wheeler's cavalrymen, along with twenty-five hundred infantrymen under Beauregard, were the only enemy forces opposing Sherman's army as it lumbered north from Columbia. Rebel militia displayed signs of defeatism, with Georgia militia and reserves refusing to enter South Carolina, and South Carolina militiamen—for the most part, men between fifty and sixty years old—prohibited by Governor Magrath from crossing into North Carolina. Confederate War Department clerk John B. Jones hoped these reports were false. "If this be true Sherman may march whither he chooses! This is very bad, if it be true."

Union troops captured one hundred of the South Carolinians after they turned back but immediately paroled them because they were physically incapable of keeping up with the army. "The people of the North can form no conception of the barrenness of the South in able-bodied men; they have all been absorbed," wrote Major Osborn. "An able-bodied white man of military age is a curiosity in the South."

The Yankees, now living entirely off the land, denuded the countryside of edibles, forage, and even blankets. "We have left on the wide strip of country we have passed over no provisions which will go any distance in supporting the people," wrote Osborn. "We have left no stock by means which they can get more. All horses, mules and cattle, sheep and hogs have been taken." Becoming refugees was their best hope of survival, "and many of them must go quick, as we scarcely ever leave provision enough to last three days and often not a meal of victuals for a single person." The South Carolinians feared the worst. "It is feared famine will possess the land," wrote Dr. Samuel McGill. "Our army is demoralized and the people panic stricken."[142]

Sherman's men captured two Confederate captains as they were about to duel over a woman. Union officers wanted them to fight it out at the first opportunity, but one of the captains escaped before that happened.[143]

꒰ꙮ꒱

Fresh disasters in the Carolinas staggered the Confederacy. Hardee evacuated Charleston on February 17, and Braxton Bragg withdrew from Wilmington five days later. Hardee's ten thousand men marched toward Cheraw, the place where he and Beauregard intended to make a stand against Sherman. Cheraw's warehouses were crammed with military stores and personal valuables sent from Charleston.

Two weeks before Bragg's withdrawal General John Schofield had arrived at Fort Fisher from Tennessee with XXIII Corps, which had helped George Thomas crush John Bell Hood's army in December at Franklin. With his twenty-one thousand troops and nine thousand men from General Alfred Terry's Provisional Corps, Schofield pushed up the west bank of the Cape Fear River, forcing the Rebels to evacuate Fort Anderson. His army halted across the river from Wilmington.

Bragg's overmatched sixty-five hundred men withdrew from the city, after setting fire to naval stores, cotton, and tobacco, and retreated to the north side of the Northeast Cape Fear River. Disturbed by Bragg's abandonment of Wilmington, Lee, in his new role as Confederate commander-in-chief, tried to inspire Bragg to continue resisting. "If you cannot arrest progress of enemy . . . hang upon his flanks, cripple and retard him. . . . Be bold and judicious," he telegraphed Bragg.[144]

Before Sherman's approach caused her to quit her South Carolina home for Lincolnton, North Carolina, the diarist Mary Chesnut was a popular hostess at her Mulberry plantation mansion near Camden. A guest at her home one day was General Hood, depressed by the slaughter of his army in Tennessee. He brooded before the fire, oblivious to the other guests, and moved around with difficulty on his prosthesis—his right leg had been amputated after he was wounded at Chickamauga. Chesnut sympathetically portrayed Hood's anguish: "How plainly he spoke out these dreadful words: 'My defeat and discomfiture'—'My army is destroyed'—'My losses'—&c&c. He said he had nobody to blame but himself."[145]

The losses of Charleston and Columbia also put John B. Jones in a black mood; he bemoaned the Confederacy's "dark and dismal" future. "My wife wept, my daughter prayed," he wrote. "South Carolina was superior to all the States in the estimation of my wife, and she regarded it as the last stronghold. Now she despairs."

Mary Chesnut wrote that the flood of demoralizing news made her never want to read another newspaper. "Shame, disgrace, beggary—all at once. Hard to bear," she said. "May our heavenly father look down on us and have pity." As February ended, it rained nearly every day, suggesting to her that "the weather represents our tearful despair on a large scale." Moreover, it was the beginning of Lent, "quite convenient, for we have nothing to eat. So we fast and pray. And go dragging to church like drowned rats, to be preached at."

New York diarist George Templeton Strong somberly noted that many of the young Charleston men who had celebrated the outbreak of war nearly four years earlier were now in their graves. "Heaven forgive them their share in the colossal crime that has cost so many lives."[146]

The man whom Hood had replaced the previous July for having "failed to arrest the advance of the enemy to the vicinity of Atlanta," General Joseph Johnston, had now been given an even more hopeless mission—stopping the same enemy, Sherman, but without the army that Johnston had had in Georgia. After gathering the medley of troops available in the Southeast and the small number coming from Mississippi, Johnson was to somehow derail the Union juggernaut barreling north through South Carolina.

Johnston's resurrection was one of the consequences of the Confederate Congress's furious reaction to Fort Fisher's capture. Besides naming Lee general-in-chief and attempting to clear out Jefferson Davis's Cabinet, Congress had restored Johnston as commander of the Army of Tennessee. He was a logical choice, with North Carolinians unhappy with Bragg and Beauregard in poor health.

Davis had quickly appointed Lee to command all Confederate forces, but he did not act on Johnston's appointment because of his intensive dislike of the general, who disliked Davis in equal measure. After a month with no movement on Johnston, Lee was compelled to ask Davis to act. Davis reluctantly obliged Lee, while irascibly writing that he had done so "in the hope that General Johnston's soldierly qualities may be made serviceable to his country acting under General Lee's orders, and that in his new position those defects which I found manifested by him when serving as an independent commander will be remedied by the control of the general-in-chief."

Confederate Senator Louis Wigfall of Texas, a close friend of Johnston's, told him that Lee had bluntly said Johnston's removal from command in July had "caused all our present difficulties." While facing Sherman in northern Georgia in 1864 Johnston had proven to be an excellent defensive tactician, although Davis, Bragg, and others deplored his over-all "strategy of withdrawal" and preferred the aggressive but reckless Hood to him.[147]

Johnston and Lee, born a month apart and both now fifty-eight years old, had been West Point classmates. Both men were repeatedly brevet-ted during the Mexican War for outstanding performance; Johnston was also wounded. In 1861 Johnston resigned his US Army commission as a brigadier general and was appointed to the same rank in the Confederate Army. He was promoted to full general for having marched to Beaure-gard's aid at First Manassas. Although Johnston was named commander of the Army of Northern Virginia, in seniority he ranked behind Samuel Cooper, Albert Sidney Johnston, and Lee, and this rankled Johnston and led to bitter arguments with Davis.

In June 1862, at Seven Pines, Johnston was severely wounded in the right shoulder and chest. With Johnston incapacitated and Richmond menaced by General George McClellan's army just east of the city, Davis turned to his then-senior military adviser, Lee, to take Johnston's posi-tion. Lee succeeded brilliantly: during the so-called Seven Days Lee's army repulsed McClellan's army and saved the Confederate capital.

Even before Johnston was wounded, he and Davis had not worked harmoniously. Although a good strategist, Johnston was prickly, nursed grudges, and flared up unpredictably at the Confederate president, who grew to dislike him. Johnston was normally a poor communicator, but when a battle loomed his correspondence with Davis practically dried up; he did not trust the administration to keep important information confidential. Sometimes days passed without Johnston informing Rich-mond of his movements.[148]

After recovering from his wounds, Johnston commanded the Depart-ment of the West and was appointed commander of the Army of Tennes-see after Bragg's defeat at Chattanooga.[149]

Relieved of that command in Georgia, "Old Joe" lived quietly with his wife, first in a rented house in Macon, Georgia, then in Columbia, and, recently, in Lincolnton, North Carolina—where Mary Chesnut encoun-tered him the day after he was recalled to command, February 23.

The appointment neither flattered nor pleased the balding, scholarly looking Virginian who was justifiably bitter over his treatment. In fact, the appointment angered him, Chesnut wrote. "He believed they were only calling him back so that he will be the one to surrender. . . . He might well be in a rage, this on-and-offing is enough to bewilder the coolest head." Johnston believed Davis was willing to sacrifice "wife, children, country and God to justify his hate of Joe Johnston," wrote Chesnut. But Chesnut also remembered from her Richmond days, when her husband was one of Jefferson Davis's aides, that Johnston was "a poor subordinate general because he is so fine a critic that he disdains to obey orders for a general campaign. He is always dissatisfied and grumbling at those above him."

Senator Wigfall tried to reassure his friend that he was not appointed to be made a scapegoat. "It was out of confidence & kindness & a real desire to obtain the benefit of your ability in this crisis." Moreover, it was Lee, not Davis, who was responsible for his resurrection, and Wigfall hoped Johnston would communicate with Lee "fully & freely & with kindness & confidence & give him the full benefit of your judgment in this hour of peril." Johnston was pleased that Lee had sought his return to command. "In youth & early manhood I loved and admired him more than any man in the world," he confessed to Wigfall.

Johnston took charge of his new command in Charlotte, the destination of the six thousand men from Hood's Army of Tennessee arriving from Mississippi. Lee ordered Johnston to "concentrate all available forces and drive back Sherman," adding in a second dispatch that Johnston should strike Sherman before Schofield could join him with his thirty thousand troops from Wilmington. Even as he pulled together all the Rebel troops capable of combat operations, the pessimistic Johnston believed victory was an impossibility, and "we could have no other object, in continuing the war, than to obtain fair terms of peace; for the Southern cause must have appeared hopeless then, to all intelligent and dispassionate Southern men."

When Sherman learned that his "special antagonist, General Jos. Johnston, was back, with part of his old army," he knew that Johnston "would not be misled by feints and false reports, and would somehow compel me to exercise more caution than I had hitherto done."[150]

Johnston asked Beauregard for his views on the situation in the Carolinas, and the Creole general told him that Sherman's "objective points are

possibly Fayetteville [North Carolina], and certainly Raleigh and Petersburg." Surprisingly, he estimated Sherman's force to be just thirty-five
thousand men. Based on that number Beauregard believed that Sherman's "plan of campaign may be signally foiled." Johnston, he advised,
must send the Army of Tennessee troops from Charlotte to Smithfield,
southeast of Raleigh, and there unite them with Bragg's sixty-five hundred men from Wilmington; Hampton's and Wheeler's five thousand
cavalrymen; and Hardee's men, now at Cheraw. When these disparate
units came together, the Confederates might muster twenty-seven thousand troops, said Beauregard, which would nearly match what he errone-
ously believed to be the size of Sherman's army.

Near Fayetteville, Beauregard continued optimistically, "we could . . .
confidently attack Sherman, expect to destroy his army, and be left free
at once to effect a junction with General Lee with all our forces." Bragg's
corps might need to remain behind to watch Schofield's army, which
Beauregard believed to number just fifteen thousand men, although it
was twice that. In fact, if it and Sherman's sixty thousand men united,
Johnston and his twenty-seven thousand men would face ninety thousand Yankees.[151]

On the day Beauregard was setting down his thoughts, Johnston was
asking Lee for reinforcements. "Would it be possible to hold Richmond
itself with half your army, while the other half joined us near Roanoke to
crush Sherman? We might then turn upon Grant." Lee could not promise any troops from Richmond or Petersburg.[152]

♌

Cheraw, located on the Pee Dee River near the North Carolina border,
was a last refuge for South Carolinians who had fled Sherman's invading
armies. Every home and warehouse in town was full of refugees. New
arrivals were compelled to live in boxcars.

Hardee's army reached Cheraw before Sherman. It had just enough
time to hold a grand review before General Joseph Mower's fast-moving
XVII Corps division burst into town, stampeding Hardee's ten thousand
men. "I have never seen troops moved with such energy as Mower moved
his division," wrote Union artillery Major Thomas Osborn. In their panicked flight the Rebels left behind twenty-four guns, thirty-six hundred
barrels of gunpowder, and two thousand muskets. With the captured

Rebel guns, Mower's men saluted President Abraham Lincoln's second inauguration on March 4—before destroying most of the guns. The Confederate rearguard, after skirmishing with the Union troops, crossed the Pee Dee Bridge and then burned it.

"We have been driven like a wild herd from our country," wrote General James Chesnut to his diarist wife during the retreat into North Carolina, "not so much from a want of spirit in the people or the soldiers, as from want of energy and competence in our commanders. Hampton and Butler are the only ones who have done anything. The restoration of Joe Johnston, it is hoped, will redound to the advantage of our cause and the reestablishment of our fortunes!"[153]

While resting and waiting for pontoon bridges to be brought up and thrown across the Pee Dee, the Yankees sacked and burned Cheraw's businesses and plundered the brimming warehouses. The frenzy of looting even infected some of the Union officers, who went about the city robbing the ladies, "tearing from the ladies their watches, their ear and wedding rings, the daguerrotypes of those they loved and cherished," wrote Dr. James Bachman, a Lutheran clergyman. One woman was forced to strip before the officers so they could see whether she was concealing valuables under her dress, he said.

To his wife, Mary, Major Henry Hitchcock wrote, "We have now marched a great army diagonally across and through the very heart of the first and most bitter and obstinate of all the rebel states, without a single check, defeat or disaster . . . sweeping everything before us, consuming their substance, burning their cotton, defeating their forces with our foraging parties and skirmish lines wherever they dared offer resistance . . . and with the loss of less than sixty men."[154]

Sherman believed that the South Carolina march surpassed the famous march through Georgia because it "will cure her pride and boasting," he told his wife, Ellen, in a letter that included verses of Adjutant Byers's lyrics to "Sherman's March to the Sea." "I think we are bringing matters to an issue. Johnston is restored to the Supreme Command [and] will unite the forces hitherto Scattered and fight me about Raleigh or Goldsboro. . . . I can whip Joe Johnston unless his men fight better than they have since I left Savannah."[155]

Captain Charles Wills of the 103rd Illinois, who had kept a record of the miles marched by the army since December 1, 1862, estimated that by the end of February it had covered three thousand miles and fought in eleven campaigns.[156]

 ❧

At dawn the cold bit deeply as Union General David Gregg's cavalry division left the Union lines south of Petersburg on February 5 and rode toward the Boydton Plank Road. The horses exhaled clouds of water vapor into the frosty air, and the infantry columns that followed in their train—two divisions each from General Gouverneur Warren's V Corps, which held the extreme left of the Union lines around Petersburg, and General Andrew Humphreys's II Corps, marching behind Warren—crunched over the frozen ground. The freezing wind knifed through both the mounted and marching men, but they were at least amply clothed.

Not so across the Petersburg lines, where the Confederates were rousted from their cold, wet trenches and the meager comfort of their winter quarters to meet the Yankees. "The cold was piercing," wrote Lieutenant J. F. J. Caldwell of the 1st South Carolina. The Rebels roundly cursed Grant for forcing them to fight in the open in cold weather.

In October, Grant's army had attempted to seize the Southside Railroad, which brought supplies to Petersburg from the southwest. Confederate troops had turned back the bluecoats three miles from the railroad, at Burgess Mill. The sawmill was near a stream known as Hatcher's Run on the Boydton Plank Road, a Rebel wagon road that curved northeastward around the extreme right of the Confederate lines southwest of Petersburg. Had Grant's men defeated the Rebels at Burgess Mill and crossed Hatcher's Run, they might have flanked Lee's thirty-five-mile-long defensive line and gained control of the railroad. But they failed to do either.

Today, Grant was going to try again, believing that a winter attack stood a better chance of succeeding than the October offensive. In committing just twenty-five thousand troops, Grant had a more modest objective this time: to seize Boydton Plank Road, severing that supply line into Petersburg, although the Rebels had all but stopped using the road because of its obvious vulnerability. If the Union attack succeeded, the Yankees might also take control of some of the Hatcher's Run crossings, which would be useful in any renewed attempt to reach the Southside Railroad.[157]

Gregg captured a few wagons, and Warren's V Corps, on his right, marched up Boydton Plank Road toward Burgess Mill while Humphreys's II Corps, on Warren's right, approached Armstrong's Mill. A salvo of Confederate artillery fire forced the Yankees to take cover. Then Lee began rushing units to the endangered area until more than twelve thousand men were committed. A division from John Gordon's Second Corps counterattacked, tried to break through II Corps, and was driven back.

The next day, after two more Union divisions were committed overnight to the offensive, Gregg and V Corps concentrated near II Corps. As a cold rain began falling, the Yankees were suddenly attacked by all three of Gordon's divisions—those of Clement Evans, William Mahone (led by Joseph Finnegan), and John Pegram—and a division from A. P. Hill's Third Corps. Some of the Confederates went into action barefooted and clad in flimsy, patched clothing. In a furious battle near Dabney's Saw Mill the two armies fought across a sawdust pile. Pegram, a popular young general who had been married for just three weeks, was mortally wounded.

The fierce Confederate counterattack briefly caused the collapse of two V Corps divisions until its third division, led by Charles Griffin, stabilized it.[158]

On February 7, after a miserable night of sleet and snow, Warren's corps pushed the Rebels back across Hatcher's Run in a pelting rain and hailstorm and then seized the Vaughn Road crossing that it had held and lost the previous day.

Hatcher's Run was a battle of small consequence, but only the pluck of the hungry, tattered Confederate regiments had prevented a disaster. Union casualties were about fifteen hundred, and the Confederates lost eleven hundred men.

General Charles Wainwright, V Corps's artillery chief, observed that many of the Union troops fought badly. "Our men were regularly stampeded. All the officers I have talked with say it was disgraceful beyond anything they have ever seen on the part of the Fifth Corps before." Warren, the corps's commander, privately confessed his dismay. "We are getting to have an array of such poor soldiers that we have to lead them everywhere, and even then they run away from us." The losses during

Grant's Overland Campaign of 1864 and the fighting around Petersburg had bled the Army of the Potomac of many of its best men. Their replacements were not of the same caliber.[159]

Uneven though it was, the offensive had nonetheless enabled Grant's army to extend its lines three miles to the west. In so doing, the Union Army compelled Lee to further stretch his already thin lines around Richmond and Petersburg to nearly thirty-eight miles. Even better, Grant's men were now a few miles closer to the Southside Railroad, which even the lowliest private understood to be the Confederate army's lifeline and escape route.

❧

At his quarters in the Trumbull house on Petersburg's west side, Robert E. Lee performed his new duties as general-in-chief with his usual meticulousness, but without relish. As he had tried to tell Jefferson Davis, defending Richmond and Petersburg against Grant's larger, better-equipped army already absorbed all of his time and energy.

Indeed, the Army of Northern Virginia's myriad problems were undermining its effectiveness. Besides the epidemic of desertions, it was not uncommon to see hungry Rebels picking up corn that had fallen under the horses while they were being fed and then to wash, parch, and eat it. Scurvy and pneumonia raged unchecked through the weakened ranks. There was a shortage of Confederate arms. Men in one unit might have five types of rifles and muskets, from muzzle-loaded muskets, to rifle muskets, to breach-loaders, to repeating rifles—whatever had been confiscated from prisoners or found on the battlefield—each requiring different ammunition. The equipment shortages, desertions, illness, disease, and enemy sharpshooters were pushing the army to the brink of collapse, Lee believed.[160]

As he had informed Davis, he had scant time to devote to the defense of the Carolinas, much less to the problems in the Deep South and Southwest. Yet, being above all a man of duty, Lee did everything possible, rising before dawn and working late into the night with his small staff. More often now, he was being required to peer into the abyss.

One night in February, Lee met privately with his old friend Senator Robert Hunter, one of the three Confederate commissioners at the Hampton Roads peace conference, to sound him out on the prospects for peace. They talked nearly all night. "He [Lee] said if I thought there was a chance for any peace which would secure better terms than were likely to be given after a surrender at discretion, he thought it my duty to make the effort," Hunter wrote. Hunter told Lee that Davis had already rejected this course, and he believed that Davis had spread the rumor that Hunter had given up hope. Lee said that if he, as general-in-chief, were to propose peace terms, "it would be almost equivalent to surrender." Lee did not pursue the matter further.

Shortly after Lee met with Hunter, Confederate War Secretary John C. Breckinridge went to Hunter and proposed just what Lee had, but Hunter told Breckinridge that he "saw no hope for peace unless the President would pledge himself to co-operate, which I hardly thought he would do."[161]

With Grant even in the wintertime nudging the Union army ever closer to the Southside Railroad and with the Confederate army becoming weaker by the day, Lee knew what the coming Union spring offensive likely meant: closure of the last rail line to Petersburg; Grant's union with Sherman's and Schofield's armies, giving him more than two hundred thousand men; and the destruction of the Army of Northern Virginia and, with it, the Confederacy. Lee began urging civilian leaders to prepare to evacuate Richmond and Petersburg.

"It is necessary to bring out all our strength and, I fear, to unite our armies, as separately they do not seem able to make head [sic] against the enemy," he wrote to Breckinridge on February 19. "I fear it may be necessary to abandon our cities, and preparations should be made for that contingency." In another message to Breckinridge two days later Lee elaborated further about his plans when the army abandoned Petersburg and Richmond. "I shall endeavor to unite the corps of the army about Burkeville [where the Southside and Richmond & Danville railroads met fifty miles west of Petersburg] so as to retain communication with the north & south as long as practicable, & also with the west. I would think Lynchburg, or some point west, the most advantageous place to which to remove stores from Richmond."[162]

News spread through Petersburg that a contingency plan was under discussion to remove or destroy warehoused cotton and tobacco. People understandably concluded that Lee's army was poised to abandon the city, and an exodus began. "People are leaving Petersburg rapidly, and everything certainly looks badly for the 'little cockade city,'" wrote artillery Lieutenant William Clopton. Army leaders tried to tamp down the rising anxiety. "There is no intention of evacuating this place if it can be held," General Henry Wise, the former Virginia governor, wrote to his wife.[163]

Breckinridge raised the subject of evacuation at a Cabinet meeting on February 25, but Davis refused to entertain it. However, over the next two days this topic was explored in conversations among Davis, Lee, and Breckinridge. Davis agreed to allow government officials to begin sorting documents and packing up nonessential material. Lee bluntly said that he probably would abandon Richmond and Petersburg but could hold on for two weeks or more. Davis did not dispute Lee's gloomy appraisal. If Richmond fell, he said, he would move the capital south to Danville. Davis now believed that the war must end with either independence or the South's destruction. "The war came, and now it must go on till the last man of this generation falls in his tracks, and his children seize his musket and fight our battle," wrote Davis apocalyptically.[164]

Longstreet, Lee's most reliable general, had returned to command the First Corps in September, his right arm and hand paralyzed and in a sling; in May Longstreet was accidentally shot through the neck and right shoulder by his own men in the Wilderness. While recovering he had taught himself to write left-handed. Lee told Longstreet to be ready "to take the field at a moment's notice, and to accumulate all the supplies you can." Grant, said Lee, was massing men and supplies on his left flank near Hatcher's Run.[165]

❧

For his part, Grant worried that the enemy might at any moment attempt to escape from Richmond and Petersburg. He exhorted his subordinates to increase their vigilance. His greatest fear was that "I would awake from my sleep to hear that Lee had gone, and that nothing was left but a picket line." The Confederates moved faster than Grant's army, and "if he got the start, he would leave me behind so that we would have the same army to fight again farther south—and the war might be prolonged another year." The general-in-chief suspected that the Rebels were already quietly sending men, stores, and ordnance down the open railroad to Danville, holding back only necessities for immediate defense.[166]

As a result of the Hampton Roads Conference, Grant permitted prisoner exchanges to resume after nearly a year's suspension. Concern in the North about starving Union prisoners was one reason; the other was that the crumbling Confederacy could not feed the troops that it had, much less tens of thousands of returning war prisoners.

Several thousand Union prisoners were exchanged at Wilmington. Northerners were appalled at the condition of the skeletal, disease-ridden former captives when they reached hospitals in the North. "They have been starved into idiocy—do not know their own names, or where they are, or where their home is," George Templeton Strong angrily wrote after sitting on the US Sanitary Commission board and hearing the eyewitnesses' testimony. "I almost hope this war may last till it becomes a war of extermination."[167]

Grant cracked down on the clandestine trade with the enemy that had long been tolerated by Union commanders in Norfolk, New Orleans, and along the lines inland. Even Lincoln sometimes permitted favored businessmen to trade Northern sugar, bacon, salt, coffee, and other military necessities needed by the Confederacy for Southern cotton.

On February 7 Lincoln sent Grant a letter that authorized a former Illinois state legislator, James Singleton, to bring Southern cotton and tobacco through Grant's lines—"if you consent." Grant suspected that Singleton was involved in a speculation scheme, but he allowed Singleton to proceed to Richmond. Then Grant changed his mind, and he urged War Secretary Stanton to cancel all permits allowing military necessities from the North to be bartered for Southern cotton and tobacco.

When Lincoln found out, he pointed out that Grant had allowed Singleton to proceed to Richmond. But he did not interfere with Grant's decision to suppress all such trading with the enemy or attempt to change his mind.

Told in early March by Unionist spies in Richmond that the Confederates planned to secretly ship tobacco across the Potomac River to the North, Grant ordered Colonel S. H. Roberts to seize and destroy the tobacco, which was in Union-occupied Fredericksburg. Roberts's men swooped down on twenty-eight railroad cars full of tobacco and burned all of it—it was valued at $400,000—and captured more than four hundred Rebels. The plume of tobacco smoke was visible fifty miles away in Washington.[168]

෧෮

Grant asked his friend, Representative Elihu Washburne of Illinois, to expedite General George Meade's elevation to major general through Congress. Grant had earlier recommended promotions for Meade along with William Sherman and Phil Sheridan. Sherman's and Sheridan's promotions had gone through in January, but not Meade's. "General Meade is one of our truest men and ablest officers," Grant told Washburne, urging him to make another attempt.

Meade had a good working relationship with Grant, but had mixed feelings about him. He thought Grant was "the best man the war has yet produced," even as he resented Grant's incremental usurpation of Meade's authority over the Army of the Potomac. Grant, he wrote, did not even recognize what he had done. "There is the difference between us," he told his brother-in-law, Henry Cram, "I over-sensitive, and he deficient in sensibility."

Meade got his promotion.[169]

MARCH 1865

With malice toward none; with charity for all; with firmness in the right, as God gives us to see the right, let us strive on to finish the work we are in; to bind up the nation's wounds; to care for him who shall have borne the battle, and for his widow, and his orphan . . .

—ABRAHAM LINCOLN,
SECOND INAUGURAL ADDRESS[1]

When this war began I was opposed to it, bitterly opposed to it, and I told these people that unless every man should do his whole duty, they would repent it. And now, they will repent.

ROBERT E. LEE,
SPEAKING TO HIS SON CUSTIS[2]

1

March 2, 1865
PETERSBURG, VIRGINIA

Outside the besieged city, a Confederate officer carrying a flag of truce appeared. Curiosity gripped both armies. Rumors of peace negotiations had waxed and waned in recent weeks, and soldiers who had endured a long, miserable winter in the cold, muddy trenches were eager to seize upon any slender hope of a denouement of the armies' dreary eight-month stalemate.

The emissary bore a letter to Ulysses S. Grant from Robert E. Lee. Its genesis had been a conversation on February 21 between Confederate General James Longstreet and Union General Edward Ord—prewar friends who now commanded troops on opposite sides of the battle line. Under a flag of truce Ord had confided to his old friend his wish that Grant and Lee would meet to discuss peace. Afterward Longstreet reported to Lee what Ord had said.

In February, efforts by Lee and War Secretary John Breckinridge to persuade members of the Confederate government to consider peace talks had gone nowhere. No one wished to incur Jefferson Davis's disfavor.

But a military convention was another matter, and during a meeting at the Confederate White House, Davis, Breckinridge, and Davis's advisers decided to explore this possibility. Lee was authorized to contact Grant.[3]

On the very day that Lee was attempting to arrange a parley with Grant he was also expressing his pessimism to Davis about the expected outcome of this initiative. "I must confess that I am not sanguine. My belief is that he will consent to no terms, unless coupled with the condition of our return to the Union. Whether this will be acceptable to our people yet awhile I cannot say."[4]

Lee's letter to Grant proposed "the possibility of arriving at a satisfactory adjustment of the present unhappy difficulties by means of a military convention.... Sincerely desiring to leave nothing untried which may put an end to the calamities of war, I propose to meet you at such convenient time and place as you may designate." If Lee and Grant were to meet, said

Lee, they might find it "practicable to submit the subjects of controversy between the belligerents to a convention of the kind authorized. . . . I am authorized to do whatever the result of the proposed interview may render necessary or advisable." Lee suggested that he and Grant meet at 11 a.m. on Monday, March 6.[5]

Grant promised to reply to Lee's letter by noon on March 4—which happened to be the hour of Lincoln's second inauguration in Washington. He forwarded Lee's message to War Secretary Edwin Stanton and requested instructions.

After conferring with Lincoln, Stanton forbade Grant to meet with Lee. "The president," Stanton wrote, "wishes you to have no conference with General Lee unless it be for the capitulation of General Lee's army . . . you are not to decide, discuss, or confer upon any political question. Such questions the President holds in his own hands. . . . Meantime, you are to press to the utmost your military advantages."

Indeed, Grant's advantages were manifold: he already held a twofold numerical edge over Lee at Petersburg, Sheridan was on his way to Petersburg from the Shenandoah Valley, and Sherman was marching into North Carolina and appeared unstoppable.[6]

Grant informed Lee on March 4 that the president alone had the authority to negotiate peace terms; Grant was permitted to discuss only matters "purely of a military character." There would be no meeting.[7]

***

Lee had continued to make plans as if Grant's refusal were a foregone conclusion. The night before Grant's rebuff arrived, Lee summoned General John Gordon, his Second Corps commander, to Lee's headquarters, the home of William Turnbull on Edge Hill.

Gordon, knife-thin and ramrod-straight, was Lee's best young general. A lawyer by training, Gordon was helping his father run a coal mining operation in north Georgia when the war began. With no formal military training, Gordon was elected captain of a mountaineer company called the Raccoon Roughs; during the first months of the war, before Confederate gray was prescribed, the Roughs wore coonskin caps, and their officers dressed in bottle-green frock coats. Gordon's rise in the Army of Northern Virginia had been meteoric; his superiors recognized his natural gifts for leadership and tactics.

Gordon was first wounded on July 1, 1862, while leading a brigade of Alabamans during the unsuccessful Confederate assault on Malvern Hill, where he lost four hundred men. Two months later at Antietam, in September 1862, he was again wounded—and promoted to brigadier general. During the 1864 Overland Campaign and Confederate General Jubal Early's campaign in the Shenandoah Valley Gordon's talents received wider appreciation. He now commanded the corps that Early had once led.[8]

Gordon arrived at the Turnbull house about 3 a.m. on March 4 and found Lee alone; he had evidently been up most of the night and wore "a look of painful depression on his face," wrote Gordon. "I realized at once, from the gravity of the commander's bearing, that I was to learn of a situation worse than I had anticipated."

The previous day Lee had received news of the destruction of the remnants of Jubal Early's Army of the Valley at Waynesboro by Phil Sheridan's Cavalry Corps. This meant that Sheridan would soon join Grant at Petersburg. Lee had sent for Gordon for counsel because the other corps commanders were unavailable; Longstreet and Richard Ewell were miles away, and A. P. Hill was on a medical furlough. Lee and Gordon sat down at a table covered with reports that Lee had been examining. The Confederate general-in-chief instructed Gordon to read them.

"Each report was bad enough," Gordon wrote. They laid bare the army's destitution—its lack of shoes, hats, overcoats, blankets, and food—and the indifference to orders and even temporary insanity exhibited by previously good soldiers. "All the distressing facts combined were sufficient, it seemed to me, to destroy all cohesive power and lead to the inevitable disintegration of any other army that was ever marshaled."

Lee shared with Gordon his estimates of the opposing armies' respective manpower: of his 50,000 men, just 35,000 were fit for duty, whereas Grant, he said, had up to 150,000 men, with more coming from the Shenandoah Valley and possibly from George Thomas's army in Tennessee. When all of the Union reinforcements arrived, Grant might very well command 200,000 men outside Petersburg and Richmond. Sherman led another 80,000 men. If Sherman and Grant united, the Army of Northern Virginia could face 280,000 enemy troops.

Lee paced the room, giving Gordon time to absorb those figures. What should he do? Lee asked him.

Gordon proposed three options, giving them to Lee in the order he believed they should be attempted: to make the best terms possible with the enemy; to abandon Richmond and Petersburg, join Johnston in North Carolina, and attack Sherman before turning on Grant; and, "lastly, we must fight, and without delay."

When Gordon had finished, there was silence. "Is that your opinion?" Lee finally asked.

Gordon, thinking he might have offended Lee with his outspokenness, reminded the Confederate commander that he had sought Gordon's opinion. He boldly added that he had a right to solicit Lee's opinion.

Lee agreed that Gordon was perfectly entitled to his opinion, and he gave it: "I agree with you fully."

Taken aback, Gordon asked Lee whether he had shared his views with Davis or Congress. Lee had not; he did not feel comfortable, he said, advising the Confederacy's civil authorities to make terms with the US government. Lee did not tell Gordon that he had already written to Grant.

Lee said he would abandon Richmond and Petersburg if Davis permitted it, but "the deplorable plight" of his soldiers and his weakened, starving horses made an evacuation problematic. The army's horses, he said, "could not move one half of his artillery and ammunition and supply trains."

The next day, Lee went to Richmond to meet with Davis. Grant's reply to Lee's letter arrived while he was with the president. For the moment, it ended any discussion of negotiations, and Lee did not press the issue with Davis, believing it was not his place to do so. The president restated his categorical refusal to accept any terms that did not include Southern sovereignty. When Lee broached the subject of evacuation, Davis said that if it must be done, it should be done without delay. But Lee said muddy roads and the poor condition of his animals required him to wait.

Lee returned to Petersburg on Sunday, March 5, after attending services at St. Paul's Episcopal Church in Richmond for the last time during the war. Speaking with Gordon, Lee remarked on Davis's "remarkable faith in the possibility of still winning independence."

What now? Gordon asked.

We must fight, said Lee.[9]

Breckinridge had continued to quietly urge Confederate legislators to pursue a peace agreement. In early March, he met with a group of influential senators in a Richmond hotel room—the venue deliberately chosen to avoid the prying eyes of Davis's allies—and pressed them to end the war and stop the loss of life. "We should not disband like banditti . . . we should surrender as a government, and we will thus maintain the dignity of our cause," Breckinridge told them. He left them with the words, "This has been a magnificent epic. In God's name let it not terminate in a farce." But the senators recoiled from publicly opposing Davis and would not promise any action. Breckinridge could not have been surprised; the Confederate Congress had almost always avoided challenging Davis. It was now apparent to Breckinridge and Lee that there would be no further peace overtures.[10]

At Breckinridge's insistence Lee analyzed the Confederacy's military situation in a confidential letter on March 9. His appraisal was discouraging. "It seems almost impossible to maintain our present position with the means at the disposal of the Government," he wrote. "Unless the men and animals can be subsisted, the army cannot be kept together, and our present lines must be abandoned. Nor can it be moved to any other position where it can operate to advantage without provisions to enable it to move in a body." Johnston's army, he understatedly said, "gives no strong prospect of a marked success."

Then Lee let slip a statement suggesting that he had never really believed the Confederacy had better than a slim chance of winning a prolonged war. The military situation was decidedly unfavorable, he told Breckinridge, but "it is not worse than the superior numbers and resources of the enemy justified us in expecting from the beginning." The consequences of the South's inferiority in numbers, he told Breckinridge, "have been postponed longer than we had reason to anticipate."

Lee ended his desolate evaluation by asserting that the outcome depended on the Southern people's will to continue fighting. "Everything, in my opinion, has depended and still depends upon the disposition and feelings of the people. Their representatives can best decide how they will bear the difficulties and sufferings of their condition and how they will respond to the demands which the public safety requires."[11]

The letter, which Breckinridge shared with some members of Congress, spurred Virginia's congressional delegation to invite Lee to Richmond to elaborate on the army's problems. When Lee had answered all of their questions, the congressmen professed their willingness—and the willingness of Virginia—to make any sacrifice for the army. But they proposed no course of action.[12]

Exasperated with the civilian leaders' failure to do anything to reverse the decline of his army, Lee was in a foul mood when he went to his Richmond family home for dinner. Afterward, he paced restlessly before the fire while his son, General George Washington Custis Lee, who often advised his father and Jefferson Davis, read the newspaper and smoked a cigar. Lee "went to the end of the room, turned and tramped back again, with his hands behind him. I saw he was deeply troubled. Never had I seen him look so grave," Custis wrote.

He stopped before his son and said, "Well, Mr. Custis, I have been up to see the Congress and they do not seem to be able to do anything except to eat peanuts and chew tobacco, while my army is starving." He said he described the abysmal condition of his army, urging immediate action, "but I can't get them to do anything, or they are unable to do anything."

Lee resumed pacing and then paused once more before his son. "Mr. Custis," he said, "when this war began I was opposed to it, bitterly opposed to it, and I told these people that unless every man should do his whole duty, they would repent it. And now, they will repent."

The Confederate Congress finally did something: it approved a resolution to raise an additional 15,000 troops. When a group of congressmen informed Lee, he bowed to them by way of acknowledgment but said, "Yes, passing resolutions is kindly meant, but getting the men is another matter." He then tigerishly added, "Yet, if I had 15,000 fresh troops, things would look very different."[13]

Peace negotiations being a dead issue, the army must now fight, Lee had told Gordon. Gordon took Lee's admonition to heart; he devised a plan to break the Union Army's grip on Petersburg so that the Army of Northern Virginia might escape and join Johnston's forces in North Carolina.

Fort Stedman, a square fort built by Union engineers nine months earlier, would be the Rebel objective. Situated on Petersburg's east side, Stedman was flanked on either side by two batteries—Battery Nos. 10 and 9 to the north, and Nos. 11 and 12 to the south. A half-mile away, within supporting range, was Fort Haskell, yet another Union stronghold.

Fort Stedman's namesake, Colonel Griffin Stedman, commander of the 11th Connecticut, was killed in August while scouting Hare Hill, upon which the redoubt was built. This was also where the 1st Maine Heavy Artillery was butchered during the bloody Union attacks of June 18. The failure of those attacks—doomed by the Union Army's slowness and lack of coordination and the Confederates' swifter reflexes—marked the beginning of the Petersburg stalemate.

Fort Stedman intrigued Gordon, a relative newcomer to Petersburg from Jubal Early's Army of the Valley, because it was a mere 280 yards from the Rebel position. The picket lines were just 145 yards apart.

Gordon's plan called for a predawn attack. Rebel axmen would smash through the abatis and chevaux-de-frise in front of the fort, and 350 picked men would infiltrate the enemy lines. The way cleared, storming parties would overwhelm the fort's small garrison and seize its four light guns before reinforcements could arrive or supporting fire could be brought to bear.

The shock troops would seize a second Union line that Gordon believed to be on the high ground behind the fort. From this position, Gordon's men could repel any Yankee counterattack and then resume their attack, knifing into the Union rear—perhaps all the way to City Point—while turning the Yankees' flanks. Everything depended on stealth and speed.

"The tremendous possibility was the disintegration of the whole left wing of the Federal army," wrote Gordon, "or at least the dealing of such a staggering blow upon it as would disable it temporarily, enabling us to withdraw from Petersburg in safety and join Johnston in North Carolina." A small force would remain behind and hold the lines until the army got away.[14]

While Lee sought local men as guides, Gordon sent his pregnant wife to a Petersburg dry goods store to buy white cloth. Torn into strips, the white material would identify Gordon's picked infiltrators so their comrades would not shoot them by mistake.[15]

Gordon and Lee agreed the attack must be made before Sheridan's powerful cavalry columns reached Petersburg and Grant launched his anticipated offensive against the Confederate right flank.

Under a pendulous gray sky, a cold wind swept down Washington's muddy streets as a drizzle fell, but the weather could not dampen the festive mood. It was Inauguration Day, March 4, 1865, and thousands of people thronged Capitol Hill to witness the second swearing-in of President Abraham Lincoln and his new vice president, Andrew Johnson of Tennessee. Women in feathers, diamonds, and "wide crinoline" filled the gallery of the Senate, where Johnson would recite the oath of office. A much larger crowd milled about in the rain outside, eager to watch Lincoln take the oath and to hear his inauguration speech.[16]

Momentous military victories in September and October—Sherman's occupation of Atlanta, and Sheridan's triumphs in the Shenandoah Valley—had convinced the electorate to stick with Lincoln for a second term. The victories had wiped away the gloomy certainty of defeat that in August had prompted Lincoln to write and seal a letter addressed to his successor, pledging his cooperation. In November, Lincoln won 55 percent of the popular vote, and 212 electoral votes to just 12 for his opponent, Democrat George McClellan, once Lincoln's senior general in the East.

Johnson was sworn in first. Republicans had chosen the fifty-six-year-old Southern Unionist and Tennessee military governor as Lincoln's running mate on the National Union ticket, replacing Vice President Hannibal Hamblin from Maine. Party leaders hoped their selection of Johnson would signal their desire for national unity with the approach of the war's end.

Johnson had reluctantly traveled to Washington from Nashville for the ceremony; he had not fully recovered from a weeks-long bout of typhoid fever. Johnson had not wanted to attend the inauguration at all, but Lincoln, after consulting his Cabinet, ordered him to come. "While we fully appreciate your wish to remain in Tennessee until her State-Government shall be completely re-inaugurated, it is our unanimous conclusion that it is unsafe for you to not be here on the fourth of March. Be sure to reach here by that time."[17]

The president must have regretted his insistence after Johnson came forward to recite his oath and deliver what was supposed to be a brief acceptance speech.

Before the ceremony, Johnson had gone to the vice president's room in the Capitol to meet with his predecessor, Hamblin. Feeling unwell and nervous, Johnson asked Hamblin whether he had something to drink.

Hamblin produced a bottle of brandy, and Johnson drank down two tumblers before striding into the Senate chamber. The liquor evidently went right to his head.

Noah Brooks, the *Sacramento Daily Union* correspondent, wrote that Johnson was "in a state of manifest intoxication" and gave a long, rambling speech in which he reminded the Supreme Court justices, Cabinet members, and diplomats, "with all your fine feathers and gewgaws," that they were supposed to serve the public. Johnson continued talking beyond the seven minutes he had been allotted. He shook his fists and launched into what was essentially a bombastic stump speech while "in vain did Hamblin nudge him from behind, audibly reminding him that the hour for the inauguration ceremony had passed," Brooks reported.

The dignitaries whispered furiously among themselves. Navy Secretary Gideon Welles said, "Johnson is either drunk or crazy." Lincoln patiently listened, but "closed his eyes and seemed to retire into himself as though beset by melancholy reflections," one observer noted. At last Johnson finished speaking and recited his oath of office. He then grasped the Bible and said, "I kiss this book in the face of my nation the United States" and did so "with a theatrical gesture."[18]

Lincoln was heard instructing a marshal as he left the Senate chamber for his own swearing-in, "Do not let Johnson speak outside." When Lincoln emerged from the Capitol onto a temporary platform erected on the building's east side, a tremendous shout, prolonged and loud, arose from the surging ocean of humanity around the Capitol building. Just as Lincoln was about to speak, the sun appeared from behind the clouds that had concealed it all day. Some believed it portended great things.[19]

Police ejected a young man from the rotunda who tried to force his way through the police line as Lincoln passed. Weeks later, when John Wilkes Booth had become a household name, the commissioner of public buildings, Benjamin B. French, was shown a photo of Booth and identified him as the disruptive man. Records would show that Booth stayed at Washington's National Hotel from March 1 to 21 when he was starring in *The Apostate* at Ford's Theatre. Later, a Booth friend recalled him saying, "What an excellent chance I had to kill the President, if I had wished, on inauguration day!"[20]

When Lincoln began his 703-word inaugural address, his voice was strong, and it carried clearly to the crowd, numbering well in the thousands, in tones "ringing and somewhat shrill." The crowd listened to his words in "most profound silence," bursting into applause upon hearing the words, "both parties deprecated war, but one of them would *make* war rather than let the nation survive, and the other would *accept* war rather than let it perish . . . and the war came."[21]

In cadences at once biblical, uncompromising, and conciliatory, Lincoln said that the ongoing national calamity might well be God's punishment for American slavery, which God had determined to remove by "this terrible war. . . . Fondly do we hope, fervently do we pray, that this mighty scourge of war may speedily pass away. Yet if God wills that it continue, until all the wealth piled by the bond-man's two hundred and fifty years of unrequited toil shall be sunk, and until every drop of blood drawn with the lash, shall be paid by another drawn with the sword, as was said three thousand years ago, so still it must be said 'the judgments of the Lord, are true and righteous altogether.'"

Lincoln's listeners grew moist-eyed when they heard his closing words: "With malice toward none; with charity for all; with firmness in the right, as God gives us to see the right, let us strive on to finish the work we are in; to bind up the nation's wounds; to care for him who shall have borne the battle, and for his widow, and his orphan—to do all which may achieve and cherish a just, and a lasting peace, among ourselves, and with all nations."[22]

The vast audience cheered; many people wept. The Supreme Court's chief justice, Salmon Chase, then administered the oath of office as Lincoln's right hand rested upon an open page of the Bible—the 27th and 28th verses of Isaiah 5, which he afterward kissed reverently. The passage read, "None shall be weary nor stumble among them; none shall slumber nor sleep; neither shall the girdle of their loins be loosed, nor the latchet of their shoes be broken: Whose arrows are sharp, and all their bows bent, their horses' hoofs shall be counted like flint, their wheels like a whirlwind."[23]

Americans were slow to grasp the Inaugural Address's sublimity and greatness of spirit. Judgments of it generally fell along partisan lines. Predictably, two New York Democratic newspapers, the *News* and *World*, denounced it, and many American newspapers did not recognize the address's significance. The *London Spectator*, however, understood its importance. "No statesman ever uttered words stamped at once with a seal of so deep a wisdom and so true a simplicity."

The Boston Brahmin Charles Francis Adams Jr., grandson of President John Quincy Adams and now a cavalry captain in Grant's army, wrote to his father, the US minister to England, "That rail-splitting lawyer is one of the wonders of the day. . . . This inaugural strikes me in its grand simplicity and directness as being for all time the historical keynote of this war . . . Not a prince or minister in all Europe could have risen to such an equality with the occasion."[24]

After watching what he described as a "splendid" fireworks display celebrating the inauguration in New York's Union Square, diarist George Templeton Strong wrote that Lincoln's address was "unlike any American state paper of this century. I would give a good deal to know what estimate will be put on it ten or fifty years hence."[25]

The mixed reaction Lincoln's address received in the newspapers elicited a sardonic observation by Lincoln to the New York political boss Thurlow Weed: "Men are not flattered by being shown that there has been a difference of purpose between the Almighty and them."[26]

At the White House reception that evening, Lincoln shook hands steadily for three hours with about six thousand people. Police turned away one guest, Frederick Douglass, who had escaped slavery in 1838, fled to Massachusetts, educated himself, and become a prominent writer and abolitionist. He was in the House gallery when the Thirteenth Amendment passed on January 31.

From outside the White House Douglass somehow got word to Lincoln about his predicament, and Lincoln invited him to the East Room. After they shook hands, Lincoln asked Douglass what he thought of his speech. "Mr. Lincoln, that was a sacred effort," replied Douglass. Lincoln smiled. "I'm glad you liked it!" he said.[27]

The Inaugural Ball two days later was held in four enormous second-floor rooms of the Patent Office. For the occasion, the rooms' walls were adorned with the insignia and guidons of Union Army units. At 10 p.m. the ball began. Three orchestras played, with one of them performing dance music only. The $10 tickets entitled gentlemen to bring an unlimited number of female companions. Dinner was served to the four thousand guests from a 250-foot-long table crowded with meats, fowl, oysters, terrapin, hams, cakes, ice cream, and tarts—a vivid display of the North's abundance compared with the South's poverty. Later, police let in the large crowd outside the building, and it made short work of the remaining viands.[28]

☙

Family and friends remarked on Lincoln's thinness and his aged appearance. First Lady Mary Lincoln reportedly told her dressmaker, Elizabeth Keckley, "Poor Mr. Lincoln is looking so broken-hearted, so completely worn out. I fear he will not get through the next four years." *New York Tribune* editor Horace Greeley wrote, "His face was haggard with care and seamed with thought and trouble. It looked care-ploughed, tempest-tossed and weather beaten."[29]

Indeed, during the week following the Inaugural Ball the exhausted president rested in bed. Noah Brooks wrote that Lincoln's health "has been worn down by the constant pressure of office-seekers and legitimate business so that for a few days he was obliged to deny himself to all comers."[30]

On March 14, Lincoln convened a Cabinet meeting in his bedroom. Navy Secretary Gideon Welles, who attended, wrote, "The President was indisposed and in bed, but not seriously ill."[31]

When he resumed his duties, for a few days Lincoln met only with his Cabinet and men who had urgent business with him. He was reported to be still weak on March 16. He made it a rule that his office was to be closed at 3 p.m. to casual visitors.[32]

☙

The Confederate Congress's opposition to arming the slaves evaporated with the failure of the Hampton Roads Conference, which had left the Confederacy with the stark options of fighting on or surrendering. Even as strident a secessionist as the Southern agriculture reform pioneer Edmund Ruffin had reversed his previous opposition to recruiting black soldiers and now enthusiastically supported the expedient. "When commanded & led by their masters, whom they had obeyed & respected as superiors, they will fight better, than under their Yankee equals." Ruffin believed that only black volunteers should be emancipated; those who were conscripted should remain slaves so that the South could preserve its "peculiar institution." Meanwhile, Breckinridge, Lee, and others who understood the situation's hopelessness continued to quietly urge peace negotiations, but no one listened. Congress, egged on by the unyielding Davis, chose to arm the slaves and continue the war.[33]

In a message to Congress on March 13 Davis conceded that Richmond was "in greater danger than it has heretofore been during the war" but then amazingly asserted that "it is within our power to avert the calamities which menace us, and to secure the triumph of the sacred cause for which so much sacrifice has been made." He asked Congress to quickly approve measures to raise revenue and collect supplies—as well as to arm the slaves.

That bill was already on its way to Davis for signing. Before it was approved, it had been watered down. Emancipation was extended to black recruits, but only if their masters consented to it. "Much benefit is anticipated from this measure, though far less than would have resulted from its adoption at an earlier date," Davis wrote.[34]

Congress exhorted the Southern people to persevere, while Davis warned, "Failure will compel us to drink the cup of humiliation even to the bitter dregs of having the history of our struggle written by New England historians."[35]

❧

On Saturday, March 11, Sherman's army marched into Fayetteville, and its commander established his headquarters in the cream-colored buildings of the old US Arsenal, which the Confederates had enlarged and converted for their own use during the war. Fayetteville was one of the largest cities in North Carolina, with four thousand residents. It was founded by exiled Highland Scots in the eighteenth century and named for the Marquis de Lafayette after the Revolutionary War.

Sherman instructed his generals to "deal as moderately and fairly with the North Carolinians as possible"—a major change from his policy of devastation in South Carolina. But he intended to level the arsenal to the ground when he left Fayetteville. He planned to "burn it, blow it up with Gunpowder, and then with rams Knock down its walls," he told War Secretary Edwin Stanton. "I take it for granted the United States will never again trust Carolina with an arsenal to appropriate at her pleasure."[36]

Besides ordering the army to curb its wanton destruction of property now that it had left South Carolina, Sherman wanted his generals to "fan the flame of discord already subsisting between them and their proud cousins in South Carolina." General Henry Slocum, the Left Wing commander, elaborated on this theme in his order to his troops. North

Carolina, Slocum said, was one of the last Southern states to secede, and he believed that most of its residents disapproved of secession. "A strong Union party" still existed there, he wrote. General Francis Blair, in his order to the XVII Corps, said much the same thing: "The State of North Carolina is to a great extent loyal."

But it was a mistake to presume that North Carolina's reluctance to join the Confederacy in 1861 meant that it was strongly Unionist in 1865. North Carolina, after all, had contributed more men to the Confederate Army than any state except possibly Virginia, suffering a commensurate number of battle deaths.[37]

A former West Point friend of Sherman's who had sided with the Confederacy visited Sherman's Fayetteville headquarters to renew their acquaintance. Sherman's face briefly lit up with pleasure at the sight of his old friend, an aide observed. Leaning against a column, Sherman said, "You shared my friendship, shared my bread, even, didn't you?" The Southerner warmly replied, "Indeed, indeed!"

Sherman gave the man a long, steady look and replied, "You have betrayed it all; me, your friend, your country that educated you for its defense. You are here a traitor, and you ask me to be again your friend, to protect your property, to send you these brave men, some of whose comrades were murdered by your neighbors this very morning—fired on from hidden houses by you and yours as they entered the town." Sherman regarded the man contemptuously. "Turn your back to me forever," he said. "I will not punish you; only go your way. There is room in the world even for traitors." Afterward, Sherman was so upset by his encounter with his former friend that he could scarcely eat, and "the hand that held the bread trembled and for a moment tears were in his eyes," an aide wrote.

Minutes later, General Oliver Howard arrived and complained that two or three of his men had been killed by people firing from windows. "Who did this outrage?" Sherman cried in a loud, bitter voice. "Texans, I think," replied Howard. Sherman told him, "Then shoot some Texan prisoners in retaliation." Howard said he had no Texans. "Then take other prisoners, take any prisoners," said Sherman. "I will not permit my soldiers to be murdered."[38]

Now prohibited from willful home-burning and looting—although it did not altogether stop; Wadesboro and Monroe were pillaged—the bummers sated their destructive impulses by burning the pine forests and the backwoods manufactures where turpentine, rosin, and tar were made for naval stores. The towering pine trees blazed like torches, day and night.[39]

On March 12, the *Davidson* steamed into Fayetteville on the Cape Fear River from Wilmington, bearing a message from General Alfred Terry. It was the first communication Sherman had received from outside his immediate army in weeks. In anticipation of action against Johnston, Sherman sent about seven thousand ragged camp followers and refugees who had been following his army down the river road to Wilmington. He replaced his worn-out horses and mules with local livestock and asked Terry to send him food, clothing, and forage.

That day, too, Sherman wrote his first account of the Carolina expedition for Grant. "I hope you have not been uneasy about us, and that the fruits of this march will be appreciated," Sherman said. "It had to be made not only to destroy the valuable depots by the way, but for its incident[al role] in the necessary fall of Charleston, Georgetown, and Wilmington." He planned to go "straight at" Johnston as soon as his men could be resupplied. "If I can now add Goldsboro without too much cost, I will be in a position to aid you materially in the spring campaign."

Sherman's earlier feints toward Charlotte had fooled no one for very long. A *New York Tribune* reporter had authoritatively written that the army's destination was certainly Goldsboro, because supply ships were arriving on the North Carolina coast at Morehead City, connected by rail to Goldsboro. When Sherman read the brief story, he was certain that Johnston would see it, too, and that he had to be ready to face Johnston's army.

Thus, in his message to Terry, Sherman cautioned, "We must not lose time for Joe Johnston to concentrate at Goldsboro. . . . Every day now is worth a million of dollars. I can whip Joe Johnston provided he don't catch one of my Corps in flank."[40]

The troops, cocky after their easy ramble through southeastern Georgia and South Carolina, appeared to be ready for anything. "Our boys have got so used to all sorts of dangers and trials that they don't seem to mind any thing that comes along," wrote Theodore Upson of the 100th Indiana.

Sherman's men were initially pleased to be in North Carolina, "the best country since we left Central Georgia. . . . Small farms and nice white, tidy dwellings." But then it began raining without letup, until the supply wagons plunged in mud "to the wagon boxes" and the pioneers had to resume corduroying the roads.

Major Thomas Osborn of the 1st New York Light Artillery wrote to his brother that so far, "the enemy has been miserably commanded since we have been on the campaign or we should not have gotten through so easily." Things were going to change, he predicted. With Johnston in command again, Sherman "does not think he will leave us long without a battle," Osborn said.[41]

The teenaged blonde beauty Marie Boozer, who had debouched from Columbia with the Union Army, was enjoying her life enormously as the consort of Sherman's cavalry commander. General Judson Kilpatrick had lured Marie away from her mother, and she now traveled with the general.

Things took a bad turn for Marie on the foggy morning of March 10, when Wade Hampton's cavalry corps swooped down on Kilpatrick's camp in a swampy area between the South Carolina border and Fayetteville, near Monroe's Cross Roads.

Marie and Kilpatrick were staying in a small house in the middle of the encampment when a Rebel bugle call awakened them. Kilpatrick bolted from the house in his nightshirt, leaped on a horse, and rode away, leaving Marie standing in her nightclothes on the porch. A Rebel trooper swept her onto his horse and then unceremoniously dumped her in a ditch—so that she would not be shot by mistake, he told her.

The Yankees rallied and, fighting dismounted with repeating rifles, drove off the Rebel attackers—but only after Hampton's men had plundered the wagons, captured hundreds of prisoners, and freed 173 Confederate captives.[42]

As Sherman settled in at the old US Arsenal, Marie Boozer left Fayetteville on a mail boat to Wilmington, the beginning of yet more adventures—among them, marriage to a rich Northerner, followed by a highly public divorce; betrothal to a French count; and a reign as an international society hostess.[43]

Before the army left Fayetteville on March 15, its engineers "completely leveled" the arsenal with fire and explosives, wrecking all of its equipment and incidentally destroying several nearby homes that caught fire. The bone-jarring explosions that flattened the old US Arsenal heralded further destruction: Fayetteville's railroad properties, factories, cotton mills, railroad trestles, the bank, and the printing plant of the Fayetteville *Observer*, even though its editor, E. J. Hale, had staunchly opposed secession.[44]

⁂

Joseph Johnston had accepted command of the Carolinas armies believing that the Southern cause was doomed and that his sole object should be "fair terms of peace," best obtained by inflicting heavy losses on Sherman's army. Thus, Johnston applied himself fully to gathering every available soldier and unit, shaping the disparate parts into a cohesive fighting force, and readying it to be hurled at Sherman's juggernaut.

One task was to persuade prickly but extremely able General D. H. Hill, appointed to command a tiny corps of Hood's shattered Army of Tennessee, to march from Smithfield to join Braxton Bragg's sixty-five hundred men near Goldsboro and to then serve under Bragg. "I beg you to forget the past for this emergency," Johnston wrote to Hill, who could not forget that he had been relieved from corps command after Chickamauga for having criticized Bragg's performance as a field commander. Hill grumpily consented, adding, "I hope that it may be possible & consistent with [the] intents of the service to give me another commander than Genl. Bragg. He has made me the scapegoat once & would do it again."[45]

"After concentration hope for opportunity to fight his divided troops," Johnston told Lee, but if no opportunity arose, by which route did Lee want him to withdraw into southern Virginia to unite with Lee's army? Lee bluntly replied that retreating into Virginia was not an option; it would mean losing the Raleigh road—disastrous for both his and Johnston's armies. Johnston simply must stop Sherman "if there is a reasonable probability" of success. "A bold and unexpected attack might relieve us," wrote Lee.

Johnston knew the odds heavily favored Sherman's legions over his army of disparate parts. "I would not fight Sherman's united army unless your situation makes it necessary," Lee had told him. It had now become necessary.[46]

Because stopping Sherman was now paramount, the myriad problems facing Johnston as he pulled together his army receded by comparison. But these difficulties were still daunting. General Beauregard declared that desertions from the army were "now an epidemic. They deserted by the hundreds from the cars on their way here [to Charlotte from Mississippi]. The same complaint reaches us from [General Stephen] Lee's army. Only an active campaign and some brilliant success can put a stop to that disorder," Beauregard wrote.

On March 11, as Sherman's soldiers were entering Fayetteville, Johnston was informed by a Confederate payroll department major, "I have the honor to advise you that I have failed in obtaining funds to pay the troops of your command." Confederate treasury notes had run out, and it would be six weeks before there would be new funds to pay the army. The major optimistically suggested that by simply explaining the problem to the soldiers, "I firmly believe that all dissatisfaction will cease."[47]

As Johnston's forces came together, the diarist Mary Chesnut sadly watched a cavalry unit ride past where she was staying. "There they go, the gay and gallant few—doomed; the last gathering of the flower of Southern youth, to be killed." She despairingly wrote that "things are beginning to be unbearable. . . . What is the good of being here at all? Our world has gone to destruction."[48]

❧

After Bragg abandoned Wilmington, General John Schofield occupied the Rebels' last viable port city and moved inland. He divided his Army of the Ohio, sending General Alfred Terry's Provisional Corps, exhilarated by its victory at Fort Fisher, directly north along the railroad to Goldsboro, where Schofield planned to rendezvous with Sherman. Army repair crews labored to make the rail line serviceable again.

The rest of Schofield's army, with General Jacob Cox's XXIII Corps its largest element, marched northeast to New Bern, North Carolina's former colonial capital. New Bern was situated on the banks of the Neuse River and linked Goldsboro by rail with the state's other port, Morehead City, which had been Union-controlled since 1862. Protected by Cox's forces, crews worked rapidly to reopen the rail line. Together, the railroads from Wilmington and Morehead City would bring a flood of supplies to Goldsboro for Sherman's hungry, ragged men, whose clothing was in tatters after nearly two months on the march.

After withdrawing from Wilmington, Bragg moved inland ahead of Schofield's forces. On March 7 his eight thousand men—Robert Hoke's division and D. H. Hill's Army of Tennessee veterans—appeared before Cox's corps northwest of New Bern. At Wyse's Fork, Hoke and Hill suddenly assaulted Cox's left flank, capturing an entire regiment and driving back Cox's men three miles.

When told that a Union counterattack was imminent, Bragg stopped Hill's attack and ordered him to preempt it. But when Hill's troops reached the place where the enemy was reportedly massing, they found no Yankees. Hill's diversion enabled Cox's Union troops to move to stronger positions, and the Confederate attack, which had begun so well, sputtered to a halt.

On March 10, the Confederates again attacked, but Hoke's and Hill's disjointed assaults were repulsed. The Rebels withdrew toward Goldsboro with more than one thousand prisoners and three guns, but they had lost more than a thousand men.[49]

❧

Sherman, the avatar of "total war," was well pleased with the demoralizing blow he had dealt the Confederacy by his unsparing destruction of South Carolina's cities, towns, and countryside. "The simple fact that a man's home has been visited by the enemy makes a soldier in Lee's or Johnston's army very, very anxious to get home to look after his family and property," he wrote to General Quincy Gilmore, commander of the Department of the South in Charleston.[50]

Although even the *New York Tribune* had accurately predicted that Sherman would march to Goldsboro, Johnston was still unsure of his destination when Sherman left Fayetteville on March 15. Would he march north to Raleigh, or northeast to Goldsboro? Johnston stuck to his decision to cover both possibilities by making Smithfield, midway between Raleigh and Goldsboro, the rendezvous point for his converging armies. On the day of his departure from Fayetteville, Sherman ordered Schofield and Terry to meet him at Goldsboro.[51]

General Henry Slocum's Left Wing, however, upheld the pretense that Raleigh was the army's destination by marching north from Fayetteville. Confederate General William Hardee's small army awaited the Yankees a few miles ahead on the Raleigh road, at Averasboro. Johnston believed that if Hardee attacked Slocum's Left Wing while Oliver Howard's Right

Wing was a dozen miles away, he would delay their union and give him more time to assemble his army and attack them in detail.

From the neck of land between the Cape Fear River and the Black River, Hardee's men struck the Yankees. It was the first serious resistance Sherman's army met since capturing Atlanta six months earlier. Kilpatrick's cavalrymen, who were in the vanguard, bore the brunt of the attack. Besieged by the swarming Rebels, the cavalrymen fought dismounted, barely holding their own with their Spencer repeating rifles. Then, infantrymen from General Alpheus Williams's XX Corps arrived and helped the troopers repel the attack.

The next day, March 16, Slocum sent all four divisions of XX Corps into action against Hardee, now aided by Hampton's and Wheeler's troopers. The armies attacked and counterattacked all day in the swamps, mud, and quicksand between the two rivers. Remarked a Union soldier wading through a seemingly endless swamp, "I guess Uncle Billy has struck this stream endwise." Neither army was able to drive the other from the battlefield.

Johnston believed that Sherman's large ratio of wounded-to-killed compared to Hardee's numbers "proves that the soldiers of General Sherman's army had been demoralized by their course of life on Southern plantations. Those soldiers, when fighting between Dalton and Atlanta, could not have been driven back repeatedly by a fourth of their number, with a loss so utterly insignificant."

Major Henry Hitchcock, a Sherman aide, might have agreed. He disgustedly observed that Sherman and his staff spent the day "lying around in the woods" rather than aggressively prosecuting the battle. The fighting ended inconclusively at nightfall, with each side suffering about seven hundred casualties.

When the four Yankee divisions attacked again early March 17, the Rebel works were empty. During the night, Hardee had withdrawn his army after Hampton declared with absolute certainty that the Yankees were "making toward Goldsboro" and not Raleigh. The Confederates began marching to Smithfield, where Johnston had established his headquarters, and where Bragg had now joined him. Hardee had succeeded in delaying Slocum's Left Wing for two days.

Seventeen-year-old Jamie Smith, whose family home became Slocum's headquarters during the battle, indignantly told a friend that Union troops ransacked the house and stole their livestock except for "one old hen, who played sick. . . . If I ever see a Yankeewoman I intend to whip her and take her clothes off her very back."

Hardee's men—eleven hundred fewer because South Carolina Governor Andrew Magrath had recalled his state troops—camped at Elevation, six miles southwest of Smithfield. Johnston intended to attack one of Sherman's wings somewhere near Smithfield while the other wing and Schofield's army were beyond supporting range.[52]

It was a nerve-wracking period for Johnston: pulling together a patchwork army from three states and then ascertaining whether Sherman was headed to Raleigh or Goldsboro. Finally, he must determine the time and place to attack one wing of Sherman's army.

When Hampton informed Johnston early March 18 that both wings of Sherman's army were converging on Goldsboro, Johnston began planning his attack. The Left Wing, Hampton reported—Slocum's army on the road from Averasboro—was more than a day's distance from the hamlet of Bentonville, while General Oliver Howard's Right Wing was a half-day's march ahead of the Left and a dozen miles east of it. Studying his map, Johnston concluded that Sherman's two wings were a day's march apart.

Johnston ordered all of his troops to immediately converge on the Bentonville area and bivouac during the night of March 18 between the hamlet and Goldsboro Road, the route of Slocum's thirty thousand men. When Johnston's scattered forces at last coalesced at Bentonville, he would have twenty-two thousand men: Bragg's sixty-five hundred, four thousand infantrymen from the Army of Tennessee, Hardee's seventy-five hundred infantrymen, and four thousand cavalrymen.

According to Johnston's map, it was twelve miles from Elevation to Bentonville and about the same distance between the roads that Sherman's Left and Right Wings were traveling.

But the map "proved to be very incorrect," Johnston later wrote. It was inaccurate in the worst way: it exaggerated the distance between the two roads and underestimated the distance from Elevation to Bentonville. In other words, Sherman's two wings could unite quicker, and Hardee's seventy-five hundred men at Elevation would reach Bentonville later than Johnston expected.[53]

Misconceptions also plagued Sherman's generals. Slocum did not suspect that Johnston was preparing to attack him on Goldsboro Road; escaped Union prisoners reported that he was massing troops near Raleigh. Kilpatrick's cavalrymen confirmed the captives' reports. Sherman's bummers sent accurate intelligence—that a large Rebel force lay in Slocum's path—but the information did not reach Slocum's lead division. "All signs induced me to believe that the enemy would make no further opposition to our progress, and would not attempt to strike us in flank while in motion," Sherman wrote.[54]

Hampton's cavalrymen, who had camped two miles south of Bentonville on March 17, advanced the next morning to engage Slocum's Yankees, purchasing time for Johnston to get into position. The Rebel troopers skirmished with Slocum's leading units until afternoon, when they found themselves backed up to a wooded hill at Cole's plantation. The hill overlooked a large field of thickets laced with small streams—"so much marshy or spongy soil that quick maneuvering was impossible," General Howard, the Right Wing commander, later wrote.

Satisfied that this would be "a proper place for a battle," Hampton dismounted his men along the edge of the woods, placed his artillery in a position that commanded Goldsboro Road, and fended off Slocum's men until nightfall.[55]

Johnston and Bragg reached Bentonville that night with the troops from Smithfield, but Hardee, having started that morning from Elevation, was five miles away when he stopped for the night.

Expecting no fight on this particular Sunday, Sherman and his staff left Slocum's Bentonville headquarters on March 19 and joined Howard and his Right Wing, several miles away. Sherman's lack of concern about Johnston's whereabouts was evident from the telegram he sent to Schofield: "Continue to extend the railroad as fast as possible, and I expect you to move toward Goldsborough [sic] even if it be unnecessary, and I don't want to lose men in a direct attack when it can be avoided. . . . I must give my men and animals some rest. We whipped Hardee easily about Averasborough [sic]. All retreated on Smithfield and Raleigh."

Within three hours Sherman's relaxed attitude would vanish. He would order Schofield to secure and fortify Goldsboro, adding, "General

Slocum reports the enemy in force between him and Cox's Bridge; thinks it is the main army of the enemy."[56]

It was a warm day, and General W. P. Carlin's First Division of XIV Corps led Slocum's Left Wing north on Goldsboro Road. Unlike Sherman, Carlin believed that a battle was imminent, and he wore a new uniform for the occasion. He sent his wagon train to the rear. Carlin was not disappointed.

A hook-shaped Confederate battle line blocked Goldsboro Road. Believing that it was just Hampton's cavalry, the Yankees' opponent the day before, Slocum sent Carlin's brigades against the Confederate right, expecting the Confederate troopers to give way. Instead, Carlin's men slammed into General Alexander Stewart's small Confederate infantry corps and were repulsed.

Three Confederates deserted to the Union lines, claiming they were former Union prisoners who had elected to enlist in the Rebel Army rather than be sent to the South's infamous archipelago of prison camps. The deserters' spokesman, when taken to Slocum, told him that Johnston's entire army was in front of him and that Johnston intended to defeat Slocum's two corps before Howard's men arrived. Slocum placed his men in defensive positions, ordered XX Corps to come to XIV Corps's assistance, and notified Sherman.[57]

About 3 p.m. the thrilling, high-pitched Rebel yell, so seldom heard in North Carolina, rang out over the marshy field. Stewart's four thousand survivors of the Army of Tennessee counterattacked across the same ground over which they had driven back Carlin. "Closing in to the left as we advanced, we passed over the bodies of the enemy who had been killed in the assault," wrote Georgian Walter Clark, who charged with the thin line of Confederates. An eyewitness thought the Rebel attack "looked like a picture and was truly beautiful" while observing that it was "painful to see how close their battle flags were together, regiments being scarcely larger than companies."

Ferocity compensated for lack of numbers. The Union line disintegrated, the attackers forced Carlin's brigades from their fieldworks, and the bluecoats pelted back more than a mile. "The onward sweep of the rebel lines was like the waves of the ocean, resistless," wrote Alexander

McClung, a staff officer under General Jefferson C. Davis, the XIV Corps commander. If McClung exaggerated, it was understandable because Sherman's army had not been in a major battle since the previous summer.[58]

General James Morgan's division, bypassed by the swarming Rebels, raked the Confederate left flank with sheeting musket fire, slowing the attack. At 4 p.m., reinforced by Hardee's late-arriving corps, Bragg launched fresh attacks on Morgan's men, who counterattacked and were then attacked again. During the desperate fighting the 113th Ohio knelt in two lines, with the rear rank loading and handing weapons to the men in front. The desperate measure succeeded; Morgan's men held. At twilight the Confederates withdrew to their original lines.[59]

It was nightfall when a courier galloped into Howard's camp with a message from Slocum reporting that he faced Johnston's entire army at Bentonville. Sherman, who had been lying down in Howard's tent, rushed outside to hear the news without bothering to dress. "He stood in a bed of ashes up to his ankles, chewing impatiently the stump of a cigar, with his hands clasped behind him, and with nothing but a red flannel undershirt and pair of Drawers," wrote a staff officer. Sherman began barking orders to turn Howard's Right Wing toward Bentonville. "The whole army is moving to your assistance as rapidly as possible," he wrote to Slocum. "Hold fast to your position, which I take for granted is now well fortified, but be ready to attack the enemy . . . follow him as far as Mill Creek."

The first Union reinforcements arrived at dawn. By noon, all of XV Corps had taken positions near Johnston's rear, forcing the Confederates to adjust their lines and form a salient around the Mill Creek Bridge, their escape route to Smithfield. XVII Corps joined Slocum's men in the afternoon.[60]

Sherman was adamant about avoiding a "general battle" unless Johnston forced it upon his army. He later wrote that he "did not feel disposed" to fight because his army had been on the march since late January and had little food. But just in case, Sherman sent his wagon trains to Kinston for provisions. Throughout March 20 the two sides launched small, sharp attacks against one another, and Sherman paced with an unlit cigar in his mouth. When he asked an officer for a light and the officer handed him his cigar to light Sherman's, the preoccupied general walked away with both cigars, then dropped the officer's on the ground, puffing on his own. With a laugh, the officer picked up his cigar.

Hampton worried about the Confederate Army's "extremely perilous" position: its lines were thin, its flanks were in the air, and its back was against a swift-running stream with just one bridge over it. Johnston's army was in "a very weak position," practically surrounded by enemy formations many times its size, Hampton wrote.

That night, Sherman ordered Slocum to find roads around the Confederates. "Johnston hoped to overcome your wing before I could come to your relief," Sherman wrote. "Having failed in that, I cannot see why he remains. . . . I would rather avoid a general battle if possible, but if he insists on it, we must accommodate him."[61]

Slocum had not only found a road that would take his army around Johnston and back to Goldsboro Road but also discovered where he might cut off Johnston's withdrawal to Smithfield. "If you find it necessary to fight him, I shall try to carry that part of his line, as it will cut off his retreat," he told Sherman.[62]

But Sherman was not burning to destroy Johnston's army, which he believed to be far stronger than it actually was; he estimated that Johnston had thirty-seven thousand infantrymen alone. Never an aggressive combat leader like Grant or Phil Sheridan, Sherman was satisfied to let Johnston go so that he could continue to Goldsboro, unite with Schofield's and Terry's corps, and rest and refit.

Not content to leave without first attacking Johnston's jugular was the general whom Sherman once described as "the boldest young soldier we have," Joseph Mower, who commanded a XVII Corps division of Midwesterners.[63]

Mower's corps commander, General Francis Blair, had ordered Mower's division to extend its line toward Mill Creek, and Blair had not objected when Mower asked whether he could also make a "little reconnaissance." Mower's two brigades did more than that: after wading through a deep swamp tangled with tree roots, they ran cheering through a second swamp, overwhelmed a line of rifle pits, and captured Johnston's headquarters; their prizes included Johnston's horse and sword.

Mower's division had landed a crushing blow on the rear of Johnston's left flank—the exact development Hampton had most feared. Mower's men stampeded the Rebels toward Mill Creek, driving them to within fifty yards of their escape route. Stopping on a hilltop, Mower sent a messenger to General Blair to report his success and request an attack all along the line.

Hampton was riding back to the left flank after warning Johnston of the dangerous situation when couriers galloped up with news of the imperiled Mill Creek Bridge. Hampton reacted instantly, rounding up a brigade of Georgia troops and sending it with a battery to the threatened sector. He dispatched a courier to bring every mounted man he could find.

The Confederates counterattacked Mower's division, and within five minutes the 50th North Carolina and the 10th North Carolina Battalion lost one-third of their men. "The enemy was lying in line three columns deep and reserved their fire until our troops were near them struggling through a dense swamp," and then Yankee musket fire flashed out of the undergrowth, wrote Lieutenant J. C. Ellington of the 50th North Carolina.

Hampton and Hardee rushed forward a mixed cavalry and infantry force to head off Mower—with Hardee personally leading the three hundred infantrymen. They smashed into the head and flanks of Mower's column, stopping it cold.

Hardee's only son, sixteen-year-old Willie, had longed for months to join the 8th Texas Cavalry—"Terry's Rangers"—but his father had forbidden it, keeping the boy on his staff before allowing him to join a light artillery unit. That morning Willie at last received permission to transfer to the Rangers. He was mortally wounded when the Texans, along with Alabama cavalrymen, charged the Union infantry line, the shock of their attack forcing Mower's men to withdraw through the swamp. Before the war General Howard had been a friend of Hardee's, and he was Willie's Sunday school teacher when Hardee was commandant of cadets at West Point. Howard mourned the boy's death when a Rebel officer informed him of it.

The spectacular success of Mower's "reconnaissance" prompted Howard to start XV and XVII Corps marching to his support, but Sherman countermanded Howard and ordered Mower's withdrawal "lest the enemy should concentrate on him." Unhappy with the missed opportunity, Howard wrote that Sherman's decision "created much feeling at the time, and some severity of criticism" by Howard's men.

Sherman gave Howard a medley of reasons for his action: Mower's "rashness," Sherman's incorrect estimate of Johnston's strength, "that there had been bloodshed enough," and that he wished Johnston would just leave so Sherman could go to Goldsboro and obtain supplies. Clearly Sherman had no stomach for a fight.[64]

That moonless night, as a chilly, soaking rain fell, Johnston's army withdrew over the Mill Creek Bridge—which Mower's men had nearly succeeded in blocking—and toward Smithfield, traveling over roads knee-deep in mud. The Yankees shelled the empty Rebel breastworks as the pine forest burned. "At frequent intervals the crash of burning, falling trees mingled with . . . the occasional boom of cannon," a Confederate soldier wrote. He and his comrades lighted their way with blazing torches.

It had been a close call for the Confederates, Hampton wrote. "If the attacking force had been able to attain possession of the road [over the bridge] we could not have withdrawn without heavy loss, if we could have done so at all." Johnston's losses totaled 2,606, compared with 1,646 for Sherman's army. On the war's scale of battle carnage, Bentonville was a minor engagement.[65]

Sherman later expressed remorse over letting Johnston slip away. "I think I made a mistake there," he wrote, "and should rapidly have followed Mower's lead with the whole of the right wing, which would have brought on a general battle, and it could not have resulted otherwise than successfully for us, by reason of our vastly superior numbers."[66]

That night, Major Henry Hitchcock of Sherman's staff wrote to his wife, Mary, "Undoubtedly, if (yes, IF) J.J.'s attack on Slocum on Sunday had succeeded in 'mashing up' that part of our forces, it would have been a severe blow to us—but it didn't succeed, and now he is on the defensive himself."

The artillerist, Major Thomas Osborn, was impressed by Johnston's frugality with his men's lives. "Johnston is very careful of his men and will make the most of them, though it is [now only] a question of men, and who can endure the draught of blood the longest."[67]

Yet Sherman had failed to exploit a glittering opportunity to decisively defeat Johnston by utilizing his great numerical superiority and advantages of position. "Strategy was his strongest point," General Howard wrote of Sherman. "Take him in battle and he did not seem to me to be the equal of [General George] Thomas or Grant."[68]

Sherman's ragamuffin army marched into Goldsboro on March 23 and 24. "I doubt if at any time the troops of the rebel army were more ragged than we," wrote U. H. Farr of the 70th Indiana. Sherman's men were grimy and sooty-faced from countless smoking campfires and the burning pine forests. They had no socks, and some of them had no shoes and marched barefooted, or with their feet wrapped in blanket strips. The soldiers wore coats with no sleeves. Their trousers were so worn and ragged from scrambling through briar patches and swamps that many soldiers were bare legged to their knees. "Probably one man in a dozen had a full set of clothes, but even this suit was patched and full of holes," observed Farr.

Over the past year Sherman's men had marched more than two thousand miles, and now they paraded in review before their proud commander. "Splendid legs! Splendid legs!" Sherman reportedly exclaimed when he saw them. "I would give both of mine for any one of them!" Schofield's troops from Wilmington watched too. "Why, it's Sherman's greasers!" some of them shouted. They loudly cheered the ragged procession—and laughed at its appearance until tears ran down their faces. "It was as good as a picnic and three circuses," one of Schofield's men said.

The bummers, marching with their livestock, pets, and foraged food, were an arresting site. They traveled with donkeys, cattle, sheep, hogs, and in buggies and wagons packed with chickens, turkeys, and honking geese; pet squirrels perched on knapsacks; and a raccoon straining at a string leash. From every saddle and wagon dangled bacon, hams, potatoes, flour, pork, sorghum, freshly slaughtered poultry, and meat, wrote Elias Smith of the *New York Tribune*, who said their appearance "strongly recalls the memory of Falstaff's ragged army. . . . Here came men strutting in mimic dignity in an old swallow-tailed coat, with plug hats, the tops knocked in . . . and coats of every cast with broadtails, narrow tails, and no tails at all—all of the most antiquated styles." Some wore "women's bonnets or young ladies' hats, with streamers of faded ribbons floating fantastically in the wind."

"Nearly every soldier had some token of the march on his bayonet from a pig to a potato," wrote Colonel Charles Kerr of the 16th Illinois Cavalry. The spectacle soon grew tiresome for Sherman's generals, who ordered the review stopped before all the divisions could parade and sent the men back to their camps. "The review was the joke of the army for a season," wrote Kerr.

Sherman also reviewed Schofield's and Terry's handsomely attired soldiers from Wilmington when they reached Goldsboro. Sherman's men disparaged them as "bandbox soldiers," but they, too, soon received replacement shoes, uniforms, and coats.[69]

On March 25 the ambitious strategic and logistical plans Sherman had made more than three months earlier came to fruition when repairs were completed to the railroad between Goldsboro and Morehead City. That day the first train rolled into Goldsboro. No longer needing foragers, Sherman ordered the bummers dismounted and returned to their units. Sherman was overheard predicting that military men one day would judge his Carolinas campaign to be "one of the most perfect military movements in history."

Sherman's army had accomplished a feat that was arguably even greater than its march through Georgia: visiting retribution on the Rebellion's birthplace and knocking the Carolinas out of the war. It had single-handedly wrecked the South's plantation society and desolated a vast region of America. "The railroads are so completely ruined that practically the southern limit of the Confederacy is at Charlotte, North Carolina," wrote Major Thomas Osborn. The army destroyed large Rebel arsenals at Columbia, Cheraw, and Fayetteville.

Through fifty days in the middle of winter, Sherman's army had marched more than four hundred miles from Savannah to Goldsboro— farther than its march to the sea. His hardy Western men had crossed five major rivers; they had captured Columbia and Fayetteville; and Charleston had fallen. Sherman described it as "one of the longest and most important marches ever made by an organized army in a civilized country." He had lost just five thousand men in accomplishing this feat.

Terry's Provisional Corps, after capturing Fort Fisher, had pushed inland with Schofield's XXIII Corps. Now, with both railroads repaired, the combined army of nearly ninety thousand men under Sherman would be amply supplied with provisions landed at Morehead City and Wilmington when it began its push into Virginia.[70]

After retreating from Bentonville, Johnston provided Lee with a brief account of the fighting, glumly adding, "Sherman's course cannot be hindered by the small force I have. I can do no more than annoy him. I respectfully suggest that it is no longer a question whether you leave your present position; you have only to decide where to meet Sherman. I will be near him." Lee forwarded Johnston's message to Davis, adding, "Please give me your counsel." As he wrote this, Lee was poised to execute John Gordon's plan for breaking out of Petersburg.[71]

2

March 25, 1865
PETERSBURG, VIRGINIA

All night the stiffly martial figure of General John Gordon restlessly prowled the Confederate lines, seeing to the last-minute preparations before the attack. His 11,500 men silently formed three columns, "almost as noiseless and shadowy as the flitting of ghosts," wrote one observer.

It was Gordon's plan, first to last; Lee had left the details to the Second Corps commander. The day before, when Gordon had requested more men, Lee had ordered General George Pickett's First Corps division of more than six thousand men to leave its positions at Richmond to reinforce Gordon, although Lee did not think they would arrive in time. Two brigades of General Henry Heth's division from the Third Corps might be summoned too, Lee said, adding, "I pray that a merciful God may grant us success and deliver us from our enemies."[72]

In the predawn darkness, Fort Stedman, looming 280 yards from the Confederate lines, appeared to be slumbering. At 4 a.m. Gordon stood atop the Confederate works beside the private whose gunshot would launch the attack. Behind them fifty men with axes were poised to cut pathways through the Union abatis and fraises blocking the fort's approaches. Waiting behind the axmen were three one-hundred-man storming parties. Each man wore over his shoulder one of the identifying white cloth strips made by Gordon's pregnant wife. While the storming parties secured the fort, three more hundred-man teams, led by guides, would press on through the fort and occupy positions on its east side to repel counterattacks. The rest of Gordon's men would sweep past the fort to seize a secondary Union line that included three small forts believed to be behind Stedman. A cavalry division would sever Union communications, and if all went well, the Confederate Second Corps would wreak havoc in the Yankees' rear, perhaps all the way to City Point.[73]

As the axmen went to work, the noise attracted the attention of a Union picket. In close proximity day after day, the enemy pickets were on good terms, and the Confederate private standing beside Gordon called over to the Yankee picket that some Rebels were gathering corn between the lines. "You know rations are might [*sic*] short over here," he said. The Yankee picket told him to go ahead.

Just before the private fired the signal shot, he courteously warned the friendly picket he was going to shoot.

The gunshot shattered the nighttime calm, and the Confederates surged toward Fort Stedman. "The cool, frosty morning made every sound distinct and clear, and the only sound heard was the tramp! Tramp! of the men as they kept step as regularly as on drill, and the cries of the Federal picket as he ran with all speed into the fort shouting: 'The Rebels are coming! The Rebels are coming!'" wrote General James Walker, one of Gordon's division commanders.[74]

Before the Union sentinels could fire a shot, the Confederates overwhelmed them and captured the fort, its artillery, and most of its men—nine guns, eleven mortars, and nearly one thousand prisoners—while losing just five men. The enemy, Walker believed, "were all asleep" except for the pickets. But in one of the staff officers' quarters, an all-night poker game was in progress; the officers, however, had been drinking whiskey and were incapable of doing anything.[75]

It appeared that Gordon's plan had worked beautifully—just before it fell to pieces.

Gordon's half-starved men stopped to eat and stuff their haversacks with the abundant Yankee food, slowing the advance. The men who guided Gordon's three columns could not find the three small forts supposedly behind Stedman. As it turned out, two of them had fallen into disuse, and the third was at that moment filling up with regiments from General John Hartranft's IX Corps division, which occupied a new fort and battery on a nearby ridge. An advancing Union skirmish line suddenly materialized behind Fort Stedman. Gordon unhappily observed, "The full light of the morning revealed the gathering forces of Grant and the great preponderance of his numbers."[76]

The Confederates now controlled the four Union batteries flanking Fort Stedman, but they had failed to seize Fort Haskell, bristling with cannon and the rallying place for soldiers driven from Fort Stedman. The Yankees there repelled a determined Rebel attack. It and other Yankee batteries in the area then plastered Fort Stedman and the cornfield between the fort and Gordon's lines with shot and shell. In Petersburg, "our very dwellings were shaken to their foundations" by the thunderous bombardment, wrote a newspaper correspondent.

About 8 a.m. Hartranft was poised to counterattack with four thousand infantrymen. Lee ordered Gordon to withdraw. "We had failed to carry the second line by surprise," wrote General Walker. "It was manned by four times our numbers, and our task was hopeless."[77]

Union cannon and musket fire cut down the Rebels as they re-entered no man's land, now a killing zone. Gordon was slightly wounded during his recrossing. A Union major who dove into a bombproof found it filled with Rebels. He persuaded them—all 204 of them—to become his prisoners, promising them good treatment, food, and $20 each for their weapons. This sounded fine to the demoralized Confederates. The major formed them into a column and "double-quicked" them to the Union lines.[78]

General George Meade, the Army of the Potomac's commander, was at City Point with Grant and unaware of what was happening; Confederates had cut the telegraph line from Petersburg before Gordon's attack.

In Meade's absence, General John Parke, the IX Corps commander, was in charge. Urged by the commanders of II and VI corps to launch large-scale counterattacks, the cautious Parke declined. "I did not deem it advisable, under the peculiar circumstances under which I was in temporary command of the army," he wrote.

When Meade returned late in the morning, he ordered II and VI Corps to attack that afternoon. A minor success, the operation bagged 834 prisoners.[79]

After Gordon's men had withdrawn, Lee encountered his sons Rooney and Robert Jr. as they brought up their cavalry division to join the assault. He told them they were too late. "I have often recalled the sadness of his face, its creased expression," Robert Jr. recalled.

Gordon's attack cost Lee's army 2,681 men whom it could not afford to lose; Union losses totaled 1,044. "Wish they would try it every day," Meade said.[80]

Gordon's aide, Major Henry Kyd Douglas, met between the lines under a white flag with General Hartranft, and they agreed to a truce to collect their wounded and bury their dead. "Men ran over the field from each side and gathered up their comrades, taking time, when they could, to exchange pipes, tobacco, penknives, hardtack and anything that was tradable," wrote Douglas.[81]

Lieutenant Colonel Theodore Lyman of Meade's staff remarked on the rough-looking Rebel prisoners who filed past him in a long procession. "These looked brown and athletic, but had the most matted hair, tangled beards, and slouched hats, and the most astounding carpets, horse-sheets and transmogrified shelter-tents for blankets, that you ever imagined," he wrote.[82]

The Confederate soldiers' bedraggled appearances illustrated the corrosive effect of their months in the trenches waging a defensive war while subsisting on starvation rations. Suddenly required to go on the offensive, the Rebels performed unevenly; some displayed their old élan, but others succumbed to their gnawing hunger. Moreover, when Union forces quickly reacted, bombarding the fort and counterattacking, many of Gordon's men chose to surrender rather than fight.

But the attack's failure was mainly due to the odd gaps in Gordon's plan, so admirably meticulous in many small ways—the fifty axmen and three hundred shock troops, the strips of white cloth—but so deficient in two major ones. It was remarkable that Lee did not carefully examine Gordon's tactical scheme because, if he had, he surely would have spotted the two problems. Gordon did not take into account either the enemy's or his own artillery, or how his men might have utilized captured guns to press their attacks. Instead, his plan laid out only the infantry's role. Gordon also did not reconnoiter, as he should have, the three small forts that he presumed were behind Fort Stedman; they were not what they appeared to be at a distance, and in the dark they were difficult to even find. Perhaps Lee and Gordon, both careful and analytical normally, were impaired by fatigue.[83]

The attack's failure disappointed Lee. In a letter to Davis he said he had hoped to break through and compel Grant to shorten his lines "and with a select body unite with Genl Johnston" to fight Sherman. "I fear now it will be impossible to prevent a junction between Grant and Sherman, nor do I deem it prudent that this army should maintain its position until the latter shall approach too near," he wrote. Johnston could not be expected to bring to Virginia more than ten thousand effectives, Lee told Davis, too few to make his diminished army a credible match for even Sherman's army.[84]

Meade's divisions were still counterattacking when President Abraham Lincoln arrived on the battlefront that afternoon on Grant's small, black horse, "Jeff Davis," on which the lanky president looked ludicrous with his long legs awkwardly folded under him and his white shins bared. Lincoln watched units from VI Corps assault a Rebel picket line and saw Confederate prisoners being marched to the rear. He somberly viewed the Union dead and wounded and was visibly affected by the mangled bodies.[85]

The president, the first lady, and their son Tad had arrived the previous night at City Point on the *River Queen*. After reading newspaper accounts of Lincoln's recent convalescence and his careworn appearance, Julia Grant had suggested to her husband that he invite the president to City Point. Grant replied that Lincoln would come when he wished, without being asked. Then, one day in Grant's presence, Mrs. Grant questioned Captain Robert Todd Lincoln about his father's health and asked him why the Lincolns did not visit City Point. The president's son replied, "I suppose they would, if they were sure they would not be intruding." Grant promptly telegraphed an invitation, and Lincoln quickly accepted it.[86]

The day the Lincolns left Washington, Treasury Secretary Gideon Welles wrote in his diary that the president did so "partly to get rid of the throng that is pressing upon him." Because Lincoln made himself available most hours every day to one and all, he "makes his office much more laborious than he should," Welles wrote. "It is now become such that he is compelled to flee."[87]

On the morning of the 25th, as the Confederates were being driven out of Fort Stedman, the Lincolns boarded a military train from City Point to the lines outside Petersburg. On horseback, Lincoln had then gone ahead to the front and toured it with Grant. Afterward, Grant asked the president whether he had ever doubted that the Union would prevail. "Never for a moment," Lincoln replied, with an emphatic swing of his hand.[88]

His profession of unswerving confidence notwithstanding, during Grant's 1864 Overland Campaign Lincoln had haunted the War Department's telegraph office at all hours for news from the front, anxiously hoping that it would not be bad. After Grant's army had marched one hundred miles south to Petersburg, suffering a shocking sixty-six thousand casualties, Lincoln had gone to City Point to visit him in June and had toured the Union positions. When the president returned to Washington, Attorney General Edward Bates Lee wrote that Lincoln appeared "perceptably [sic] disappointed at the small measure of our success, in that region; but encouraged by Grant's persistent confidence."[89]

Grant's steadiness and Lee's months of immobility had gone far to allay Lincoln's concern, but his reelection in November was probably the greatest tonic. When a recent White House visitor had asked Lincoln about the war's progress, he confidently replied with one of his amusing colloquialisms, "Grant has the bear by the hind leg while Sherman takes off the hide."

Yet, Lincoln still craved reassurance that Grant was going to prevail. When Lincoln's old friend General Grenville Dodge, recovering from a battle wound suffered at Atlanta in August, visited the White House, Lincoln questioned him about what he had seen and heard at City Point—and pointedly asked Dodge about Grant's plans to capture Richmond. Dodge said he was convinced that Grant would eventually defeat Lee. Lincoln reached across the table, laid his hand on Dodge's, and said, "You don't know how glad I am to hear you say this."[90]

Lincoln's visit gave thousands of men an opportunity to see the president for the first time. Lieutenant Colonel Lyman, Meade's aide, thought Lincoln "the ugliest man I ever put my eyes on; there is also an expression of plebeian vulgarity in his face that is offensive. On the other hand, he has the look of sense and wonderful shrewdness, while the heavy eyelids give him a mark almost of genius. He strikes me, too, as a very honest and kindly man . . . I never wish to see him again, but, as humanity runs, I am well content to have him at the head of affairs."[91]

Admiral David Porter, the commander of the North Atlantic Blockading Squadron, would spend many hours with the president during his visit, and his admiration for Lincoln grew as their relationship matured into friendship. "He was one of the most interesting men I ever met; he had an originality about him which was peculiarly his own." Porter, who claimed "not a particle of the bump of veneration on my head," wrote that he "saw more to admire in this man, more to reverence, than I had believed possible; he had a load to bear that few men could carry, yet he traveled on with it, foot-sore and weary, but without complaint."[92]

After repairs were completed on the last section of railroad line between Morehead City and Goldsboro, Sherman boarded a train the evening of March 25. The next day, he was at sea on the steamer *Russia*. He reached Fortress Monroe early March 27 and thence sailed up the James River to City Point.

Sherman had decided that this was a good time to meet with Grant. It was Sherman's first visit to City Point, which throbbed with activity. The busy harbor at the confluence of the James and Appomattox Rivers was crowded with the masts and smokestacks of dozens of war and merchant vessels, and its wharves were lined with warehouses full of military supplies. Huts, tents, and whitewashed barracks overlooked the river. Everywhere one looked, there were Union soldiers walking and riding, teamsters driving ambulances and mule teams, and flags waving in the breeze.[93]

Sherman found Grant, with his family and staff, occupying "a pretty group of huts" near the river. When Grant saw his friend he cried out, "How d'you do, Sherman!" Sherman exclaimed, "How are you, Grant!" They had not seen one another since meeting in Nashville and Cincinnati a year earlier to plan the 1864 campaign, whose principal objectives were cryptically summarized by Sherman, "He was to go for Lee, and I was to go for Joe Johnston."

Lieutenant Colonel Horace Porter, Grant's aide, witnessed their joyous reunion at Grant's City Point headquarters: "In a moment they stood upon the steps, with their hands locked in a cordial grasp, uttering earnest words of familiar greeting. Their encounter was more like that of two school-boys coming together after a vacation than the meeting of the chief actors in a great war tragedy." Sherman was "tall, spare, and sinewy . . . with lips that shut tightly together," wrote Lieutenant Colonel Lyman, Meade's aide, "a very homely man, with a regular nest of wrinkles in his face, which play and twist as he eagerly talks on each subject; but his expression is pleasant and kindly. But he believes in hard war. I heard him say: 'Columbia!—pretty much all burned; and burned good!'"[94]

Sherman accompanied Grant to his headquarters, where he greeted Mrs. Grant. Sherman sat before the fire and launched into a colorful account of his army's march through Georgia and the Carolinas. "The story, told as he alone could tell it, was a grand epic related with Homeric power," wrote Porter. After Sherman had talked for an hour Grant told him that Lincoln was on the *River Queen* and was anxious to see him.

They met briefly with Lincoln, and afterward Mrs. Grant asked them whether they had called on Mrs. Lincoln. They had not. She playfully chided them, "Well, you are a pretty pair! I do not see how you could have been so neglectful." They promised to pay their respects to the first lady when they met with Lincoln the next morning.[95]

It was probably just as well that they had not seen the first lady. Twice in recent days Mrs. Lincoln, known for her mood swings and outbursts, had exploded in jealous rages when the wives of General Charles Griffin and Edward Ord had been permitted to ride with the president's party while Mrs. Lincoln and Julia Grant rode in an army ambulance.

Lincoln had given Mrs. Griffin a special permit to join the mounted party that had toured the Fort Stedman battlefield. The other officers' wives stayed in the rear. When Mrs. Lincoln learned about it, she exclaimed, "Do you mean to say that she saw the president alone? Do you know that I never allow the president to see any woman alone?" She demanded to be let out of the ambulance to confront Mrs. Griffin. Grant persuaded her to wait until everyone got out. By then General George Meade had mollified her with a white lie: it was War Secretary Edwin Stanton, and not the president, who had permitted Mrs. Griffin to ride with the group.

The next day, May 26, was worse. Lincoln, Grant, Ord, and their wives sailed down the James River to Aiken's Landing, from there riding to a review of Ord's Army of the James. This time, Grant let Lincoln ride his favorite horse, Cincinnati, while Grant traveled on the stocky Jeff Davis. Mrs. Ord rode with the men; Mrs. Lincoln and Mrs. Grant once again traveled in an ambulance. Grant's aides, Horace Porter and Adam Badeau, sentenced to ride with Mrs. Lincoln, witnessed her fury when she found out that Mrs. Ord was riding with the president's party.

"What does the woman mean by riding by the side of the president? And ahead of me? Does she suppose that he wants her by the side of him?" Mrs. Lincoln raged.

Mrs. Grant tried to defend her friend, but the first lady then turned on the general-in-chief's wife. "I suppose you think you'll get to the White

House yourself, don't you?" she said nastily. Mrs. Grant replied that she was happy with her present position, which was better than anything she had ever expected. The first lady shot back contemptuously, "Oh! You had better take it if you can get it. 'Tis very nice."

When the group caught up with Mrs. Ord, Mrs. Lincoln violently rebuked her. and continued her verbal assault even after Mrs. Ord burst into tears. She resumed her insults that night at a social gathering on the *River Queen* with the Grants, urging Ord's removal from command for unfitness. Grant defended his general.

Badeau deeply sympathized with the president's obvious mortification over his wife's misbehavior. "He bore it as Christ might have done; with an expression of pain and sadness that cut one to the heart, but with supreme calmness and dignity." Mrs. Lincoln "turned on him like a tigress; and then he walked away, hiding that noble, ugly face that we might [not] catch the full expression of his misery." Badeau now understood why, days earlier, when he had asked Mrs. Stanton a question about Mrs. Lincoln, she had replied, "I do not visit Mrs. Lincoln." Puzzled, he had repeated the question, provoking the response, "Understand me, sir? I do not go to the White House; I do not visit Mrs. Lincoln."[96]

Lincoln found relief from Mrs. Lincoln's viperish behavior in the company of three orphaned kittens living in the tent of the City Point telegraph operator. He took the tiny kittens into his lap and stroked them, while instructing the operator to give them plenty of milk and kind treatment. The president returned several times to visit the kittens, wiping their eyes with his handkerchief and stroking their coats. "It was a curious sight at an army headquarters," wrote Porter, who witnessed Lincoln's demonstrations of affection, "upon the eve of a great military crisis in the nation's history, to see the hand which had affixed the signature to the Emancipation Proclamation, and had signed the commissions of all the heroic men who served the cause of the Union . . . tenderly caressing three stray kittens."[97]

❧

The war's last great military conference was held March 28 in the second-floor saloon of the *River Queen*. It was more informal exchange of views than war council. Present were Lincoln, Grant, Sherman, and Admiral Porter. Before the three military men left Grant's headquarters to see the president Mrs. Grant reminded them to inquire after Mrs. Lincoln. They dutifully did so when they came aboard the *River Queen*, but the president said the first lady was unwell and could not see them.

The four men got down to business. Grant described the plan he intended to put into motion in just a few days: to maneuver around the Confederates' right flank, while Phil Sheridan's Cavalry Corps, recently arrived from the Shenandoah Valley, destroyed the railroads into Petersburg from the south. It was "the crisis of the war," and Grant confessed to the others that his great fear was that Lee would somehow escape from Petersburg and Richmond, prolonging the war another year. "I knew he could move much more lightly and more rapidly than I," Grant later wrote.

If Lee somehow slipped out of Grant's grasp, said Sherman, he could hold both Lee and Johnston until Grant got there; together they would then crush both armies. If Lee was still in Petersburg, Sherman intended to leave Goldsboro on April 10, march to Raleigh, and thence to Burkeville Station, Virginia, southwest of Petersburg, where the Southside and Richmond & Danville Railroads from Petersburg intersected before proceeding to Lynchburg and Danville. Choking off these supply lines to Petersburg and Richmond would either starve out or force Lee to fight a last battle.

"Mr. Lincoln exclaimed, more than once, that there had been blood enough shed, and asked if another battle could not be avoided," Sherman later wrote. He told the president that "we could not control that event; that this necessarily rested with our enemy," and that he expected Lee would fight "one more desperate and bloody battle."[98]

Twice Lincoln expressed anxiety about Sherman's absence from his army. Sherman assured him that he planned to return the next day, and in the meantime the army was "snug and comfortable, in good camps, at Goldsboro," under the competent supervision of General John Schofield, whom he had left in command. The president also asked whether Johnston could get away from him by using the railroads. His army had broken them up, Sherman replied. Couldn't they be rebuilt? asked Grant. "Why no," Sherman replied, "my boys don't do things by halves. When they tore up the rails they put them over hot fires made from the ties, and then twisted them more crooked than a ram's horn. All the blacksmiths in the South could not straighten them out."[99]

Another subject that surely arose was the Union campaign planned in Alabama, the last Deep South state where organized Confederate forces remained in the field. While Mobile Bay had been in Union hands since August, the city of Mobile, thirty miles up the bay and protected by forts, earthworks, and torpedoes, was still a Rebel stronghold. Alabama's interior also remained unconquered. Generals James Wilson and Edward Canby were poised to bring all of Alabama to heel, with Wilson planning to seize the military industrial center at Selma with his large cavalry corps, and Canby, at the head of forty-five thousand men, intending to overpower Mobile's defenders and capture the port city. Wilson would face the brilliant cavalry leader, General Nathan Bedford Forrest, at the head of Rebel units from three states that together scarcely equaled half of Wilson's thirteen thousand men.[100]

⁊⅊

The president was eager to discuss the postwar. "The most liberal and honorable terms," Lincoln said, should be granted the South when it surrendered. "Let them once surrender, and reach their homes, they won't take up arms again," he told his military chieftains. "Let them all go, officers and all. I want submission, and no more bloodshed. Let them have their horses to plow with, and if you like, their guns to shoot crows with. I want no one punished; treat them liberally all round. We want those people to return to their allegiance to the Union and submit to the laws." Jefferson Davis, he intimated, should be permitted to "escape the country," but Lincoln added that he could not publicly express this wish because it would provoke a loud outcry.

Lincoln illustrated his point with one of his stories, this one about a man who had taken a total-abstinence pledge and, when visiting a friend, was invited to have a drink. He declined on account of his pledge, but accepted his host's offer of lemonade. As he prepared his guest's lemonade, the host pointed to a brandy bottle and said the lemonade would be improved if he were to add a little brandy. The abstaining visitor replied that he would not object, so long as it was done "unbeknown" to him. Sherman took this to mean that Lincoln wanted Davis to escape, "'unbeknown' to him."[101]

After the fighting ended, Lincoln said, he would provisionally recognize existing Southern state governments to forestall the outbreak of anarchy—until Congress could reorder civil affairs in the former Confederacy. Sherman later said that Lincoln told him he could assure North Carolina Governor Zebulon Vance that as soon as the armies laid down their arms and the soldiers resumed their former civilian pursuits, they would be "guaranteed all their rights as citizens of a common country."[102]

Lincoln's manner intrigued Sherman. "When at rest or listening, his legs and arms seemed to hang almost lifeless, and his face was care-worn and haggard; but the moment he began to talk, his face lighted up, his tall form, as it were, unfolded, and he was the very impersonation of good humor and fellowship," Sherman wrote. "Of all the men I ever met, he seemed to possess most of the elements of greatness, combined with goodness, than any other."

Before they parted at the gangplank of the *River Queen*, Lincoln said, "Sherman, do you know why I took a shine to Grant and you?" Sherman replied that he did not, while acknowledging that the president had always treated him fairly and kindly.

Lincoln said, "Well, you never found fault with me."[103]

❧

The president had not been away from Washington even a week before members of his administration began showing up at City Point, asking to see him. The intrusions annoyed Lincoln. When Admiral Porter showed Lincoln a telegram from Secretary of State William Seward requesting permission to join Lincoln, the president said, "No, I don't want him. Telegraph him that the berths are too small, and there's not room for another passenger." Porter said he could find room, but Lincoln was adamant. The president, the admiral replied to Seward, "did not want any of his Cabinet down there to contest the views he had formed in regard to [ending the war], nor to try to turn him from his plans."

Vice President Andrew Johnson and Preston King, the former New York senator, arrived uninvited on the *Malvern*, wanting to pay their respects to the president. "I won't see either of them," Lincoln told Admiral Porter. "Send them away. They have no business here, anyway; no right to come down here without my permission." He didn't care what Porter told them, "but don't let them come near me." The admiral said that Lincoln at that moment looked "like a man it would be dangerous for any one to anger." Porter instructed the *Malvern*'s commander to bring out all the champagne, cigars, and liquor and to take Johnson and King somewhere and entertain them.[104]

⚬⚬

Phil Sheridan's Cavalry Corps was a pillar of Grant's plan to sever the railroad connections to Petersburg, to turn Lee's right flank, and to destroy the Army of Northern Virginia. The hard-riding Union troopers, aided by infantry divisions from VI and IX Corps and from West Virginia, had crushed Jubal Early's Army of the Valley in three battles the previous fall—at Winchester, Fisher's Hill, and Cedar Creek—and had seized control of the produce-rich Shenandoah Valley. Sheridan then proceeded to burn the granaries, barns, and fields and to appropriate or slaughter all of the livestock. As a consequence, Richmond suffered severe, persistent food shortages in early 1865. "Through the effect of Sheridan's raid, Richmond is rapidly approaching a state of famine," wrote Robert Kean, chief of the Confederate Bureau of War.

Indeed, Richmond's inhabitants were now acting as though apocalyptic times were upon them. Red auction flags fluttered up and down the streets, signaling an imminent exodus from the city. What couldn't be sold was given away; women donated silverware and jewelry to the Confederate Treasury to help feed the troops.

They sold their possessions so that they would have ready cash. The Confederacy's first lady, Varina Davis, sold her silk gown, laces, gloves, furniture, artwork, china, and silver through an auction house, and Davis sold all of his horses except one. The auction house sales netted the couple $28,400. Wealthy friends bought back Varina's matched team of carriage horses and presented them to the Davises.[105]

A commercial traveler who visited Richmond reported, "There seemed a death-like stillness to pervade the city; every one wore a haggard, scared look, as if apprehensive of some great impending calamity." Susan Blackford affirmed the traveler's acuity when she wrote, "Hope had ceased to be a steadying and staying comforter. All anticipated the near approach of the end . . . and yet, with rare exception, all were calm and resigned, though defiant."

Diarist Sallie Putnam saw approaching disaster in the half-starved Confederate troops passing through Richmond. "Many of them, from their rags and tatters, would have made admirable scare-crows had they made their appearance in the spring in our corn-fields." The cavalrymen and their horses were in worse shape, though—"tatterdemalions mounted on poor, weak, miserable animals, scarcely more than moving skeletons."[106]

Edward Fontaine, too, bleakly noted the harbingers of imminent defeat. "I fear that God has ceased to work miracles," he wrote. "He certainly seems now to be on the side of our oppressors. We are in our last struggle, & without his mighty aid the Southern Confederacy will cease to exist in the next four months . . . while our enemies insultingly exalt over the glorious battle fields where our greatest defenders died in vain."[107]

Jefferson Davis designated March 10 as a day of fasting and prayer. Captain Charles Blackford, a judge advocate in Richmond's military courts, drolly remarked, "To name one day as a fast-day seems almost amusing when every day is a fast day to all, whether citizens or soldiers. . . . I have never known a day so devoutly kept by every class of the community." When he learned of Davis's pronouncement, War Department clerk John B. Jones indulged in some black humor by noting, "Four days hence we have a day of fasting, etc., appointed by the President; and I understand there are but three day's rations for the army—a nice calculation."[108]

Sheridan's troopers left Winchester on February 27 and rode south, up the valley, turning east toward Richmond at Staunton. On March 2, in the pouring rain, the forty-five hundred men of General George Custer's division struck the remnants of Early's army at Waynesboro. Needing troops in Petersburg and Richmond, Lee had stripped Early of all but fifteen hundred infantrymen and five hundred cavalrymen. It was "one of the most terrible panics and stampedes I have ever seen," wrote Jedediah Hotchkiss, the Confederate Army topographer. Simultaneously flanking Early and attacking frontally, Custer's troopers routed the Confederates and took sixteen hundred prisoners. They proceeded to Charlottesville, whose leaders, "with medieval ceremony," presented Custer with the keys to the city's public buildings. At the University of Virginia, a delegation of professors flourishing a white handkerchief on a walking cane asked Custer to protect the campus, which Thomas Jefferson had designed. Custer placed a provost guard around the college to prevent vandalism. Early, who escaped Waynesboro with his staff, went home to Lynchburg and was not recalled to command.

The Cavalry Corps wrecked the James River canal and tore up the Virginia Central Railroad west of Richmond, severing those supply arteries to Richmond and Lee's army. Heavy rains turned the roads into quagmires as the Union cavalry slogged east toward Richmond.

Grant's orders had called for Sheridan to march to Lynchburg, destroy the Rebel supply depot there, and then proceed to North Carolina to join Sherman's army. But Sheridan did not wish to join Sherman when he could be with Grant's army, and he made no effort to march to Lynchburg. The Confederates, he said in explaining his decision to go to City Point and not Lynchburg, had destroyed the James River bridges, and the river was running so high and fast that it could not be forded. Later, Sheridan truthfully wrote, "Feeling that the war was nearing its end, I desired my cavalry to be in at the death." The death, he was certain, would come with Lee's defeat in southern Virginia.

As Sheridan's men rode east toward Richmond, Lee, concerned that they might be planning a raid on the capital, sent two of General James Longstreet's First Corps divisions and some cavalry to intercept them. The Confederate task force struck the Cavalry Corps at Ashland, northwest of Richmond. While a Union cavalry brigade held off the Rebels, the rest of Sheridan's men crossed the South Anna River and rode north and east of Richmond.[109]

When Sheridan reached City Point, Grant invited him to accompany Grant and Lincoln to the same review of the Army of the James that was marked by the first lady's tirades against Mrs. Ord. As the party sailed downriver to its disembarkation point, Lincoln, Grant, and Sheridan watched the Cavalry Corps cross a pontoon bridge over the James, and Lincoln questioned Sheridan about his men and their exploits.[110]

Lincoln was dubious about Sheridan when he was appointed commander in the Shenandoah Valley in August; the president thought him "too young." It was true that Sheridan's small stature and wiriness made him appear younger than his actual age, thirty-three. Moreover, the president was one foot taller than Sheridan. Sheridan had dispelled Lincoln's doubts by defeating Early and taking firm control of the Shenandoah Valley. At City Point, Lincoln displayed genuine fondness for Sheridan. "When this peculiar war began I thought a cavalryman should be at least six feet four inches high," Lincoln reportedly said, "but I changed my mind. Five feet four will do in a pinch."[111]

When Sheridan left the Shenandoah Valley to join Grant, he gave up his independent command of the Middle Military District. To compensate him for the loss of that command and to demonstrate his absolute faith in Sheridan, Grant removed Sheridan and the Cavalry Corps from the Army of the Potomac's command structure. Sheridan would no longer report to Meade; he would report directly to Grant. This was a singular honor, for it elevated Sheridan to a position equal to that of Sherman, Meade, and Ord. In addition, six thousand cavalrymen were going to be added to Sheridan's nine-thousand-man Cavalry Corps by April 1.

"General Grant felt that [Sheridan] was entitled to every consideration which could be shown him," wrote Lieutenant Colonel Horace Porter, a Grant aide. Grant's intimates knew just how much the general-in-chief admired Sheridan—as someone who "would fight, always," and as "incomparably the greatest general our civil war produced." Someone described Sheridan as "the left-hand man of Grant the left-handed." The Confederates had begun calling him "Sheridan the inevitable."[112]

Sheridan was undoubtedly pleased by his new status in the Union Army, but he disliked his anticipated role in the coming campaign. The Cavalry Corps was to move south and west of Petersburg to cut the railroads and attempt to slip around Lee's right flank and into his rear, or at least draw him out of Petersburg to fight. Sheridan was agreeable to that part of his mission, but the rest of his orders disturbed him: his troopers were to then join Sherman in North Carolina to supersede Sherman's erratic cavalry general, Hugh Judson Kilpatrick, and support Sherman's army as it marched north to join Grant.[113]

Sheridan forcefully argued against joining Sherman; if he left Petersburg, he believed, the Army of the Potomac would not move. Sherman would then end the war with the Cavalry Corps's help. Sheridan had correctly divined Sherman's intentions. In fact, Sherman had been pressuring Grant to delay his offensive until Sherman's army arrived in Virginia, "and make a sure thing of it." But Sheridan told Grant that the Union forces at Petersburg should end the war.

Grant's chief of staff, General John Rawlins, sided with Sheridan, and Grant then abruptly reversed himself. The orders sending Sheridan to North Carolina had been a "blind" to deceive peace advocates in Washington, said Grant, somewhat unconvincingly. If the maneuver against Lee's right failed, he would be able to say that he was only trying to close the gap between his army and Sherman's. Grant told Sheridan that he had all along intended to keep Sheridan with his army outside Petersburg. "I mean to end this business here," Grant said.

Sheridan slapped his leg, and his face "brightened at once," wrote Grant aide Lieutenant Colonel Adam Badeau, "and he replied with enthusiasm, 'That's what I like to hear you say. Let us end this business here.' The two natures struck fire from each other in the contact."[114]

Afterward, Sheridan was in camp with his troopers when he found out that Sherman was at City Point, conferring with Grant. Concerned that Sherman might change Grant's mind, Sheridan set out for Grant's headquarters, prepared to again argue for keeping the Cavalry Corps at Petersburg.

Just as Sheridan had expected, upon his arrival Sherman immediately proposed that he bring his cavalrymen to North Carolina. Sheridan would have none of it, and he forcefully—perhaps too forcefully—reiterated his opposition to that plan. "My uneasiness made me somewhat too earnest, I fear," he later confessed. After Sherman had left, Grant assured Sheridan that he was not leaving Petersburg.

Early the next morning, before he left for Goldsboro, Sherman slipped into Sheridan's tent while he was asleep and again tried to convince him to unite his army with Sherman's. Sheridan didn't budge; he was resolved to end "this business" in Virginia.[115]

❧

On March 29, Grant's divisions began their massive shift westward. To be close to the action, Grant and his staff decided to move their headquarters from City Point. Lincoln accompanied Grant and his aides to the train, and the president shook hands solemnly with each of them. As the train pulled away, Grant and his staff raised their hats in a salute to the president, who lifted his hat in reciprocation. In an emotion-choked voice Lincoln called, "Good-bye, gentlemen. God bless you all! Remember, your success is my success!"[116]

Lincoln was unsure whether he should stay at City Point or return to Washington. "I begin to feel that I ought to be at home, and yet I dislike to leave without seeing nearer to the end of General Grant's present movement," he told War Secretary Edwin Stanton.

Stanton urged him to remain. "I have strong faith that your presence will have great influence in inducing exertions that will bring Richmond; compared to that no other duty can weigh a feather.... A pause by the army now would do harm; if you are on the ground there will be no pause."[117]

The movement had begun when General Ord led his four Army of the James divisions to the works held by General Andrew Humphreys's II Corps and Gouverneur Warren's V Corps, freeing the two corps to begin advancing toward Lee's right flank. Sheridan, with his three cavalry divisions, rode down the Weldon and Petersburg Railroad south of the marching infantry corps. In August the Yankees had severed the railroad; it no longer carried supplies to Petersburg from North Carolina. Instead, they came by wagon train via the Boydton Plank Road, about ten miles west of the railroad. If all went according to plan, that road would fall into the hands of Humphreys, Warren, and Sheridan. Grant's ultimate objective lay ten miles beyond the Boydton Plank Road: the Southside Railroad and Lee's right flank.

About fifteen miles south of Petersburg, the Cavalry Corps turned to the northwest and rode toward Dinwiddie Court House. At some future time Sheridan and the two infantry corps would unite north of there and together push around the Rebels' right rear.

In his instructions to Sheridan, Grant told him not to "go after the enemy's roads at present" but to press on and "get onto [Lee's] right rear.... We will act altogether as one army here until it is seen what can be done with the enemy." Grant added, "I now feel like ending the matter if it is possible to do so before going back."[118]

Scarcely had the campaign begun when heavy rains started to fall. The downpours began during the evening of March 29 and continued without interruption for the next thirty-six hours. The low-lying terrain south of the Appomattox River was transformed into "glutinous mud." By the evening of the 30th "whole fields had become beds of quicksand," wrote Horace Porter, "in which the troops waded in mud above their ankles."

Always trying to coax celerity from an army known for sluggishness, Grant had hoped to speedily put the Eastern troops astride the Southside Railroad and on Lee's right flank. But because of the weather, the maneuver became a slog along roads that had become "sheets of water." Horses plunged into seemingly bottomless mudholes, and one soldier nearly drowned in one, weighed down by his weapons, a full haversack, and his ammunition. A train of six hundred wagons, aided by a thousand engineer soldiers who all but carried the wagons from quagmire to quagmire, covered just five miles in fifty-six hours.

The rain did not altogether rob the waterlogged Yankees of their sense of humor. Soldiers would call out to officers as they rode by, "I say, fetch along the pontoons," and, "When are the gunboats coming up?" It seemed to Horace Porter that the "saving of that army would require the services, not of a Grant but of a Noah."[119]

❧

Sheridan's troopers had just reached Dinwiddie Court House on the Boydton Plank Road when the rain began. The diminutive, fierce-looking cavalry leader—with his high cheekbones and almond-shaped eyes, he might have been a Cossack chieftain—established his headquarters at the Dinwiddie Hotel. There was no supper, but the two young women refugees who lived there made coffee for the cavalry officers—and asked them not to fight a battle where the women would have to see men killed. Lieutenant Colonel Frederick Newhall, Sheridan's adjutant general, said they pledged to not bring "red war to the doorstep of the Dinwiddie Hotel." Sheridan and his staff slept that night on the floor, wrapped in their cloaks.[120]

March 30 was a lost day because of the rain, and then, late in the day, Grant suspended offensive operations until the roads dried. "The heavy rains of today will make it impossible for us to do much until it dries up a little or we get roads around our rear repaired," he wrote. When Sheridan read the order, he instantly concluded that it "would be a serious mistake." He ordered his groomsman to saddle his gray, Breckinridge—so named because it had belonged to a staff officer of General John Breckinridge when captured on Missionary Ridge. Sheridan set off in the rain to talk to Grant.

"Plunging at every step and almost to his knees in the mud," Breckinridge carried Sheridan the few miles to where the general-in-chief had made his headquarters in an old cornfield beside Gravelly Run. Grant's staff was ranged around a campfire, while Grant was inside a tent arguing with Rawlins, his chief of staff, about the suspension; like Sheridan, Rawlins believed Grant was making a mistake. Sheridan stepped into the tent long enough to hear Grant say disconsolately to Rawlins, "Well, Rawlins, I think you had better take command." Sheridan withdrew.[121]

The cavalry chief returned to the staff officers around the fire and began to energetically describe the coming campaign, taking "a decidedly cheerful view." Pacing "like a hound in the leash," Sheridan declared, "I can drive in the whole cavalry force of the enemy with ease, and if an infantry force is added to my command, I can strike out for Lee's right, and either crush it or force him to so weaken his entrenched lines that our troops in front of them can break through and march into Petersburg."

Someone asked how he would get forage if the rain continued. "Forage!" cried Sheridan. "I'll get up all the forage I want. I'll haul it out, if I have to set every man in the command to corduroying roads, and corduroy every mile of them from the railroad to Dinwiddie.

"I tell you, I'm ready to strike out tomorrow and go to smashing things!" he exclaimed.

His speech was a "tonic" for the staff officers, and they encouraged him to repeat to Grant what he had just said. Because Sheridan was reluctant to intrude, one of the officers entered the tent where Grant and Rawlins were still talking and told Grant that Sheridan had some interesting things to discuss. Grant and Sheridan went to another tent to speak privately. There, Grant told Sheridan that his officers had convinced him to suspend the offensive because they believed the rain and mud made it impossible to move the trains.

Sheridan urged Grant not to suspend the campaign, warning that if he did, he would be "surely ridiculed, just as General [Ambrose] Burnside's army was after the mud march of 1863." Soon after that failed maneuver Burnside was relieved of command of the Army of the Potomac. The cavalry, Sheridan said, was ready to push on toward Lee's right.

Sheridan's arguments and abundant confidence buoyed Grant. "We will go on," Grant said.

Sheridan asked Grant to send him VI Corps, which had been his primary infantry force in the Shenandoah Valley; the Cavalry Corps and VI Corps had grown fond of one another during their joint operations the previous fall. With VI Corps, Sheridan said, the Cavalry Corps could turn or break through the Confederate lines.

VI Corps was too far away, replied Grant; he offered him V Corps, which was nearby. Although Sheridan had little confidence in the ability of General Gouverneur Warren, V Corps's commander, he accepted Grant's offer. After parting with Grant, Sheridan encountered Warren who, evidently affected by the rainy weather, began "speaking rather despondently of the outlook." Sheridan was unimpressed.[122]

The day after Gordon's attack at Fort Stedman was repulsed, Lee wrote a long letter to Jefferson Davis explaining what the operation had hoped to achieve—a breakout to join Johnston in North Carolina, forcing Grant to shorten his lines—and what its failure portended. Unable now to prevent the union of Sherman and Grant, Lee did not think it "prudent that this army should maintain its position until [Sherman] shall approach too near." But, as Lee usually did when dealing with the Confederate president, he humbly said he wished only to inform Davis of "the condition of affairs, knowing that you will do whatever may be in your power to give relief." Davis did not act on Lee's letter.[123]

Amid the growing sense that their cause was doomed, the Confederate troops remaining in Petersburg—half-starved, frequently ill, but unwilling to quit—turned more than ever to religion, always their great comfort in trying times. "From the commander-in-chief to the privates in the ranks, there was a deep and sincere religious feeling in Lee's army," wrote Gordon. "Whenever it was convenient or practicable, these hungry but unyielding men were holding prayer meetings."[124]

On March 29, Confederate scouts reported large numbers of Union troops at Hatcher's Run and Dinwiddie Court House moving toward Lee's right. Lee and his corps commanders knew this meant that Grant's army would try again to sever the Southside Railroad.[125]

Lee faced a dilemma. If he extended his thirty-eight-mile-long defensive line further in anticipation of Grant's westward shift, he must stretch it another four miles. The Rebel lines were thinly manned already, with only 1,140 men defending each mile on average. Another extension would invite a powerful Union attack against one of the defensive line's vulnerable points, with a breakthrough the probable result.[126]

Lee and his advisers chose another course: to combine all of the available Confederate cavalry units in Richmond and Petersburg and to strike Sheridan's Cavalry Corps at the Five Forks crossroad or at Dinwiddie to preempt its lunge toward the railroad. The Rebel mounted force, however, mustered just 5,500 troopers on worn-out horses. They were armed with muzzle-loaded carbines and a medley of captured weapons, no match for Sheridan's 13,000 mounted men—including additional Army of the James troopers—and their Spencer repeaters. Longstreet proposed a novel if imperfect solution: converting George Pickett's First Corps infantry division, now in reserve, into a mobile force that would operate with the Rebel cavalry. The combined task force, which also included two brigades from General Bushrod Johnson's division, totaled 10,600 men, with a six-gun battery commanded by Colonel William Pegram. The task force rendezvoused at Five Forks on March 30, the day Sheridan convinced Grant to "go on" despite the rain and mud.[127]

On the 31st Bushrod Johnson's remaining brigades on the Petersburg line and General Samuel McGowan's South Carolina brigade, all entrenched on the Rebel right, lashed out at the large V Corps columns marching westward on the White Oak Road. The previous day, Lee had perched on a fence rail in the rain with his aides, and they had sketched the day's attack by marking the muddy ground with a stick. They worked out the details while crouched down eating bread and sardines.[128]

The plan was audacious and very nearly worked. Although outnumbered three-to-one, the Confederates broke two of Gouverneur Warren's three divisions and drove them back a mile to Gravelly Run. "I have no idea that the brigade ever killed more men, even in the most sanguinary engagements, than it did this day," wrote Lieutenant J. F. J. Caldwell of McGowan's brigade. "Our loss was slight."

A shocked Warren and his staff officers rallied the routed divisions behind his only intact one, that of General Charles Griffin. With II Corps aiding with diversionary attacks, Griffin regained the lost ground. The Confederates withdrew to where they began the attack that morning. Lee, who had ridden out from Petersburg to observe the battle, was pleased by his overmatched men's heroic performance.

Confederate General Eppa Hunton returned from the fight with his scabbard doubled over by flying metal and three bullet holes in his clothing. Lee said to him, "I wish you would sew those places up. I don't like to see them." Hunton replied, "General Lee, allow me to go back home and see my wife and I will have them sewed up." Amused, Lee retorted, "The idea of talking about going to see wives; it is perfectly ridiculous, sir."

Not everyone was attuned to the crisis facing Lee and his army. Lee's twenty-three-year-old daughter Agnes chose to visit her father in Petersburg just as Grant was beginning his westward shift and as Lee was attempting to foil the maneuver. He regretfully wrote Agnes, "I am too sorry I cannot go in to see you, but I must go to the right. The enemy in strong force is operating in that direction. I do not yet know to what extent or when I can visit you."[129]

❧

Grant's confidence in General Warren had ebbed steadily since the previous May, when he first had occasion to doubt Warren's ability during the fighting at Spotsylvania Court House. At one point Grant had nearly relieved Warren of his command for balking at orders to attack. At Cold Harbor and Petersburg, Grant's dissatisfaction had increased; he thought Warren too slow and not aggressive enough.

Warren's performance on March 31, when two of his divisions had fled before the Confederates, deepened Grant's disaffection. "I don't understand why Warren permitted his corps to be fought in detail when [General Romeyn] Ayres pushed forward. He should have sent other troops to their support," wrote Grant. After Sheridan had sent him intelligence about Rebel movements, Meade had warned Warren late March 30 that Ayres "should be put on his guard and that he should be re-enforced without delay, as the enemy may attack him at daylight." Whatever Warren had done, it was not enough.

Warren was a brilliant topographer whose eye for tactically advantageous terrain had probably saved the Union Army at Gettysburg. As chief engineering officer of the Army of the Potomac, he had understood the importance of Little Round Top and had rushed Union troops there before the Confederates could seize it. For this deed he was elevated to corps command.

While V Corps fought its pitched battle on White Oak Road, the Pickett task force advanced on Dinwiddie Court House with three cavalry divisions under General Fitzhugh Lee and five infantry brigades. Sheridan's forward cavalry brigades fought a delaying action as they slowly withdrew from just south of Five Forks to within a mile of Dinwiddie. There, the Cavalry Corps had constructed a series of barricades; from behind them, Sheridan's men fought dismounted. The advancing Rebels drove Sheridan's men backward from barricade to barricade.[130]

Needing reinforcements, Sheridan summoned Custer's division, which had drawn the unenviable job of shepherding the Cavalry Corps's wagon train through the endless mud. An Ohio sergeant described the laborious process, "Wagons in the mud up to the Hubs, and men with Rails or poles lifting the wheels out only to be repeated a few feet farther on." Liberated from this thankless duty, Custer's men raced to the battlefield. On a hilltop, they threw up breastworks and brought up the field artillery just in time to repel a Confederate cavalry attack on the Cavalry Corps lines at Dinwiddie.[131]

Then, Pickett's infantry brigades emerged from the woods as sunset approached. "They had an air of abandon, a sort of devil-may-care swing in their long stride as they advanced over a field, that was rather disheartening to men that did not want to get shot," wrote Lieutenant Colonel Frederick Newhall, Sheridan's adjutant general.

To inspire his men, Sheridan, cap in hand, galloped along his line with his staff officers, Custer, and General Wesley Merritt, while "mud and bullets flew" around them. "Sheridan seemed to have infused his own indomitable spirit among his subordinates," wrote Major Henry Tremain of General George Crook's staff. As the firing on both sides intensified, "the repeating Spencers [were] puffing out their cartridges like Roman candles." A *New York Herald* reporter riding with Sheridan was hit in the shoulder by long-range musket fire. Two attacks by Pickett's brigades were repulsed by Custer's men, their "repeating rifles pouring out such a shower of lead that nothing could stand up against it," Sheridan proudly wrote. The Confederates withdrew to the woods, where they continued to exchange gunfire with Sheridan's men. Night fell, and the shooting slackened.[132]

Sheridan sent Grant a battle report, estimating that he had lost up to 450 men killed or wounded. "This force is too strong for us," he conceded, but added, "I will hold on to Dinwiddie Court-House until I am compelled to leave." Meade immediately ordered V Corps's remaining twelve to fifteen thousand men and General Ranald Mackenzie's fifteen hundred cavalrymen from the Army of the James to go to Sheridan's aid. Grant told Meade to instruct Warren "not to stop for anything." While one division marched directly to Dinwiddie, Warren's other two divisions were to push south of White Oak Road and attack Pickett's rear. Grant's faith in Sheridan's aggressive leadership persuaded him to give Sheridan command of Warren's corps as well as his own.

After sending Warren his orders, Grant told Sheridan that V Corps should be in position by midnight. This was highly improbable; Warren did not receive the order until nearly 11 p.m., and his divisions were dispersed in camps six miles away. It would be several hours before any V Corps units could come to Sheridan's aid.

Sheridan told Grant's aide, Horace Porter, that when V Corps came under his command the next morning, he intended to go on the offensive. Pickett's force, he declared, "is in more danger than I am." If Pickett cut him off from the Army of the Potomac, Pickett's men, at the same time, would be cut off from Lee's army, "and not a man in it [Pickett's force] should ever be allowed to get back to Lee. We at last have drawn the enemy's infantry out of its fortifications, and this is our chance to attack it."[133]

Pickett also came to that conclusion after cavalrymen that night brought him two captured Yankees from V Corps. They told him that Warren's men were marching toward Pickett's left flank. Pickett might be able to handle Sheridan's cavalry, but not fifteen thousand Union infantrymen, too.

At daybreak on April 1 Sheridan's scouts probed the woods where Pickett's men were last seen. The woods were empty. The Confederates had withdrawn during the night to Five Forks.

President Abraham Lincoln, in his "Five Dollar Bill" portrait. *Library of Congress*

General Ulysses S. Grant, the Union Army's general-in-chief. *Library of Congress*

General Robert E. Lee, commander of all Confederate Army forces. *Library of Congress*

Confederate President Jefferson Davis. *Library of Congress*

General George Meade, commander of the Army of the Potomac. *Library of Congress*

Union troops captured Fort Fisher, North Carolina, on January 15, 1865, closing the Confederacy's last major port, Wilmington. *National Archives*

BELOW: General Sherman's men burned Columbia, South Carolina, the so-called cradle of secession, during a chaotic night in February 1865, burnishing Sherman's reputation as a modern-day Attila. *Library of Congress*

ABOVE: General William T. Sherman, whose army's incendiary march through South Carolina sent shock waves through the Confederacy. *National Archives*

McPhersonville was one of the many South Carolina communities destroyed during Sherman's march. *Library of Congress*

Confederate General Joseph Johnston pulled together a patchwork army to try to stop Sherman's troops after they entered North Carolina. *National Archives*

Confederate General John Gordon, one of Robert E. Lee's best young generals, led the failed breakout at Fort Stedman in March 1865. *Library of Congress*

Rebel soldiers killed in action await burial. *Library of Congress*

General Phil Sheridan's Cavalry Corps secured the Shenandoah Valley and rejoined General Ulysses Grant's army outside Petersburg in March 1865. The aggressive Sheridan was eager to be part of the war's final act. *National Archives*

At the Battle of Five Forks outside Petersburg on April 1, 1865, General Phil Sheridan's Cavalry Corps and V Corps shattered General George Pickett's Confederate task force, making Petersburg untenable for Lee's army. *Library of Congress*

Union forces launched a successful all-out attack on Petersburg on April 2, 1865, ending the nearly ten-month siege. Confederate troops evacuated Petersburg and fled westward. *Library of Congress*

Confederate General A. P. Hill, who commanded the Third Corps, was killed by a Union soldier during the April 2 assault on Petersburg. *Library of Congress*

Dead Confederate soldiers in a trench at Petersburg. *Library of Congress*

Confederate and Union dead lie side by side at Petersburg. *Library of Congress*

BELOW: Union Admiral David Porter (center), shown with his staff on the *U.S.S. Malvern*, accompanied President Abraham Lincoln to Petersburg and Richmond immediately after their capture. *Library of Congress*

ABOVE: Confederate General James Longstreet, whose First Corps led the retreat from Petersburg. *Library of Congress*

Richmond's business district lay in ashes after fires set by retreating Confederates swept through the city during the night of April 2–3. *Library of Congress*

Wilmer McLean's home at Appomattox Court House, where General Robert E. Lee surrendered the Army of Northern Virginia to General Ulysses Grant. *Library of Congress*

The US flag was raised over Fort Sumter at Charleston, South Carolina, on April 14, 1865, exactly four years after it was lowered in surrender during the war's first action. *Library of Congress*

President Abraham Lincoln was mortally wounded on April 14, 1865, while watching *Our American Cousin* at Ford's Theatre in Washington. The manhunt for Lincoln's assassin, John Wilkes Booth, ended twelve days later with Booth's death in a northeastern Virginia barn. *Library of Congress*

The "Grand Review" of the victorious Union armies on May 23 and 24, 1865, was the largest parade in US history until that time. About 150,000 troops marched and rode down Pennsylvania Avenue before massive, adoring crowds. *Library of Congress*

APRIL 1865

There seemed to be no front nor rear, for firing and fighting might be heard ahead and behind and on both sides at once.

—CONFEDERATE STAFF OFFICER,
DESCRIBING THE RETREAT FROM PETERSBURG[1]

My God! Has the army been dissolved?

—ROBERT E. LEE,
AT SAILOR'S CREEK[2]

Let the thing be pressed.

—ABRAHAM LINCOLN,
AFTER SAILOR'S CREEK[3]

1

April 1, 1865
FIVE FORKS, VIRGINIA

General Warren and V Corps were late in reaching Sheridan. Hours after the midnight arrival promised by Grant, General Romeyn Ayres's division joined Sheridan's Cavalry Corps, which was advancing from its entrenchments at Dinwiddie Court House toward Five Forks several miles away. The delay occurred because Warren stopped to rebuild a bridge the Confederates had destroyed over Gravelly Run. With a touch of exasperation, George Meade ordered Warren to send troops to Sheridan by other routes, even if he had to abandon the planned attack on George Pickett's left rear.

That was out of the question anyway. During the night Pickett had withdrawn his ten-thousand-man task force from Dinwiddie to Five Forks after learning that V Corps was approaching his left flank. General Wesley Merritt's cavalry division harried the Rebels into fortifications they had built around Five Forks.[4]

About 11 a.m. Grant's aide, Lieutenant Colonel Horace Porter, assigned by Grant to shadow Sheridan that day and send him updates, rode up to Sheridan, who was impatiently waiting for Warren and the rest of his corps.

Minutes after Porter's arrival Warren appeared. Sheridan got down to business immediately, sketching his battle plan in the dirt with his saber. While Warren positioned V Corps opposite Pickett's left flank at Five Forks, Sheridan's cavalrymen would pin down the Confederates by pouring a steady fire into their center and right flank. Then, V Corps and the Cavalry Corps would simultaneously strike the center and left flank. Sheridan was certain that the joint assault by more than thirty thousand infantrymen and cavalrymen would overwhelm Pickett's men. He told Warren to move quickly.

Since his momentous day at Gettysburg, Warren had seldom acted with the sense of urgency—which Sheridan possessed in abundance—that Grant or Meade wished. With rising irritation, Sheridan watched Warren sit down on a log and write out his orders, handing them to aides to deliver, rather than riding to his division commanders to brief them in person—as Sheridan surely would have done. Then Warren rode away.

Not long afterward, Lieutenant Colonel Orville Babcock, another Grant aide, rode up to Sheridan and verbally delivered an extraordinary message from the general-in-chief: "General Grant directs me to say to you that if, in your judgment, the Fifth Corps would do better under one of its division commanders, you are authorized to relieve General Warren and order him to report to him [General Grant] at headquarters." V Corps's erratic performance on White Oak Road the previous day and Warren's dilatoriness in reaching Sheridan had pushed Grant to the very limits of his tolerance.[5]

While waiting for Warren to bring up V Corps, Sheridan positioned his cavalry before Pickett's entrenchments, and the troopers commanded by Generals George Custer and Thomas Devin opened a steady fire that pinned down the Rebels.

Hours passed, and V Corps did not attack. The Union cavalrymen began to run low on ammunition. Sheridan "became as restive as a racer struggling to make the start," Porter wrote. "He made every possible appeal for promptness, dismounted from his horse, paced up and down, struck the clenched fist of one hand against the palm of the other, and fretted like a caged tiger." At one point Sheridan exclaimed, "This battle must be fought and won before the sun goes down!"[6]

Sheridan finally rode out to where Warren was forming his divisions to find out why they were not attacking. To Sheridan's annoyance, Warren, the very picture of contentment, was resting under a tree making a sketch of the terrain. Sheridan's irritation increased when Warren quietly said that he, too, was impatient to begin the attack but deliberately suppressed any expression of it "as it would but tend to impair confidence in the proposed operations." Sheridan's officers remarked to one another that "there would be a deuce of a row if the Fifth Corps was not ready to move out soon." In his report to Grant, Sheridan said of Warren, "His manner gave me the impression that he wished the sun to go down before dispositions for the attack could be completed."[7]

At 4 p.m., V Corps was finally ready. Ayres's division began to march west on the White Oak Road to strike Pickett's angled left flank. To Ayres's right was General Samuel Crawford's division, with General Charles Griffin's division in reserve behind Crawford. Crawford's mission was to get into Pickett's rear and cut off, capture, or destroy the Rebels before they could return to Petersburg or flee to the west. Custer would lead the frontal attack on the Rebels' center. General Ranald Mackenzie's cavalry division, roving V Corps's right flank, scattered a Confederate cavalry brigade on White Oak Road that tried to interfere with V Corps's preparations.

When the attack began, Warren's corps was out of alignment, and a gap quickly opened between Ayres's division and the division on its right, Crawford's, which veered too far north, missing the Rebel lines altogether. Warren raced after Crawford to correct his division's trajectory. Ayres's division initially had to fight Pickett's infantrymen alone, and its skirmish line wavered under the intensive Rebel artillery and musket fire in the rough, wooded terrain, cut up by many ravines. The division, which had broken the day before on White Oak Road, was in danger of doing so again.

Sheridan ordered Griffin's reserve division to fill the widening gap between Ayres's and Crawford's divisions. Then, grasping his two-starred swallowtail pennant, Sheridan and his staff rode to the front of Ayres's line. The fiery general darted back and forth along the line, shouting encouragement to every regiment. "Come on, men," he cried, "go at 'em with a will! Move on at a clean jump, or you'll not catch one of 'em!"

Blood suddenly spurted from the neck of one of Ayres's skirmishers. "I'm killed!" the man cried, falling to the ground. Sheridan rode up and said, "You're not hurt a bit! Pick up your gun, man, and move right on the front." The man got to his feet, rushed forward a dozen paces, and fell dead.[8]

With his battle flag, Sheridan made a splendid target. A musket ball pierced the flag, another killed a color sergeant beside him, and an aide fell wounded. Rebel gunfire struck three horses ridden by Sheridan's staff officers.

"All this time," wrote Porter, "Sheridan was dashing from one point of the line to another, waving his flag, shaking his fist, encouraging, entreating, threatening, praying, swearing, the true personification of chivalry, the very incarnation of battle."

He rode past Ayres's infantrymen, swinging his clenched fist in the air and shouting, "Smash 'em! Smash 'em!" They responded by swarming

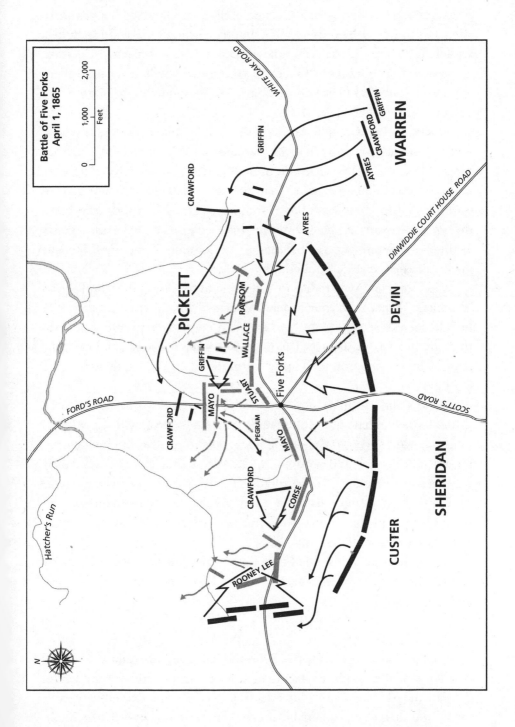

Battle of Five Forks
April 1, 1865

0   1,000   2,000
Feet

WHITE OAK ROAD

WARREN

GRIFFIN

CRAWFORD

GRIFFIN

AYRES

CRAWFORD

GRIFFIN

DINWIDDIE COURT HOUSE ROAD

CRAWFORD

AYRES

DEVIN

PICKETT

RANSOM

WALLACE

GRIFFIN

Five Forks

STUART

SCOTT'S ROAD

FORD'S ROAD

CRAWFORD

MAYO

PEGRAM

MAYO

CRAWFORD

CORSE

SHERIDAN

Hatcher's Run

ROONEY LEE

CUSTER

N

over the Rebel breastworks at the angle. Sheridan spurred his warhorse Rienzi over the earthworks, landing among a group of crouching Rebels who had just surrendered. Sheridan directed them to the rear. "Get right along now," he told them. "Oh, drop your guns; you'll never need them any more. You'll all be safe over there. Are there any more of you? We want every one of you fellows."[9]

General Joshua Chamberlain was the Maine college professor whose 20th Maine had valiantly held Little Round Top at Gettysburg against repeated Confederate attacks. Wounded in the White Oak Road fighting on March 29 and in great pain, Chamberlain nonetheless led a brigade of Griffin's division in the scrubby woods between Ayres's and Crawford's diverging divisions. As he was putting his men into action beside Ayres's at the Confederate angle, Chamberlain encountered Sheridan. He was greatly pleased to see Chamberlain.

"By God! That's what I like to see! General officers at the front!" cried Sheridan. "Where are your general officers?" Chamberlain replied that he had seen Ayres in a tight spot and had come to help him. Sheridan told him to take command "of all the infantry around here and break this dam." Chamberlain rounded up two hundred men and led them into the fighting.[10]

Custer's and Devin's troopers assaulted the earthworks and crashed through the Confederate center. Warren had caught up with Crawford's division, which overran General Thomas Munford's cavalry men guarding the extreme left and scooped up Rebels as they tried to make their way back to Petersburg. "We could do nothing but shoot and run," wrote Munford. The Virginia troopers fired a volley and "then turned and scooted through the woods like a flock of wild turkeys" all the way to Ford's Road, two miles away.[11]

As the defenders crumbled and broke, the question asked by many Confederates was: Where were Pickett and Generals Fitzhugh Lee and Thomas Rosser?

⁂

Lee's instructions to Pickett that morning had been unequivocal: "Hold Five Forks at all hazards. Protect road to Ford's Depot and prevent Union forces from striking the Southside Railroad. Regret exceedingly your forced withdrawal, and our inability to hold the advantage you had gained."

When Pickett withdrew from Dinwiddie Court House before dawn, he had considered occupying stronger positions north of Hatcher's Run, where he had sent his wagon train. But then he received Lee's order, with its mild reproach of his failure to remain at Dinwiddie and its acknowledgment, too, that the withdrawal was compelled by V Corps's appearance near his left rear.

Consequently, Pickett pulled back only as far as Five Forks and dug in. Although the White Oak Road crossroad wasn't an ideal defensive position, it blocked the Union Army's principal route to the Southside Railroad. Pickett placed W. H. F. "Rooney" Lee's cavalry on his right, Munford's cavalry on his left, and his infantry brigades between them, with General Matthew Ransom's brigade holding the angled left flank. William Pegram positioned his guns wherever there were cleared fields of fire. Behind the infantry entrenchments, near Hatcher's Run, were Fitzhugh Lee's troopers.

Because they had seen nothing more of the Union infantry that had hovered near their flank late the previous day, Pickett and his officers believed they now faced only Sheridan's Cavalry Corps, and not a mixed force of more than thirty thousand cavalry and infantry. Pickett's half-infantry, half-cavalry force, they were convinced, could repulse any attacks by Sheridan, and if Union infantry then joined Sheridan, Pickett expected General Richard Anderson's brigades to reinforce them from the Petersburg lines. But Grant's drive westward had forced Lee to stretch his right flank to the extent that no more men could be spared for Pickett. In fact, Lee had asked General James Longstreet to send men from his First Corps, north of the James River, to support the Confederate right.[12]

When noon passed without a Yankee attack, Pickett and Fitz Lee assumed there would be no major battle that day. They accepted Thomas Rosser's invitation to attend a shad bake at his camp north of Hatcher's Run, where his cavalry was in reserve. Two days earlier, Rosser, somewhat of a gourmand, had caught a mess of shad on the Nottaway River. Not wanting to pass up an opportunity to ingratiate himself with his superior officers, Rosser invited Fitz Lee and Pickett to join him for a feast.[13]

Good fortune had eluded forty-year-old George Pickett since his doomed attack on Cemetery Hill at Gettysburg on July 3, 1863, when a hurricane of musketry and artillery fire swept away more than half of his division. Afterward, he commanded the Department of Virginia and

North Carolina with mixed results. In 1864 his efforts had thwarted the Army of the James's drives toward Richmond and Petersburg, but the stress had made him ill. Now, Pickett, at the consequential hour of the critical day, chose to leave his small army to attend a party.[14]

Amazingly, Fitz Lee and Pickett left their commands without telling anyone where they were going. By 2 p.m., while Sheridan was waiting impatiently for Warren to bring up his men, they were eating the shad prepared by Rosser's commissary officer and imbibing Rosser's liquor. Rooney Lee, the senior officer remaining with Pickett's task force, was with his cavalry division on the far right of the Five Forks line and was unaware that he was nominally in command.

When Munford saw Union infantry and cavalry massing to attack, he sent couriers to tell Lee and Pickett. After a good deal of searching, Sergeant J. B. Flippin found them, more than two miles away, sitting under a fly tent "with a bottle of whiskey or brandy, I don't know which for I was not invited to partake of it." When Flippin delivered Munford's message about the impending Union attack, Pickett instructed Flippin to tell Munford to "do the best [he] could," and then resumed eating and drinking.[15]

The party broke up when Pickett dispatched a courier to carry orders to Five Points, and the courier was captured while in plain view. Then, Union infantrymen emerged from the woods and crossed the road in front of the generals. Pickett and Fitz Lee hastily mounted their horses and raced for Five Forks.

After crossing Hatcher's Run, Pickett encountered a line of Fitz Lee's cavalrymen, now commanded by Munford. They were facing east and retreating slowly before an approaching Union infantry formation one hundred yards away.

Pickett asked Munford to hold the Yankees so that he could slip past them and get to Five Forks. Overhearing Pickett's request, Captain James Breckinridge of the 3rd Virginia Cavalry launched his men in a headlong attack straight at the enemy. Clinging to his horse's neck, Pickett bolted through a gantlet of infantry fire and escaped. Breckinridge's valiant attack cost him his life.

Sheridan's attacks shattered the Confederate left and center, precipitating a panicked flight. Of Pickett's task force only General Montgomery Corse's infantry brigade and Rooney Lee's cavalry division remained intact, serving as rallying places for the retreating Rebels. At one point,

Rooney Lee's troopers suddenly attacked Custer's division as it was rolling up the Confederate line. "The shock of the collision was terrible," wrote Private Paul Means of the 5th North Carolina Cavalry. "Sabers rang on each other with a cold steel ring . . . this saber slashing lasted longer than I ever saw one."

Shot through the left arm and side while beside his guns was the brilliant artillery commander Colonel William Pegram. The bespectacled twenty-three-year-old was the younger brother of General John Pegram, killed a month earlier at Hatcher's Run, three weeks after his marriage. After being wounded, "Willie," as he was called, said to his aide, Gordon McCabe, "Oh! Gordon I'm mortally wounded, take me off the field." McCabe managed to get Pegram into an ambulance just as they were being overrun. Pegram died the next morning.[16]

❧

Warren at last caught up with Crawford and his misguided division north of the battlefield. He turned it toward the south with the intention of blocking White Oak Road and the shattered Rebel regiments' retreat westward. Reaching the road, Crawford's men found themselves facing Corse's brigade, which had erected breastworks at the edge of a cotton field. Seeing that Crawford's jumbled brigades were not responding to his exhortations to attack the Confederates, Warren snatched up V Corps's flag and ordered his men to charge with him. As Warren galloped toward the enemy line, his horse was shot out from under him. The attack continued without Warren, and Crawford's men flattened Corse's brigade, taking hundreds of prisoners.[17]

At dusk, a Confederate colonel with a broken regiment led a desperate counterattack. "Twice they halted, and poured in volleys, but came on again like the surge from the fog, depleted, but determined," wrote correspondent Alfred Townsend of the *New York Herald*. Union cavalry suddenly struck the attacking regiment's flank, and "the charging column trembled like a single thing." The regiment formed a hollow square from which the Confederates continued to fight until the colonel and most of his men were killed or wounded.[18]

Only the Confederate cavalry escaped the bluecoats swarming in from all directions. The Yankees corralled five to six thousand prisoners, seizing so many Rebel muskets that they used them to corduroy the roads.

❧

Five Forks was the Army of the Potomac's first important battlefield victory since Gettysburg and arguably the most consequential of the war. By destroying Pickett's task force, the Cavalry Corps and V Corps had made Petersburg and Richmond untenable for Lee's besieged army. Lee could not stop Grant's men from capturing the Southside Railroad and smashing his right flank—or, for very long, from capturing the Confederate capital. The Confederacy's downfall was imminent.

"This has been the most momentous day of the war so far, I think," wrote Colonel Charles Wainwright, who commanded V Corps's artillery brigade, "a glorious day, a day of real victory."[19]

Couriers rode hard to City Point with a clutch of captured Rebel battle flags to present to Lincoln. The president was delighted. "Here is something material—something I can see, feel, and understand. This means victory. This *is* victory."[20]

❧

Warren's strenuous efforts to reorient Crawford's division and trap Pickett's army went unappreciated by Sheridan, fuming over Warren's slowness and his unavailability during Ayres's attack on Pickett's left flank. When Sheridan saw Crawford's division veering off course and a gap open between Ayres and Crawford, he had sent one courier after another to overtake Warren and have him reel in Crawford. "Warren could not be found," Sheridan later wrote. Then, when Ayres's men began to waver during their attack on the Confederate left flank, it was Sheridan, in Warren's absence, who took charge, inspired Ayres's men, and drove them through the Rebel fortifications.[21]

Sheridan was in no mood to savor the victory. When an officer galloped up to him to announce that his men had captured three guns, Sheridan barked, "I don't care a damn for their guns, or you either, sir! What are you here for? Go back to your business, where you belong! What I want is that Southside Road."

Then Sheridan stood in his stirrups, waving his hat overhead at the large group of men gathered around him. With his "face as black as his horse," he roared, "I want you men to understand we have a record to make, before that sun goes down, that will make hell tremble! I want you there [the Southside Railroad]!" But daylight ebbed before anything more could be done.[22]

As the sound of fighting faded, Horace Porter remarked to Sheridan that he had exposed himself more to enemy gunfire than seemed proper for an army commander. Porter was struck by Sheridan's response: "I have never in my life taken a command into battle, and had the slightest desire to come out alive unless I won." Porter thought this "the true key to his uniform success on the field."[23]

∂◊

As his men savored their victory, Sheridan was prepared to settle his grievances with Warren. The unfortunate recipient of Sheridan's pent-up anger was Warren's inspector general, Colonel H. C. Bankhead. Warren had sent Bankhead to tell Sheridan that he was with Crawford's division, which now stood between Pickett's former positions and Petersburg.

The instant Bankhead delivered his report, Sheridan exploded. "By God, sir, tell General Warren he wasn't in that fight!" Sheridan shouted. Stunned, Bankhead asked Sheridan to write down what he had just said. "Take it down, sir!" he ordered Bankhead. "Tell him by God he was not at the front."

This broadside was followed by an even more shocking message delivered to Warren by Sheridan's aide, Lieutenant Colonel George Forsyth. "Major-General Warren, commanding the Fifth Army Corps, is relieved from duty, and will report at once for orders to Lieutenant-General Grant, commanding Armies of the United States."

Sheridan's action was unprecedented; no Union corps commander had ever been relieved of command on the battlefield. Sheridan named General Charles Griffin, Warren's most aggressive division commander, to succeed him.

When he read the order stripping him of his corps command, Warren went to Sheridan and asked him to reconsider. "Reconsider?" Sheridan shot back. "Hell, I don't reconsider my determinations."[24]

That night some of V Corps's officers were relaxing with their new commander, Griffin. The tired officers, speaking in murmurs, were subdued after the dismissal of Warren, who "had been part of the best history of the Fifth Corps from the beginning," wrote Joshua Chamberlain.

From the shadows emerged a stocky figure. It was Phil Sheridan, who had come to seek their forgiveness for his harsh words to some of them during the battle. He did not intend to offend them, he said, only to "carry this place." Sheridan told them, "I know it is hard for the men, too; but we must push. There is more for us to do together. I appreciate and thank you all."

His amazingly contrite words buoyed the officers. "All the repressed feeling of our hearts sprang out towards him," wrote Chamberlain. "We had had a taste of his style of fighting, and we liked it. Sheridan does not entrench. He pushes on, carrying his flank and rear with him, —rushing, flashing, smashing."*[25]

Grant later wrote that he regretted not having reassigned Warren to other duties before Five Forks. Warren's problem, wrote Grant, was that he overanalyzed every situation, which kept him from acting quickly. "He could see every danger at a glance before he encountered it," said Grant.[26]

❧

Horace Porter and an orderly rode to Grant's headquarters at Gravelly Run to announce the great victory. As they passed a group of soldiers on the Boydton Plank Road, the orderly shouted the news, to which a disbeliever among them retorted, "No, you don't—April fool!"—it was the first of April, after all. Porter reached Grant and his staff ahead of the couriers from the battlefield, and he had the honor of informing them of Sheridan's triumph. "For some minutes, there was a bewildering state of excitement, and officers fell to grasping hands, shouting, and hugging each other like school-boys." They recognized that "it meant the beginning of the end, the reaching of the last ditch."

---

*Warren repeatedly requested a court of inquiry to review his dismissal, but Grant, first as general-in-chief and then as president, denied every request over the next twelve years. Warren remained in the Army Corps of Engineers during this time. Finally, in 1879, two years after Grant left the White House, a military court heard the case at Governor's Island, New York. In November 1882, the court exonerated Warren of the most serious charges, his alleged neglect of duty at Five Forks, but found fault with his actions on March 31 during the White Oak Road battle and with his dilatoriness in marching to Dinwiddie Court House that night. By then, the partial exoneration didn't matter to Warren, who had died three months earlier. Even so, Sheridan, commander of Army forces throughout much of the West, thought the findings were "not in accordance with the evidence. They are more in the nature of apologies" (Sheridan Papers, reel 94, 14).

Porter, caught up in the celebratory spirit, rushed up to Grant and clapped him on the back, "to his no little astonishment and to the evident amusement of those about him."

As Porter gave a recitation of the battle, Grant, impassive as always, asked the one question that he always did: How many prisoners? Over five thousand, replied Porter, which evoked "a responsive expression." Grant then went into his tent and wrote out several dispatches. When he emerged, he told his officers, "as coolly as if remarking upon the state of the water," that he was ordering an immediate, all-out attack on the Petersburg lines.[27]

At his camp near Five Forks, Sheridan lay on the ground before a fire, his head resting on a saddle, as he helped a reporter from the *New York World* write an account of the battle. Later that night Sheridan made his plans for the next day. Lieutenant Colonel Frederick Newhall rode to brief Grant, arriving around 3 a.m. on April 2 after negotiating "shockingly bad" roads filled with muddy water. Grant approved of Sheridan's plan to attack Lee's right. He told Newhall that the general attack he had ordered would begin at 4 a.m.[28]

That night too, General John Rawlins, Grant's chief of staff, wrote to his wife, "The hero of the Shenandoah [Sheridan] stands affront of all on the Appomattox. His personal gallantry and great genius have secured us a great success to-day."[29]

Just before learning about the disaster at Five Forks, Lee had warned Jefferson Davis that Sheridan's presence at Dinwiddie Court House "obliged us to prepare for the necessity of evacuating our position on the James River at once." The new Union position, said Lee, meant that his army no longer could receive forage over the Boydton Plank Road, and that Sheridan and his troopers were a mere seven miles from the Southside Railroad. Lee urged Davis to come to Petersburg to discuss the situation.[30]

When reports of the Five Forks debacle began trickling in, Lee knew that his defenders, now totaling just forty thousand, were stretched beyond their capabilities. Just over eleven thousand men defended the eleven-mile line on Lee's right—a soldier every two yards. Compelled to move men from less-imperiled sectors to reinforce threatened ones, Lee summoned

General Charles Field's forty-six-hundred-man First Corps division from north of the James River along with the corps's commander, Longstreet, Lee's most trusted adviser. "It is important beyond measure that no time be lost," Field's orders said. His brigades immediately withdrew from the lines, leaving only pickets to guard them until troops from General Richard Ewell's Richmond command took their place. "Hurry out the local troops as rapidly as you can," Ewell was urged. Trains shuttled Field's men over the river and down to Petersburg, but a small division was a paltry counterweight to the onslaught that Grant planned to unleash.[31]

Leading the all-out attack at Petersburg that Sunday morning would be Horatio Wright's VI Corps and John Parke's IX Corps. Supported by John Gibbon's XXIV Corps of the Army of the James on his left, Wright's men would stab northwestward into the sector occupied by A. P. Hill's Third Corps. Parke would assault the Confederate line east of Petersburg defended by John Gordon's Second Corps.

Andrew Humphreys's II Corps was to exploit opportunities that opened on the Rebel right flank and to prevent the Confederates from striking Sheridan's cavalry and infantry at Five Forks. In all, four Union army corps, with more than eighty thousand troops, would storm the entrenchments the Rebels had tenaciously defended for more than nine months. General Edward Ord's other Army of the James infantry corps was the all-black XXV Corps that General Godfrey Weitzel had commanded since its formation in December. It faced Richmond's eastern defenses and was poised to break into the Confederate capital city.

While the attacks were under way, Sheridan with his Cavalry Corps and V Corps were to march north to sever the Southside Railroad and strike the retreating Rebels. The plan jibed perfectly with Grant's philosophy of hitting the enemy at several points simultaneously. Grant intended to transform every sector around Petersburg into a crisis zone. The Rebel line would surely give way somewhere, he believed.

Grant had initially wanted the four army corps to attack right away because he feared Lee might lash out at Sheridan in a desperate attempt to recapture Five Forks, "risking everything upon the cast of a single die." But nightfall made an immediate attack impracticable: troops couldn't be sent groping in the darkness; better to wait until daybreak. In the meantime, Grant ordered a bombardment of all the Confederate lines north and south of the James River.[32]

No other Union Army bombardment during the war equaled this one. For three hours, 150 guns crashed and heaved, emitting "a constant stream of living fire" on the Confederate lines around Petersburg and Richmond. An awed soldier of the 126th Ohio wrote that the bombardment set "the very earth beneath quaking and trembling at each discharge of those war monsters which sent shot and shell into the enemy's camp." The gunners fired so rapidly that there was "a constant flash as of lightning in intense darkness." It was "indescribably wild and grand," wrote an Ohio officer. Confederate batteries responded with fury.[33]

Recognizing that the metal storm was only the prelude to the climactic battle they had anticipated for weeks, the soldiers wrote letters home and otherwise prepared for what might well be their last hours of life. "You need not send clothes, nor flour, nor anything else to me, my dearest," Colonel Samuel Walkup of the 48th North Carolina wrote to his wife. "We will either be killed or captured or the road will be destroyed before this letter reaches you. . . . Be prepared for bad news from Lee's army. There is no reasonable prospect of good news."

In the Union ranks on this misty, moonless night some soldiers wrote letters home; others wrote messages that they left with noncombatants in case they did not return. As the hour of attack neared, they discarded nonessential clothing as well as their playing cards—to disassociate themselves from a petty vice that could send them to the fiery regions if they were killed.

In what had become standard procedure for many Union infantry units, the soldiers wrote their names on slips of paper and pinned them to their uniforms so that their bodies could be identified. "All knew that bloody work was before us," wrote General Lewis Grant, commander of VI Corps's Vermont Brigade. Another VI Corps officer, Colonel Hazard Stevens, wrote that he overheard many of his comrades say, "Well, good-bye, boys, this means death."[34]

VI Corps had fought under George McClellan, Ambrose Burnside, Joe Hooker, and George Meade. Five days into Grant's 1864 Overland Campaign, VI Corps's beloved commander, John Sedgwick, the bachelor general known by his men as "Uncle John," was killed by a Rebel sharpshooter at Spotsylvania Court House.

John Sedgwick's successor, competent but unspectacular Horatio Wright, would lead VI Corps into action against the Rebel center. This sector included Forts Fisher and Welch and was defended by A. P. Hill's Third Corps. Wright's men would advance in an inverted "V" formation behind General George Getty's division, which had slugged it out toe-to-toe with the Third Corps for two days the previous May at a crossroads in the densely wooded Wilderness. Now Getty's division, with Colonel Thomas Hyde's brigade at the tip of the spear, once more faced two of Hill's divisions, commanded by Cadmus Wilcox and Henry Heth—mere shades of the powerful formations that had fought Getty's men to a standstill in the Wilderness eleven months earlier.

Yankee pickets had spotted a gap in the enemy's abatis just outside the trenches, used by Rebel woodcutters to come and go from their lines. There was always a large fire burning behind the Rebel forts, the pickets said, and it lined up with the opening; it might guide the attackers through the obstacles.

As Hyde's brigade and Lewis Grant's Vermont Brigade moved quietly to their attack positions, a Union soldier accidentally fired his weapon, and the Confederates replied with a fusillade of picket fire whose accuracy "could be told by the thuds and stifled outcries." One of the casualties was Lewis Grant.

At 4:40 a.m. on April 2, a signal gun at Fort Fisher fired, and the attackers lunged forward, cheering, as Confederate gunfire scorched their ranks. The Yankees swept over the Rebel picket pits and through the abatis "like a hurricane," reaching the ditch in front of the enemy fortifications. "They were soon over the works like so many cats, giving and receiving bayonet thrusts and the [Rebel] cannon were hardly silent before they were fired the other way," wrote Colonel Hyde.

One of Hyde's regiments, the 61st Pennsylvania, broke apart during the attack. Three hundred bounty men and substitutes—"white slaves," one soldier contemptuously described them, "from the almshouses, from the cots of venereal hospitals, . . . from prison cells"—took to their heels along with some recent draftees, "and we never heard of them afterwards." But the 61st's two hundred "old men" distinguished themselves by capturing two enemy flags.

In the path of the VI Corps juggernaut was General James Lane's North Carolina brigade, part of Wilcox's division. Major James Weston

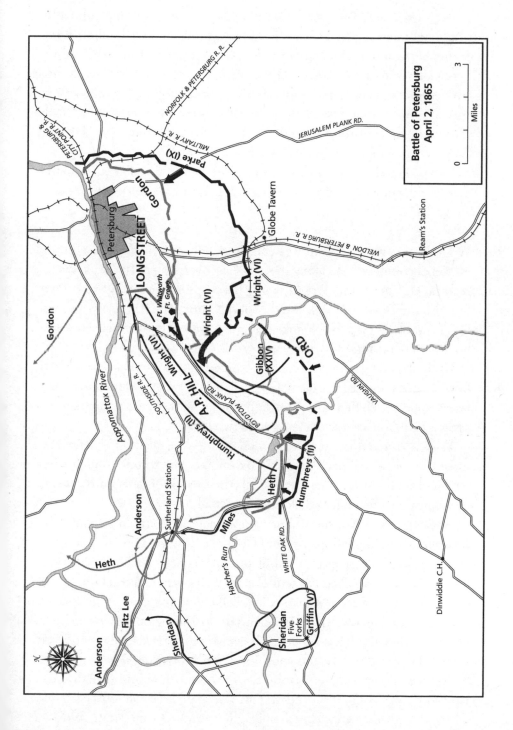

Battle of Petersburg
April 2, 1865

0   3
Miles

NORFOLK & PETERSBURG R. R.

JERUSALEM PLANK RD.

PETERSBURG & CITY POINT R. R.

Parke (IX)

MILITARY R. R.

Gordon

Globe Tavern

Petersburg

LONGSTREET

WELDON & PETERSBURG R. R.

Ream's Station

Gordon

Ft. Whitworth
Ft. Gregg

Wright (VI)

Wright (VI)

Appomattox River

Wright (VI)

Gibbon (XXIV)

ORD

A. P. HILL

BOYDTON PLANK RD.

VAUGHAN RD.

SOUTHSIDE R. R.

Humphreys (II)

Heth

Humphreys (II)

Anderson

Sutherland Station

Heth

Miles

WHITE OAK RD.

Hatcher's Run

Fitz Lee

Dinwiddie C.H.

Anderson

Sheridan

Sheridan
Five
Forks

Griffin (V)

of the 33rd North Carolina wrote that the Yankees were unstoppable. "We fought desperately, but our thin line was pushed back by sheer force of numbers until it was broken in pieces." General William McCombs's Tennessee brigade was also overpowered. Sergeant Lester Hack of the 5th Vermont opened fire on a squad of Tennesseans guarding their colors and, after wounding several of them, demanded their surrender. Hack captured several prisoners and the colors of the 23rd Tennessee. He was later awarded the Congressional Medal of Honor.[35]

In less than thirty minutes VI Corps had broken the Confederate line that for nine months had stood like a wall between it and Petersburg.

Wright's men stormed southwest, all the way to Hatcher's Run, fending off Rebel counterattacks along the way. Discovering that II Corps was already at Hatcher's Run, Wright swung his corps northeast toward Petersburg on the Boydton Plank Road, where Gibbon's XXIV Corps joined it. The Yankees could see smoke rising from the city; the tobacco warehouses were burning.[36]

In their path were two exposed Confederate redoubts constructed from timbers and earth—Forts Gregg and Whitworth, named after the farms upon which they stood. Ord, the Army of the James's commander, ordered Gibbon's corps to capture the two forts.

Wilcox ordered the forts defended to the last man. The defenders must be sacrificed if necessary, Wilcox said, so that troops coming from Richmond could reinforce a secondary line south of Petersburg; it was imperative that that line be held until nightfall.

Some of Lane's North Carolina troops occupied Fort Gregg, joined by Georgians and Mississippians from Generals Edward Thomas's and Nathaniel Harris's brigades until about 350 Rebels, armed with muskets and a pair of field guns, filled the redoubt. Its walls were eight feet thick, and a ditch, fourteen feet wide and six feet deep, guarded its approaches.[37]

Before leaving Fort Gregg's defenders to their fate, Wilcox made a speech. "Men, the salvation of Lee's army is in your keeping; you must realize the responsibility, and your duty; don't surrender this fort."

A short time later General Robert Foster's four-thousand-man division from Gibbon's corps advanced on Fort Gregg in three columns, each one a brigade. "It was a grand but awful sight," wrote a Confederate soldier.

Firing massed volleys from loopholes and aided by artillery and musket fire from nearby Fort Whitworth, where Nathaniel Harris commanded two hundred defenders, the Rebels, "rebel-yelling as was never heard before," repulsed Foster's first attack. The second assault, in which Gibbon threw in a two-thousand-man brigade from the division facing Whitworth, came in a flood. The Yankees plunged into the chest-deep waters of the moat surrounding the fort and then scaled the fort's muddy walls, planting their battle flags. From the parapet the Rebels rapid-fired muskets, loaded and passed to them by bloody-handed wounded men.

From Fort Whitworth, Harris cheered on Fort Gregg's defenders by waving the flag of the 48th Mississippi over his head and shouting, "Give 'em hell, boys!"

There was no possibility that the Rebels could stop the thousands of Yankees converging on Fort Gregg, but they tried. When the bluecoats reached the parapet and swept into the rear of the fort, the Confederates, nearly out of ammunition, fought them with artillery shells used as grenades, fireplace bricks, bayonets, and fists. The Rebels broke their muskets and used the barrels as clubs. The fighting "was the most desperate I ever witnessed," wrote Foster. "Savage men!" wrote Captain A. K. Jones of the 12th Mississippi. "The curses and groaning of frenzied men could be heard over and above the din of our musketry." The last operable Confederate gun, aimed at the troops charging across the ditch, was loaded and a gunner gripped a taut lanyard, ready to fire. "Don't fire that gun! Drop the lanyard or we'll shoot!" the Yankees shouted, aiming their muskets at him. The Rebel gunner retorted, "Shoot and be damned!" and pulled the lanyard. Canister balls cut a bloody swath through the attackers as the Yankees riddled the gunner with bullets.[38]

Inside the fort, Union troops splashed through pools of blood. During the hour-long attack 714 men in Foster's division were killed or wounded. "For one hundred yards in front of the work the ground was completely covered with one trembling mass of human beings," wrote a Mississippi soldier. Of the Confederates, 56 were killed, and 200 were wounded and captured; 30 uninjured Rebels also became prisoners.[39]

Foster's men now turned to Fort Whitworth, but the fighting at Fort Gregg had achieved Wilcox's object: Charles Field's First Corps division was already filing into Petersburg's secondary defensive line. Wilcox ordered Harris to withdraw from Fort Whitworth.[40]

Two Baltimore brothers, fighting on opposing sides, were wounded at about the same time during the day's fighting and ended up in the same VI Corps field hospital. Until their chance meeting there, Major Clifton Prentiss, commander of the 6th Maryland, and his younger brother, Confederate Private William Prentiss, had not seen one another since the war began. The brothers' wounds were ultimately fatal. William, whose left leg was amputated, died in June, and Clifton, shot in the chest, survived William by just two months.[41]

A. P. Hill, the Third Corps's frail-looking, thirty-nine-year-old commander, only two days earlier had returned to duty, but he was far from well. Illness had been his constant companion since, as a rising West Point junior twenty years earlier, he had contracted gonorrhea in New York City. With no known effective treatment, the venereal disease had progressed to increasingly painful symptoms, which included chronic prostatitis and repeated urinary and kidney infections that interfered with his sleeping and urination. Invalided for much of the winter, Hill had briefly returned to his command, only to go back on sick leave March 20, staying at the home of an uncle outside Richmond. On March 31 he was informed that Grant was moving against Lee's elongated right flank—Third Corps's position. Hill left his sick bed to rejoin his corps.[42]

Throughout the South in 1862, Hill and his "Light Division" of Stonewall Jackson's army were acclaimed for reinforcing Lee in the nick of time at Antietam. It was the acme of Hill's career. After Jackson's death at Chancellorsville, Lee reorganized his army and appointed Hill to corps command, but he never distinguished himself as a corps commander as he had while leading the Light Division.[43]

On April 1, Hill spent fifteen hours in the saddle inspecting his lines; subordinates remarked that he looked especially thin and sickly. Hill's sergeant of couriers, George Tucker, wrote that Hill said little that day and "seemed lost in contemplation." That night, he returned to the cottage in Petersburg where he was staying with his wife and two small children. Across the road was his corps headquarters. The intensive artillery fire that night made sleep elusive. Hill rose at 3 a.m. and went to his headquarters tent to read the latest reports. Then he mounted "Champ" and rode out to see Lee at the Turnbull house on Edge Hill, a mile and a half away.[44]

At dawn, Union troops suddenly appeared within sight of the Turn-bull house. The Third Corps lines to the south had been breached. Lee turned to one of his officers and said, "Well, Colonel, it has happened as I told them it would at Richmond. The line has been stretched until it is broken."[45]

Hill, Tucker, and Colonel Charles Venable of Lee's staff immediately mounted their horses and rode toward the lines to rally Hill's men. Blue-coats were all around. Venable turned back, but Hill and Tucker con-tinued riding to the right—westward—looking for the Third Corps. Hill told Tucker that if anything happened to him, he must notify Lee. Pre-monitory or not, his words were tinged with the same fatalism as those he had uttered recently in Richmond: that he did not wish to outlive the capital's downfall.[46]

Hill and Tucker approached two Yankees who, when they saw Hill and Tucker, attempted to conceal themselves behind a clump of trees. The Union soldiers leveled their guns. "We must take them," Hill said, draw-ing his Colt navy pistol. Tucker told Hill to stay where he was and rode ahead, demanding their surrender. Confederate troops were right behind them, Tucker announced to the Yankees, hoping to bluff them into giving up. But Corporal John W. Mauk of the 138th Pennsylvania of VI Corps told his companion, "I can't see it. Let's shoot them." Mauk then shot Hill. The bullet took off the thumb of his pistol hand and entered his heart. Hill fell to the ground, dead. The second Yankee's gunshot missed Tucker, who, seeing Hill sprawled on the ground, seized Champ's bridle. Leaping on Hill's horse, which was fresher than Tucker's, he rode back to tell Lee what had happened.

Lee was stricken by the news; tears filled his eyes. "He is at rest now, and we who are left are the ones to suffer," he said softly. While a detail retrieved Hill's body—it was found undisturbed where he had fallen—and brought it to Petersburg, Lee sent Colonel William Palmer, Hill's adjutant general, to tell Mrs. Hill. "Colonel, break the news to her as gently as possible," Lee said. When Palmer reached the Hills' cottage, he heard Mrs. Hill singing, her habit when doing housework. When she saw Palmer standing in the doorway, the singing stopped. Mrs. Hill said, "The general is dead; you would not be here unless he was dead."[47]

Shortly after Hill's death, men from VI Corps neared Turnbull house on Edge Hill. A Confederate battery raked the Yankees with enfilading fire, changing position after each volley. "A fine-looking old officer, on a gray horse ... seemed to be directing [the defenders'] movements," wrote Colonel Thomas Hyde, the Union brigade commander. When the Rebel battery moved to Edge Hill, the guns' "audible presence became more annoying than ever." Hyde's brigade tried and failed three times to seize the hill. Then he sent fifty men from the 1st Maine around the hill with orders to shoot the battery's horses.

Another assault through a swamp carried the Yankees to the hilltop, where the dead and wounded horses and abandoned guns betokened the Maine men's success. Hyde asked a dying artillery officer who the man on the gray horse was. He gasped out, "General Robert E. Lee, sir, and he was the last man to leave the guns." As Lee and his adjutant, Walter Taylor, evacuated their headquarters of the past five months, Lee remarked, "This is a bad business."[48]

The spectacle of massive Union troop formations on the march transfixed even the Confederates who were supposed to stop them. Captain John Gorman described one approaching large unit "marching in line of battle, three columns deep, apparently by divisions, their guns glistening and sparkling in the sun, and their blue uniforms seemingly black in the distance." The Yankees attacked through Confederate artillery fire and carried a line of breastworks with "a loud huzza, that drowned the sound of battle on other parts of the line."[49]

❧

The Confederate line did not collapse everywhere. John Gordon's Second Corps held a six-mile sector along Petersburg's southeastern side with fifty-five hundred men when John Parke's IX Corps—at least fourteen thousand men with dozens of light artillery pieces—attacked shortly after 4 a.m. The centerpiece of Gordon's defenses was Fort Mahone, the Petersburg line's most formidable Rebel stronghold, protected by ditches full of water, abatis, chevaux-de-frise, and other obstacles. Lee had sent a reserve artillery unit under General William Pendleton to reinforce Gordon.

Charging up both sides of the Jerusalem Plank Road, through a blazing gantlet of artillery fire, the IX Corps infantrymen plunged into the moats along the Rebel entrenchments; some of them drowned. The Yankees burst into the fort and tenaciously clung to a foothold inside.

Confederate General Bryan Grimes's division made three counterattacks, retrieving some of the ground taken by Parke's men. The battle raged all day long, the soldiers fighting from traverse to traverse. "I saw the men of my regiment load their guns behind the traverses, climb to the top, fire down into the ranks of the enemy, roll off and reload and repeat the same throughout the day," wrote Sergeant Cyrus Watson of the 45th North Carolina, part of Grimes's division. Late in the day Watson encountered a soldier from his company "whose cheeks from the corner of his mouth to his ears were almost black as lampblack" from the frequent tearing of cartridges. When Watson asked the soldier how many rounds he had fired, he estimated more than two hundred.

Unlike VI Corps, which cracked the Confederate lines southwest of Petersburg, IX Corps was unable to break through Gordon's gritty defenders. By dusk, the Union troops had captured a few hundred yards of trenches and only part of Fort Mahone—at a cost of seventeen hundred casualties. "I was never so glad to see the sun go down," confessed a Pennsylvania soldier. Gordon stopped counterattacking when he was told that Petersburg was going to be evacuated that night.[50]

Because his Second Corps had fought a force three times its size to a standstill, Gordon was justifiably proud, but there was another reason, too: his wife Fanny, who had made the white bandoleers for Gordon's shock troops before the Fort Stedman attack, had given birth in Petersburg to the couple's third son.

Yet another life-affirming event occurred amid the disasters that befell Lee's army on this day, one upon the other. Walter Taylor, Lee's twenty-six-year-old adjutant general, got married on this of all days. Lee had given Taylor permission to leave the army for several hours to travel to Richmond to marry his fiancé, Bettie Saunders. That night, the Reverend Charles Minnigerode, the rector of St. Paul's Episcopal Church, would perform the wedding service in a private home.[51]

Grant rode to a place where he could better monitor the fighting, now just three miles from the center of Petersburg. Near a farmhouse, he sat on the ground to receive reports. The cloud of Union staff officers and orderlies around Grant attracted the attention of enemy gunners, who began shelling the hilltop. "The place seemed hot for a while, even to men who were used to battle," wrote Lieutenant Colonel Adam Badeau, Grant's military secretary and aide. Several officers arrived just as the shelling began, and Grant remained to read their reports and write orders. Aides urged him to move to a less hazardous spot, "but he sat unmoved, with his back to a tree, until the reports directed to this spot had all arrived," wrote Badeau. Lieutenant Colonel Horace Porter, another Grant aide, said, "He kept on writing and talking without the least interruption from the shots falling around him." When he at last finished writing his orders, Grant remarked, "The enemy seems to have the range of this place. Suppose we ride away." With relief, Grant's aides accompanied him to a less exposed place.[52]

That afternoon Grant telegraphed War Secretary Edwin Stanton: "Everything has been carried from the left of the Ninth Corps," he wrote. "We are now closing around the works of the line immediately enveloping Petersburg. All looks remarkably well." When Lincoln, at City Point, read Grant's words, he jubilantly wrote to Mrs. Lincoln, "General Grant telegraphs that he has Petersburg completely enveloped from river below to river above and has captured, since he started last Wednesday [March 29], about 12,000 prisoners and 50 guns."

During this day's assault on Petersburg, Grant's army had suffered about four thousand casualties and captured five thousand Rebels, whose numbers of killed and wounded were not known. To Grant, Lincoln wrote, "Allow me to tender to you and all with you the nation's grateful thanks for this additional and magnificent success. At your kind suggestion I think I will meet you to-morrow."[53]

⁂

When Humphreys's II Corps turned north toward Petersburg, General Nelson Miles's First Division split away from it and continued to push to the west toward the Southside Railroad. Phil Sheridan, leading the Cavalry Corps and V Corps, had also made the railroad his objective. Miles struck the Southside a few miles closer to Petersburg than did Sheridan's advance units.

At Sutherland Station, Confederate General Henry Heth took charge of four Third Corps brigades belonging to his and Cadmus Wilcox's divisions—they had been cut off from the main Rebel Army by VI Corps—and with them attempted to defend the railroad. Heth was the senior division commander of the Third Corps and first in line to succeed Hill, but his corps command would be brief; Lee would consolidate the Third and First Corps under Longstreet.

Heth had just placed the four brigades in a line protecting the railroad when Miles's division appeared. "All the length of the crest of the ridge before us began, in a few minutes, to glitter with arms, and then to grow blue with the long lines of the enemy swarming to the attack," wrote Lieutenant J. F. J. Caldwell of the 1st South Carolina. The Confederates repulsed Miles's first two attacks. During a pause in the action, while Miles's men prepared for a third attack, a Yankee lying on the field with a broken thigh begged the Confederates to shoot him; they refused. Before their eyes, the wounded man cut his own throat with a pocketknife.

Weight of numbers—Miles's eight thousand men, twice Heth's force— told in the third assault. Aimed at the Rebels' left flank, held by General Samuel McGowan's South Carolina brigade, the Union onslaught struck the Rebel front and flank simultaneously. "The entire line was enveloped in one living cloud of blue coats, whose muskets spurted fire and smoke and death," wrote Captain William Dunlap. The Confederate line broke, and Miles's men captured hundreds of prisoners. Grant's army at long last was in possession of the Southside Railroad.

General Wesley Merritt's Cavalry Corps division reached the Southside Railroad at Ford Station, a few miles southwest of Sutherland Station, and began riding toward Petersburg, destroying the tracks along the way.[54]

⊙⟨⊙

Hungry and exhausted, the Union troops pushing toward Petersburg— II, VI, IX, and XXIV Corps—stopped to consolidate the day's unprecedented gains. Grant rode over to congratulate VI Corps for breaking Lee's lines. When they saw Grant, the troops cheered loudly. He doffed his hat and bowed his thanks to them. The general-in-chief shook hands with General Wright and his division commanders and then joined Meade to plan the next phase of their attack.[55]

Many of Grant's officers urged him to immediately assault Petersburg's inner lines and to capture the city before nightfall. But Grant, who believed that the Rebels intended to abandon the city that night, did not want to incur unnecessary losses. Instead, he looked ahead to interdicting the Confederates' likely line of retreat, anticipating a final, decisive battle with Lee's army somewhere west of Petersburg.[56]

That night, Grant wrote to his wife, Julia, "Altogether this has been one of the great victories of the war. Greatest because it is over what the rebels have always regarded as their most invincible Army and the one used for the defense of their capital."

Lieutenant Colonel Theodore Lyman, Meade's aide, in his brief letter that night to his wife, conveyed the jubilant spirit gripping Union headquarters:

> My dear Mimi:
> THE
> REBELLION
> HAS
> GONE UP![57]

His right flank broken, A. P. Hill dead, driven from his headquarters, Lee recognized that his army could not remain where it was. "I see no prospect of doing more than holding our position here till night. I am not certain that I can do that," he telegraphed War Secretary John Breckinridge in Richmond. After nightfall Lee intended to withdraw his army from both Petersburg and Richmond. "I advise that all preparation be made for leaving Richmond to-night. I will advise you later, according to circumstances." If possible, he would concentrate Confederate forces from Richmond and Petersburg near the Richmond & Danville Railroad, he told Breckinridge.

Lee selected Amelia Court House as the place where columns from Petersburg and Richmond would rendezvous. Amelia was a logical choice; from there, the united army could then march down the Danville railroad into North Carolina to join Joseph Johnston. Moreover, Amelia was nearly equidistant from Richmond and Petersburg: thirty-nine miles southwest of Richmond and thirty-six miles northwest of Petersburg. Amelia was a convenient rendezvous, a dot on the map—one of those placid, isolated places into which this war so often veered, inflicting its horrors on unsuspecting townspeople and farmers.[58]

The shocking news of the Confederate Army's disaster at Petersburg spoiled a warm, hazy Sunday morning in Richmond, where daffodils were in bloom and the stately hardwood trees were beginning to flood the city with their bright green aura. As usual, the churches were crowded, largely with women, many wearing black mourning clothes, but there were also a few men in uniform, pale from wounds or recent illnesses, some of them on crutches.

Jefferson Davis was in his usual spot, Pew No. 63 at St. Paul's Episcopal Church. It being the first Sunday of the month, it was communion Sunday. The rector, Reverend Minnigerode, who that night would preside at the wedding of Walter Taylor and his bride, was in the pulpit. The soothing routine was broken when the church sexton, William Irving, approached Davis's pew with a message that a courier from the War Department had handed him: "General Lee telegraphs that he can hold his position no longer. Come to the office immediately. Breckinridge." Pale and grim, Davis rose and walked "rather unsteadily out of the church," fathering a thousand whispered questions. Then the sexton returned to fetch Josiah Gorgas, the Confederacy's chief of ordnance, sitting behind Davis's pew; weeks earlier, Gorgas had had the foresight to send Richmond's gun-making equipment and machine operators to Danville and North Carolina. Overcome by curiosity, the congregants rose in groups and went outside to find out what was happening. There they saw piles of documents being burned outside the nearby government offices.[59]

The Reverend Moses Hoge paused while conducting services at the Second Presbyterian Church when a messenger walked up the aisle and handed him a note. He read it, briefly bowed his head, and then said to the assembled worshippers, "Brethren, trying times are before us. General Lee has been defeated; but remember that God is with us in the storm as well as in the calm. We may never meet again. Go quietly to your homes, and whatever may be in store for us, let us not forget that we are Christian men and women."[60]

At the War Department, Davis read Lee's telegram to Breckinridge. The president sent a testy response that suggested he had been unaware that he might have to leave Richmond quickly: "To move to-night will involve the loss of many valuables, both for the want of time to pack and of transportation. Arrangements are progressing, and unless you otherwise advise, the start will be made."

Lee had been warning Davis since February 21 to prepare for this emergency, and this day had been one of the worst of Lee's life, so it was understandable when he irritably tore up Davis's telegram. "I am sure I gave him sufficient notice," he tersely said. His usual patience had returned by the time he replied that it was "absolutely necessary" for the army to abandon Petersburg and Richmond that night. Lee said he would send an officer to Davis to explain how he planned to move his troops to Amelia Court House and to furnish the president with a guide and any assistance that he might need.[61]

Captain Charles Blackford, the army's assistant adjutant general, was inside St. Paul's when Davis left. Blackford returned to his own office, where he learned that Lee's line had been broken. He began packing documents, and he carted them to the Danville train station. Then Blackford put his clothes in a valise, cooked some rations, mounted his horse, and headed for the James River canal towpath.

"The streets were full of scared people, ladies and gentlemen, all in great distress, but all powerless to accomplish anything," Blackford wrote. Indeed, many of them were frantically trying to find transportation out of the city, while porters bustled about with huge loads, and wagons, piled high with luggage, clattered through the streets.

The banks all opened, despite it being Sunday, and depositors withdrew their savings while directors took the bullion. Confederate officials packed barrels full of government gold, trundled them into wagons, and drove to the Richmond & Danville Railroad depot, the destination of many of the civilians attempting to leave the city.

Before he left Richmond, Blackford told his slave Gabe that he was free and recommended that he find employment with the Yankees when they arrived. Then he rode west on the canal towpath, all the way to Charlottesville, where he joined his wife.[62]

❧

The Petersburg Common Council met in emergency session that morning. The soft spring breeze carried the sounds of cannon fire from south and east of the city, mingled with the tearing sound made by massed musketry. The streets were choked with smoke from the burning tobacco warehouses. People helped themselves to food from the commissary warehouses, thrown open to one and all. Many people already were streaming out of the Cockade City.

The council members wanted Lee to inform them when he made the decision to evacuate the city. After Lee notified them, a committee of city officials would then surrender Petersburg and request the Union Army's protection of its citizens and their property. Mayor William Townes and two councilmen rode out to Cottage Farm, where Lee had established his new headquarters. At 10 p.m., he told them, he would send a courier into town to inform them of his plans. Promptly at ten, a staff officer arrived; the army would be gone by midnight, he said.[63]

※

"It is absolutely necessary that we should abandon our position to-night, or run the risk of being cut off in the morning," Lee had written Breckinridge late in the day. "I have given all the orders to officers on both sides of the river. . . . It will be a difficult operation, but I hope not impracticable."

Indeed, it was an incredibly complex operation, whose details Lee and his staff completed by mid-afternoon. The plan was carried out during the night with calm efficiency, a reflection of Lee's unruffled demeanor throughout the long day of shocks and catastrophes. "There was no apparent excitement and no sign of apprehension as he issued his orders for the retreat of his sadly reduced army and the relinquishment of the position so long and successfully held against the greatly superior force opposed to him," wrote Walter Taylor.

After Lee had dictated all of the necessary orders, he and Longstreet dined with the Cox family at their Clover Hill plantation. "As General Lee entered the house, everything and everybody was under the spell of his presence and dignity," wrote one of the Cox children, Kate. It was Lee's last dinner in Petersburg. During the meal, Kate professed her unwavering faith in him and his army, "General Lee, we shall gain our cause, you will join General Johnston, and together you will be victorious." Lee, aware of the near impossibility of this happening, replied obliquely with a profession of his own. "Whatever happens, know this, that no men ever fought better than those who have stood by me."

The tread of marching men, the clatter of cavalry horses, and the creak of wagons filled the streets of Richmond and Petersburg as the long-suffering Army of Northern Virginia converged on the bridges over the James and Appomattox Rivers. Even after the desperate fighting around Petersburg that day, the thin, weary, ragged soldiers tramped along with their usual economy of motion. The greater concern was whether the half-starved teams pulling the supply wagons would last; if they did not, the army would starve.[64]

ॐ

That night, the Confederate government and the last Rebel units in Richmond abandoned the Confederacy's capital. The government's leaders were going to Danville, a small city three miles from the North Carolina border. Danville's weapons and clothing manufactures, its relative isolation, and its ready access to the Richmond & Danville Railroad had magnified the city's importance during the war.

Jefferson Davis and his advisers boarded a special train waiting for them at the Richmond depot. Treasury Secretary George Trenholm arrived with a hamper of food and drinks; he shared a bottle of his peach brandy with Secretary of State Judah Benjamin, Attorney General George Davis, Postmaster General John Reagan, and Navy Secretary Stephen Mallory.

Two days earlier, Davis had sent away his wife Varina—over her strenuous objections—along with their children, in the care of his private secretary, Burton Harrison. Traveling with them were Varina's sister Margaret and Trenholm's daughters. Davis gave Varina a Colt revolver and grimly exhorted her to "force your assailants to kill you" if captured.

The Confederacy's president nearly broke down when he bid his family farewell after seeing them onto the train that would take them to North Carolina. He told his wife, "If I live you can come to me when the struggle is ended, but I do not expect to survive the destruction of constitutional liberty." He believed that "he was looking his last upon us," wrote Varina.[65]

In bulging bags and boxes, gold and silver from the Confederate treasury and Richmond's banks were taken to another train. When its loading was completed, the treasure train contained at least a half million dollars' worth of double-eagle gold pieces, Mexican silver dollars, gold nuggets and ingots, and silver bricks. A detail of soldiers and sailors ringed the train until it left the station a little after midnight. Government wagons laden with the Confederacy's archives also rolled up to the Danville depot. The records filled eight trains.

Meanwhile, piles of worthless government paper money were burned in Capitol Square.

⁂

People clogged the streets leading to the city's rail depots. Decorum broke down: there were oaths and blasphemous shouts, and pale women and shoeless children struggled through the throngs. Eighty-year-old Richmond Mayor Joseph Mayo was seen on the street, "excited, incoherent, chewing tobacco defiantly, but yet full of pluck." At the crowded depots, the people with baggage and trunks became panicky and desperate. Some of them turned around their wagons and carriages and took to the roads; others found places on packet boats headed west on the James River canal.[66]

A slave dealer named Lumpkin herded a coffle of fifty slaves, chained together by their ankles, to the railroad station, intending to take them with him to the Deep South. An armed, uniformed sentry turned Lumpkin away, and he had little choice but to unshackle the slaves—"merchandise" once worth $50,000.[67]

At the Richmond commissary Confederate soldiers loaded hundreds of wagons with bacon, flour, and whiskey and galloped away to join the army. Looters had been waiting for this moment. With a roar, they descended on the commissary and plundered it of everything that remained.

In the hope of preventing widespread drunkenness, the authorities poured whiskey from the government warehouses into the gutters. The looters scooped up the liquor in pans and pitchers. "The gutters ran whisky, and it was lapped as it flowed down the streets," wrote Captain Clement Sulivane, who commanded a detached brigade guarding Mayo's Bridge over the James. The alcohol inspired a frenzy of pillaging.

The quartermaster stores and government bakery were thrown open, and people snatched sacks of sugar, coffee, and pork, carting them away in wheelbarrows. When those places had been picked clean, the mob proceeded down Main Street and looted the city's business establishments.[68]

"Bare-headed women, their arms filled with every description of goods plundered from warehouses and shops, their hair hanging about their ears, were rushing one way to deposit their plunder and return for more, while a current of the empty-handed surged in a contrary direction," wrote Lieutenant Colonel Edward Boykin of the 7th South Carolina Cavalry, part of the Confederate rearguard. It was, he said, "the saddest of many of the sad sights of war—a city undergoing pillage at the hands of its own mob."[69]

Admiral Raphael Semmes and his *CSS Alabama* crewmen had become famous throughout the North and South for their rapacious plundering of Union merchantmen from Borneo to the North Atlantic. The *USS Kearsage*, however, had sunk the *Alabama* off Cherbourg, France, the previous summer, and Semmes had returned to the Confederacy. Promoted to rear admiral, in February 1865 Semmes was given command of the James River Squadron—three ironclads and five wooden vessels.[70]

Now, just weeks after Semmes's appointment, Navy Secretary Mallory ordered him to destroy his squadron. "Sick at heart," he instructed the crews to pack their vessels with powder and shells. The first to go was Semmes's flagship, the ironclad ram *Virginia*. "The spectacle was grand beyond description," he wrote. "Her shell-rooms had been full of loaded shells. The explosion of the magazine threw all these shells, with their fuses lighted, into the air. . . . The pyrotechnic effect was very fine." The explosions jolted Richmond's homes and broke windows two miles away. Lieutenant Royal Prescott of the 24th New Hampshire described how "there flashed out a glare of light as of noonday." Someone described the percussive sound as "the wreck of matter and the crushing of worlds."

As Semmes and his men traveled upriver in wooden gunboats, he saw entire blocks of Richmond in flames, and a conflagration raging at the Tredegar Iron Works, where shells were exploding. The Navy men disembarked and burned their boats at Manchester, where hundreds of distraught men and women milled about. The sailors commandeered an abandoned train, ship's engineers got it running, and the naval contingent chuffed away, traveling all the way to Danville, where it joined Jefferson Davis and his Cabinet.[71]

On Richmond's north side, a powder magazine exploded in a deafening thunderclap, killing eleven people in a nearby almshouse. Then, more than three hundred inmates escaped from the state penitentiary after the guards fled. "A cry of dismay rang all along the streets . . . and I saw a crowd of leaping shouting demons in parti-colored clothes, and with heads half shaven," wrote Mary Tucker McGill. "Many a heart which had kept its courage to this point quailed at the sight."[72]

On their way out of Richmond, the retreating Confederate soldiers fired the James River bridges—keeping only Mayo's Bridge open until the last troops had departed—and also set fire to two warehouses full of tobacco on the waterfront. The tobacco was burned by order of General Richard Ewell, who obdurately insisted that the Yankees would not get a shred of it. The eccentric, one-legged former corps commander had transferred all of the tobacco into the two warehouses and a third one that was not ignited because it was also a collection point for wounded Rebel soldiers.

Mayor Mayo and two councilmen had entreated Ewell not to burn anything in Richmond, fearing that the fires would spread to the business and residential districts. Ewell rejected their pleadings. The city officials could only post city firemen, with hoses and pumping equipment, near the warehouses.[73]

As Mayo and the councilmen had warned, a strong breeze sprang up from the southeast early April 3 and carried the flames into Richmond's business district. Then, arsonists set fire to the national arsenal and the Richmond armory. When firemen tried to extinguish the blazes, their fire hoses were cut. At the arsenal, packed with an estimated 750,000 loaded shells, the explosions continued for hours. "The earth seemed fairly to writhe as if in agony, the house rocked like a ship at sea, while a stupendous thunder roared around," a diarist wrote.

Not since British troops burned Richmond in 1781 had there been fires in the city of this magnitude. Driven by the strong winds, the flames swept into the city center before dawn. After deploying his men around Mayo's bridge, Captain Sulivane had nothing else to do but observe "the terrible splendor of the scene . . . the two cities, Richmond and Manchester, were like a blaze of day amid the surrounding darkness. Three high arched bridges were in flames. . . . Every now and then as a magazine exploded, a column of white smoke rose up as high as the eye could reach, instantaneously followed by a deafening sound."

Lieutenant Colonel Boykin rode through the city with General Martin Gary's cavalry brigade, the army's rearguard. The cavalrymen were forced from Main Street when flames blocked their path, and they entered a residential area. "At the windows," Boykin wrote, "we could see the sad and tearful faces of the kind Virginia women." Around daylight, the cavalry column, behind a column of ambulances, reached Mayo's Bridge. When they had all crossed over, General Gary rode up to Sulivane. "Touching his hat to me he called out, 'All over, good-bye; blow her to hell,' and trotted over the bridge." Sulivane and his brigade followed Gary over the span, the bridge was ignited, and flames and smoke quickly enveloped it.[74]

The South Carolinians sat their horses on a hill in Manchester and gazed at the conflagration engulfing Richmond. "The old war-scarred city seemed to prefer annihilation to conquest," wrote Boykin.[75]

The sun rose "like an immense ball of blood" in a pall of granular smoke. The air in central Richmond was full of burning brands, sparks, and, of course, billowing black clouds. Pulverized glass carpeted the streets. Thousands of men, women, and children converged on Capitol Square, a green oasis where they hoped to breathe pure air. None was to be had there. The dazed citizens wandered the green slopes, coughing, wheezing, and blinking away ash and cinders. The square began to fill up with piles of furniture dragged by homeowners from their blackened residences.[76]

❧

The Cary Street warehouse known as the infamous Libby Prison was empty save for Major Thomas Turner, the prison commandant. As the fires roared through Richmond, Turner was in his office, burning records and gathering his belongings. The fifteen hundred Union officer captives were gone—having been sent to prisons in Georgia and South Carolina when the Yankees neared Richmond. The prisoners had tried to burn down Libby when they left, but failed. Confederate officials had also removed the ten thousand Union enlisted prisoners held on the cruelly misnamed Belle Isle in the James River. Gaunt and ill, they had gladly left the hellish island where so many of them had died, never dreaming that they were going someplace worse—Andersonville, Georgia.[77]

In a nearby home on a hill overlooking the James River, Elizabeth Van Lew eagerly awaited the arrival of the Union Army. A spinster who moved in elite Richmond social circles, Van Lew was a secret Unionist who had helped many Union officers escape from Libby Prison. She was also a spy whose informants and couriers had supplied valuable information to the Union high command. Today was her day of liberation.

She retrieved a large American flag that had been smuggled to her from General Benjamin Butler when he commanded the Army of the James, and she ran it up her flagpole. Union troops, she knew, would march into Richmond from the east; she hoped hers would be the first American flag seen by the Yankees. It was. After four years, Van Lew's Stars and Stripes, snapping in the smoky breeze, was the first to fly over Richmond.

Grant had received Van Lew's reports—sometimes secreted in servants' shoe soles, other times in hollowed-out eggs—for months at City Point. When the Union Army marched into the enemy capital, the general-in-chief dispatched an officer to Van Lew's home to protect her from vengeful Southerners.[78]

Early April 3, Mayor Mayo and a committee of city councilmen rode east of the city in two hacks with the intention of surrendering Richmond to a federal commander. Over Mayo's carriage fluttered a white flag. Inside was a box containing Richmond's official seal and a letter addressed to "the General Commanding the United States Army in front of Richmond." The letter read, "The Army of the Confederate Government having abandoned the City of Richmond, I respectfully request that you will take possession of it with an organized force, to preserve order and protect women and children and property."[79]

Captain George Bruce's 13th New Hampshire led the first column of infantrymen into the city. Part of the XXIV Corps division commanded by General Charles Devens, the New Hampshire troops for months had occupied the works opposite Richmond. Bruce's first sight of Richmond on this day was unforgettable: "The city was wrapped in a cloud of densest smoke, through which great tongues of flame leaped in madness to the skies. . . . Added to the wild tumult of the flames, ten thousand shells bursting every minute in the Confederate arsenals and laboratories were making an uproar such as might arise from the field when the world's artillery joins in battle." Weirdly juxtaposed across the way, as cinders from the burning capital fell around him, a farmer plowed a field.[80]

Around Bruce's marching column galloped two companies of the 4th Massachusetts Cavalry of XXV Corps, which General Godfrey Weitzel, the corps commander, had ordered to enter Richmond first. The

Massachusetts cavalrymen quickly clattered up to the state Capitol, ringed by sooty, numb citizens husbanding their salvaged belongings. Two majors climbed to the Capitol roof to plant their companies' yellow guidons. It was 7:30 a.m. on April 3.

A half-hour later, the Capitol's Confederate flag was lowered and a large US flag was run up. A heartbroken witness to this historical event wrote, "We covered our faces and cried aloud. All through the house was the sound of sobbing. It was as the house of mourning."[81]

A Richmond woman never forgot her first sight of the Yankee infantry: "Stretching from the Exchange Hotel to the slopes of Church Hill . . . was the array, with its unbroken line of blue, fringed with bright bayonets. . . . As the line turned at the Exchange Hotel into the upper street, the movement was the signal for a wild burst of cheers from each regiment." Through the chaos of fires and bursting shells, she wrote, came "the garish procession of the grand army, with brave music, and bright banners and wild cheers."[82]

Dancing, shouting, and cheering, hundreds of Richmond's blacks crowded around Bruce's regiment at the head of Devens's division. They hugged and kissed the legs of the mounted officers and their horses, shouting hallelujahs. Devens, riding beside Bruce, was overcome with emotion. His eyes brimming with tears, Devens said huskily, "This is a great sight for us to behold—the deliverance of a race."

When the soldiers reached Main Street, three bands were brought up, and they began playing. With colors flying, the musicians launched into the thrilling "Yankee Doodle," followed by "Rally Round the Flag" and "Battle Cry of Freedom" to celebrate the Union Army entering the Confederacy's inner sanctum for the first time. "The step was exact; arms at right shoulder and distances kept with the precision of a parade drill," wrote Colonel Joel Baker of the 9th Vermont.[83]

Bruce's regiment stacked arms on Capitol Street and beheld "a scene of indescribable confusion" in Capitol Square. "Men, women, and children, black and white—exhausted, anguished, disconsolate—were scattered promiscuously" while the wind was "blowing like a hurricane," wrote Bruce. "The heated air, dim with smoke and filled with innumerable particles that float from the surface of so great a fire, rendered it almost impossible to breathe. At every gust the crowd turned to escape its fury as men turned to escape the blast of a driving snowstorm."[84]

General Weitzel accepted Mayor Mayo's surrender and established his headquarters in the Senate chamber of the Capitol. General Charles Ripley, Bruce's brigade commander, was assigned to bring order to the city.

The first task was putting out the fires. Union troops commandeered the few fire trucks still functioning and blew up buildings in the fires' paths. With great effort, the fires were at last extinguished, but by then, smoldering ruins were all that remained of twenty blocks in the city center.

Ripley organized a police force to patrol the streets. By noon, commandeered printing presses were churning out circulars announcing the terms of the temporary martial law now in effect. Only Union soldiers detailed to Richmond's protection were allowed into the city; the rest of the army remained outside.[85]

Among the units not permitted to enter Richmond were Weitzel's two XXV Corps divisions of US Colored Troops, and Lieutenant Colonel Charles Francis Adams's black 5th Massachusetts Cavalry.

Adams, grandson and great-grandson of Presidents John Quincy Adams and John Adams, asked Weitzel as a "special favor" to permit his troopers to march through downtown Richmond. Not only would this please Adams's men, but it would also be a deeply symbolic gesture. Weitzel granted Adams's request.

"This fine regiment of colored men made a very great impression on those citizens who saw it," Weitzel later wrote. White Richmond residents were unimpressed, though. Mary Fontaine said the cavalrymen "thundered at a furious gallop," and the city's servants "were completely crazed."[86]

Many citizens whose homes had not burned remained inside behind shuttered windows. Others streamed into the churches, "whole congregations sobbing the Litany." At one church, loud weeping stopped the singing of a hymn. As worshippers left another church after services, a blaring Union military band passed by, rubbing salt into raw emotional wounds. "The great swell of its triumphant music seemed to mock the shabby, broken spirited congregation defiling out of the gray old church buried in shadows."[87]

A momentous telegram from Fortress Monroe arrived at the War Department office in Washington:

Here is the first message for you in four years from
Richmond, Va., April 3, 1865
Hon. Edwin M. Stanton, Secretary of War, Washington, D.C.: We took
Richmond at 8:15 this morning. I captured many guns. The enemy left in
great haste. The city is on fire in two places. And making every effort to
put it out. . . .

G. Weitzel, Brig-Gen'l Comd'g.

When he received the telegram, the jubilant war secretary, in his shirt-sleeves, picked up a fifteen-year-old telegraph operator and held him up to the open window so that he could announce the news to the crowd below. Stanton then ordered an eight-hundred-gun salute.[88]

The news threw Washington into a celebratory uproar, Navy Secretary Gideon Welles wrote in his diary, with "immense gatherings in the streets. . . . It seemed as if the entire population, the male portion of it, was abroad in the streets. Flags were flying from every house and store that had them."[89]

In New York, too, the streets quickly filled with dense crowds. They sang "Old Hundred," "John Brown," and "The Star-Spangled Banner," repeating the last two lines of the latter again and again as the crowd roared. "It seemed a revelation of profound national feeling," wrote diarist George Templeton Strong, who walked around shaking hands with strangers amid booming cannons.[90]

When the momentous news reached the 116th Pennsylvania in Nelson Miles's division southwest of Petersburg, "all fatigue, sufferings and trials were on the instant forgotten," wrote Colonel St. Clair A. Mulholland. "Exhausted men who were scarcely able to drag their limbs along leapt with delight and felt fresh and strong enough to start in immediate and rapid pursuit of the flying foe."[91]

Diarist Mary Chesnut wrote, "Richmond has fallen—and I have no heart to write about it. . . . They are too many for us . . . Blue-black is our horizon."[92]

⁂

At Petersburg the night of April 2–3, Lee hurried his army across the Appomattox River and ordered the bridges destroyed. He wanted to interpose the river between the Rebels who had gotten to the north bank and Grant's five infantry corps and Sheridan's Cavalry Corps on the south bank. Five routes were utilized to evacuate two hundred guns, more than one thousand wagons, and about thirty thousand troops. Most of the Rebels and their trains went over the Pocahontas and Battersea Bridges, which were both burned after the army had gotten across them. The Confederates' immediate objective was Amelia Court House, more than thirty miles to the northwest. If the Richmond & Danville Railroad was still open, the Confederate Army might proceed southwest to Burke-ville Station, and thence to Danville and a union with Joseph Johnston. If Sheridan's Cavalry Corps had closed that escape route, Lee would push on to Lynchburg in the west.

Of Lee's three infantry corps, only John Gordon's Second Corps, oc-cupying the defenses east and southeast of Petersburg, marched through the city. Gordon's men never forgot what they saw that night: weeping women on the streets and sidewalks in an "agony of despair" as the sol-diers passed them, and towering flames from the burning warehouses illuminating the city with a strange, dancing light. A woman wrote that when the last soldiers had left the city, there was an unsettling stillness, a "dreadful anticipation."[93]

Lee sat astride his horse, Traveller, at the Hickory Road crossing on the Appomattox River's north bank, pointing Gordon's men to the right and James Longstreet's to the left. When the rearguard had passed, Lee rode on.[94]

General Samuel McGowan's brigade shambled through the country-side beyond Sutherland Station, from which it and the remnants of three other Third Corps brigades had been driven that afternoon by Nelson Miles's division. The hungry, dispirited men kept no regular pace or for-mation. They fell out when they became tired, rejoining the column later. "An indescribable sadness weighed upon us," wrote Lieutenant J. F. J. Caldwell of the 1st South Carolina. "The men were very gentle toward each other—very liberal in bestowing the little food that remained to them."[95]

Grant and Meade entered Petersburg early April 3 while the Rebel evac-uation was still under way. The Appomattox River bottom was jammed with retreating Confederates, whose musket fire forced the Union generals to take cover behind a house. The packed roads were potentially rich targets for artillery, but Grant humanely chose to let the opportunity pass. "I had not the heart to turn the artillery upon such a mass of defeated and fleeing men, and I hoped to capture them soon," he wrote.[96]

The Rebels were sometimes too hasty in firing the Appomattox bridges; not all of the troops were across when the flames consumed them. The unlucky ones stranded on the south bank either quickly found another way over the river or became prisoners.

Corporal J. S. Kimbrough of the 14th Georgia and two companions dropped out of the Third Corps's stumbling, nighttime hegira when fatigue overcame them. They spread their blankets on the ground about fifty yards from the road and fell into a deep sleep that lasted all night. When they awakened, the sun was up and the road was empty. Hearing "the hoarse huzzas" of Yankees celebrating their entry into Petersburg, the Rebels leaped to their feet, grabbed their muskets, and ran to the nearby river bridge. Nothing remained of it but the abutments, charred and still smoking. "No language can describe my feelings as I gazed across that muddy, swollen stream and realized that there was no chance to cross nor time to escape," wrote Kimbrough. A squad of Union soldiers approached. Kimbrough bent his musket over a rock, threw it in the river, and surrendered.[97]

⁂

Of the Union Army corps deployed around Petersburg, just IX Corps entered the city, and only because Petersburg lay across IX Corps's path as it marched west; Grant's other corps were south or west of the city, pursuing Lee. About 4 a.m., after Union commanders ascertained that the Rebels had abandoned the city, two Michigan sharpshooter regiments raced into Petersburg, eager to be the first to raise their regimental colors. For nine months, Petersburg's church steeples had lay tantalizingly close, yet just beyond the Yankees' reach.

The 1st Michigan Sharpshooters got there first. Reaching Petersburg's courthouse, the troops known for their deadly marksmanship scrambled up the winding steps of the courthouse's clock tower in the darkness. They opened the clock face and thrust their flag out. It was 4:28 a.m. "Our hearts were too full for utterance," wrote one of the soldiers, "so we clasped hands and shed tears of joy, for we knew that the beginning of the end had come."[98]

The conquerors were initially greeted by a "remarkable silence. Stores, shops and all public buildings were closed; nearly all the inhabitants had fled with the army, save women and negroes," wrote Chaplain Edwin Haynes of the 10th Vermont. In the streets, the blacks, the first to venture out, sang spirituals and, falling to their knees, gave prayerful thanks. A few hours later, when it was apparent there would be no pillaging or destruction of private property, the disconsolate white inhabitants began emerging from their homes. Others could be seen gazing out the windows. "When the truth came to me that we are in the Federal lines, I could not keep my tears back, my heart was so sick," wrote Bessie Callender.

With keen interest, the Union soldiers studied the city they had for so long dreamed of occupying. "The main part of the town resembles Salem [Massachusetts], very much, plus the southern shiftlessness and minus the Yankee thrift," wrote Lieutenant Colonel Theodore Lyman, Meade's aide, yet allowed that the "haute noblesse" dwellings on Market Street were as well kept as any in Salem.

The Yankees observed that the Union shelling had scarcely touched the upper city and, although damage was more evident in the lower city, which had been within artillery range, "it was certainly wonderful that so little damage had been done," a New York Herald reporter wrote. "Nearly every other building in some localities had been struck; but, with the exception of now and then a chimney knocked down, or a hole through the building that a few dollars would repair, the injuries were scarcely perceptible." An estimated twenty thousand shells had landed in the city the previous summer and fall. Besides inflicting little damage, the shelling caused few casualties.[99]

Mayor William Townes and Councilman Charles Collier breasted the waves of retreating Confederates for hours to reach Petersburg's east side so that they could formally surrender the city. Before sunup, masses of bluecoats were streaming past them and steadfastly ignoring the men's entreaties to accept the city's surrender. Then New York Herald reporter Sylvanus Cadwallader appeared on a horse that bore a staff officer's insignia on its harness, and Townes and Collier tried to surrender the city to him. Cadwallader curtly dismissed them, and the city leaders returned to the courthouse to find it covered with American flags.[100]

Lyman ventured out of Petersburg to see the abandoned entrenchments close up. "Upon these parapets, whence the rifle-men have shot at each other, for nine long months, in heat and cold, by day and by night, you might now stand with impunity and overlook miles of deserted breastworks and covered ways," he wrote.[101]

Councilman Collier conceded that the Union authorities made every effort to protect Petersburg's citizens and their property. Guards were sent to every householder who requested one. "Comparative order and quiet reigned under martial law," Collier conceded. After city employees took the oath of allegiance, they received their salaries in greenbacks instead of worthless Confederate scrip. Relief agencies set up operations, and needy residents began receiving food and clothing.[102]

ༀ

Hours after Lee's army evacuated Petersburg, a man claiming to be a Confederate Army engineer informed Grant and Meade that Lee had prepared strong entrenchments west of Petersburg. He intended to fight a last battle there, the man claimed. Meade wanted to immediately cross the Appomattox River and attack Lee's army in its last redoubt. But after a year of matching wits with Lee from the Rapidan River to Petersburg, Grant was highly skeptical. "I knew that Lee was no fool, and he would have been to have put himself and his army between two formidable streams like the James and Appomattox rivers" and allow Grant's army to box him in. It was a "ruse," Grant concluded, designed to disrupt his army's pursuit so the Confederates might escape to North Carolina. Grant, determined to block Lee's flight, did not alter his army's line of march along the Appomattox's south bank.[103]

ༀ

President Lincoln arranged to travel by military train to see Petersburg, which had defied Grant's army for so long. When Lincoln told War Secretary Edwin Stanton of his plan to go see Grant, Stanton, believing it too dangerous, urged the president to reconsider. "Allow me respectfully to ask you to consider whether you ought to expose the nation to the consequence of any disaster to yourself," Stanton wrote. "Commanding

generals are in the line of their duty in running such risks; but is the political head of a nation in the same situation?"[104]

Lincoln went anyway. Traveling with him were his son Tad; his bodyguard, William Crook; Naval Captain John Barnes; and Admiral David
Porter, whose flagship, the captured blockade-runner *Malvern*, was now
Lincoln's home away from Washington. Porter and Lincoln had become
friends during the president's visit; they admired and respected one another, and probably more importantly, they shared a good sense of humor.

When the president first came aboard Porter's small vessel, he declined the admiral's offer to let Lincoln use his quarters; instead, the six-
foot-four Lincoln slept in a stateroom measuring just six by four and a
half feet. When he retired for the night, Lincoln put his socks and boots
outside his door. The next morning, the president's socks, full of holes
when he took them off, were darned, and his boots had been cleaned.

Lincoln said to Porter, "A miracle happened to me last night. When
I went to bed I had two large holes in my socks, and this morning there
are no holes in them. That never happened to me before; it must be a
miracle!"

Porter asked him how he had slept. Soundly, said Lincoln, although
adding, "but you can't put a long blade into a short scabbard. I was too
long for that berth."

While Lincoln and Porter were ashore that day, carpenters dismantled
Lincoln's stateroom, added two feet to both its length and width, and
replaced the mattress with a wider one before putting the room back together. Nothing was said to Lincoln about the changes.

The president emerged smiling from his expanded quarters the following morning. "A greater miracle than ever happened last night," he
told Porter. "I shrank six inches in length and about a foot sideways. I
got somebody else's big pillow, and slept in a better bed than I did on the
River Queen."[105]

The night of April 2, during the massive bombardment of Petersburg,
Lincoln turned to Porter. "Can't the Navy do something at this particular
moment to make history?" he asked. Porter replied that the Navy was
doing all it could do by keeping the Confederate ironclads bottled up on
the James River.

"But can't we make a noise?" asked Lincoln. "That would be refresh-
ing." Porter said his squadron could do that. "Well, make a noise," said

the president. Porter sent a telegram, and the ships upriver began firing broadsides toward the Petersburg forts. Lincoln listened attentively and thought the noise "a very respectable one."[106]

After Lincoln took his seat in the special train taking his party to Petersburg, Porter walked through the car, closing doors. As he stood by the car's front door, waiting for the locomotive to connect with it, three stocky young men in white cravats approached the admiral and, evidently mistaking him for a train conductor, demanded to see Lincoln. Porter refused to let them in, but two of the men tried to force their way past him. Porter threw them into the mud and warned them that he would shoot them if they tried to mount the platform again. Lincoln laughed when he saw the two men sprawled on the ground, and he asked Porter what he "would sell that trick for." The men left.[107]

Lieutenant Robert Todd Lincoln, the president's other son, met the train in Petersburg with a cavalry escort. There were horses for Tad and the president—Grant had lent Lincoln his horse, Cincinnati—but not for Porter. The admiral persuaded a soldier to give up his mount. Unfortunately for Porter, the raw-boned white horse was "a hard trotter, and a terrible stumbler."

When they reached the house where Grant and his staff were waiting, Lincoln overheard Porter asking one of Grant's staff officers whether he could buy the horse. Lincoln objected. "Just look at him first; his head is as big as a flour barrel." The president continued itemizing the horse's many flaws: sprung knees, advanced age. "His hoofs will cover half an acre. He's spavined and only has one eye. What do you want with him? You sailors don't know anything about a horse." Lincoln told the officer not to sell Porter the horse. Porter said he wanted the horse for a special purpose. "I want to buy it and shoot it, so that no one else will ever ride it again." The president laughed in delight.[108]

❧

At the Thomas Wallace house, Grant was waiting for Lincoln on the front porch. The president entered the yard with long strides and seized Grant's hand, shaking it for a long time and "pouring out his thanks and congratulations with all the fervor of a heart which seemed overflowing with its fullness of joy." Lincoln said to him, "Do you know, general, that I have had a sort of sneaking idea for some days that you intended to do something like this." But the president thought Grant would delay his attack until Sherman's army reached Virginia and could join in.

Sounding much as Sheridan had when they had discussed Sherman's role, Grant told the president that the Army of the Potomac alone should finish the job. "If the Western armies should be even upon the field, operating against Richmond and Lee," he said, "the credit would be given to them for the capture, by politicians and non-combatants from the section of the country which those troops hailed from. It might lead to disagreeable bickerings between members of Congress of the East and those of the West." The Eastern armies, Grant said, should "vanquish their old enemy single-handed." Lincoln replied that he had never considered the matter from that angle, but that he could see Grant's point.[109]

In his eagerness to help Grant destroy Lee and the Confederacy, Sherman never suspected that he was being excluded from the war's finale. His congratulatory telegram to Grant after the fall of Petersburg and Richmond anticipated an imminent union of their armies to finish off Lee's and Joseph Johnston's armies. "It is to our interest to let Lee & Johnston come together just as a billiard player would nurse the balls when he has them in a nice place," wrote Sherman. "Lee has lost in one day the Reputation of three years, and you have established a Reputation for perseverance and pluck that would make Wellington jump out of his Coffin."[110]

Grant, however, now made it clear to Sherman that he was unneeded in Virginia. "Should Lee go to Lynchburg with his whole force and I get Burkeville there will be no special use in you going any farther into the interior of North Carolina," he told Sherman. "There is no contingency that I can see except my failure to secure Burkeville that will make it necessary for you to move to the Roanoke [River] as proposed when you were here."[111]

⁓

Lee's objective was also Burkeville Station on the Richmond & Danville Railroad, but it would be a longer march for the Rebels than for Grant. During the 1864 Overland Campaign, Lee had always traveled the shorter chord of the bow, while Grant made the longer march along the arc. Their roles were now reversed. Also ironic was that Lee must cross the Appomattox River twice, while Grant need not cross at all—the reverse of the armies' circumstances in 1864 on the North Anna River. To reach Burkeville, Lee's men must march fifty-five miles in better time than Grant's could cover thirty-six miles. Another wrinkle in Lee's plan was Phil Sheridan's powerful Cavalry Corps, which could cover ground more quickly than either army's infantrymen. Lee's plan appeared to be a hopeless one.

Before Lee's army could reach Burkeville Station and thence proceed to North Carolina to join Joseph Johnston's army, his half-starved men had to eat. Lee had ordered 350,000 rations sent to Amelia Court House, where the Petersburg army would join Richard Ewell's Richmond forces.

Lee's divisions were one day ahead of their pursuers, but the Confederates were in poor physical shape. Weeks of meager rations and inactivity in the trenches had enfeebled the infantrymen, and the underfed horses struggled to pull their loads. Without provisions, neither men nor horses could last long.

Rooney Lee ordered General Rufus Barringer's North Carolina cavalry brigade to make a stand at Namozine Church to delay Sheridan's men, who were harrying the Rebels' rear and rounding up hundreds of prisoners. Barringer tried to persuade Lee to give the job to another brigade; his men were exhausted by days of hard duty, he said. But Lee did not change his mind, and in the last organized fight of Barringer's division, Sheridan's cavalrymen quickly overwhelmed and scattered the Rebel troopers.

The roads the Rebels traveled were strewn with burning caissons, ambulances, wagons, and discarded artillery ammunition. The Confederate army was unraveling. "One of our men, recaptured, reports that not more than one in five of the rebels have arms in their hands," Sheridan told Grant.[112]

❧

After supervising the withdrawal of the Confederate First Corps's artillery batteries from the James River bluffs outside Richmond, General Edward Porter Alexander had ridden to the Richmond freight depot of the Richmond & Danville Railroad. There he stumbled upon an extraordinary stockpile of military supplies and food. Availing himself of the chance to improve his equipment, Alexander appropriated an English bridle and felt saddle blanket for his horse and "a magnificent side of English bacon" that he hung on a ring on his saddle.

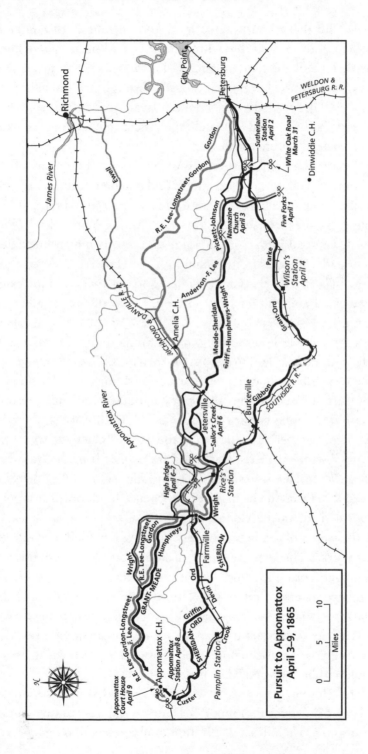

**Pursuit to Appomattox
April 3–9, 1865**

Puzzled by the cornucopia of food and supplies, Alexander made inquiries and discovered that a huge mistake had been made. The provisions that Lee's men so anticipated had been sent from Danville to Amelia Court House, but the train passed through Amelia without being unloaded and proceeded to Richmond instead. Its contents were heaped on the depot siding. "Unfortunately, the officer in charge of it misunderstood his orders," wrote Alexander.

It was more than unfortunate; it was calamitous. The Army of Northern Virginia and the troops from Richmond reached Amelia Court House on April 4 after marching for more than twenty-four hours straight— "sleepless, foodless, cheerless," reported Major Henry Kyd Douglas, previously General John Gordon's aide and now commanding a Second Corps brigade. Boxcars from Richmond, not Danville, awaited them on a siding. In a drizzle the Confederates opened them to find caissons, harnesses, and ammunition, but no food. Lee ordered the ammunition blown up.[113]

Lee's men had little or nothing to eat. Some units, such as the Texas Brigade, had the foresight to put aside provisions for such an emergency; the Texans made a thin gruel that they ate without salt. Now numbering roughly thirty-eight thousand, the army had persevered until now on élan, but it could not long endure starvation. The troops appropriated their horses' corn, parched it in the coals, and ate it. "Chewing the corn was hard work," wrote artillerist Carleton McCarthy. "It made the jaws ache and the gums and teeth so sore as to cause almost unendurable pain."[114]

Forced to halt at Amelia in order to procure food for his hungry men, Lee appealed to Amelia County citizens "to supply as far as each one is able the wants of the brave soldiers who have battled for your liberty for four years." The army needed "meat, beef, cattle, sheep, hogs, flour, meal, corn, and provender in any quantity that can be spared," Lee wrote, promising vouchers for future payment. But the countryside had already been stripped bare, and the foraging wagons returned nearly empty. Moreover, the Confederate Army's one-day head start over Grant's army—purchased at great effort—had evaporated. "The delay was fatal, and could not be retrieved," Lee later wrote.[115]

General Rooney Lee's cavalry scouts probed southwest of Amelia Court House down the Richmond & Danville Railroad toward Burkeville Station, twenty-five miles away. If the rail line was still open and rations

could be sent by rail from Danville to Burkeville, Lee's army might yet
march to Danville.

The scouts were outside of Jetersville, ten miles from Amelia, when
they saw that Union troops had blocked the railroad; dismounted Union
cavalry were arrayed behind entrenchments, with bluecoat infantrymen
marching to their support. Lee rode over to consult with his son, and
he studied his sketchy maps and interviewed area farmers. After scanning the terrain with binoculars, Lee concluded that the position was too
strong to attack. Instead of following the rail line to Danville, Lee had no
choice but to march west to Farmville, twenty-three miles away, where
he might obtain rations from Lynchburg. From Farmville he might yet
be able to swing south toward Danville, bypassing Burkeville Station.[116]

Before Lee changed his plans, Union pickets captured a man on a mule
with identical messages from Lee's commissary general to quartermasters in Danville and Lynchburg, requesting that each send three hundred thousand rations to Burkeville. The telegrams enabled Sheridan to
gauge the strength of the Rebels, which he now knew were concentrated
at Amelia Court House. Always the opportunist, Sheridan saw a way to
disrupt Lee's resupply plan while obtaining Confederate rations to resupply his own men, who had outrun their supply train. Sheridan gave
the Rebel courier's messages to two of his scouts and ordered them to
find working telegraph lines over which to send the messages to Danville
and Lynchburg. Sheridan's men would intercept the rations when they
reached Burkeville.[117]

That night, General Martin Gary's cavalry brigade camped near a
Union outpost. "All around us through the stillness floated the music of
the Yankee bands, mocking with their beautiful music our desperate condition; yet our men around the fires were enjoying it," a Rebel trooper
wrote.[118]

❧

April 5 dawned gray and drizzly, and many of Lee's men were missing
from the Army of Northern Virginia's morning roll call. Lee's men began
marching west toward Farmville. Straggling and desertions carved great
gaps in the ranks. Weakened veterans left the column to lie down in the
fields. An officer in Fitzhugh Lee's cavalry "beheld the first signs of dis-
solution of that grand army"—stragglers swarming over the hills in every

direction. The ground was littered with discarded muskets, haversacks, and canteens.

Longstreet's First Corps, which had absorbed the remnants of A. P. Hill's Third Corps, was at the head of the long column, followed by General Richard Anderson's small Fourth Corps and Richard Ewell's Richmond defense forces and reserves. John Gordon's Second Corps brought up the rear. The orchards were in bloom, but there was no joy in the ranks; Lee intended to keep his starving men on the march all day and through the moonless night.

The troops begged for food at homes along the way. From the marching columns soldiers shot pigs, chickens, and cattle and ate the meat raw. It was "almost absolute starvation," wrote General Pendleton, Lee's artillery chief. "One day a tiny bit of raw bacon, another a handful of uncooked corn, part of the scanty horse-feed." Private William Quattlebaum of the 14th South Carolina was so hungry that he paid $10 for the heels of a butchered beef. "The heels were gluey and sticky when cooked and was a nauseating meal, but it kept body and soul together," wrote Quattlebaum.

Driven onward without rest or food, Lee's army was falling to pieces. The forced marches were "incomparably trying, in lack of food and rest and sleep," wrote artillery Major Robert Stiles, "and because of the audacious pressure of the enemy's cavalry. The combined and continued strain of all this . . . can hardly be conceived and cannot be described."

Union cavalry struck Rebel baggage trains just west of Amelia Court House. Yankee troopers rode up and down the column, setting fire to two hundred wagons and caissons. Other raids destroyed some of Lee's headquarters records and left Fitz Lee's headquarters baggage in flames. The attacks soon came without respite, and the mounted Yankees hung on the flanks and rear of Lee's army like packs of wolves. "There seemed to be no front nor rear, for firing and fighting might be heard ahead and behind and on both sides at once," wrote a Confederate staff officer.[119]

Commissary General Isaac St. John, joining the column from Richmond, told Lee that he had loaded wagons with rations in Richmond after learning about the mix-up with the supply train, but he was unable to send the wagons to him at Amelia Court House in time. St. John instead dispatched eighty thousand rations by wagon to Farmville, where Lee also anticipated getting rations that he had ordered from Lynchburg before they continued on to Burkeville, now held by Sheridan.[120]

Through the night of April 5–6 the ragged gray column stumbled along the muddy road to Farmville. "When the batteries halt to rest, the men throw themselves upon the ground and immediately go to sleep," wrote Lieutenant William Owen of the Washington Artillery, a Louisiana battery that had fended off repeated cavalry raids throughout the day. "Tired and hungry we push on. When the order is given to move forward, the horses often move on without their drivers, so hard is it to arouse the men. It is now a race for life or death. We seldom receive orders now." During the night, the column inched forward at such a glacial pace that by morning it had advanced just three to four miles. Whenever the miserable procession stopped, men fell asleep standing up, waking long enough to trudge ahead a few yards more. "The horrors & privations of the retreat have never been told," wrote Major Campbell Brown, General Richard Ewell's assistant inspector-general and stepson. He watched starving Confederates kill a fifty-pound pig, cut it up, and eat it raw.[121]

Phil Sheridan had gotten to Burkeville before Lee with two corps— one infantry, one cavalry. It had been an extremely demanding march for General Charles Griffin's V Corps infantrymen, whom Sheridan had expected to keep up with his troopers. Marching harder and faster than they ever had, Griffin's men joined the Cavalry Corps at Jetersville, foiling Lee's plan to follow the railroad to Danville. Sheridan and his hard-bitten troopers had accomplished what no other corps in Grant's army could have done.[122]

Sheridan intended for his more than thirty thousand men to continue marching westward, south of the Appomattox River, as it shadowed Lee's army traveling along the north bank. If Sheridan's men each day continued making prodigious marches as they had, he was certain he could block Lee's escape route and compel him to fight a climactic battle.

Sheridan's scouts, the very best in the Union Army and commanded by Major Harry Young, kept their commander apprised of Lee's every move. Young's scouts were drawn from different regiments and were chosen for their special abilities. They roved the countryside in small groups, clinging to the enemy flanks. Disguised as Confederates or Southern planters, they visited homes and enemy outposts, talked to many people, and spied on Rebel camps. "Seldom is a general in active campaign better acquainted with the moves of his enemy than was Sheridan," wrote cavalry Major Henry Tremain.[123]

Late in the day on April 5, Sheridan's scouts informed him that Lee's army was about to march either around Jetersville to try to reach Danville or westward toward Farmville. Sheridan wanted to attack Lee immediately, as soon as II Corps arrived.

General George Meade rejected Sheridan's plan. Although ill with fever, chills, and nausea and riding in an ambulance, Meade remained in command of the Army of the Potomac and was senior in rank to Sheridan, although no longer his superior officer. Meade planned to march on Amelia Court House but not until II, V, and VI Corps had all reached the railroad. He ordered a general advance by the three infantry corps up the Richmond & Danville Railroad to Amelia early the next morning, April 6, "in conjunction with General Sheridan."[124]

Sheridan fumed over Meade's decision; he was certain Lee would no longer be at Amelia by the time the Army of the Potomac got there the next morning. "Unless we [attacked immediately] he [Lee] would succeed in passing by our left flank and would thus again make our pursuit a stern-chase," Sheridan wrote.[125]

Having failed to convince Meade of the sense of his plan, Sheridan appealed directly to Grant, the general-in-chief. Confident of his ability to bring Grant around to his thinking—he had talked Grant out of sending Sheridan's corps to Sherman, and had persuaded Grant to not suspend his campaign because of heavy rains—Sheridan urged Grant to act immediately. "I feel confident of capturing the Army of Northern Virginia if we exert ourselves. I see no escape for Lee," Sheridan wrote. "I wish you were here yourself." Sheridan enclosed a letter that he hoped would clinch the argument he would make to Grant if he did ride out to see Sheridan. The intercepted letter, written by Confederate Colonel William B. Taylor to his mother, began, "Our army is ruined, I fear. . . . My trust is still in the justice of our cause and that of God. . . ."[126]

⊗

Sheridan had risen steadily in Grant's esteem during the three years Grant had known him, first in Mississippi and at Chattanooga, and then, beginning in 1864, while commanding the Cavalry Corps during Grant's Overland Campaign, and leading the Army of the Shenandoah. Sheridan was Grant's most aggressive general, he was tireless, he inspired his men, and he was a competent strategist and tactician. Three days earlier, when Grant had cracked Lee's lines at Petersburg, he had written to Lincoln at City Point, "I have not yet heard from Sheridan, but I have an abiding faith that he is in the right place at the right time."[127]

When Grant read Sheridan's message, the general-in-chief promptly saddled Cincinnati and went to see him, although it was nighttime and Sheridan was fifteen miles away at Jetersville. Grant, with General John Rawlins, Lieutenant Colonel Horace Porter, newspaper correspondent Sylvanus Cadwallader, and a fourteen-man trooper escort, rode through the shadowy woods and quiet fields between his camp and Sheridan's. "The ride was lonely, somewhat hazardous, and made at a slow pace part of the way," wrote Cadwallader, "the scouts, or couriers acting as guides, riding from one to two hundred yards in advance in perfect silence."

Sheridan's headquarters was a log cabin in a tobacco field, and when Grant's party rode up, it was nearly midnight. Sheridan, sleeping on the floor in the loft, scrambled down the ladder in his shirt-sleeves. Unrolling his maps, he showed Grant where his scouts had seen Lee on the move, and stated his objections to riding to Amelia and pursuing Lee. He proposed instead to push westward on a route parallel to Lee and to close off his path of retreat. "Sheridan . . . ended by declaring this to be the final battle ground," wrote Cadwallader. "He was enthusiastic, positive, and not a little profane in expressing his opinions."

While listening to Sheridan, it was apparent to Cadwallader that Grant was "brimming over with quiet enjoyment of Sheridan's impetuosity." For argument's sake, Grant said that if he were Lee, he would still believe that he could slip away with part of his army. Sheridan insisted that not a single regiment would escape. Grant calmed Sheridan, saying "in his quiet, pleasant way that we were doing splendidly; everything was now in our favor . . . but it was too much to expect to capture the whole Confederate army just then."[128]

Grant proposed that he and Sheridan see Meade without delay. He was in his ambulance, close by. "We did not want to follow the enemy," Grant told Meade, "we wanted to get ahead of him." Meade's orders for the next morning might enable Lee, who was moving west even then, to get away, said Grant. Meade said he would change his orders. After a short discussion the generals decided that Sheridan would continue to ride westward in order to sever Lee's line of retreat, while II and V Corps marched toward Amelia according to Meade's original plan.

Grant asked Meade to detach VI Corps so that it could operate with the Cavalry Corps under Sheridan's command. They had cooperated seamlessly in the Shenandoah Valley, and Sheridan had wanted VI Corps to support his cavalrymen at Five Forks but had gotten V Corps instead. Now the hard-riding general was getting his favorite infantry corps.[129]

It was that night, wrote General Joshua Chamberlain, a Sheridan admirer who commanded a V Corps brigade, that "Meade was no longer in reality commander of the Army of the Potomac, but only the vanishing simulacrum of it." Grant and Sheridan were in command in actuality.[130]

❧

At daylight April 6, II and V Corps marched toward Amelia Court House while VI Corps peeled away to join Sheridan's corps. When they entered Amelia, Meade's infantrymen found that Lee's army was no longer there, just as Sheridan had predicted. The starving Confederates had tramped westward all night without food or rest; no march in the history of the Army of Northern Virginia had ever been this punishing. Stragglers and deserters lurked in the woods and fields.

General Henry Davies's cavalry brigade, sent by Sheridan to make contact with Lee's army, struck a supply train, destroying 180 wagons and capturing a thousand prisoners.[131]

Later in the day, Chamberlain's division of V Corps reached the spot where Davies's men had fallen upon the supply train. Davies's troopers had "burst across the flying column and left a black and withered mark behind him like the lightning's path." Continuing their pursuit, Chamberlain's infantrymen came to a low, swampy spot where the muddy, deeply rutted road was littered with wreckage from Lee's army—"abandoned cannon and battery-wagons stuck fast in the mire, the trembling mules still harnessed to the wreck; horses starved and overtasked, but still saddled or packed, turned loose by their masters."[132]

❧

While Grant pursued Lee, Lincoln paid a visit to Richmond, ignoring the grave danger he was inviting by entering the Confederate capital just a day after its fall. Incredibly, Lincoln said that no one there wished to hurt him. "I must go on the course marked out for me," he said when a Confederate deserter told his staff about a rumored assassination plot, "and I cannot bring myself to believe that any human living would do me any harm."[133]

The journey alone to Richmond would be perilous and laborious enough, even with Admiral David Porter's assurances that it would be fine. Torpedoes, sunken boats, and debris from the destruction of the James River Squadron saturated the thirty-mile stretch of the river that the president must first negotiate. Lincoln, his son Tad—who turned twelve on this memorable day—Porter, and Lincoln's aides left City Point on the *River Queen*, accompanied by Admiral Porter's flagship *Malvern* and several other vessels.

One by one, the president's escorting vessels fell away because of the obstacles in the water and problems breasting the strong river current. Before long sunken boats blocked the *River Queen* and the *Malvern*. Lincoln, his party, and a dozen sailors transferred to Porter's shallow-draft barge, towed by the tugboat *Glance*, which carried Lincoln's security guard of thirty Marines. Then, the tug ran aground while trying to aid another boat that had become pinned against a bridge. The Marines were left behind; the barge carrying Lincoln, Porter, Lincoln's aides, and the twelve sailors pushed on toward Richmond, with the sailors manning the oars.

The dwindling flotilla, Lincoln told Admiral Porter, reminded him of a supplicant who had asked him for a ministerial appointment. Lincoln turned him down. The man requested a more modest position; denied that, he asked to be made a tide-waiter. "When he saw he could not get that, he asked me for an old pair of trousers," Lincoln said. "But it is well to be humble."[134]

The barge put the presidential party ashore in Richmond about one hundred yards downriver from Libby Prison. Lincoln and his companions began walking toward the fire-blackened center of the city, over a mile away.

A dozen black men digging nearby dropped their spades when they saw Lincoln, and crowded around the president and his companions, their leader shouting, "Glory, allelujah!" He fell to his knees and kissed Lincoln's feet. When the other black men worshipfully followed his example, Lincoln said, "Don't kneel to me. That is not right. You must kneel to God only and thank him for the liberty you will hereafter enjoy. I am but God's humble instrument." The president's face, wrote Admiral Porter, was "lit up with a divine look as he uttered these words—though not a handsome man . . . in his enthusiasm he seemed the personification of manly beauty. . . . He really seemed of another world."

When news spread through the black community that Lincoln had come to Richmond, hundreds of blacks spilled into the lower downtown district streets, eagerly reaching out to touch Lincoln's hand or clothing, as if they might possess miraculous properties. The blacks flung their hats in the air and threw themselves on the ground to demonstrate their reverence for Lincoln. A woman held her sick child aloft as Lincoln passed, and when the child refused to look at the president, the mother said, "See here, honey, look at the savior and you'll get well. Touch the hem of his garment, honey, and your pain will be done gone."[135]

The sailors, armed with carbines, formed two lines—six of them in front of Lincoln and six behind him. On Lincoln's right were Porter and Captain Charles Penrose; on his left, holding Tad's hand, was the president's bodyguard, William Crook. As Lincoln walked past the infamous Libby Prison, someone shouted, "Pull it down!" The president replied, "No, leave it as a monument."

The crowd of spectators increased as the little procession proceeded along Main Street toward Richmond's center. Lincoln's protectors became anxious for his safety. Unlike the blacks who had initially greeted Lincoln, this crowd was predominantly white and largely silent. "There was something oppressive in those thousands of watchers without a sound, either of welcome or hatred," wrote Crook. "Wherever it was possible for a human being to find a foothold there was some man or woman or boy straining his eyes after the President. Every window was crowded with heads. Men were hanging from tree-boxes and telegraph-poles." The lone sign of welcome was an American flag draped over the shoulders of a young woman standing on a pedestrian bridge.

And then Crook's eye was drawn to a house's second-story window, where the blinds were partly opened. "A man dressed in gray pointed something that looked like a gun directly at the president." Crook dropped Tad's hand and stepped in front of Lincoln, expecting to be shot. No bullet came. "It seemed to me nothing short of miraculous that some attempt on his life was not made," Crook wrote.[136]

Lincoln's impulsive visit to the Rebel capital caught the Union command in Richmond by surprise. It had neither expected Lincoln in Richmond, nor knew that he at that moment was walking through crowds on Main Street with a light guard. When the news finally reached General Godfrey Weitzel's headquarters at the Capitol the general immediately dispatched a cavalry detachment to escort the president to the Confederate White House.

There, in the Confederacy's former command center, Lincoln settled into Jefferson Davis's office chair and drank a glass of water. After a luncheon served in the mansion, the cavalry escort returned and a carriage was brought around for the president. Lincoln, Tad, and Admiral Porter toured the city. Sallie Putnam wrote that "sable multitudes of both sexes" surrounded the carriage to "press or kiss his hand" and then ran after it "in furious excitement." Weitzel joined Lincoln on his tour and asked him what should be done with the Southern people. Lincoln turned to Weitzel and said, "If I were in your place, I'd let 'em up easy, let 'em up easy."[137]

Lincoln spent that night aboard the *Malvern*, whose crew had managed to bring the vessel into Richmond. He met the next day with John Campbell, who was one of the Confederate Hampton Roads commissioners. The president reiterated his peace terms: Southern submission, acceptance of abolition, and disbandment of Confederate armies. Any state that withdrew its troops and its support from the Confederacy, said Lincoln, would recover all of its confiscated property, slaves excepted.

Campbell obtained Lincoln's consent to reconvene the Virginia legislature in Richmond to take those steps and return to the Union. Lincoln instructed Weitzel to permit the legislature to meet, but to disperse it at the first sign of hostility toward the Union. The president was certain that his Cabinet would support his attempt to pacify Virginia.[138]

When Lincoln returned to City Point, he learned that Secretary of State William Seward had suffered a broken jaw, deep head lacerations, and a dislocated shoulder in a carriage accident in Washington. War Secretary Stanton had telegraphed the news to Lincoln, adding, "I think your presence here is needed." But when doctors determined that Seward was not as badly hurt as initially believed, Stanton told Mrs. Lincoln, en route to City Point with a party of dignitaries, that the president need not hurry back to Washington.[139]

Judith McGuire, who had decamped to Richmond when Union troops occupied her native Alexandria, regarded it as "a bitter pill" when Lincoln entered the Confederate president's home. "I would that dear old house, with all its associations, so sacred to Southerners, so sweet to us as a family, had shared in the general conflagration," she wrote. "Then its history would have been unsullied."[140]

From his walks around Richmond's devastated central district, John B. Jones estimated that seven hundred buildings had been destroyed, including his former place of employment, the War Department. The Union troops quietly kept order, he wrote, without interfering with the people. Robert E. Lee's family had remained in Richmond, and a Union guard paced outside their door, "his breakfast being just sent to him from within." Jones reported that Confederate money was no longer being accepted as payment.[141]

The Union army extended an olive branch to Richmond's citizens by holding military band concerts on the Capitol grounds each afternoon. At the first concerts, "except the Federal officers, musicians and soldiers, not a white face was to be seen," wrote Phoebe Pember, a nurse at the Confederacy's vast Chimbarozo Hospital. "The negroes crowded every bench and path."

The next week there was a new policy: no blacks would be admitted to the concerts. "The entertainers went alone to their own entertainment," said Pember. A few days later "the music ceased altogether, the entertainers feeling at last the ingratitude of the subjugated people," she wrote.[142]

During the first days of the Union occupation, the Richmond women stayed home, "clad in their mourning garments, overcome but hardly subdued." If required to run an errand or to go to church or the hospital, they did it "with veiled faces and swift steps," observed Pember. "By no sign or act did the possessors of their fair city know that they were even conscious of their presence. If they looked in their faces they saw them not: they might have supposed themselves a phantom army."[143]

But hunger drove Richmond's citizens to the US Relief Commission for ration tickets; 128,132 were issued during the first seventeen days of the occupation. Before being issued the tickets, applicants were required to pledge an oath of allegiance to the Union. At first, this was too much for many people. One day a young girl in line for rations was asked whether she had taken the oath; she replied that she had not, and that she had never sworn in her life. The agent insisted that she take the oath before he gave her rations. "Well, sir, if you say I must starve unless I do such a horrid, wicked thing as swear, then d—n the Yankees!" she declared, and held out her hand for the rations.[144]

2

April 6, 1865

SAILOR'S CREEK

Fifteen miles west of Amelia Court House, General George Crook's cavalry division rode up on Lee's wagon train near Sailor's Creek, a small, northwest-flowing tributary of the Appomattox River. The Confederate wagons seemed to stretch for miles. Pleased with his good fortune, Crook formed his troopers into a line and attacked. The Rebels instantly went on the defensive and, with roaring musket and artillery fire, repelled Crook's assault.

Sheridan ordered Crook to break off the action and to find a more vulnerable place in the train to attack. Sheridan summoned General George Custer's division and sent VI Corps to the area.[145]

Lee's army, starving and sleepless, had staggered along the rutted, muddy roads all night and much of the day. Exhausted men were dropping out of the column by the hundreds to beg or steal food, to lie down to rest, or to desert and go home. A Confederate staff officer wrote, "It was a period in which no note was taken of day nor night; one long, confused, dreadful day."

When Sheridan's scouts informed him of Confederates begging provisions from people along the road, he passed the intelligence to Grant and urged an all-out attack. "The [Confederate] trains and army were moving all last night and are very short of provisions and very tired indeed," Sheridan wrote. "I think that now is the time to attack them with all your infantry."[146]

Longstreet's First Corps, which had absorbed the remnants of the late A. P. Hill's shattered Third Corps, led the retreating Confederates toward Farmville, where eighty thousand rations awaited them. Behind Longstreet's men—now more than a half-mile or more behind—were General Richard Anderson's Fourth Corps, which included Joseph Kershaw's First Corps division, the remnants of George Pickett's task force, and the Richmond brigades under Richard Ewell. John Gordon's Second Corps brought up the rear.

Sheridan's harassing attacks had forced Anderson and Ewell to stop and fight—and to lag even farther behind Longstreet. It had become a gap of catastrophic proportions, as events would show. For whatever reason, Anderson had not told William Mahone, in charge of the rear division of Longstreet's corps, about the delays, and so the van of Lee's army, unaware of the dangerous interval behind it, marched on obliviously.[147]

Then Custer's division burst through that gap, dismounted, and blocked Marshall's Crossroads. Pickett's and Bushrod Johnson's divisions from Anderson's corps immediately attacked the Yankee cavalrymen. The cavalry divisions of Crook and Thomas Devin fell in alongside Custer's men, forming a solid barrier and menacing the Confederate flanks.

Sheridan had cut Lee's army in half. At the head of Lee's column, Longstreet's men pushed on, insensible to the disaster unfolding behind them. The distance steadily grew between the two halves of Lee's army.

Bluecoat infantry formations—Horatio Wright's VI Corps—suddenly appeared behind the marooned Confederate divisions. Ewell, hoping to save the wagon train in his rear, diverted it to another road that crossed Sailor's Creek two and a half miles to the northwest. Unfortunately Ewell failed to inform Gordon, whose depleted corps was following the wagon train and served as the column's rearguard. Instead of closing up behind Ewell, Gordon's corps plodded after the train, deepening the crisis by unknowingly exposing Ewell's rear to VI Corps's assaults.[148]

The Confederates' situation rapidly deteriorated. Wedged between Sheridan in front and two of Wright's infantry divisions in the rear, Anderson and Ewell were compelled to fight separate battles. While Anderson tried to break through Sheridan's troopers at Marshall's Crossroads, Ewell fought Wright's powerful infantry corps in a battle that gravitated to Hillsman's farm, on a hill overlooking Sailor's Creek.

Sheridan snapped shut the jaws of his trap. Four mounted brigades advanced on Anderson's corps. "It was grand and imposing; it was morally sublime," wrote Major Henry Tremain of Crook's staff. "As bugle after bugle echoed 'the charge' along that line of cavalry, there was one grand jump into the conflict. All was dust and confusion; horses and men fell dead across the rebel works. . . . The rebel line was gone, and squads, companies, and regiments were flying over the hills." Sheridan, riding among his cavalrymen, shouted, "Never mind your flanks! Go through them! They're demoralized as hell!"

Custer's young brother, Lieutenant Tom Custer of the 6th Michigan Cavalry, leaped his horse over the breastwork at Marshall's Crossroads and captured a Confederate battle flag. Wounded in the face and neck by the Rebel color bearer, Custer shot him and seized the flag, Custer's second flag capture in a week. Lieutenant Custer was returning to the battle when his brother ordered him to the rear to receive medical treatment.[149]

Anderson counterattacked, but the Rebel assault failed just minutes after it began. "The troops seemed to be wholly broken down and disheartened," Anderson wrote. The exception was General Henry Wise's brigade, which forced its way out of Sheridan's vise and escaped, along with a brigade from Bushrod Johnson's division. Anderson's other troops became prisoners.[150]

At the same time, VI Corps's infantry divisions launched a massive assault, supported by a powerful artillery barrage, on Ewell's Richmond troops, deployed at Hillsman's farm. Unfortunately for Ewell's men, their guns were all in the wagon train that had vanished into the hills with Gordon's corps. Major Robert Stiles, whose artillery battalion had no guns with which "to reply and thus disturb their aim," lay down so that it would present a smaller target for the bucking Yankee guns lined up on the hill across the creek. Stiles paced his line to keep up his men's morale. A shell struck in front of him, "nearly severing a man in twain, and hurling him bodily over my head, his arms hanging down and his hands almost slapping me in the face as they passed."

Wright's infantrymen advanced over Sailor's Creek in two lines and strode up the hill toward Hillsman's farm, where Stiles' battalion and other Confederate units had withstood the terrific bombardment. Stiles told his men, still flat on the ground, that when he said, "Ready!" they were to rise up on their right knee; when he said, "Aim!" they were to aim at the attackers' knees, then fire on his command. Moments later, Stiles barked out the sequence of orders, and his men unleashed a devastating volley into the bluecoats.

"The earth appeared to have swallowed up the first line of the Federal force in our front," wrote Stiles. "The second line wavered and broke." Without orders, Stiles's artillerists, joined by a brigade of Confederate Marines, chased Wright's men down the hill and drove them back across Sailor's Creek "with an élan which has never been surpassed," wrote Sheridan's highly impressed aide, Lieutenant Colonel Frederick Newhall. On the creek bank they planted the Stars and Bars. Horatio Wright wrote, "I was never more astonished." Then, massed Union musketry and artillery fire tore the gallant attackers to pieces and drove the survivors back to their starting point.[151]

As VI Corps's decisive attack on Hillsman's farm began, "the water in the creek was dancing over the dropping bullets . . . a good many men were falling," wrote Newhall. A cry arose from the ranks, "There's Phil! There's Phil!" It was Sheridan. His fierce features and too-small brimmed hat were as instantly recognizable as the way he characteristically "rolled and bounced upon the back of his steed much as an old salt does when walking up the aisle of a church after a four years' cruise at sea." The infantrymen loudly cheered the general they had come to idolize in the Shenandoah Valley. Major Evan Jones wrote, "The sight of that man on the field was more gratifying than rations, more inspiring than reinforcements."

The Rebels "fought like a tiger at bay," wrote Sheridan, but Wright's attack broke their line. From both the front and the rear, Yankees swarmed over Stiles's battalion in "overwhelming numbers." The fighting devolved into brute encounters with clubbed muskets and bayonets. Soldiers fired pistols into one another's faces. "I saw numbers of men kill each other with bayonets and the butts of muskets, and even bit each others' throats and ears and noses, rolling on the ground like wild beasts," wrote Stiles. "I saw one of my officers and a Federal officer fighting with swords over the battalion colors." A soldier of the 37th Massachusetts, Samuel E. Eddy, was pinned to the ground by a bayonet that pierced his chest and protruded from his back. Eddy coolly loaded his rifle and shot his attacker through the heart. The Rebel fell on top of Eddy, dead. The doughty Yankee shoved the Confederate's body off him, agonizingly withdrew the bayonet from his chest, and walked to the rear.

At Hillsman's farm the Yankees captured hundreds, if not thousands, of Confederates, including Stiles. An officer of the 47th Virginia was captured "with an empty seven-shot revolver and bloody sword" in his hands—testament to the battle's ferocity.[152]

Many Southerners had once considered Ewell as Stonewall Jackson's tactical and strategic heir, but the loss of his left leg during Second

Manassas seemed to have muted his previous aggressiveness, and Lee had eased him from command of the Second Corps in 1864. But the nadir of Ewell's career was surely on this day, when, believing that further resistance would be a pointless waste of his men's lives, he surrendered his polyglot Richmond command, which included a division commanded by Custis Lee, the general-in-chief's son; the Marine brigade; Stiles's heavy artillery battalion; and a cadre of reservists—boys under eighteen and men over forty-five. Custis Lee, who had just recently been commissioned a major general and given his first combat command, now joined Ewell as a prisoner.

Custer's men captured Kershaw and thirty-two battle flags. Five other Confederate generals also were taken prisoner.[153]

The Confederate dead lay in bloody heaps, some of them frozen grotesquely in the posture in which they died. In a ravine that the Rebels had used as a rifle pit, a Union officer saw many bodies, including one soldier "apparently kneeling, his eyes open, and his hands uplifted as if in prayer." At first the officer thought the man was alive, but then he saw that his eyes were "dazed in death, and beneath him in this awful ditch the bodies of his brave companions lay at least six feet deep."[154]

*

Unbeknownst to the men fighting the two battles at Sailor's Creek, John Gordon's Second Corps was waging a third battle—a desperate rearguard action at Lockett's Farm against Andrew Humphreys's II Corps, which had harried Gordon's column all the way from Amelia Court House. When Gordon had veered from the main road behind the wagon train and marched west toward Farmville, II Corps had followed him.

Between Amelia and Sailor's Creek Gordon's men had had a bad enough time. Every mile or two they had been compelled to stop and battle Humphreys's pressing divisions just so that the wagon train could advance. Then Gordon's corps would close up behind the wagons and fight yet another delaying action. The sharp actions had followed one upon the other and were so numerous that Gordon had lost count of them.

When Gordon left the Rice Station road, on which Ewell was following Longstreet, Humphreys's divisions did not take their eyes off Gordon. "It was a sort of running fight," wrote a member of the 148th Pennsylvania, part of General Nelson Miles's division. "As fast as their rear guard took position, we were hurried forward to drive them out." While crossing Sailor's Creek below Lockett's Farm, the Confederate wagons broke the bridge, and a huge traffic jam developed. The Yankees pounced.

The exhausted Confederates counterattacked and forced them back, but Gordon sent a plea for help to Lee: "I have been fighting heavily all day. My loss is considerable and I am still closely pressed. I fear that a portion of the train will be lost as my force is quite reduced & insufficient for its protection. So far I have been able to protect [the wagons] but without assistance can scarcely hope to do so much longer."

No help came, and Gordon's line was broken. Yet somehow he reformed what remained of his corps on the creek's west bank, after losing seventeen hundred men, many of them surrounded and captured behind the stopped wagons. In the abandoned Confederate wagons Miles's men found piles of mail. "Groups of our boys [were] reading letters by their camp fires far into the night," wrote a Pennsylvania infantryman.[155]

When told that morning that his wagon trains were under attack, Lee ordered General William Pendleton, his army's artillery chief and incidentally an Episcopal minister, to gather up every available man and stop the attacks. Lee did not yet know that the rear half of his army was under assault from all sides, but the absence of Anderson's corps concerned him. While waiting for Anderson, Lee rode north toward the Appomattox River.

At the mouth of Sailor's Creek near the Appomattox, Lee met a cavalry brigade from his son Rooney Lee's division. The cavalrymen were watching Gordon's corps battle II Corps near the broken bridge at Sailor's Creek. Lee was puzzled; Gordon was supposed to be the rearguard, so where were the other divisions?

Intending to find out, Lee rode back to where he had expected Gordon and the rest of the army to be. There, he met his aide, Lieutenant Colonel Charles Venable, and General William Mahone, who commanded the rearguard of Longstreet's corps. Now genuinely worried about the fate of Anderson's and Ewell's men, Lee ordered Mahone to turn his division around and return to Sailor's Creek. Lee went with him.

Lee and Mahone rode along a ridge that suddenly provided a panoramic view of the creek and the surrounding valley. Lee stopped and stared in disbelief at what he was seeing—a sight he had never witnessed in the three years he had commanded the Army of Northern Virginia. Streaming out of the valley toward him on the ridge were hundreds, if not thousands, of routed, demoralized Confederates: teamsters without wagons, infantrymen without muskets, units without officers.

"My God!" Lee cried in horror. "Has the army been dissolved?"

Beside him, Mahone, momentarily struck mute by the sight, fumbled out a reply, "No, General, here are troops ready to do their duty."

Lee quickly recovered his usual equanimity. "Yes, General, there are some true men left. Will you please keep those people back?"

While Mahone formed a battle line, Lee attempted to rally the beaten men coming toward him. He picked up a battle flag and, seated on Traveller, held it aloft, the breeze whipping the flag around his body. Recognizing their commander, some of the fleeing soldiers stopped and gathered around Lee. Generals Anderson and Bushrod Johnson turned up later without their commands, abashed by what had happened.[156]

⟳⟲

Lee chose the "High Bridge" as the escape route for Gordon, the wagon train, and the remnants of Ewell's and Anderson's commands. High Bridge was a 2,400-foot-long railroad bridge that soared 160 feet over the Appomattox River northwest of the battlefield and four miles north of Rice Station. Crossing the bridge to the north bank would interpose the river between Gordon's corps and Grant's army so that the Rebels might continue their march to Farmville. Lee sent Mahone's division to secure High Bridge. After Confederate units had finished crossing it, Mahone's men were to burn the bridge.

Longstreet's corps had continued its march to Rice Station, seven miles southeast of Farmville. Lee had hoped that Rice Station would exceed the range of Sheridan's cavalry. If so, the rations sent to Farmville could be forwarded there and the army might still march to Danville. The day's events had proven otherwise: the tireless Union cavalry was hovering off Lee's left flank, and its range appeared limitless. The Union troopers would exact a high price if Lee tried to turn south from Rice Station. He instead redirected Longstreet to Farmville to obtain rations and join Gordon's corps on the Appomattox River's north bank.

Earlier in the day, High Bridge was the scene of a furious battle between Union "bridge burners" and a hastily assembled Rebel response team.

General Edward Ord, commander of the Army of the James, had sent nine hundred infantrymen and cavalrymen to destroy the High Bridge. General Theodore Read, Ord's chief of staff, commanded the two Ohio and Pennsylvania infantry regiments; Colonel Francis Washburn led an eighty-man battalion of the Fourth Massachusetts Cavalry.

When Longstreet learned that Union troops planned to destroy High Bridge, he knew he must preserve it until Gordon's men could get across the Appomatox, but no cavalry was available. Providentially, General Tom Rosser rode up with a small mounted division, and Longstreet sent him to pursue and destroy the Union force, "if it took the last man of his command to do it." After Rosser left, General Thomas Munford reported to Longstreet with Fitzhugh Lee's cavalry division. Munford was sent after Rosser.[157]

Near High Bridge, Rosser's and Munford's men overtook Read's task force. Read drew up his men in a battle line and made a speech he hoped would inspire them. They attacked the Confederate troopers, driving them into a wood. Then the Rebels counterattacked and overwhelmed the Union infantrymen, many of whom were killed or wounded; the rest were captured. Read and Washburn led a futile cavalry charge—eighty men against up to one thousand Confederate troopers—to free their captured comrades. In the melee Read and Confederate General James Dearing fought on horseback with sabers. Dearing "cut [Read] down from his horse," killing him, but then Read's orderly shot Dearing before he, in turn, was shot. Dearing later died of his wounds. Washburn also was mortally wounded in the hand-to-hand fight, which ended with most of the eighty Yankee troopers dead, wounded, or captured. Rosser later claimed to have bagged eight hundred captives.[158]

That night—a cold one, with snow reported at Burkeville Station—the Confederates crossed High Bridge. Mahone's division entrenched around High Bridge and at a wagon bridge down on the riverbank. Gordon's men, the survivors of the Sailor's Creek battle, and what was left of the wagon train crossed to the river's north bank. The Rebels knew that the bridge soared above the Appomattox River, but "the night was so dark that they could not see the abyss on either side," wrote artillerist Carleton McCarthy of Gordon's corps. "Arrived on the other side, the worn-out soldiers fell to the ground and slept, more dead than alive."

Mahone ordered the engineers to burn the bridge, but they waited too long. Just two of the bridge's twenty-one arches were in flames when General Regis de Trobriand's II Corps division got there. A detachment of Yankees with axes cut away the burning spans and sacrificed a third span, while their comrades skirmished on the riverbank and saved the wagon bridge, which Confederate engineers had set ablaze at the last minute. It sustained little damage. The Yankees lost no time in crossing the river and continuing the pursuit.[159]

Two of Lee's army corps no longer existed. During this blackest of days for the Army of Northern Virginia, Lee lost about one-fourth of his army, with 7,700 men killed, wounded, or captured. Union losses totaled 1,180. Lee, with no more than 20,000 exhausted, starving men, and shedding stragglers hourly, faced Union forces more than four times his number.[160]

⁊⧉

Sailor's Creek, Sheridan's second great victory in five days, was the death knell for Lee's army. The Army of Northern Virginia's unspooling could be seen in its growing trail of detritus that now included a new, portentous feature—a plethora of abandoned Dutch ovens, "their little legs kicked up in the air in a piteous manner," wrote Lieutenant Colonel Theodore Lyman of Meade's staff. Hillsides were covered with adjutants' papers, broken boxes, and ammunition cases. Trunks lay everywhere. "It was strange to see the marks on the wagons, denoting the various brigades, once so redoubtable!" wrote Lyman. More piteous were the horses and mules dying in the mud and the wounded Rebels occasionally found lying among the retreating army's discards. "The constant marching and fighting without sleep or food are rapidly thinning the ranks of this grand old army," wrote Lieutenant Colonel William Owen, a Confederate artillery officer.[161]

Sheridan jubilantly reported the great victory to Grant: "I attacked them with two divisions of the Sixth Army Corps and routed them handsomely, making a connection with the cavalry. . . . If the thing is pressed I think that Lee will surrender."

When Lincoln, at City Point, read Sheridan's dispatch, forwarded to him by Grant, he immediately replied, "Let the *thing* be pressed."[162]

That night, Sheridan and Custer shared their campfire, blankets, coffee, sugar, hardtack, and broiled ham with Ewell, Custis Lee, Kershaw, and the five other captured generals. Lieutenant Colonel Frederick

Newhall, Sheridan's adjutant general, described them as "mostly staid, middle-aged men, tired to death nearly, and in no mood for a chat; and so the party is rather a quiet one." While most of the officers stood, Ewell sat on the ground hugging his knees, a picture of "utter despondency." Ewell said the Confederate army was finished, and he urged Sheridan to send a flag of truce to Lee and demand his surrender. Sheridan obliquely replied that he hoped that Grant would move faster and end Lee's flight.[163]

John Wise, the son of General Henry Wise and bearing a message from Jefferson Davis at Danville, found Lee and an aide that night camped in a field north of Rice's Station and east of High Bridge. After reading the dispatch by firelight, Lee told Wise to say to Davis that he could not reach Danville, and was instead retiring in the direction of Lynchburg, "governed by each day's developments." He said to Wise, "A few more Sailor's Creeks and it will be over—ended—just as I have expected it would end from the first."[164]

On the morning of April 7, as Sheridan's cavalry men passed by the captive Confederate generals, arrayed disconsolately around their campfire, Custer raised his hat and bowed to them, and his staff followed his example. One of the Rebel generals proposed three cheers for Custer, whom he characterized as "the very embodiment of chivalry." After the Rebels cheered Custer, Custer's band, which had been playing "Bonnie Dundee," returned the compliment by switching to "The Bonnie Blue Flag." "Confederate enthusiasm was unbounded," wrote an eyewitness.[165]

General Henry Wise, who had broken out of Sheridan's trap at Sailor's Creek with one brigade and had taken charge of a second, spent a miserable night shivering on the ground. In the morning, he washed his face in a pool of water stained red by the clay dust, but he had nothing with which to dry himself. "With a face painted like an Indian, with [a] gray blanket around me, and with the Confederate Tyrolese hat on . . . and muddy all over," Wise led his two brigades on foot to Farmville. There, he met Lee on Traveller. When Lee saw Wise, he said, "Good morning, General Wise, I perceive that you, at any rate, have not given up the contest, as you are in your war-paint this morning."[166]

Lee, who habitually sought the opinions of others, asked Wise to assess their situation. "There is no situation," the former Virginia governor irritably shot back. "Nothing remains, General Lee, but to put your poor men on your poor mules and send them home in time for the spring plowing. . . . I say to you, Sir, emphatically, that to prolong the struggle is murder, and the blood of every man who is killed from this time forth is on your head, General Lee."

With a pained look Lee said, "Oh, General, do not talk so wildly. My burdens are heavy enough! What would the country think of me, if I did what you suggest?"

"Country be d—d!" replied Wise. "There is no country. There has been no country, General, for a year or more. You are the country to these men. They have fought for you. They have shivered through a long winter for you. Without pay or clothes or care of any sort, their devotion to you and faith in you have been the only things that have held this army together. If you demand the sacrifice, there are still left thousands of us who will die for you." To that Lee made no response.[167]

Longstreet's hungry, ragged men marched into Farmville, and this time the promised rations—eighty thousand of them—were there. They were the first rations to reach Lee's men since their retreat began April 2. Some units collected their French soup, meat, and bacon and began preparing their highly anticipated repasts over bonfires in Farmville's streets. But then there was an outbreak of heavy firing in the east, north of the river. It was puzzling at first, because High Bridge and the wagon bridge had supposedly been destroyed; no Union infantry should have been on the north bank.

When Lee learned that the two bridges had not been destroyed as he had ordered, in a rare flash of anger he condemned the grievous failure, which killed all hope of a respite at Farmville and placed his army in mortal peril.[168]

Longstreet's men hastened to Farmville's two river bridges and prepared to fire them. Lieutenant J. F. J. Caldwell and his 1st South Carolina regiment crossed one of the bridges as it began burning; enemy cavalry pressed the South Carolinians from behind. Reaching the north bank, they were attacked from three sides and shelled.

Then the rest of Longstreet's men got over the river and drove off the Yankees. Commissary General Isaac St. John put the unclaimed food on a train and sent it up the railroad, hoping that soldiers who had not received rations might obtain them later.[169]

II Corps had pursued Mahone and Gordon all morning along the Appomattox's north bank. When Longstreet's corps crossed the river, II Corps found itself suddenly confronting Lee's entire army. Grant sent VI Corps, which had pursued Longstreet's columns south of the Appomattox, across the Appomattox to reinforce the besieged II Corps, and Crook's cavalry division waded the river and struck the Confederate wagon trains. While Lee watched, the cavalry divisions of his nephew, Fitzhugh Lee, broke up the attack and made a prisoner of one of Crook's brigade commanders, Colonel Irvin Gregg.[170]

As the confused fighting shifted to the heights north of Farmville, Mahone's men and one of Longstreet's divisions fended off the swarming bluecoats near Cumberland Church. Virginian James Hall wrote a short time later, "Every one knows and feels that we are fighting against hope itself—when everything is even now lost forever."[171]

With Grant's legions harrying their flanks and rear, the Confederates converged on the Lynchburg Road. Short-lived Confederate successes enabled the march to continue, but otherwise made little difference; Grant's relentless pursuit—"let the *thing* be pressed," Lincoln had urged him—continued. When darkness fell, Lee's men continued marching. Gordon's corps, which had neither eaten nor rested, was melting away.

With Lee clearly headed to Lynchburg and not Danville, Sheridan was free to ride ahead of the Confederates to try to block their way. Remaining south of the river, the Cavalry Corps rode southwestward toward Prince Edward Court House and, beyond it, Appomattox Station on the Southside Railroad. Straining to keep up with the troopers were the fast-marching infantrymen of V and XXIV Corps.[172]

The two armies couldn't have been more different. Grant's men, cheerfully pushing ahead in the belief that the war's end was in sight, applauded their general-in-chief as he rode along the marching columns. In Farmville, Grant sat on a hotel porch, watching Horatio Wright's VI Corps parade past him on their way to join II Corps north of the river. The soldiers cheered him and lustily sang "John Brown's Body."

"We were filled with new life," wrote Assistant Surgeon Alfred Woodhull of General Edward Ord's Army of the James. "Lee was in retreat, and we were in full cry after him. . . . We were like so many schoolboys on a holiday." As Ord's men marched westward, the sun shone upon the "fairly-reflecting steel of the arms," said Woodhull. "As far as the eye could reach, the curving country road was vivid with . . . blue and steel."[173]

Had the Rebels burned High Bridge and the wagon bridge, Grant's infantrymen would have had no easy way to cross the Appomattox River and Lee would have regained the one-day lead over Grant that he lost at Amelia Court House. But the bridges had survived, and the day had been squandered in rearguard actions, many troops had gotten no rations, and the Confederates faced another night march. Lee switched Gordon's and Longstreet's corps so that the fresher First Corps became the army's rearguard.

"The roads were terrible in consequence of the rain and we had to leave behind a great many useful & necessary . . . cannons, caissons, wagons, ammunition, stores, &c., &c.," wrote Chaplain William Wiatt of the 26th Virginia at 10:30 p.m. on April 7. "Our teams are in very bad order and can't pull them; a distressing time we had; the straggling continues to an alarming extent; a great many of the men are going into the enemy's hands." A British newspaper correspondent described a Dante-esque scene of "exhausted men, worn-out mules and horses, lying down side by side—gaunt Famine glaring hopelessly from sunken, lackluster eyes— dead mules, dead horses, dead men everywhere." Lieutenant Edward Tobie of the 1st Maine Cavalry came upon a dead Rebel soldier in the road, "with every appearance of having died from hunger and exhaustion."[174]

Remarkably, even after a week of calamities, many of the crumbling Confederate Army's surviving stalwarts—although thin, dull eyed, ragged, and covered with mud—still refused to consider themselves beaten. They clung to their faith in Lee; he would find a way out for them.[175]

෨෬

A conversation with a captured Virginia doctor from Lee's army inspired Grant to initiate a correspondence with Lee about surrendering his army. The doctor told Grant that General Ewell, a relative of the doctor's and a fellow captive, believed that the war was lost and that it was time for the Confederates to make the best peace terms possible. He said that Ewell was unsure whether Lee would surrender—and only after first consulting Jefferson Davis—but Ewell hoped that he would give up soon.

Late April 7 Grant wrote to Lee,

GENERAL: The result of the last week must convince you of the hopelessness of further resistance on the part of the Army of Northern Virginia in
this struggle. I feel that it is, and regard it as my duty to shift from myself
the responsibility of any further effusion of blood by asking of you the surrender of that portion of the C.S. Army known as the Army of Northern
Virginia.[176]

General Seth Williams, Grant's inspector general and in a more tran-
quil time Lee's adjutant at West Point, rode to the front with a flag of truce
to deliver Grant's message. About 9 p.m., Williams appeared before the
picket line in Longstreet's sector and handed Grant's letter to Colonel
Herman Perry, who carried it to the cottage where Lee was staying.[177]

Lee read Grant's letter without comment and passed it to Longstreet.
After carefully reading it, Longstreet handed it back. "Not yet," he said.[178]

By candlelight Lee composed a reply,

GENERAL: I have received your note of this date. Though not entertaining
the opinion you express of the hopelessness of further resistance on the
part of the Army of Northern Virginia, I reciprocate your desire to avoid
useless effusion of blood, and therefore, before considering your proposition, ask the terms you will offer on condition of its surrender.[179]

That night, too, there was a meeting of a group of Lee's senior officers who were convinced of the hopelessness of the situation. Lee, they
decided, should be told that, in their opinion, "the contest should be
terminated and negotiations opened for a surrender of the army." They
wanted to "lighten his responsibility" by sharing accountability for such
a momentous decision. Designated to tell Lee of the officers' consensus
opinion was General William Pendleton, Lee's artillery commander, West
Point contemporary, and friend.[180]

❧

Lee began moving early Saturday, April 8, toward Appomattox Court
House on the Lynchburg Road, and so it was not until that afternoon
that Pendleton caught up to him. He found Lee resting under a large
pine tree. Lee listened while Pendleton stated his case, and he expressed
his gratitude that the officers had wished to relieve him of some of his

burdens. Then he said, "I trust it has not come to that. We certainly have too many brave men to think of laying down our arms. They still fight with great spirit, whereas the enemy does not." Lee added that Grant would demand the army's unconditional surrender if Lee suggested that he was ready to listen to terms. "Sooner than that I am resolved to die. Indeed we must all determine to die at our posts," Lee grimly said. Chastened by Lee's steely resolve, Pendleton told Lee "every man would no doubt cheerfully meet death with him in discharge of duty."[181]

For the first time since Lee's army abandoned Petersburg and Richmond on April 2–3, no Union cavalry harried the Confederates' rear. The Rebels, in fact, were disturbed little during their march on this pleasant spring day, passing through a part of Virginia that was largely untouched by the war. George Meade exhorted II and VI Corps to march faster and catch the Confederates, but Lee's tatterdemalion columns managed to stay a few miles ahead of the Yankees all day.

The Confederate units continued to unravel, with even leathery veterans of many campaigns—and some of their senior officers—straggling, discarding their weapons, and lying down on the ground. Major John Claiborne, a surgeon inspector, encountered Colonel Henry Peyton, Lee's inspector general, as Peyton was positioning about two hundred infantrymen on a knoll. When Claiborne asked whose command this was, Peyton replied, "slowly and sadly," that it was all that remained of the 1st Virginia, the unit assigned to protect the army's left flank. Incredulous, Claiborne asked Peyton, "Does General Lee know how few of his soldiers are left, or to what extremities they are reduced?" Peyton did not think so, but he could not bring himself to tell Lee. "Choking with tears," Claiborne said to his companions, "I cannot see of what further use we can be here; let us push on ahead, maybe we can get to Johnston's army."

Lee relieved Generals Richard Anderson, George Pickett, and Bushrod Johnson of their commands, apportioning the remnants of their units to Longstreet's and Gordon's divisions. Lee never explained why he relieved the three men. He might have blamed Anderson and Johnson for the Sailor's Creek disaster, and Pickett for the defeat at Five Forks, or he might have only wanted to consolidate his fragmented divisions and corps.[182]

That day, Lee received Grant's answer to his question about surrender terms. There was just one condition that he would insist upon, Grant wrote, "that the men and officers surrendered shall be disqualified from taking up arms again against the Government of the United States until properly exchanged." Grant offered to meet with Lee anywhere that he wished to arrange his army's surrender.[183]

After sending this message and informing Sheridan of Lee's request for terms, Grant said, "I think Lee will surrender today. . . . We will push him until terms are agreed upon."[184]

Although Lee's foot-weary infantrymen might have been grateful for the respite from Sheridan's flying cavalry attacks, Fitzhugh Lee, whose job was to protect the column with his cavalry, was suspicious. Every day since leaving Petersburg, the Union Cavalry Corps had struck the Confederates' flanks and rear—with spectacular results at Sailor's Creek two days earlier. Now Sheridan had disappeared.

Fitz Lee suspected that Sheridan was riding to Appomattox Station to intercept the Confederates' supplies, and that he was planning to throw his troopers across the path of Lee's army. He dispatched scouts to locate Sheridan. They found the Cavalry Corps on the Southside Railroad at Pamplin Station adjacent to Prince Edward Court House, about fifteen miles from Appomattox Station. Fitz Lee inexplicably concluded that the Union cavalry, which covered six miles per hour on average, would not reach Appomattox until the next day. Lee's army, he believed, would undoubtedly get there first.[185]

Near Prince Edward Court House, the energetic Sheridan stopped to speak to a middle-aged Southern gentleman, who was dressed rather flamboyantly in a swallowtail coat, vest, pantaloons, and morocco slippers. Sitting down on the step of the man's large home, Sheridan lit a cigar and asked him whether Lee's troops had passed by. The man replied with a patriotic Confederate tirade and refused to answer Sheridan's question.

Sheridan gave a soft whistle and inquired how far away Buffalo Creek was. The man said he did not know.

"The devil you don't," Sheridan said. He asked the man how long he had lived there.

All his life, he replied.

"Very well, sir," said Sheridan. "It's time you did know." He ordered a captain to put the man under guard and, when the army moved, to walk him down to Buffalo Creek "and show it to him." The man was led away in his Moroccan slippers, shooting Sheridan "a savage glare," and was compelled to walk the five miles to the creek.[186]

The Cavalry Corps departed from Prince Edward Court House that afternoon after feeding the horses and resting. Sheridan's column traveled at route step, the horses having acquired a "long, slinging walk" during the Cavalry Corps's many campaigns. At this pace "10,000 cavalry [could march] on one road from daylight to dark, and never change the gait in a single regiment, and never turn a hair," wrote Lieutenant Colonel Frederick Newhall, Sheridan's aide.[187]

⁂

As the cavalry rode on, one of Major Harry Young's top scouts, Sergeant James White, brought Sheridan welcome intelligence: four railroad trains, laden with provisions from Lynchburg, were stopped at Appomattox Station, awaiting Lee's army. These were the rations requested in the intercepted Rebel telegram that White, at Sheridan's direction, had forwarded to Lynchburg. Clad in Confederate gray, as were all of Young's scouts, White had encountered the trains west of Appomattox Station. Brandishing a copy of the intercepted ration order, White told the railroad crews to run their trains into the station—he did not say this would make their capture easier for Sheridan's approaching troopers.[188]

Late in the afternoon, Custer's division, at the head of Sheridan's column, reached the outskirts of Appomattox Station, five miles southwest of Appomattox Court House. The four trains were unguarded, and Lee's army was miles northeast of the village.

To ensure that the railroad crews, when attacked, could not quickly run the trains back to Lynchburg, Custer sent two of his regiments around the station to tear up the tracks west of it. When he saw a plume of smoke in the sky from the burning crossties, Custer swooped down on the station with the rest of his troopers and captured the trains. They were packed with canned goods, crackers, quinine, canteens, and other provisions. Some cavalrymen who had been railroad engineers in civilian life began running three of the trains around the station, ringing their bells and blowing their whistles, while their comrades burned the fourth train. The whistles' "unearthly screeching" got on Sheridan's nerves, "and I was on the point of ordering the [rest of the] cars burned." The engineers grew tired of their amusement before that happened, however, and drove the three trains eastward to the infantry column following Sheridan's troopers. "It is impossible to overestimate the value of this day's work," Union cavalry General Wesley Merritt reported. "The enemy's supplies were taken, as it were, out of their mouths."[189]

Custer's cavalrymen repelled Confederate infantry and cavalry units that had been sent—too late—to protect the trains. The chaotic battle raged for hours in the woods. The Union troopers then probed toward the Lynchburg Road west of Appomattox Court House, and they stumbled upon Lee's reserve artillery, commanded by General Reuben Lindsay Walker. The sixty guns had been sent ahead of Lee's army, and were parked a couple of miles beyond Appomattox Court House.

Around dusk, Custer's troopers burst from the woods, surprising the artillerists in their camp. The Rebels fought back with muskets and their cannons. The gunfire flared and crashed through the woods and could be seen and heard from Lee's camps east of Appomattox village. The artillerists drove off the dismounted troopers' repeated charges long enough to withdraw most of their guns, but twenty-five were captured, along with a hospital train and some wagons.

General William Pendleton, rebuffed by Lee earlier that day when he broached the sensitive subject of surrender, had ridden out from Lee's camp to meet with Walker at his bivouac. Pendleton arrived just as the shooting began; he was present during most of the fierce skirmish.

Riding back toward Lee's camps, Pendleton was nearly captured by Sheridan's cavalrymen, who came thundering down the Lynchburg Road, "firing upon everything" as they pursued Walker's artillery train. Pendleton spurred his horse over a fence into a clump of bushes and, avoiding the road, reached Appomattox village. Advancing Confederate infantry dispersed the Union cavalry at the village outskirts.[190]

A bright moon rose that night, and Lee's army then saw a chilling sight. To the west, to the east, and to the south the skies glowed orange with the campfires of tens of thousands of Union troops. Only in the north was the sky black. The portentous glow graphically demonstrated that the Army of Northern Virginia was nearly surrounded.[191]

It was a magnificent achievement by Sheridan and his hard-riding troopers: they had boxed in Lee's army, blocking the road to Lynchburg. "Although Sheridan had been marching all day, his troops moved with alacrity and without any straggling," wrote Grant. "Nothing seemed to fatigue them. They were ready to move without rations and travel without rest until the end."

The same could be said for the infantrymen of Edward Ord's Army of the James—XXIV Corps and two brigades of black troops from XXV Corps—and Charles Griffin's V Corps. They had struggled all day to keep up with Sheridan's mounted troopers, covering twenty-nine miles before collapsing beside the road that night. In a note to XXIV Corps's commander, General John Gibbon, recounting the Cavalry Corps's successes at Appomattox Station, Sheridan closed by saying, "If it is possible to push on your troops we may have handsome results in the morning."[192]

⁂

Lee stalled for time to break out of the trap enveloping him. Responding to Grant's letter that Lee's surrender was an essential condition of peace and expressing his willingness to meet, Lee parsed and equivocated. He never intended to propose his army's surrender, Lee wrote, only to learn Grant's conditions. "To be frank, I do not think the emergency has arisen to call for the surrender of this army." If Grant wished to discuss terms for "the restoration of peace," Lee would meet him at 10 a.m. the next day, Sunday, April 9, between the armies' picket lines. But if the plan forming in Lee's mind succeeded, at the hour of his proposed assignation with Grant, Lee and his army would be marching toward Lynchburg.[193]

The citizens of Appomattox Court House were shocked by the Confederates' ragged appearance. Their very attire—or lack of it—signified to them an army in its death throes. They "were, many of them, shirtless, hatless, and barefooted," observed one resident. "A sadder looking lot of men I never saw."[194]

That night, Lee summoned his senior generals to his spartan bivouac east of Appomattox Court House. "There was no tent there, no tables, no chairs, and no camp-stools. On blankets spread upon the ground or on saddles at the roots of the trees, we sat around the great commander," wrote John Gordon, who was joined by Fitz Lee and Longstreet. Lee read aloud the letters he had exchanged with Grant. Afterward, the generals proposed a plan to force their way westward through Grant's lines. It was quixotic at best, for the Rebels were nearly surrounded and heavily outnumbered.

The cavalry would lead the assault, beginning at 1 a.m. on April 9. Fitz Lee was given wide latitude on when to begin the movement, depending on circumstances. Gordon's Second Corps would follow Fitz Lee. Gordon's men would wheel to the left to protect the passage of the wagon train, pared to two artillery battalions and ammunition wagons. Longstreet would close up behind the wagons in a defensive line.

If they broke through, "the utmost that could be hoped for was that we might reach the mountains of Virginia and Tennessee with a remnant of the army and ultimately join General Johnston," wrote Gordon. In that event, Lee and Johnston would continue the war until the Union grew weary of fighting and granted the South sovereignty. In their hearts Lee and his generals knew that, with the army starving, broken down, and demoralized, this was improbable. Addressing the likelihood that the next morning's "forlorn hope" would fail, Lee "stood calmly facing and discussing the long-dreaded inevitable"—surrender.[195]

About 1 a.m., General Pendleton reached Lee's bivouac after his harrowing experience west of Appomattox Court House. To his surprise, Pendleton found Lee "dressed in his neatest style, new uniform, snowy linen, etc." He wore embroidered gauntlets, a ceremonial sword that had been presented to him by Virginia's ladies, and a red silk sash. When Lee saw Pendleton's reaction to his attire, he explained, "I have probably to be General Grant's prisoner, and thought I must make my best appearance."

Lee declined the poor breakfast prepared by his aides, who had slept on the ground, as had Lee, using coats for blankets and saddles for pillows. For their repast they boiled water in a shaving tin and added corn meal. "Each man in his turn, according to rank and seniority, made a can of corn meal gruel, and was allowed to keep the can until the gruel became cool enough to drink," wrote Colonel Charles Marshall, Lee's military historian. "This was our last meal in the Confederacy. Our next was taken in the United States."[196]

Throughout the night the Confederates heard large numbers of enemy troops moving along their lines. Heavy early-morning ground fog made it impossible for Fitz Lee's cavalrymen to see what lay in their path west of the village. Fitz Lee elected to wait until visibility improved. At 5 a.m., his twenty-four hundred cavalrymen advanced.

Chaplain Wiatt and the 26th Virginia, now attached to Gordon's corps, had marched into Appomattox Court House when Walker's artillerymen were under attack. Although drawn up into a battle line, the regiment was never ordered into action. After awhile the exhausted men lay down and slept. At daybreak on this Palm Sunday, the Virginians were rousted and ordered forward.[197]

Sheridan and his staff spent the night in a small frame house south of Appomattox Station, too keyed up to sleep, even though they had had little rest during the past eight days. "Everybody was jubilant," observed a Sheridan staff officer, because of rumors that Lee was going to surrender. Sheridan, however, nervously paced the floor, worrying that Generals Ord and Gibbon from the Army of the James would not reach him in time with their XXIV and XXV Corps columns—although those units in fact were marching through the night to join him.

Without infantry support, Sheridan knew that his cavalry alone could not hold Lee's infantrymen for long. Because he couldn't very well hurry troops who were already straining to reach him, Sheridan, wanting to do something, sent messages to V Corps, which was behind Ord's and Gibbon's divisions. One dispatch reached General Joshua Chamberlain, the V Corps brigade commander whom Sheridan had praised at Five Forks when he saw him leading his troops from the front. "If you can possibly push your infantry up here tonight, we will have great results in the morning," Sheridan wrote.

Chamberlain promptly turned out his two brigades, which had collapsed in exhaustion a few hours earlier along the road to Appomattox Station. They rose, "sleepless, supperless, breakfastless, sore-footed, stiff-jointed, senses-benumbed," and double-timed toward Appomattox alongside Ord's Army of the James troops, taking their turns in the fields and on the road, with "[General William] Birney's black men [from XXV Corps] abreast with us, pressing forward to save the white man's country."[198]

Grant and his staff were staying in a large farmhouse twenty miles east of Appomattox village when the general-in-chief received Lee's message proposing that they meet at 10 a.m. the next day, Palm Sunday. After General John Rawlins, Grant's chief of staff, read it aloud, Rawlins angrily asserted that Lee was trying to "entrap us" into a peace agreement more far-reaching than his army's surrender. It was a ploy to buy time and receive better terms, Rawlins said, urging Grant to reject Lee's request. Grant concurred, observing, "It looks as if Lee still means to fight." In his reply to Lee, Grant wrote, "I have no authority to treat on the subject of peace; the meeting proposed for 10 a.m. today could lead to no good." He recommended that Lee's men lay down their arms.[199]

Grant was afflicted with one of his pounding migraine headaches, a result of stress and lack of sleep; he had tried the usual home treatments—a hot foot bath and mustard plasters on his wrists and the back of his neck—but the headache had not gone away. The piano playing and singing by his staff officers downstairs had made it worse; the tone-deaf Grant asked them to stop.

A dispatch from Sheridan arrived at Grant's headquarters at 4:20 a.m. By that time Sheridan's Cavalry Corps had been in ranks and under arms, facing east, for twenty minutes. "If General Gibbon and the Fifth Corps can get up to-night we will perhaps finish the job in the morning. I do not think Lee means to surrender until compelled to do so," wrote Sheridan.[200]

Just before sunup, Ord, exhausted from his army's all-night march, gave Sheridan the news that he had so hoped for: Ord's Army of the James and Griffin's V Corps were just two miles away.[201]

But they could already hear firing from Sheridan's front. The Cavalry Corps, which had thrown up fieldworks in Lee's path during the night, need only delay Lee's army until Ord's and Griffin's thirty-five thousand infantrymen took up positions beside and behind it. To the east II and VI Corps's infantry forces were already moving to envelop the Confederate rear, guarded by Longstreet's corps, and its flanks. With Sheridan's cavalry, the Union Army had eighty thousand troops in the vicinity of Appomattox village—to Lee's fifteen thousand. Only a miracle could save Lee's army.

Lieutenant J. F. J. Caldwell of the 1st South Carolina described the ramshackle Confederate formations that assembled for battle in the dim early-morning light. The soldiers' "faces were haggered [sic], their steps slow and unsteady. Bare skeletons of old organizations remained, and these tottered along at wide intervals." About 250 men closed up with the rear of Caldwell's brigade and lay down. Someone asked whose regiment it was. "With a strange smile" a soldier replied that it was "[General Joseph] Kershaw's division! One brigade in our corps numbered eight men."[202]

Fitz Lee's cavalry and Gordon's small infantry corps, followed by Longstreet's artillery, marched through Appomattox village and advanced on the breastworks blocking the Lynchburg Road that were manned by Custer's and Thomas Devin's dismounted troopers.

The Rebel yell rang out over a contested battlefield for the last time as "the footsore and starving men of my command with a spirit worthy of the best days of Lee's army" attacked, wrote Gordon. "We did just what we had always done before; raised a shout and made a dash at Sheridan's line," said Sergeant Cyrus Watson of the 45th North Carolina. Fitz Lee's men swept around the Union left. The Rebel troopers drove Sheridan's men from their breastworks, "shooting the gunners and support down with our Colt Navies" and capturing two guns, wrote Virginia cavalryman John Bouldin.[203]

From atop a small rise behind his men, Sheridan sat on his coal-black warhorse, Rienzi, watching the action. Observing a heavy line of infantry—Longstreet's corps—in the village streets behind the Confederate wagons, he decided "it would be unwise to offer more resistance than that necessary to give Ord time to form." He ordered Devin and Custer to fall back to the right, to make room for Ord's men, who at that moment were filtering into the woods behind Sheridan. George Crook's and Ranald Mackenzie's cavalry divisions on Sheridan's left were instructed to hold their ground, but to not needlessly sacrifice men.[204]

As the Union cavalry pulled back, the advancing Confederates keened their high-pitched foxhunters' cry, believing they might yet break out of Grant's trap.

But then the Rebels' hope vanished; as the Cavalry Corps divisions withdrew, it was like a curtain opening. Ten thousand men from Ord's Army of the James emerged from the woods behind Sheridan's cavalrymen and stood shoulder to shoulder facing Gordon's right flank. Ord's divisions had accomplished the remarkable feat of marching more than 110 miles in four days, in the daytime and in the nighttime, in the heat and in the rain, often without food or rest.

More bluecoat infantrymen appeared in front of Gordon's and Fitz Lee's men every minute: from the XXIV and XXV Corps, from Griffin's

V Corps. Soon thirty thousand troops, ranked three deep, stretched along a three-mile line behind Sheridan. "The undulating lines of the infantry, now rising to the crest of a knoll, now dipping into a valley or ravine, pressed on grandly across the open," wrote Sheridan aide Frederick Newhall. To the east, II and VI Corps began pressing Longstreet's corps, the Confederate rearguard behind Gordon's men.[205]

Joshua Chamberlain's two brigades were in the middle of the V Corps column when a Sheridan staff officer rode up. Sheridan wanted Chamberlain and his brigades to leave the column—without waiting for orders through regular channels—and to march at once to Sheridan's support. Chamberlain and his men raced through the woods, emerging at the edge of a smoky field where they saw Sheridan's swallow-tailed red-and-white battle flag.

As Chamberlain approached Sheridan, mounted on Rienzi, both man and horse seemed, to Chamberlain, to possess the same "unearthly shade of darkness, terrible to look upon, as if masking some unknown powers." Before him, Gordon's men were attacking Devin's division. With "a dark smile and impetuous gesture," Sheridan indicated that Chamberlain's brigades should support Devin. Sheridan rode off to his cavalry, "smiting his hands together" and crying, "Now smash 'em, I tell you, smash 'em!"[206]

When Gordon's men saw the massed Union infantry blocking the road, the cheering died on their lips, and they stopped. The ranked bluecoats began advancing toward them. Union cavalry suddenly rode out to drive a wedge between Gordon and Longstreet; Gordon detached a brigade to intercept them. Daunted by the enemy's massive numbers, Gordon's Confederates reflexively pulled back to a ridge near the village to await developments. "A death-like stillness prevailed," wrote Captain W. T. Hill of the Texas Brigade. "Faces grew grave and serious, and men when they talked at all spoke in whispers."[207]

About 8 a.m. Lee aide Charles Venable galloped up to Gordon to find out whether he was going to be able to break out. Gordon replied, "Tell General Lee, I have fought my corps to a frazzle and I fear I can do nothing unless I am heavily supported by Longstreet's corps." Gordon's men continued fighting, but without hope now.[208]

When Venable brought him Gordon's pessimistic appraisal, Lee knew that if his most aggressive field commander could do nothing, it was over. He said, "Then there is nothing left me but to go and see General Grant, and I would rather die a thousand deaths." Lee's aides reacted with "passionate grief, many were the wild words which we spoke as we stood around him." One officer cried, "Oh, general, what will history say of the surrender of the army in the field?" People would say "hard things of us," not understanding that they had been overwhelmed by numbers, Lee said, but the question was, "Is it right to surrender this army? If it is right, then *I* will take *all* the responsibility."[209]

For a moment Lee gazed over the field, where the fog was now lifting, and said with emotion, "How easily I could be rid of this and be at rest! I have only to ride along the line and all will be over." His fit of darkness passed, and with a deep sigh Lee added. "But it is our duty to live. What will become of the women and children of the South if we are not here to protect them?"[210]

Lee summoned Longstreet from his corps's rearguard. Longstreet brought with him his artillery commander, General Edward Porter Alexander, and Mahone. Holding back Meade's II and VI Corps was "all the work that the rear-guard could do," Longstreet said. He could spare no one to aid Gordon.

Lee asked Longstreet what he should do. "I asked if the bloody sacrifice of his army could in any way help the cause in other quarters," Longstreet wrote. Lee did not think so. "Your situation speaks for itself," Longstreet replied. Mahone agreed. A wispy man once described as "a mere atom with little flesh," Mahone was shivering, but he made it clear that it was from the morning chill and not fear.[211]

Alexander told Lee that his men wanted to cut their way out, but Lee said he did not have enough men who could still fight. Alexander argued that rather than surrender, it would be better to allow the men to make their way under arms to their home states. Lee asked how many could get away. Perhaps two-thirds, said Alexander. "We would be like rabbits and partridges in the bushes, and they could not scatter to follow us."

Estimating that he had fifteen thousand men in all—in reality, there were only about ten thousand Confederates under arms, eight thousand of them infantry—Lee said that two-thirds of that number scattered among the states was too small a force to accomplish anything. Moreover, he said, a guerrilla war would demoralize the South even further. "If I took your advice, the men would be without rations and under no control of officers," said Lee. "They would be compelled to rob and steal in order to live. They would become mere bands of marauders, and the enemy's cavalry would pursue them and overrun many wide sections they may never have occasion to visit." It would take years for the South to recover, he said.

Alexander had no response to Lee's perceptive analysis. "He [Lee] had answered my suggestion from a plane so far above it, that I was ashamed of having made it," Alexander wrote.[212]

Still believing that he was to meet Grant at 10 a.m. between the armies' lines, Lee rode to the rear with Walter Taylor and Charles Marshall, his adjutant and military secretary, and Sergeant George Tucker, the courier who was with A. P. Hill when he was killed and who now served Lee. Tucker bore a white handkerchief on a stick—a flag of truce—as the party rode eastward toward the Union lines. They stopped when they saw Yankee skirmishers.

A staff officer of General Humphreys and an orderly with a white flag rode toward them. The officer knew nothing about a meeting, but he had a letter for Lee. It was Grant's reply to Lee's proposal that they meet: Grant had no authority to discuss peace terms; Lee's men must simply lay down their arms and "save thousands of human lives, and hundreds of millions of property not yet destroyed."

Lee dictated a letter to be sent to Grant stating that he was now ready to discuss unconditional surrender "at such time and place as you may designate." Meade, who was suffering from chills and fever in a nearby ambulance, passed the message on to Grant, who was on his way to see Sheridan on the other side of Appomattox Court House. When Meade's officer overtook Grant, shortly before noon, the general-in-chief dismounted and read it.

"When the officer reached me, I was still suffering from the sick headache; but the instant I saw the contents of the note I was cured." Grant rapidly scratched out a reply, "I am writing this about four miles west of Walker's Church, and will push forward to the front for the purpose of meeting you. Notice sent to me on this road where you wish the interview to take place will meet me." He gave the note to Colonel Orville Babcock, his aide, to carry to Lee. Babcock rode to Sheridan's lines, believing that he could reach Lee quicker from that direction.

Meade had not opened Lee's note to Grant, but had only forwarded it, unread. When Colonel Marshall, under another flag of truce, requested a ceasefire while the two generals met, Meade bristled. "Hey! What!" he barked. "I have no sort of authority to grant such suspension.... Advance your skirmishers, Humphreys, and bring up your troops! We will pitch into them at once!" After considerable persuasion by his staff, Meade agreed to wait before resuming his attack.[213]

◈

Just as Sheridan was poised to unleash an attack by Devin's and Custer's cavalry divisions, supported by Chamberlain's brigades, a Confederate officer approached his lines under a white flag. The Union advance stopped.[214]

About that time, Fitz Lee's cavalrymen were quietly slipping away from the battlefield west of Appomattox Court House and riding away to the northwest. Gordon had agreed to notify Fitz Lee if enemy infantry blocked his corps's advance—so that the Rebel cavalry could escape. Gordon gave the signal, and the troopers of Generals Rooney Lee, Thomas Rosser and Thomas Munford scattered to their homes, "subject to reassembling for a continuation of the struggle," wrote Fitz Lee. He feared that Grant's men would seize their horses, which were the Rebel cavalrymen's personal property.[215]

The Union Cavalry Corps's warrior general fumed at the prospect of a truce. "Everybody seemed acquiescent and for the moment cheerful—except Sheridan. He does not like the cessation of hostilities, and does not conceal his opinion," wrote Chamberlain. Sheridan "thinks we should have banged right in and settled all questions without asking them."

Colonel Babcock, bearing Grant's latest note to Lee through Sheridan's lines, stopped to speak with Sheridan, pacing and manifestly unhappy with the ceasefire. "Damn them, I wish they had held out an hour longer and I would have whipped hell out of them." Then Lieutenant Colonel Adam Badeau of Grant's staff rode up, and Sheridan bombarded him with questions: "What do you think? What do you know? Is it a trick? Is he negotiating with Grant? I've got 'em—I've got 'em like that," he declared, thrusting a clenched fist into the air.[216]

Babcock rode on, and found Lee resting under an apple tree alongside the road. After Lee read Grant's message, he and two aides saddled their horses and began riding up the hill to Appomattox Court House.

Although it was quiet east of Appomattox village, to the west the fighting did not so easily die down, and Sheridan was nearly shot. He was fired on while riding toward the Confederate line to meet with Gordon. Sheridan waved his hat and shouted, "Truce!" but it made no difference. The gunfire came from General Martin Gary's South Carolina cavalry brigade, which had just joined Gordon's men and was unaware of the truce. To avoid getting shot, Sheridan rode down into a swale until he was out of range.

As Sheridan neared Gordon's lines, some Confederates leveled their muskets at him, but their officers stopped them from firing. A Rebel tried to take Sheridan's flag, and when Sheridan's sergeant drew his saber to "cut the man down," Sheridan ordered him not to. Sheridan sent a staff officer to Gordon to demand an explanation. Gordon and General Cadmus Wilcox invited Sheridan to join them, and he rode on. There was more firing—Gary's men again, this time shooting at cavalrymen led by Generals Custer and Wesley Merritt. Sheridan turned to Gordon and asked, "What does this mean, General Gordon?" Gordon said it appeared that his order to cease firing had not reached this unit, but he would send someone to stop it. Sheridan shrugged impatiently. "Oh, let them fight it out," he said.

Sheridan then suggested that Gordon send a staff officer to inform Gary of the truce, but Gordon had none to send. Sheridan volunteered Lieutenant Vanderbilt Allen for the dangerous assignment. When Allen reached Gary's line, the combative Gary refused to accept any orders from a Yankee. "I don't care for white flags; South Carolinians never surrender," he declared. Just as Allen was about to be made a prisoner, Confederate Colonel W. W. Blackford, an engineer dispatched by Gordon, rode up and told Gary that the army had surrendered. "He quivered as if he had been shot," wrote Blackford. Gary replied, "I'll be damned if I surrender"—although he later did, along with his men.[217]

Amid the contretemps with Gary, Sheridan and Gordon conversed. Sheridan reminded Gordon that they had met in the Shenandoah Valley— on the battlefield at Winchester and Cedar Creek. "I had the pleasure of receiving some artillery from your Government, consigned to me through your commander, General Early." Gordon replied that although that was true, "I have this morning received from your government artillery consigned to me through General Sheridan," referring to the two artillery pieces the Rebels had captured that morning.

Gordon later said that Sheridan was never discourteous, but his conversation and bearing displeased him. "There was an absence of that delicacy and consideration which was exhibited by other Union officers." Neither was Sheridan especially happy about his encounter with Gordon and his men; he dashed off notes to Lee protesting the ceasefire violations by Gary's men.[218]

The flamboyant Custer, with his red kerchief and flowing locks, had confronted Gordon before Sheridan met with him, and had demanded Gordon's unconditional surrender. If he refused, Custer warned him, the Union army "can annihilate your command in an hour." Unflustered, Gordon refused, explaining that Lee had requested a truce. If Sheridan resumed hostilities, said Gordon, he would be responsible for any additional bloodshed.[219]

Having no answer to that, Custer asked to see Longstreet. The request was highly unusual, but no more unusual than the present circumstances. Gordon ordered a staff officer to take Custer to Longstreet.

Longstreet was waiting for Lee to return from the meeting with Grant that had not materialized when Custer rode up. In a loud voice, Custer insisted that Longstreet surrender to him. Longstreet replied that Lee was already in communication with Grant and, furthermore, that he would not recognize the demands of a subordinate Union officer.

Custer said that he and Sheridan that day were operating independently of Grant. "Unless you surrender at once, we will destroy you."

On this day of catastrophes, Longstreet was in no mood to hear ultimatums from enemy subordinate officers. He upbraided Custer for trampling on military courtesy—and if he did it again, Longstreet warned, Custer's ignorance would not save him. "Now, go and act as you and Sheridan choose and I will teach you a lesson you won't forget! Now go!" Without another word, Custer rode away.[220]

⁂

Lee had been waiting for half an hour when Grant arrived at their meeting place about 1:30 p.m. It was a spacious, two-story brick home in the middle of Appomattox Court House—in fact, the finest home in town, owned by Major Wilmer McLean, who had prospered in the wartime sugar market. Lee, Colonel Marshall, Colonel Babcock from Grant's staff, and the orderly, Sergeant Tucker, had ridden into the village looking for a suitable place for the conference. Lee and Babcock had waited while Marshall and Tucker canvassed the town. McLean had first shown them a sitting room in another home, but it was too small. McLean had then volunteered the large parlor of his own home.

It was the strangest of coincidences. McLean and his family had lived in the house since 1863. In this out-of-the-way corner of Virginia, McLean was certain that the fighting would remain safely distant. But in one of the Civil War's great ironies, the war had found McLean, just as it had in July 1861 during the first major battle, at Manassas. Then, Confederate General P. G. T. Beauregard had made his headquarters in the McLean farmhouse near Bull Run, and Union artillerists had put a shell through the house.[221]

At the edge of town, Grant and his staff encountered Sheridan, who was with a group of dismounted officers. "No one could look at Sheridan at such a moment," wrote Lieutenant Colonel Horace Porter, "without a sentiment of undisguised admiration"—for he, more than any one man in the army, was responsible for bringing Lee to bay. Grant greeted his warrior general with, "How are you, Sheridan?" Sheridan replied, "First-rate, thank you. How are you?" Grant nodded in reply and pointed up the road. "Is Lee over there?" he asked. "Yes," answered Sheridan, "he is in that brick house, waiting to surrender to you." "Well, then, we'll go over," said Grant.[222]

Grant rode up to the McLean home with a dozen staff officers and Generals Sheridan and Ord. Grant's assistant adjutant general, Colonel Theodore Bowers, and Lieutenant Colonel Ely Parker accompanied Grant into the McLean parlor, where Babcock, Marshall, and Lee waited; the others remained in the hallway or on the porch.[223]

Lee rose and shook hands with Grant. Tall, commanding, and wearing his clean dress uniform with a sash and ceremonial sword, the Confederate general made a striking contrast to the shorter, slighter Grant, clad in a private's uniform flecked with mud from his sixteen-mile ride to the village. Grant's only mark of rank was his lieutenant general's shoulder straps.

After they sat down Babcock slipped away to invite the other Union officers into the parlor, where they stood quietly along the walls. Grant told Lee he remembered their meeting during the Mexican War. Lee said he knew that they had met, but he could not remember what Grant looked like then. This might have been because Grant was clean shaven in Mexico but now had a dark, heavy beard. Grant and Lee reminisced about that distant war until Lee brought Grant back to the present one.[224]

The surrender terms, Grant said, would be what he had previously outlined: Confederates who surrendered would be paroled, allowed to go home, and disqualified from taking up arms until they had been exchanged. Arms, ammunition, and supplies would be handed over to the Union Army.

Lee said those terms were acceptable, and he asked Grant to put them in writing. Grant lit a pipe and wrote them out in pencil. When he had finished, he went over the draft with Colonel Parker, who made minor editing changes. Grant's written terms also permitted officers to keep their horses and sidearms, a subject that Grant and Lee had never discussed.[225]

Lee drew a pair of steel-rimmed spectacles from his pocket, put them on, and read what Grant had written. He inquired whether Rebel cavalrymen and artillerists, who also owned their army horses, might also be allowed to retain them. Grant said his terms did not allow it, and he would not change them. But he said any man who claimed to own a horse or mule could keep it and "take the animals home with them to work their little farms." Lee appeared relieved. "This will have the best possible effect upon the men. It will be very gratifying and will do much toward conciliating our people."[226]

Lee handed the draft to Colonel Bowers to copy in ink. But Bowers, who was quite nervous and did not think he had a steady enough hand, passed it to Parker. With an inkstand supplied by Colonel Marshall, Parker copied out Grant's terms. Lee told Marshall to draft an acceptance letter:

GENERAL: I have received your letter of this date containing the terms of the surrender of the Army of Northern Virginia as proposed by you. As they are substantially the same as those expressed in your letter of the 8th inst., they are accepted. I will proceed to designate the proper officer to carry the stipulations into effect.[227]

While copies were being made, Grant introduced Lee to the other officers in the room. Lee showed little emotion during the introductions, until he was presented with Colonel Parker. From Parker's swarthy features,
Lee correctly surmised that he was of American Indian lineage.

Parker was a Seneca; a trained lawyer, although barred from practicing
law because of his Native American heritage; a civil engineer; and the last
Grand Sachem of the Iroquois League of the Five Nations. He had become friends with Grant before the war when he helped build a customs
house and hospital in Galena, Illinois, where Grant was working in his
brothers' leather-goods store.

Lee, Parker later wrote, extended his hand to him and said, "I am glad
to see one real American here." Parker said that he replied, "We are all
real Americans."[228]

There were other, minor matters to settle. Lee's army had Union prisoners that Lee said would be returned to Grant's army. Lee's men had no
food, but he expected several trainloads from Lynchburg to reach Appomattox Station at any hour—the same four trains that Sheridan's men had
captured the previous day. "When they arrive I should be glad to have the
present wants of my men supplied from them," said Lee.

The Union officers in the parlor all looked at Sheridan. Grant asked
Sheridan to send Lee the rations that he needed; they decided that
twenty-five thousand rations containing fresh beef, salt, hard bread, coffee, and sugar would be sufficient.[229]

Sheridan approached Lee and asked him for the two notes of protest
that he had sent Lee that morning after being fired upon by Gary's men;
Sheridan had not had an opportunity to make copies. Lee handed the
notes to Sheridan. "I am sorry," Lee said. "It is probable that my cavalry
at that point of the line did not fully understand the agreement."[230]

Two hours after it began, the meeting was over. Lee emerged from the
McLean parlor onto the porch. The Union officers waiting there sprang
to their feet and raised their hands in a military salute. Lee returned it
and then stood on the top of the steps, gazing down the small valley. The
Union officers now had an opportunity to observe close up the Confederate chieftain who had frustrated the Army of the Potomac for nearly a
year. They noted Lee's sturdy physique, his bronze cheeks, his aura of
dignity, and that he was "sad-eyed and weary."

Lee mechanically pulled on his gauntlets, "smiting his gloved hands into each other several times after doing so, evidently oblivious to his surroundings," observed Lieutenant Colonel George Forsyth, a Sheridan aide. Lee ordered Sergeant Tucker to bring Traveller around, and mounted the gray horse. As he settled into the saddle, "there broke unguardedly from his lips a long, low, deep sigh, almost a groan in its intensity, while the flush on his neck and face seemed, if possible, to take on a still deeper hue." Grant emerged from the house and touched his hat brim in salute to Lee, who responded in kind as he passed through the yard and went to his army, his "arrival there being announced to us by cheering."[231]

Grant rode away from the McLean house in silence, his face betraying no emotion. "If he was very much pleased by the surrender of Lee, nothing in his air or manner indicated it," wrote Lieutenant Colonel Frederick Newhall, Sheridan's adjutant general.[232]

Grant later confessed that he was "sad and depressed. I felt like anything rather than rejoicing at the downfall of a foe who had fought so long and valiantly," he wrote, "and had suffered so much for a cause, though that cause was, I believe, one of the worst for which a people ever fought."[233]

On the ride back to the army's headquarters, an aide reminded Grant that he had not yet informed the government in Washington of Lee's surrender. Grant dismounted, sat down on a large rock, and asked for pencil and paper. After noting the time, 4:30 p.m., he wrote:

Hon. E.M. Stanton
Secretary of War
Washington

General Lee surrendered the Army of Northern Virginia this afternoon on terms proposed by myself. The accompanying additional correspondence will show the conditions fully. U.S. Grant, Lieut.-General.[234]

The message was taken to a nearby telegraph station for transmission while Grant and his officers resumed their ride. Hearing cannon fire along the Union lines celebrating Lee's surrender, Grant ordered it stopped. "The war is over; the rebels are our countrymen again," he said, "and the best sign of rejoicing after the victory will be to abstain from all demonstrations in the field."

Grant may have squelched loud, overt demonstrations, but there were quiet exhibitions of joy and thanksgiving up and down the Union lines. The 121st Pennsylvania erupted in rejoicing when the news reached it. "Hats, clothing, boots, anything that could be laid hold of, were sent flying through the air, that at times was almost black with missiles." "Stern officers who have never failed on the bloody field of battle, wept like children, for joy," wrote Major Holman Melcher of the 20th Maine. "I cried and laughed by turns," wrote Lieutenant Colonel Elisha Rhodes of the 2nd Rhode Island. "I never was so happy in my life." Cheer after cheer arose from the Union lines. "Speeches were made, songs were sung, the various bands of the army discoursed patriotic and national airs," wrote a soldier from the 17th Maine.[235]

After the commanding generals had gone, furious bidding began by the Union officers who remained at the McLean home for the parlor furniture. Sheridan handed McLean two $10 gold pieces as payment for the table on which Grant had drafted the surrender terms; he made a gift of it to Custer's wife, Libbie, who had befriended Sheridan during a dance the previous July at City Point. "Permit me to say, Madam," Sheridan wrote, "that there is scarcely an individual in our service who has contributed more to bring this [the surrender] about than your very gallant husband." Custer galloped back to camp with the table on his shoulder.

Ord paid $40 for the marble-topped table where Lee had sat, later presenting it to Mrs. Grant, who insisted that it be given to Mrs. Ord. After the officers departed with their choice treasures, Union soldiers, also seeking relics, descended on the home. "Cane bottomed chairs were ruthlessly cut to pieces; the cane splits broken into pieces a few inches long, and parceled out among those who swarmed around," wrote newspaper correspondent Sylvanus Cadwallader. "Haircloth upholstery was cut from chairs, and sofas were also cut into strips and patches and carried away." When the frenzy ended, the room was practically bare.[236]

Lee returned to the apple grove where Babcock had found him a few hours earlier, before the meeting with Grant. He paced back and forth "like a caged lion," wrote Colonel W. W. Blackford. "General Lee seemed to be in one of his savage moods, and when these moods were on him, it was safer to keep out of the way." Visitors arrived, one after another; they were Northern men whom Lee had known before the war. His staff made the introductions, but Lee shook no one's hand. "They would remove their hats entirely and stand bareheaded during the interview, while General Lee sometimes gave a scant touch to his hat in return and sometimes did not even do that." When he finally mounted Traveller and started for his headquarters, souvenir hunters swarmed the grove and carved up the apple tree where Babcock had found Lee resting. Chips sold briskly for $5 and $10 apiece.[237]

When Lee's men saw their general-in-chief approaching, they formed solid ranks along both sides of the road, the lines extending all the way to the general's headquarters. As they cheered him loudly, they asked disbelievingly whether the army had been surrendered. Yes, he replied, yes. The soldiers cursed, roared, and wept in their despair, and they crowded around Lee and Traveller to say their good-byes. Tears streamed down Lee's cheeks as he passed along the road, hat in hand, bowing his acknowledgments, while Traveller tossed his head. "Grim bearded men threw themselves on the ground, covered their faces with their hands and wept like children. Officers of all ranks made no attempt to conceal their feelings, but sat on their horses and cried aloud," wrote Blackford.[238]

In the Rebel camps, soldiers walked about in a daze of incredulity. "We were very silent, and moved as passively as if we had no volition of our own," wrote Lieutenant J. F. J. Caldwell of the 1st South Carolina. "We broke ranks, some wandering slowly through the open field, some falling helplessly upon the ground, some standing and staring about them as in a dream." A friend told Caldwell, "I did not think I should live till this day. I hoped I should die before this day!" Heavy rain began falling, a fitting backdrop to the desolation of Caldwell's regiment. The South Carolinians "lay huddled together, silent and sorrowful."[239]

Others burned their regimental flags after first tearing off strips as personal mementoes. Some officers, fearing retaliation by the Yankees, ripped off their rank insignia. When Chaplain William Wiatt of the 26th Virginia saw Lee returning from his meeting with Grant at the McLean house, "I could not refrain from shedding tears again; it has been a sad day to us." The chaplain said the army's defeat was the manifestation of God's will. "May we have grace to bear our troubles & trials with faith & patience." Wiatt knew it would not be easy.[240]

In Richmond, the news of Lee's surrender, announced by Union cannon salutes and Navy vessels sounding their whistles on the James River, plunged ardent Confederates into despondency. Lee and his army had personified their dream of Southern nationalism just as George Washington and his army had embodied the fight for American independence. "We cannot believe it, but my heart became dull and heavy, and every nerve and muscle of my frame seems heavy," wrote Judith McGuire. "We passed the night, I cannot tell how—I know not how we live at all." "It is true!" former Confederate War Department clerk John B. Jones wrote in his diary. "Yesterday Gen. Lee surrendered the Army of Northern Virginia. . . . This army was the pride, the hope, the prop of the Confederate cause. . . . All is lost!"

On street corners, knots of people quietly discussed the desolating news. "Upon every countenance rested the shadow of gloom, and on every heart the paralyzing torpor of despair," wrote Sallie Brock Putnam. Their sole consolation was that the killing was at an end. "We moved about, little more than breathing automatons, and were slow to receive all the dreadful truth, and slower still to say, 'Thy will be done, oh Lord!'"[241]

"Oh, I wish we were all dead," wrote a Florida woman. "It is as if the earth had crumbled beneath our feet."[242]

The news swept away the last hopes of diarist Mary Chesnut, now back home in Chester, South Carolina. "We are scattered—stunned—the remnant of heart left alive with us, filled with brotherly hate. . . . Only the dead heroes left stiff and stark on the battlefield escape."

Yet it wasn't a complete surprise; from the window of her home Chesnut had seen disaster's portents days earlier. "Men are moving the wrong way all the time. They slip by with no songs and no shouts now . . . the marching now is without tap of drum."[243]

In Lee's last report to Jefferson Davis, he described the events leading to his army's surrender, which "it is with pain that I announce." The tipping point was the twenty-four-hour delay at Amelia Court House, which erased the army's one-day head start and "could not be retrieved." The Union corps pushed Lee's army beyond its human limits and destroyed half of it at Sailor's Creek. "If we could have forced our way one day

longer it would have been at great sacrifice of life, and at its end I did not
see how a surrender could have been avoided," Lee concluded.[244]

Grant's army awakened on April 10 to find its camps overrun by friendly,
curious Confederate soldiers. "They stood over our very heads now—the
men whose movements we used to study through field glasses, or see
close at hand framed in fire," wrote General Joshua Chamberlain. The
Yankees shared their food with their former enemies, and the men bartered for knives, pipes, tobacco, and cash. "The inundation of visitors
grew so that it looked like a county fair, including the cattle show," Chamberlain wrote.[245]

Sheridan's Cavalry Corps, which, more than any Union Army unit,
was responsible for Lee's surrender, was sent away from Appomattox
early April 10 to Burkeville Station and thence to Petersburg. Sheridan's
men had been forbidden to fraternize with the Rebels, evidently to prevent clashes between the aggressive troopers and the Confederates who
so loathed them. Lee was rumored to have requested that the Union cavalry be excluded from the surrender ceremony April 12, when the Confederates would turn over their arms and battle flags and receive their
paroles.

Lee later attributed his army's defeats in early April to a lack of cavalry; he had sent away thousands of troopers to obtain fresh horses in the
Carolinas and to aid Johnston and Hardee. "Our small force of cavalry
was unable to resist the united Federal cavalry under Sheridan," Lee told
General Wade Hampton, one of the exiled cavalrymen. Fitzhugh Lee and
Rooney Lee remained behind with forty-five hundred men to face Sheridan's fifteen thousand.[246]

Sheridan, however, gave Grant the credit for the victory. With Grant's
appointment as general-in-chief in March 1864, Union leaders "knew
that henceforth, systematic direction would be given to our armies in every section of the vast territory. . . . Harmony of plan was the one thing
needed to end the war," and Grant provided it. Against Grant, Lee "was
now, for the first time, overmatched," Sheridan wrote.[247]

The Cavalry Corps, however, did not quietly ride away from Appomattox on April 10. In a final defiant gesture, Sheridan led his troopers,
four abreast and closed up, through the middle of Appomattox Court

House, waiting until 8 a.m. so as to maximize its visibility to both Yankees and Rebels.[248]

Although the Rebels might have pointedly kept Sheridan's cavalrymen away from the Army of Northern Virginia's formal surrender, they were not the only Union units sent to Burkeville. The railroad junction was an ideal resupply point; rations could be easily transported there from Richmond and Petersburg. All of Grant's corps marched eastward from Appomattox on April 10 except XXIV and V Corps, and General Ranald Mackenzie's small cavalry division from the Army of the James.[249]

Grant and Lee conversed again during the morning of April 10, before Grant left Appomattox for Washington. They met on horseback between the lines as a light rain fell and, for half an hour, had "a very pleasant conversation," wrote Grant. Once before, they had exchanged good-natured verbal ripostes. On March 3, when Lee had proposed peace talks to Grant, the Union general, who declined Lee's offer, had jokingly told their intermediary that he knew what Lee ate for breakfast each morning. Lee had replied that if Grant knew how meager his breakfasts were, he would have shared his with Lee.

Lee now said that he hoped no more men would die. Grant advised Lee to use his considerable influence in the South to urge the surrender of all Confederate armies. "I had no doubt his counsel would be followed with alacrity." Lee replied that he could not do that without first consulting President Jefferson Davis. Grant did not press the issue. "I knew there was no use to urge him to do anything against his ideas of what was right," he wrote.

Grant proposed that Lee meet with President Lincoln either at Richmond, City Point, Fortress Monroe, or Washington. If the men could agree on terms acceptable to both the North and South, fighting would end everywhere, Grant said. Lee replied that he would like to arrange such an agreement, but as a soldier he could not parlay with Lincoln; only Davis had that authority. Lee and Grant's next meeting would be at the White House, during Grant's first months as president.[250]

Lee turned to Colonel Marshall, his bespectacled military historian, when he decided to issue a farewell address to his army. Marshall was a lawyer, the great-grandnephew of the late Supreme Court chief justice, John Marshall, and, most importantly, fluent in the South's chivalric idiom. However, so many interruptions kept Marshall from beginning his task that Lee ordered him to remain in his ambulance until he completed the address. Lee posted an orderly to prevent any intrusions.

Marshall wrote the draft in pencil and gave it to Lee, who made some minor changes and then "struck out a paragraph, which he said would tend to keep alive the [antagonistic] feeling existing between the North and South." Marshall returned to the ambulance, made the revisions suggested by Lee, and gave the draft to a clerk to copy in ink. Lee signed the address and copies of it that were distributed to the corps commanders and Lee's staff.[251]

Issued as General Orders No. 9, Lee's farewell address began,

After four years of arduous service, marked by unsurpassed courage and fortitude, the Army of Northern Virginia has been compelled to yield to overwhelming numbers and resources. I need not tell the brave survivors of so many hard-fought battles, who have remained steadfast to the last, that I have consented to the result from no distrust of them.

He said further loss of life would serve no purpose. After receiving their paroles, the men could return home until exchanged.

With an increasing admiration of your constancy and devotion to your country, and a grateful remembrance of your kind and generous considerations for myself, I bid you all an affectionate farewell.[252]

Later in the day, three Union generals and three of their Confederate counterparts returned to the McLean house to settle the details of the Army of Northern Virginia's official surrender. The Union commissioners were John Gibbon, Charles Griffin, and Wesley Merritt; the Confederates were James Longstreet, John Gordon, and William Pendleton. They decided where the Rebels would stack their weapons and flags, where they would surrender horses and mules belonging to the Confederacy, and how the Rebels would apply for and receive their paroles.[253]

❧

On April 12, the chilly, overcast weather reflected the dour mood of the Army of Northern Virginia's men as they formed ranks for their last march under arms—to the place where they would surrender their battle flags and weapons.

Because of Joshua Chamberlain's outstanding leadership during the past ten days, Grant had named him over dozens of more senior generals to the place of honor overseeing the surrender of Lee's army. Chamberlain requested the brigade that he had commanded at Gettysburg for the ceremony. He placed its regiments in ranks facing one another across the village's main street.

The long gray column made its appearance. Foremost was John Gordon's Second Corps, led by the 210 survivors of the legendary Stonewall Brigade—the renowned "foot cavalry." Gordon rode at the head of his corps.

"On they came," wrote Chamberlain, "with the old swinging route step and swaying battle flags." On this day, the banners were crowded so thickly together because of the corps's shockingly thin ranks that the column seemed to consist entirely of red flags. The men were "thin, worn, and famished, but erect." Gordon appeared tired and dejected.

As the Confederates approached his formation, Chamberlain, out of respect for his adversaries' fighting ability and their "proud humiliation," ordered his bugler to sound "carry arms"—calling the Yankees to shift from "order arms" to the marching salute, muskets held to their right shoulders.

Gordon's downcast expression vanished, and he wheeled his horse to face Chamberlain, dropping the point of his sword to his boot toe. Then, he commanded his men to return the Union brigade's salute.

An "awed stillness" fell over Chamberlain's men, a "breath-holding, as if it were the passing of the dead."

The famous Rebel divisions continued to pass. Chamberlain was struck by the aspect of George Pickett's few remaining men, "so thin, so pale, purged of the mortal—as if knowing pain or joy no more." "With what strange emotion I look into these faces," wrote Chamberlain. "It is by miracles we have lived to see this day—any of us standing here."

The Confederates stacked their arms and cartridge boxes. When they laid down their flags, it was a heartbreaking moment for men who had fought for years and watched their comrades die under those same banners. Grizzled veterans, their cheeks wet with tears, burst from the ranks to press the flags to their lips. One hundred battle flags were surrendered.[254]

Afterward, Chamberlain spoke with many high-ranking Rebel officers. Although most of them were conciliatory, at least one remained angrily obdurate: General Henry Wise, the former Virginia governor who had hanged John Brown and who, almost alone among the commanders of Anderson's corps at Sailor's Creek, had managed to escape with two brigades.

When Chamberlain told Wise that he hoped "brave men may become good friends," Wise sharply corrected him. "You're mistaken, sir. You may forgive us, but we won't be forgiven. There is a rancor in our hearts which you little dream of. We hate you, sir."[255]

A total of 28,356 Confederates were paroled; half of them had not fought in the final battle at Appomattox, but had instead hungrily roamed the woods and fields looking for food. Another 19,132 were captured between March 29 and April 9, a period when an unknown number of other Rebels were killed, wounded, or went missing. The parole certificates inoculated the bearers against arrest and gave them access to Union transportation and rations as they made their way home.[256]

Colonel Charles Francis Adams Jr. was sent with his black 5th Massachusetts Cavalry to Petersburg. Writing to his father, the ambassador to Great Britain, Adams said, "For the first time I see the spirit of the Virginians, since these last two battles, completely broken; the whole people are cowed—whipped out." It was "a curious region of desolation," where "all landmarks are defaced, not only trees and fences, but even houses and roads. . . . It will be years and years before the scars of war disappear from this soil, for nature must bring forth new trees and a new race of men must erect other habitations."[257]

❧

Waves of applause greeted President Lincoln on April 10 when he appeared at the second-floor White House window where he often delivered public speeches. His son Tad waved a captured Rebel flag, which earned him "a great shout of applause." News of Lee's surrender had inspired daylong celebrations throughout Washington. A thunderous five-hundred-gun salute early that rainy morning had broken windows in homes near Lafayette Square. Even now, in the nighttime, bonfires and rockets flared along the muddy streets, where there wandered throngs of happily dazed people.

The crowd outside the White House called on Lincoln to give a speech, but he was unready "to say anything that one in my position ought to say. Everything I say, you know, goes into print." The exuberant assembly laughed and applauded appreciatively, and Lincoln said that he would have something to say the next night. He asked the band to play "Dixie," followed by "Yankee Doodle," and he called for three cheers for Grant and his men.[258]

During Lincoln's departure from City Point on April 8, a military band had come aboard the *River Queen* and serenaded the president, first lady, and their guests. Lincoln had twice requested "La Marseillais"—for the Marques de Chambrun, a guest of the Lincolns, because its performance was banned in France by the royalist government. "You have to come over to America to hear it," Lincoln said to the marquis. The president also requested "Dixie." "That tune is now Federal property," he declared, "and it is good to show the rebels that, with us in power, they will be free to hear it again."[259]

Before leaving Virginia, Lincoln had once more toured Richmond and Petersburg, this time with the first lady and other dignitaries, and he visited the military hospital at City Point. He shook hands with hundreds of the nearly six thousand wounded Union and Confederate soldiers under medical care there.

He extended his hand to Colonel Harry Benbow, a South Carolina soldier shot through both hips at Five Forks. "I hope a Confederate colonel will not refuse me his hand," Lincoln said. "No, I will not," replied Benbow, and clasped Lincoln's hand in both of his.

Lincoln stopped at the bed of Captain Charles Houghton of the 14th New York Heavy Artillery, who had lost a leg at Fort Stedman. The president placed his hand on the man's brow and kissed him on the cheek. When doctors pulled back covers so that Lincoln could see the raw stump of Houghton's leg, Lincoln bent low, shaking with sobs. "You must live!" he said. "Poor boy, you must live!" The twenty-two-year-old whispered, "I intend to, sir."

Afterward, the head surgeon remarked that Lincoln's right arm must ache from all of the hand shaking that he had done. Lincoln smiled, stepped outside, and picked up an ax. Slowly, with his right arm, the former rail-splitter raised the ax at arm's length from his side until it was level with his shoulder.[260]

On the eve of the final battle between Grant and Lee, the presidential steamer cast off from City Point and sailed downriver to the Chesapeake Bay, before proceeding up the Potomac to Washington. Lincoln read aloud for several hours from Shakespeare's *Macbeth* and was transfixed by the passages about Duncan's assassination. "Now and then he paused to expatiate on how exact a picture Shakespeare here gives of a murderer's mind when, the dark deed achieved, its perpetrator already envies his victim's calm sleep," wrote the Marquis de Chambrun. He said Lincoln read the scene twice. The president also reportedly recited from Henry Wadsworth Longfellow's "Resignation": "The air is full of farewells to the dying, and mournings for the dead . . ." And there was a William Knox poem, "Mortality," that Lincoln was fond of reciting: "'Tis the wink of an eye; 'tis the draught of a breath / From the blossom of health to the paleness of death, / From the gilded saloon to the bier and the shroud; / why should the spirit of mortal be proud?"[261]

Lincoln's recent dreams might explain his memento mori state of mind. The week before, he had related a disturbing dream to intimates that included Mrs. Lincoln and Ward Lamon, his friend, former law partner, and self-appointed bodyguard. In the dream, Lincoln said, he was awakened in the White House by what he believed were sobs. He wandered room to room looking for their source. In the East Room was a wrapped corpse on a catafalque. Lincoln asked one of the soldiers guarding it who had died. "The president," the soldier replied. "He was killed by an assassin!"[262]

When the *River Queen* reached Washington the night of April 9, Lincoln's carriage met the president's party at the wharf. Riding to pay their respects to the injured secretary of state, William Seward, who was recovering in bed from his carriage accident of April 5, they found the streets full of exultant people. Bonfires burned everywhere. Someone asked a bystander what had happened. "He looked at us in amazement, not recognizing Mr. Lincoln," wrote William Crook, a Lincoln bodyguard. "Why, where have you been? Lee has surrendered."[263]

❧

Lincoln had carefully prepared his first speech after Lee's surrender. Already he was looking ahead to the challenge of restoring the South to the Union and mending its broken places. Earlier in the day, he had issued a proclamation closing most of the South's ports until the United States was able to establish control over Southern commerce. Foreign vessels entering the closed ports would be subject to seizure, along with their cargoes. The proclamation heralded the end of blockade running.[264]

Already, while he was in Virginia, Lincoln had taken tentative steps toward reestablishing civil government. He granted Assistant Confederate War Secretary John Campbell's request to convene the Virginia legislature so that it could recall Virginia's troops and end its support for the Confederacy. "I do not think it very probable that anything will come of this," Lincoln had told Grant, but he authorized General Godfrey Weitzel to allow the legislature to meet if he believed no harm would come from it. Five legislators met without taking any action. Three days later, Lee surrendered.[265]

The president persisted in believing that the South's antebellum leaders could best lead their states back into the Union and reestablish civil order. He had permitted Louisiana to begin establishing a reconstruction government, although Congress had balked at recognizing it. But Lincoln hoped that now Virginia, too, might be nudged toward reviving its ties with the United States. He anticipated that Virginia legislators would "come together and undo their own work," he told his Cabinet when he returned to Washington.

Cabinet members strongly disagreed with him; they did not think that Virginia, the Confederacy's heart and soul, was eager to reconcile with the Union. Navy Secretary Gideon Welles said he "doubted the policy" and feared that Virginia's leaders would begin again to conspire against the Union. Seeing that all of his advisers were against him, Lincoln conceded that "he had perhaps made a mistake, and was ready to correct it if he had." He promptly rescinded his order to General Weitzel. "Do not now allow them to assemble; but if any have come, allow them safe-return to their homes," he wrote.[266]

Lincoln had momentarily abandoned normalizing relations with Virginia, but he was unwilling to give up on Louisiana. Its new state government was the subject of his speech on April 11, in which he revealed the outlines of his moderate reconstruction policy: reconciliation with the South, not punishment, predicated on the South's recommitment to the Union and its acceptance of black emancipation.

Now, as Lincoln looked out over the crowd gathered outside the White House, he held in his hand the rolled-up manuscript of the address that he would deliver. It was an important speech, and he did not want to be misunderstood. It would be Lincoln's last public speech.

His audience, anticipating a triumphal recounting of Lee's final defeat, got a policy speech instead, prefaced by Lincoln's grateful acknowledgment that "to General Grant, his skillful officers, and brave men, all belongs." As newspaper correspondent Noah Brooks stood behind a curtain holding a candle for the president to read by, Lincoln quickly moved on to reconstruction, which, he said, "is pressed much more closely upon our attention. It is fraught with great difficulty." Indeed, while Lincoln favored a moderate, relatively speedy reknitting of the North and South, Radical Republicans already were demanding that Southern states meet stringent benchmarks before being readmitted to the Union—and that they be denied representation in Congress until then. Louisiana had become the flashpoint for the competing views of reconstruction held by Lincoln's administration and Congress. It was understood that Louisiana was the prototype for postwar reconstruction everywhere in the South.

Lincoln defended what Louisiana had already accomplished. Twelve thousand Louisiana voters had sworn allegiance to the Union, cast ballots in elections, organized a state government, adopted a constitution, opened public schools to both blacks and whites, and empowered their legislature to allow blacks to vote, Lincoln told the crowd. The Louisiana legislature had ratified the US constitutional amendment abolishing slavery. The president said his Cabinet had welcomed Louisiana's plan to form a new government and write a new constitution, and it had met no objections in Congress—until "the people of Louisiana had begun to move in accordance with it." Congress had then rejected Lincoln's plan. Lincoln, in turn, had pocket-vetoed Congress's alternative plan. Early in 1865, Congress had refused to seat Louisiana's congressional representatives; Radical Republicans demanded that Louisiana blacks first be permitted to vote.

Accept Louisiana's new state government, Lincoln exhorted. "If we reject and spurn them, we do our utmost to disorganize and disperse them," he warned. "We would in effect say to the white men, 'You are worthless, or worse—we will neither help you, nor be helped by you.' To the blacks we say, 'This cup of liberty which these, your old masters, hold to your lips, we will dash from you.'" In conclusion, Lincoln said, "I repeat the question, 'Can Louisiana be brought into proper practical relation with the Union sooner by sustaining or by discarding her new State government?' What has been said of Louisiana will apply to other states." But he added that "no exclusive and inflexible plan can be prescribed as to details and collaterals" for all states. Lincoln also suggested that he might soon "make some new announcement to the people of the South."[267]

Lincoln's audience applauded the speech, but not with loud cheers; it was too much of a reasoned argument to move a large crowd. Afterward Lincoln turned to Brooks, his candle-holder, and said, "That was a pretty fair speech, I think, but you threw some light on it." The *New York Tribune* said the speech "fell dead, wholly without effect on the audience," and "it caused a great disappointment and left a painful impression." The *Tribune*'s reaction reflected the views of Radical Republicans, bitterly opposed to Louisiana's constitutional government. Their leader, Senator Charles Sumner of Massachusetts, wrote, "The President's speech and other things augur confusion and uncertainty in the future, with hot controversy. Alas! Alas!" These critics were in a minority. The *New York Herald* wrote that the reconstruction speech had been "very generally canvassed and meets with approbation from a large majority of the people" despite "a very active minority of the more radical of the Republicans [being] much chagrined at the indications of a disposition to heal up existing difficulties." In his report on the speech for the *Sacramento Daily Union,* Brooks wrote that the American people "have an implicit and trustful faith in Lincoln . . . he has so often proved himself wiser than his critics and advisers."[268]

The end of major combat operations, it sometimes seemed, had only opened new fields of bitter contention, although characterized by flying words, not bullets. Disputation had become a deeply engrained habit. While Radical Republicans sought to punish the South and possibly even demand reparations, moderates such as Lincoln favored reconciliation and a swift return to the antebellum status quo, slavery excepted. The battle lines were drawn the previous year when it became apparent that the Union would prevail. With the fighting practically ended, issues profound and petty were being contested—even the prayers uttered in Richmond Episcopal churches.

At Sunday services during the war, Richmond ministers had routinely offered a prayer for President Jefferson Davis. After Richmond's capture, General Weitzel ordered the practice stopped. On April 9, Palm Sunday, at St. Paul's Episcopal Church, the minister called for a prayer for "all in authority" rather than for Davis. "How fervently did we all pray for our own President!" wrote Richmond diarist Judith McGuire. "Thank God, our silent prayers are free from Federal authority!"

This wasn't good enough for War Secretary Edwin Stanton, who had expected Weitzel to demand that the churches pray on Palm Sunday for President Lincoln instead of Davis. He fired off a telegram to Weitzel, demanding to know what had happened. Weitzel replied, "No orders were given as to what would be preached or prayed for, but only as to what would not be permitted." Stanton said that was unsatisfactory; Weitzel must require all religious denominations to show "no less respect for the President . . . than they practiced toward the rebel chief . . . before he was driven from the capital."[269]

Lincoln briefly weighed in and told Weitzel that he had supported his prohibition of the prayer for Davis without the requirement that in its place one be said for Lincoln. "I have no doubt you have acted in what appeared to you to be the spirit and temper manifested by me while there [in Richmond]," the president said.[270]

In obedience to Stanton's demand, however, Weitzel published an order stating that a prayer must be offered for President Lincoln at all Sunday services. The churches refused to make the change until Richmond's Episcopal bishop authorized it, and he was away from the city. Consequently, Episcopal churches throughout Richmond canceled Easter Sunday services.[271]

3

April 14, 1865

GOOD FRIDAY

Hush'd be the camps to-day,
And soldiers let us drape our war-worn weapons,
And each with musing soul retire to celebrate,
Our dear commander's death

—WALT WHITMAN[272]

In Charleston, South Carolina, the Stars and Stripes were raised with ceremonial formality over the ruins of Fort Sumter, whose thirty-four-hour bombardment in April 1861 had begun the orgy of slaughter and destruction. Four years to the day after Fort Sumter's surrender, General Robert Anderson, who in 1861 had lowered the flag in surrender, hoisted the same battered ensign over the fort as Army and Navy guns boisterously consecrated the moment, along with bands and singers. The Reverend Henry Ward Beecher offered gratitude for God's beneficence. Among those bowing their heads in thanks was the old antebellum agitator, William Lloyd Garrison. "Remember those who have been our enemies," said the Reverend Doctor R. S. Storrs of Brooklyn, "and turn their hearts from wrath and war, to love and peace."

In Washington, General Grant and War Secretary Stanton were stopping all military recruiting and the draft, and curtailing military purchases. Indeed, with the surrender of Robert E. Lee's army, it was a mere matter of time before all hostilities ceased. On the night of April 13, Washingtonians celebrated by illuminating the federal buildings—six thousand lights burned in the Patent Office alone—and strolling along the brightly lit streets.

On the 14th, Lincoln met for two hours with his Cabinet. For the first time, Grant attended, and reconstruction was discussed. Each Southern state presented a unique set of problems that should be addressed separately, Lincoln said. He reiterated his support for Louisiana's constitution, although he acknowledged that he was disappointed that black suffrage had not been written into it. The president did not want to require the Rebels to pay restitution. As for the Confederacy's leaders, Lincoln said, "Frighten them out of the country, open the gates, let down the bars, scare them off. Enough lives have been sacrificed. We must extinguish our resentments if we expect harmony and reunion."

He had had another premonitory dream. The president had had several throughout the war. There was the recent dream in which he was awakened by the sound of sobbing and learned that the catafalque in the White House East Room was his.

In the dream of the night before, he told his Cabinet, he was in "some singular, indescribable vessel," moving rapidly to an "indefinite shore." Lincoln said that he had had this same dream before some of the war's pivotal events: Fort Sumter, Bull Run, Antietam, Gettysburg, Stones River, Vicksburg, and the capture of Wilmington. "We shall, judging from the past, have great news very soon," Lincoln said. "I think it must be from Sherman. My thoughts are in that direction, as are most of yours."[273]

But what also might have been on his mind were the murder plots targeting him. They had proliferated the previous fall when it became clear that he was going to be reelected and that the Union would win the war. He once showed newspaperman John Forney a pigeonhole in his office desk where he kept the threatening letters. There were scores of them. "I know I am in danger," said Lincoln, "but I am not going to worry over threats like this."[274]

Yet he did worry. On his way to the War Department earlier that day with his bodyguard, William Crook, they passed some drunken men. Lincoln said, "Crook, do you know, I believe there are men who want to take my life?" Almost as though speaking to himself, he added, "And I have no doubt they will do it." As they continued walking, Lincoln said he had confidence in his bodyguards. "I know no one could do it and escape alive," he said. "But if it is to be done, it is impossible to prevent it."[275]

From his first inauguration in March 1861, Lincoln had labored every hour of every day under the burden of waging an increasingly bloody war with an uncertain outcome. Now that he could see the end of it, his mood had become almost buoyant.

On the afternoon of April 14, he took Mary on a carriage ride to the Navy Yard. No aides or bodyguards accompanied them—just as Lincoln liked it. He visited with the sailors and went aboard the monitor *Montauk*. He was "cheerful—almost joyous," the first lady observed, and when she remarked to him on this, he replied, "We must both be more cheerful in the future—between the war and the loss of our darling Willie [their eleven-year-old son, who became ill and died in 1862]—we have both been very miserable."[276]

The Lincolns planned to go that night to Ford's Theatre to attend the farcical three-act play *Our American Cousin*, featuring Laura Keene, the renowned actress and Broadway theater owner who now managed a traveling production show; *Our American Cousin* would close out her two-week engagement at Ford's. The Stantons and the Grants were invited to join the Lincolns in the president's box, but Mrs. Stanton had told Mrs. Grant that if she did not attend, neither would Mrs. Stanton; she could not stand to be alone with Mrs. Lincoln. Mrs. Grant was in no mood to endure an evening with the difficult Mary Lincoln either; she declined the invitation, saying that she was leaving Washington that night to visit her children at their New Jersey boarding school. Mrs. Stanton promptly sent her regrets, too. Yet, the notice that theater manager James Ford had placed in the afternoon newspapers announced that Grant, the Lincolns, "and other distinguished personages" would be present.

Ward Lamon, Lincoln's self-appointed bodyguard, was not going. Before leaving for Richmond, Lamon had warned the president against going out at night. War Secretary Stanton also urged Lincoln not to mingle with the theater crowd. It was an unusually dangerous night for the president to be abroad, Stanton said, because of the newspaper notice that both he and Grant would be in the president's box, where they would be in plain sight.[277]

❧

John Wilkes Booth, twenty-six years old and darkly handsome, was the youngest member of America's foremost theatrical family. His father, the famous English-born stage actor Junius Brutus Booth, had become an instant sensation after immigrating to the United States. When Junius died in 1852, Edwin Booth, one of John's two older brothers, assumed the family patriarchy and became the nation's best-known tragedian. In March 1864, Edwin Booth gave a command performance for Lincoln in Washington to celebrate the third anniversary of his inauguration.

Although a well-known leading actor in his own right, John did not have Edwin's prodigious talents, and he never matched his brother's achievements on the stage. Before the war Edwin had decided that rather than compete for audiences against his brother John, he would perform on Northern stages, while John would tour the South, a less lucrative territory.

Living in the South, John became infatuated with the region and its culture, and as war approached, he enthusiastically supported the Confederacy. But when the shooting war began, John moved North, although his passion for the Confederacy intensified—to the extent that his ardent Unionist brother Edwin expelled John from his home after a violent quarrel over the war.

By late 1864 John was telling his friends that he had handsomely profited from the oil wells he owned in Pennsylvania and might retire from the stage. But oil wasn't absorbing his energies so much as his growing radicalism on behalf of the Confederacy. When Lincoln's reelection became fact, all but dooming the South to defeat, Booth was spurred to act.

Radical measures were now being openly proposed in the South. The *Richmond Whig* on November 1 even raised the subject of tyrannicide: "Some brave democrat, devoting himself for his country, would surely with bullet or pontard [*sic*] rid the world of that grotesquely horrible Frankenstein." The newspaper, however, shrank from openly advocating Lincoln's assassination. "Not what we desire to see Abraham Lincoln put out of the way either by that method or any other," the *Whig* wrote. "He suits us exactly as the ruler of an enemy's country; and our suggestion is altogether in the interest of any of his unfortunate subjects who may still possess the spirit of men and of freemen."

While Southerners despaired about the future, the romantic Booth, who had spent the war in comfort in the North, perversely resolved to share "the last ditch" with his Southern brethren. In November, he met in Montreal with high-ranking Confederate spies and committed himself to a far-fetched plot to kidnap President Lincoln. The scheme was concocted with the knowledge of Jefferson Davis, who authorized gold to be sent to one of the ringleaders, Thomas Conrad. The Rebel agents gave Booth money to put the plan into action.

In a letter to his mother Mary, Booth melodramatically announced that the time had come for him to perform "a noble duty for the sake of liberty and humanity due to my Country. . . . For four years I have lived a slave in the north. . . . Not daring to express my thoughts or sentiments, even in my own home. Constantly hearing every principle, dear to my heart, denounced as treasonable. . . . And knowing the vile and savage acts committed on my countrymen their wives & helpless children, that I have cursed my willful idleness. . . . For four years I have borne it mostly for your dear sake . . . but it seems that uncontrollable fate, moving me for its ends, takes me from you, dear Mother, to do what work I can for a poor oppressed downtrodden people."[278]

In December, Booth was busy enlisting potential allies in pro-Confederate southern Maryland for his plot, and meeting with a small group at various Washington saloons and Mary Surratt's boarding house. Booth intended to seize the president when he was riding alone, as he often did, to the Soldiers' Home outside Washington and smuggle him through southern Maryland and down to Richmond. With the money he had received in Montreal, Booth bought two Spencer repeating rifles, six revolvers, two Bowie knives, handcuffs, and ammunition. He purchased a boat and found an oarsman at Port Tobacco to take him across the Potomac River to Virginia when the time came.

But Booth was uncomfortable with the idea of kidnapping the president in a rural area; he was far more at home in the Washington theaters than in the countryside. Booth revised his plan—he would seize the president while he was attending a play, rather than while riding outside Washington. Booth's coconspirators objected, but could not dissuade him.[279]

Booth shadowed Lincoln for weeks, and even had a seat at the president's swearing-in on March 4, thanks to his secret fiancée, Lucy Hale, a New Hampshire senator's daughter, who obtained a ticket for him. In early April, the Confederacy's collapse convinced Booth that kidnapping the president would not be enough; he resolved to murder Lincoln. Booth later boasted to a friend, "What an excellent chance I had to kill the president, if I had wished on Inauguration Day! I was on the stand, as close to him nearly as I am to you." The shocked friend asked Booth why he wanted to kill the president. "I could live in history," replied Booth.

On April 11, he was at the front of the crowd when Lincoln delivered his reconstruction speech at the White House. When the president advocated black voting rights Booth reportedly said, "That means n—r citizenship. Now, by God, I'll put him through."[280]

Booth decided to also kill William Seward, and assigned the mission to a hulking, twenty-year-old Confederate combat veteran named Lewis Powell, whose service included more than a year with John Mosby's famed Rangers. It was curious that Booth targeted the secretary of state instead of War Secretary Stanton. But Booth and others like him had nursed a profound hatred of Seward for years because his views were so diametrically opposed to theirs. Moreover, they believed that Seward, because of his strong convictions, would pose a greater threat to their interests than any other Cabinet member if Lincoln were killed.[281]

During the day on April 14, Booth slipped into Ford's Theatre, whose layout he knew intimately, and drilled a peephole in the door that opened directly into the presidential box. A narrow hallway and a second, outer door separated the box from the balcony corridor. Booth armed himself with a .44-caliber derringer and a dagger and waited for nighttime.

He attempted to explain himself in a rambling letter "To the Editors of the National Intelligencer." "Baffled and disappointed" by previous efforts to advance "my object"—evidently the kidnapping plot—"the hour has come when I must change my plan," he wrote, to "a bolder and more perilous one. . . . If the South is to be aided it must be done quickly. It may already be too late." He compared himself to Brutus, who murdered Caesar when his power "menaced the liberties of the people. . . . The stroke of his dagger was guided by his love of Rome. It was the spirit and ambition of Caesar that he struck at."

"Many, I know—the vulgar herd—will blame me for what I am about to do, but posterity, I am sure, will justify me," wrote Booth. "Right or wrong, God judge me, not man. Be my motive good or bad, of one thing I am sure, the lasting condemnation of the North."[282]

The Lincolns arrived at Ford's Theatre at 9 p.m. Ward Lamon and William Crook, the president's usual bodyguards, were absent. Instead, a metropolitan policeman named John Parker accompanied the president and first lady. Concerned about the light security, Stanton assigned Major Henry Rathbone to sit with the Lincolns. Rathbone escorted his fiancée, Clara Harris, daughter of New York Senator Ira Harris.[283]

The Lincolns, Rathbone, and Harris settled into their seats in the box. The play had already begun, but a murmur ran through the theater when the audience saw the president and first lady.

Parker sat down in a chair outside the door where Booth had made the peephole, but he neither noticed the peephole nor remained in place for long. A poorer bodyguard than Parker would have been hard to find in the metropolitan police department. He had been disciplined numerous times—for using disrespectful language, for having lived five weeks in a house of prostitution, and for sleeping on the job. On this night, Parker left his post outside the presidential box, where he could hear but not see the actors. He slipped into an aisle seat in the audience where he could watch the play. Later, the delinquent bodyguard went outside for a drink.[284]

At the beginning of Act Three Booth entered the narrow hallway, barred the balcony door behind him, and peered through the peephole at Lincoln, who was sitting in a rocking chair. Booth moved quickly, bursting into the box with his derringer in his right hand and a dagger in his left, and shot the president behind his left ear from less than five feet away.[285]

Major Rathbone sprang from his seat and grappled with the slender, dark-haired assailant dressed in black. During the struggle, Booth dropped his pistol, slithered out of Rathbone's grasp, and lunged at him with the dagger, slicing his left bicep when Rathbone threw up his arm protectively.

Booth agilely leaped to the railing at the front of the box, and as Booth began to jump to the stage ten feet below, Rathbone managed to grab a handful of Booth's jacket, throwing him off balance and causing his spur to catch on one of the flags draped over the front of the box. Booth landed awkwardly on the stage, injuring his left leg. In the glare of the footlights Booth thrust his long dagger above his head and cried, "Sic Semper Tyrannis"—the state of Virginia's motto, meaning "thus always to tyrants." Many of the theatergoers instantly recognized the famous actor before he darted from the stage, slashing the air in front of him to clear a path. He ran out the theater back door to an alley and galloped off on a mare waiting for him there.[286]

From the president's box came a piercing scream that broke the stunned silence that had fallen over the open-mouthed audience. Someone shouted, "Our president! Our president is shot!" Pandemonium erupted, with men crying, "Kill the murderer! Shoot him! Catch him! Stop that man!" Someone bellowed, "Burn the theater!" A chant arose, "Booth! Booth! Booth!" Angry men smashed seats, and the crowd surged toward the stage, pinning people against the orchestra.[287]

Laura Keene stepped to the front of the stage and shouted to the audience for order. Then someone in the president's box called for her to bring a pitcher of water and a glass. Keene found them backstage and made her way to the box. There she saw the president lying on the floor. He appeared dead, but Captain Charles Leale, a twenty-three-year-old Army surgeon, and two other surgeons were trying to resuscitate him. Lincoln was bleeding from the entry wound, and his right eye bulged where the bullet had lodged behind it. Keene sat on the floor and cradled the president's head in her lap, with her palms on either side of his face. Keene's clothing became crimson stained.

Leale rounded up volunteers to carry the president out of the theater. Lincoln's carriage was readied to take him to the White House, but Leale said the president could not survive the bumpy six-block ride and should be taken to the nearest private home instead. Lincoln was carried across the street to a small bedroom in the rear of William Petersen's four-story brick boarding house.[288]

While Booth had been closing in on Lincoln, Lewis Powell was arriving at the door of William Seward's home, where the secretary of state was in bed recovering from his carriage accident injuries. Powell told the doorman, William Bell, that he was delivering medicine. When Bell refused to admit him, Powell brushed past him and bolted up the stairs to the third floor, where Seward's son Frederick confronted him. Powell tried to shoot him, but the pistol jammed, and so he savagely beat the young man with the pistol butt until the gun fell to pieces. Bursting into the room with the wreck of a revolver in one hand and a knife in the other, Powell punched Seward's daughter Fanny, pinned Seward to his bed with one hand, and began slashing him in the face and neck with the knife.

Fanny screamed, "Murder!" bringing a male nurse and Seward's other son, Augustus. Powell flung both of them aside and ran down the stairs.

On his way out the front door Powell stabbed a State Department messenger in the back before mounting his horse and riding away.[289]

☙

At 10:30 p.m., Navy Secretary Gideon Welles was awakened from a sound sleep and plunged into the middle of a nightmare: Lincoln had been shot and Seward attacked in his home. Welles quickly dressed and walked to Seward's home just across the square. Stanton arrived in a carriage about the same time. They found the sixty-three-year-old secretary of state in a "bed saturated with blood," a cloth covering part of his head and eyes. Frederick was in worse condition, "weltering in his own gore."

Although everyone urged them not to, the two Cabinet members got into Stanton's carriage and went directly to the Peterson boarding house, where Lincoln lay dying. A doctor told Welles that Lincoln "was dead to all intents," but might cling to life for a few more hours. Welles and Stanton entered a bedroom where the president had been laid diagonally across a bed that was too short for him. Part of Lincoln's face was discolored, and his right eye was swollen. Without clothing Lincoln was impressive, Welles thought, with his large rail-splitter's arms, remarkable for a man of his thinness.

The rest of the Cabinet, Seward excepted, piled into the small bedroom, and it became uncomfortably warm and overcrowded. Every hour during the long night, wrote Welles, Mrs. Lincoln would come to her husband's bedside "with lamentations and tears."

Outside, the large crowd that had gathered in the street could hear Mrs. Lincoln's hysterical shrieks. While sitting with her husband, she at one point cried out in anguish, "Kill me! Kill me! Kill me, too! Shoot me, too!"

In another room Stanton organized a manhunt for Lincoln's and Seward's assailants, barking orders to subordinates and couriers. He asked New York City's police chief to send down three or four of his best detectives. Stanton stopped all rail and ship traffic in and out of Washington and Baltimore and ordered troops to seal the roads into those cities. He and Attorney General James Speed also interviewed witnesses, whose accounts were taken down by a shorthand reporter. The war secretary shuttled between his provisional headquarters and the bedroom where Lincoln lay dying.

"He lay with his head on [the] pillow, and his eyes, all bloodshot almost protruding from their sockets," wrote the boarding house owner's son, fifteen-year-old Fred Petersen. "His jaw had fallen down upon his breast, showing his teeth." Each breath made a "dismal, mourning, moaning" sound.

Ulysses and Julia Grant were in a Philadelphia restaurant for a late-evening meal as they waited to cross the Delaware River on a ferry to New Jersey when three telegrams were delivered to their table. Grant blanched as he read them. Julia asked what was wrong. "Something very serious has happened," Grant said. "Do not exclaim. Be quiet and I will tell you. The President has been assassinated at the theater, and I must go back at once." Later, Grant was heard to mutter, "This is the darkest day of my life."

Stanton also telegraphed Sherman, warning him to be on guard because of "evidence that an assassin is also on your track." General Henry Halleck, the Army chief of staff, sent Sherman a description of the would-be killer that was so vague that it could have matched thousands of men in Sherman's own army. The assassin's name was Clark, said Halleck.

At 7:22 a.m. on April 15, Lincoln died. Surgeon General Joseph Barnes folded Lincoln's hands across his chest and rose from his bedside. "He is gone," Barnes said.

The Cabinet moved to a back parlor, officially convened, and signed a letter prepared by Attorney General Speed to be delivered to Vice President Andrew Johnson. The letter informed him of Lincoln's death and his accession to the presidency. Two other men—John Tyler and Millard Fillmore—had become president when the chief executive died of natural causes; Johnson was the first vice president to succeed a murdered president. Chief Justice Salmon Chase swore him into office at 11 a.m. at the Kirkwood House hotel.[290]

Vengeful mobs materialized in Washington early that morning, and one of them converged on the Old Capitol Prison after hearing rumors that its four hundred Confederate prisoners were at that moment escaping. They were not. "Hang 'em! Shoot 'em! Burn 'em!" the men cried, preparing ropes to carry out their spurious sentence on the Rebels, who neither knew that Lincoln was dead, nor that their lives were in peril.

Congressman Green Smith of Kentucky and some friends barred the mob's way. While Smith pleaded with the crowd, others ran for help. Union soldiers arrived in time to prevent a massacre.[291]

But the public mourning was mostly peaceful. "Everywhere, on the most pretentious residences and on the humblest hovels, were black badges of grief," wrote newspaper correspondent Noah Brooks of the observances in Washington. The weather matched the city's funereal mood. "The wind sighed mournfully through the streets crowded with sad-faced people, and broad folds of funeral drapery flapped heavily in the wind over the decorations of the day before," Brooks wrote.[292]

Julia Ward Howe, who wrote the lyrics for "The Battle Hymn of the Republic," set to the tune of "John Brown's Body," learned of Lincoln's death while at her Beacon Hill home in Boston. "Nothing has happened that has given me as much personal pain as this event," she wrote. A reporter in Springfield, Illinois, wrote that Lincoln's hometown was bowed down in sorrow as if "the Death Angel had taken a member from each family."

Lincoln's death deeply upset Frederick Douglass, who described the assassination as both "a personal as well as national calamity; on account of the race to which I belong and the deep interest which that good man ever took in its elevation." Brooks summarized Lincoln's achievements in moving words, "A martyr to the national cause, his monument will be a nation saved, a race delivered, and his memory shall be cherished wherever Liberty hath a home."[293]

New York diarist George Templeton Strong wrote after learning of Lincoln's death, "There is a profound, awe-stricken feeling that we are, as it were, in the immediate presence of a fearful, gigantic crime, such as has not been committed in our day and can hardly be matched in history." Two days later he added, "Death had suddenly opened the eyes of the people (and I think of the world) to the fact that a hero has been holding high place among them for four years."[294]

The Union Army grieved—and thirsted for vengeance. "Everyone seems to feel as though his Father had been assassinated and all they [long] for was only another 6th of April [Sailor's Creek] to Avenge his death on the rebel Army," Sergeant John Hartwell wrote to his wife.[295]

Fearing that his men would run amok in nearby Farmville, Virginia, Joshua Chamberlain posted a double guard around his brigades' bivouac outside the town. His men, he said, "could be trusted to bear any blow but this . . . he had taken deep hold on the soldier's heart, stirring its many chords." Later, Chamberlain and two other generals went to see their commander, General George Meade. "We found him sad—very sad."[296]

Most Southern military and civilian leaders experienced "a shudder of horror at the heinousness of the act, and at the thought of its possible consequences." But others received the news with bitter joy, regarding Lincoln's death "as a sort of retributive justice," wrote John Wise, the son of General Henry Wise and a courier for Jefferson Davis. "Lincoln incarnated to us the idea of oppression and conquest. We had seen his face over the coffins of our brothers and relatives and friends, in the flames of Richmond, in the disaster at Appomattox," he wrote. "We greeted his death in a spirit of reckless hate, and hailed it as bringing agony and bitterness to those who were the cause of our own agony and bitterness."[297]

Some of Lincoln's detractors in the North made the mistake of blurting out their approval of the assassination in front of grief-stricken countrymen. James Hall was sentenced to two years in prison for loudly declaring in a Baltimore saloon, "John Wilkes Booth done right." Samuel Peacock got thirty days' hard labor for saying, "He ought to have been killed long ago." There was even ill-considered jubilation in the Union Army's ranks; nearly seventy Union soldiers and sailors were prosecuted for expressing satisfaction with the assassination.

In San Francisco, mobs destroyed the offices of two anti-Lincoln newspapers. A citizens' group ordered the editor of the Westminster, Maryland, *Democrat*, Joseph Shaw, to leave town. He did, but then returned; he was killed. Laura Keene and her theatrical company were repeatedly arrested while traveling to Cincinnati, despite having been cleared in Washington of any connection to the assassination.[298]

A rumor circulated in Washington that Booth was seen among Confederate prisoners being marched through the streets, and a mob attacked the prisoners, guarded by Union troops. Several people were wounded in the melee, including some of the guards, before the crowd was satisfied that Booth was not there.

It was unsurprising that there were such outbursts, with revenge being preached from church pulpits across the country. In Auburn, New York, the Reverend Henry Fowler said, "Each American seemed called to avenge the blood. . . . The President, living teaches us mercy, and we listen with consent to amnesty and re-construction; but the President murdered, teaches us retribution, and we swear above his open grave, extermination against treason and its plotters." Mercy for the penitent but not for "those who will murder from behind," added Fowler. "I call upon government to unsheathe the sword of justice, and I do it in the name of moral law and of Infinite Righteousness."[299]

꧁꧂

On April 17, Lincoln's body was placed in a mahogany, lead-lined coffin and taken to the White House East Room, where it lay in state. An honor guard of Army and Navy officers stood watch over the murdered president day and night, while an estimated thirty thousand people passed through the black-draped room to view the remains.

On the 19th, the day of Lincoln's funeral, the Union Army suspended operations everywhere. Officers and men wore black crepe on their left arms, and the headquarters' tents and unit colors also bore badges of mourning. General Chamberlain's men formed a square and listened to an address by the senior chaplain, Father Egan Irish.[300]

In the White House East Room, the Reverend Doctor Phineas Gurley, Lincoln's pastor, delivered the homily to six hundred dignitaries. "God be praised that our fallen chief lived long enough to see the day dawn and the day star of joy and peace arise upon the union. He saw it and he was glad," said Gurley. In a closing prayer, the Reverend Doctor E. H. Gray, the chaplain of the US Senate, said, "God of justice, and avenger of the nation's wrong, let the work of treason cease, and let the guilty author of this horrible crime be arrested and brought to justice."

There was no music, underscoring the ceremony's solemnity. Members of Congress, Grant, General Henry Halleck, and Admiral David Farragut were honorary pallbearers. The Supreme Court was there, along with many governors and the new president, Andrew Johnson. Undone by her husband's death, Mrs. Lincoln did not attend; she had still not left her room and was turning away nearly all visitors. Grant sat apart from the others at the head of the catafalque. Tears ran down his cheeks during the service.[301]

The casket was carried outside and placed in a hearse, around which crowded thousands of people. Throughout the city, cannons boomed, bells tolled, and bands played dirges during the hearse's journey down

Pennsylvania Avenue to the Capitol. Grim spectators, up to sixty thousand of them, thickly lined the road to glimpse the president's casket, the riderless horse, and the flag, torn by the assassin's spur, which had adorned the president's box at Ford's Theatre. The solemn pageant passed Seward's home, and the injured secretary of state sat up in bed to see it. The coffin was placed in the Capitol rotunda on public display until the next evening. Twenty-five thousand people stood in line to pay their respects.

On the evening of the 20th, the president's remains began their sixteen-hundred-mile, meandering rail journey that would end in Springfield, Illinois. Making the trip with Lincoln's body was the exhumed coffin of his son Willie. Mrs. Lincoln remained at the White House, "more dead than alive, shattered and broken by the horrors of that dreadful night," wrote Noah Brooks.[302]

Over twelve days, Lincoln's funeral train traveled to ten cities, including Philadelphia, New York, Albany, Cleveland, Columbus, Indianapolis, Chicago, and, finally, Springfield. Between Washington and Springfield an estimated 7 million people lined the train's route. About 300,000 people filled Philadelphia's streets to view the coffin at Independence Hall. Squashed and trampled, Philadelphians waited up to eight hours to glimpse their dead president. In New York up to 120,000 people passed Lincoln's remains at City Hall; many women tried to kiss the dead president on the lips. Nearly a million people watched the procession wend its way through New York's city streets to the railroad station. From a second-floor window of a mansion along the route, the two young sons of Cornelius Roosevelt observed the austere pageant: six-year-old Theodore Roosevelt, the future president, and his younger brother, Elliott, the future father of Eleanor Roosevelt, who would become the wife of another Roosevelt president.[303]

Early May 3, Lincoln's remains reached Springfield, from which he had set out for Washington in February 1861 and to which he had not returned until now, in death. The coffin was taken to the state Capitol, where Lincoln had delivered his "House Divided" speech, and was displayed in the rotunda for the next twenty-four hours. About seventy-five thousand people filed past the dead president.

The procession to Oak Ridge Cemetery began at 11:30 a.m. on May 4. Lincoln was buried at noon, Willie reinterred beside him. At the graveside services, as thousands of people strained to hear the words, one of the three officiating ministers read Lincoln's Second Inaugural Address as a testament to his principles and hopes for the nation.[304]

General William T. Sherman was in an excellent mood as he boarded the train that would take him to Durham, twenty miles to the west, to meet with Confederate General Joseph Johnston. Three days earlier, Johnston had requested a truce "to stop the further effusion of blood and devastation of property" so that civil authorities might meet to end the war.

This was the best concession that Johnston could wrest from the now nearly delusional Jefferson Davis. When they met in Greensboro on April 13, Davis refused to even listen to arguments to end the fighting, claiming that within three weeks he could raise a large new army of repentant deserters and conscripts and fight on.

The next day, War Secretary John Breckinridge arrived from Virginia to report Lee's surrender, and Breckinridge and Johnston agreed that Davis needed to end the war. Even with Lee's army defeated, Davis wasn't ready to quit; he asked Breckinridge and Johnston for a comparison of the Confederate forces with Grant's. Twenty-five thousand Confederates faced Union forces exceeding three hundred thousand, they said—a fifteen-to-one disparity. "It would be the greatest of human crimes for us to attempt to continue the war," Johnston declared. Davis replied to Johnston's assertion, "as if somewhat annoyed by it," that he could not negotiate because the Union did not recognize his authority.

Davis then polled his Cabinet; only Secretary of State Judah Benjamin was for continuing the war. It was now apparent to Davis that his determination to fight on was very much a minority opinion. He grudgingly dictated a letter for Johnston—the one that Johnston sent to Sherman under his signature—seeking an armistice so that civil authorities could make "needful arrangements."

Sherman replied to Johnston that he was authorized to arrange terms. When Johnston returned to Greensboro to show Davis the response from Sherman, Davis wasn't there; he had left for Charlotte. Without Davis's participation, Johnston and Sherman agreed to meet April 17 outside Durham.[305]

Sherman had just entered his railroad car at Raleigh's North Carolina Railroad depot when the telegraph operator ran to the train and said he was receiving an important dispatch that Sherman should see. Sherman held the train until the message could be deciphered.

The dispatch was from Stanton and contained the worst of news: "President Lincoln was murdered about ten o'clock last night in his private box at Ford's Theatre in this city, by an assassin who shot him through the head with a pistol ball." The telegram also informed Sherman of the knife attack on Secretary of State Seward and his son, concluding with, "I have no time to add more than to say that I find evidence that an assassin is also on your track, I beseech you to be more heedful than Mr. Lincoln was of such knowledge." Sherman instructed the operator to not tell anyone about the telegram's contents until he returned that afternoon.[306]

After resting and refitting in Goldsboro, fifty-five miles southeast of Raleigh, Sherman's ninety-thousand-man army had set out on April 10 for Raleigh and a climactic battle with Johnston's army. Sherman intended to heed Grant's words, "Rebel armies now are the only strategic points to strike at." On the 11th, the Yankees captured Smithfield, midway between Goldsboro and Raleigh, after a sharp fight with Rebel cavalry and infantry in Smithfield's streets.[307]

The news of Lee's surrender reached the army twelve miles east of Raleigh on April 12. "Billows of tumultuous cheering . . . rolled along the lines as brigade after brigade came along by our Headquarters and were told the news," Major Henry Hitchcock of Sherman's staff told his wife. "We were all pretty gay that morning, you may believe, and haven't got over it yet." Bands played "John Brown's Body" and "Marching Through Georgia." The 100th Indiana's band played—and drank, too. "The Band finally got so they were trying to play two or three tunes at once," wrote Sergeant Theodore Upson.

"All glory to God!" said Sherman's proclamation to his troops announcing Lee's surrender. "All honor to our brave comrades toward whom we have been marching! A little more toil; a few days of labor, and the great race is won."[308]

Sherman telegraphed his congratulations to Grant. "I hardly know how to express my feelings, but you can imagine them. The terms you have given Lee are magnanimous and liberal. Should Johnston follow Lee's example I shall of course grant the same."[309]

Before marching north to join Grant, Sherman indulged himself in a self-congratulatory letter to his wife Ellen: "The last March from Savannah to Goldsboro, with its legitimate fruits, the capture of Charleston, Georgetown and Wilmington, is by far the most important in conception and execution of any act of my life."[310]

Sherman also reorganized his army. Henry Slocum's Army of the Left Wing became the Army of Georgia; John Schofield's Army of the Center was now the Army of the Ohio; and Oliver Howard's Army of the Right Wing was renamed the Army of the Tennessee. Each consisted of two corps. Sherman promoted General Joseph Mower, the XVII Corps division commander who had nearly severed Johnston's escape route from Bentonville over Mill Creek, to command of XX Corps, replacing Alpheus Williams, demoted to division command. Sherman prized Mower's boldness, even if he had balked at capitalizing on Mower's impetuous attack at Bentonville.[311]

After driving the Confederates from Smithfield, Sherman's powerful army encountered little opposition as it neared Raleigh. Rebel cavalrymen tried to harry the columns of bluecoats, but their tentative efforts had no effect. "They have not yet hurt a man on our road, and we don't know that more than two of them have been hit," wrote Captain Charles Wills of the 103rd Illinois. "They keep shooting all the time, but are afraid to wait until we get within range of them."[312]

Raleigh officials surrendered the city to Sherman on April 13, and his army moved into the enemy capital. Sherman reviewed his troops, clad in the new blue uniforms issued in Goldsboro. In keeping with his policy of nonretribution in North Carolina, Sherman honored Governor Zebulon Vance's request to spare the city, issuing an order prohibiting the destruction of public or private property. He made the governor's mansion his headquarters.

Before withdrawing from Raleigh, General Joe Wheeler's cavalrymen looted the mansion, plundered downtown shops, and burned the railroad depot. To pleas by townspeople for restraint, a Confederate trooper shouted, "Damn Sherman and the town, too!" A defiant Confederate cavalry lieutenant lingered long enough to empty his revolver at the advancing Yankee troopers before galloping away, with the Union cavalrymen hard on his heels. The lieutenant's horse fell while turning a corner, and the Rebel officer was captured and brought before General Hugh Kilpatrick, who ordered him put to death for violating Raleigh's surrender. A short time later, the Confederate was hanged a few blocks from the capital.[313]

⤙⤚

From Durham Station, Sherman, with a cavalry escort, rode west to meet Johnston, who was traveling east with his own escort. The generals met between Durham and Hillsborough and went to the nearby farmhouse of James and Nancy Bennett to discuss peace.

Sherman showed Johnston the telegram reporting Lincoln's assassination and carefully observed Johnston's reaction. "The perspiration came out in large drops on his forehead, and he did not attempt to conceal his distress," Sherman wrote. Johnston told Sherman "the event was the greatest possible calamity to the South." Sherman replied that he did not believe Johnston or Lee had any involvement in Lincoln's murder, but he was unsure about Davis "and men of that stripe." Sherman "dreaded the effect" the news would have on his men, who loved Lincoln and who might retaliate by wrecking Raleigh.

Sherman offered Johnston the same terms that Grant had given Lee: his army's surrender and the parole of his men to their homes. This was the extent of his authority. Johnston replied that he had wanted an armistice so there could be negotiations "between the 'civil authorities' of the two countries." Impossible, said Sherman; the US government acknowledged neither the existence of the Confederacy nor its civil authorities. Sherman said he could not accept any proposition made by Southern civilians.

Johnston suggested that he and Sherman, acting as military authorities, "might do more than [Sherman] proposed" and arrange a permanent peace for the entire South, as European armies had done in the past. Forgetting Grant's instructions, Sherman said that his recent conversations with Lincoln had convinced him that restoration of the Union was the US government's primary object. Moreover, Sherman was aware that Lincoln had granted the Virginia legislature permission to meet in order to withdraw from the Confederacy and recall Virginia's troops— although that permission was later rescinded. They discussed amnesty; Sherman asserted that it could not include Davis and his Cabinet. Unable to resolve this issue that afternoon, the generals agreed to resume their discussion at the farmhouse at noon the next day.[314]

⌘

Confederate War Secretary John Breckinridge accompanied Johnston to the next day's meeting. Sherman objected to the presence of a Confederate Cabinet member. Johnston pointed out that Breckinridge was also a Confederate general, and said that they "might sink his character of Secretary of War." Sherman said that was acceptable, and he produced a bottle of bourbon, which he shared with the two Confederates.

Sherman rejected a surrender agreement written by Confederate Postmaster General John Reagan and brought to the meeting by Breckinridge; it was too verbose, said Sherman. He sat down and composed his own version. "Recalling the conversation of Mr. Lincoln, at City Point, I sat down at the table, and wrote off the terms, which I thought concisely expressed his views and wishes." It proposed a truce; a general amnesty; that all remaining Confederate forces be disbanded and repair to their respective state capitals to deposit their arms and public property in state arsenals; federal recognition of Southern state governments after their officers pledged their loyalty to the Union; and restoration of Southerners' political and property rights. Nowhere did it mention slavery. Sherman and Johnston signed the agreement, and it was sent to Washington by courier for approval.

Before their meeting ended, Sherman advised Breckinridge to leave the country. The Northern people were particularly hostile toward the South's political leaders—and especially Breckinridge, he being a former US vice president. Jefferson Davis should also go abroad, added Sherman.[315]

While he was writing the agreement, Sherman had absently risen, poured himself another drink, and returned the bottle to his saddlebag without thinking to share it with Breckinridge and Johnston. After Sherman departed, Breckinridge, a Kentuckian who liked his bourbon, vented his indignation to Johnston over Sherman's oversight. "He is a bright man, a man of great force," said Breckinridge. "But General Johnston, General Sherman is a hog. Yes, sir, a hog. Did you see him take that drink by himself?" No Kentucky gentleman would have acted that way. "He knew we needed it, and needed it badly."[316]

While Sherman and Johnston negotiated, the Confederate cavalry commander, General Wade Hampton, waited outside the farmhouse with a group of Union officers. Stretched out on a bench, Hampton radiated his contempt for the Yankees and exchanged taunts with Union cavalry General Kilpatrick about their battles. An eyewitness wrote that the argument progressed to the point where the cavalry leaders stood toe-to-toe "expressing a desire that the issue of the war should be left between the cavalry." Sherman and Johnston emerged from the farmhouse before the argument went further.[317]

Hampton was so upset that Johnston had agreed to terms with Sherman that he wrote directly to Davis in protest. Although the agreement ostensibly was made to stop further suffering by the Southern people, "nothing can be more fallacious than this reasoning," Hampton wrote. "*No* suffering which can be inflicted by the passage over our country of the Yankee armies can equal what would fall on us if we return to the Union." If Davis would furnish Hampton with "a good force of cavalry," he would lead the troopers and Davis safely across the Mississippi to fight another day.[318]

At Durham Station, Union troops plundered a warehouse owned by J. R. Greene that was filled with "bright leaf" tobacco, a variety that was heat cured with charcoal. The tobacco was lighter and sweeter than the kind the soldiers usually smoked. They quickly acquired a taste for Greene's product, and requests for it poured into Greene's factory then and in the years following. Greene and a partner gave their mild-tasting product the name, "Genuine Bull Durham Smoking Tobacco."[319]

When he returned to Raleigh, Sherman told his senior officers that Lincoln had been assassinated. As the news filtered down through the ranks, grief and rage followed in its wake. "The army is crazy for vengeance," wrote Captain Charles Wills of the 103rd Illinois. "If we make another campaign it will be an awful one." He and many other soldiers hoped that Johnston would not surrender. "God pity this country if he retreats or fights us."

Some men wanted to loot and burn Raleigh that day. "It is a Rebel hole and ought to be cleaned out," one man was heard to say as a mob of two thousand troops started for the North Carolina capital. General

John Logan interposed himself between the angry men and the city and ordered them to return to camp. They ignored him. Then, Logan announced that if they persisted, he would order the artillery, which was in plain view, to fire canister at them. The mob dispersed. "General Logan saved the City and it owes him a debt it never can pay," wrote Theodore Upson, a soldier in Logan's XV Corps.[320]

When the Sherman-Johnston agreement reached Grant in Washington on April 21, he instantly recognized that Sherman had exceeded his instructions and authority. Grant asked War Secretary Stanton to summon the president and Cabinet to a meeting that night to discuss what Sherman had done.[321]

Sherman believed that he had acted in accordance with Lincoln's wishes, but he had in fact badly misread the mood of the US government. Moreover, he was missing a key piece of information. On March 3, when Lee tried to arrange a parley with Grant to discuss peace terms, Grant had forwarded Lee's message to Stanton and requested instructions. After conferring with Lincoln, Stanton forbade Grant to meet with Lee, except for the purpose of accepting his surrender. "You are not to decide, discuss, or confer upon any political question," Stanton wrote. Sherman never saw that telegram.[322]

Sherman's proposed agreement could not have arrived in Washington at a worse time. The government remained unhinged by Lincoln's assassination. Stanton was directing the largest manhunt in US history, while continuing to oversee the herculean task of winding down the war. Earlier that day, Lincoln's casket had been transported with great ceremony to the Baltimore and Ohio Railroad depot and placed on the black crepe-shrouded train that would take the dead president to Springfield.[323]

His nerves frayed by days of stress and lack of sleep, Stanton exploded in anger when he read the agreement. At that night's stormy Cabinet meeting, Stanton, "who came charged with specific objections," counted them off on his fingers: permitting the South to preserve its state governments, the generous amnesty, and the failure to address slavery—in effect, he claimed, permitting Southerners to keep their slaves. Stanton and Attorney General James Speed "were emphatic in their condemnation," wrote Navy Secretary Gideon Welles, while Grant defended his friend. He "was tender to sensitiveness of his brother and abstained from censure." But Grant, the Cabinet, and President Johnson unanimously rejected the Bennett farmhouse agreement. Grant was directed to immediately inform Sherman of the agreement's rejection, to relieve Sherman and take command of his army, and to resume combat operations against Johnston's army.

In Richmond, General Henry Halleck, the Union Army's chief of staff, sent Stanton an uncorroborated report that said the exiled Confederate government, with its Rebel treasury and Richmond bank funds, intended to bribe Sherman or another Union commander to permit them and their "gold plunder, to go to Mexico or Europe. Johnston's negotiations look to this end." Halleck told Stanton that Sherman and other generals should be warned. But fearing that Sherman might already have been compromised, Halleck ordered Meade, Sheridan, and Horatio Wright, the VI Corps's commander, "to pay no regard to any truce or orders of General Sherman respecting hostilities."

Grant dispatched Sheridan, with his Cavalry Corps and VI Corps, to Danville to block Johnston's retreat in the event that fighting resumed in North Carolina. The general-in-chief then decided to go to Raleigh to tell Sherman in person about his government's rejection of the peace agreement.[324]

Seldom has a hero as dazzling as Sherman become a goat so quickly. The conqueror of Atlanta, Savannah, and Columbia, whose exploits in the Carolinas had thrilled newspaper readers, was now being pilloried by those same publications.

Stanton led the public scourging of Sherman by taking the highly unorthodox step of sending newspapers the text of Sherman's agreement; Lincoln's instructions of March 3, which Sherman had never seen, forbidding what he had just done; and Stanton's own point-by-point evisceration of the agreement. Stanton's critique began with the words, "It was an exercise of authority not vested in General Sherman," and proceeded to the Cabinet's other objections—nine in all. "It undertook to re-establish the rebel state governments, that had been overthrown at the sacrifice of many thousand loyal lives," Stanton wrote, and "by the restoration of the rebel authority in their respective states, they would be enabled to re-establish slavery." In conclusion, Stanton said the agreement would have "left them in condition to renew their effort to overthrow the United States government."[325]

Newspapers piled on editorially. The *Boston Evening Transcript* wrote, "This revelation of qualities of mind and character in Gen. Sherman, the existence of which no one imagined, is almost appalling . . . two qualities, latent until now, have blazed out—inordinate ambition and a conceit so enormous as almost to touch the edge of insanity." The *Philadelphia North American* concluded that Sherman had been "completely outwitted by Jeff. Davis and Jo. Johnston. . . . The terms agreed to by Sherman are an entire forfeiture of what we have gained by the war."[326]

Attorney General Speed, egged on by Stanton, speculated wildly about Sherman's supposed motives: that he intended to march on Washington "at the head of his victorious legions" and seize the government, and that he might even arrest Grant when he reached Raleigh and then take command of the entire Union Army.

Welles did not believe any of it; he was convinced that the terms Sherman made were only "a liberal construction of President Lincoln's benevolent wishes." "We have permitted ourselves amid great excitement and stirring events to be hurried into unjust and ungenerous suspicions by the erroneous statements of the Secretary of State." Stanton would "now reinstate himself with Grant by prostrating Sherman," Welles wrote, after having gone to Savannah "to pay court to Sherman when that officer was the favored general and supposed to have eclipsed Grant."[327]

Sherman had been so confident of the government approving his agreement with Johnston that he had halted the depredations of two independent cavalry commands—those of General George Stoneman, rampaging through western North Carolina, and General James Wilson, busy wreaking havoc in Georgia after marching five hundred miles in thirty days, capturing sixty-three hundred prisoners, and destroying every railroad and factory in his path. Moreover, Sherman had trustingly sent the orders suspending those operations in Union cipher over Johnston's telegraph lines in the hope that they would reach Stoneman and Wilson more quickly.[328]

~~~

Wilson and his twelve thousand troopers were riding through Georgia on the tide of their Alabama triumphs, minor though they seemed when compared to the more consequential Union victories in Virginia and North Carolina. They had driven General Nathan Bedford Forrest, the former hobgoblin of the West, and his much-diminished army before them in a chain of running battles across northern Alabama that ended at Selma. Forrest's men, facing an enemy twice their number and lacking Wilson's Spencer repeating rifles or fresh mounts, dug in outside the Southern manufacturing center. On April 2, Wilson's troopers overwhelmed Forrest's army, capturing twenty-seven hundred Rebels. Before riding unopposed through Montgomery, the Confederacy's first capital, and thence into Georgia, the Union cavalrymen reduced Selma's factories to smoldering rubble.[329]

Ten days later, Alabama's submission became complete when Mobile was surrendered after a two-week siege by General Edward Canby's army of the forts guarding upper Mobile Bay. The previous August, Union forces had seized the lower bay and its forts.

Confederate General Richard Taylor formally surrendered his forces to Canby, and Forrest informed his troops in words that must have greatly pained him to write, "The cause for which you have so long and so manfully struggled, and for which you have braved dangers, endured privations and sufferings, and made so many sacrifices is to-day hopeless." The former slave trader and feared cavalry leader urged his men to submit to the "powers that be." "The terms upon which you were surrendered are favorable," he wrote. "You have been good soldiers, you can be good citizens."[330]

A few days after ordering Wilson and Stoneman to suspend their offensives, Sherman sensed that his peace agreement with Johnston might encounter trouble after receiving a batch of Northern newspapers. He read about the anger and fury in the North over Lincoln's assassination, and he learned that the permission granted by Lincoln to reconvene the Virginia legislature had been rescinded.

Sherman sent Johnston a note warning him that because of the president's murder, "the feeling North on this subject is more intense than anything that ever occurred before." The agreement's recognition of "existing local governments" might prove problematic, Sherman said, but he still hoped that "good sense" would win out.[331]

Grant had not told Sherman that he was coming to Raleigh, and so when he arrived in Raleigh at dawn on April 24 it was a tremendous surprise to Sherman and his generals. "I was both surprised and pleased to see the general," Sherman wrote. So was General Henry Slocum. "All is well," Slocum wrote. "Grant is here. He has come to save his friend Sherman from himself."[332]

Grant handed Sherman a letter that he had written on April 21 about the unanimous disapproval of the peace agreement, and then explained the reasons for the rejection, omitting the Cabinet members' biting denunciations. Grant also shared a Stanton letter that said Sherman must follow the same guidelines that Stanton had given Grant on March 3. "It would have saved a world of trouble" if he had seen the March 3 instructions earlier, Sherman wryly observed.

Grant directed Sherman to inform Johnston of the agreement's rejection, and to also tell him that there was "a disapproval of the negociations [sic] altogether, except for the surrender of the Army commanded by Johnston."[333]

"I am instructed to limit my operations to your immediate command, not to attempt civil negotiations," Sherman obediently wrote to Johnston that day. The truce they had made would expire in forty-eight hours, he said. "I therefore demand the surrender of your army on the same terms as were given General Lee at Appomattox, of April 9, instant, purely and simply."[334]

After reading Sherman's letter, Johnston asked War Secretary Breckinridge for instructions on how to proceed. "We had better disband this small force to prevent devastation to the country," Johnston added. His army was shrinking daily. Since the armistice, thousands of Rebels had deserted from every branch of service.[335]

But Jefferson Davis did not wish to disband his last major fighting force. Probably at Davis's direction, Breckinridge proposed that Johnston "bring off the cavalry and all of the men you can mount from transportation and other animals, with some light field pieces" to begin marching to the Southwest, where they could continue the war. Johnston refused. His men would not fight again, his commanders had told him. "We think your plan impracticable," Johnston wrote, and agreed only to send Davis a cavalry escort.

Receiving no encouragement from Breckinridge or Davis to resume negotiations with Sherman, Johnston acted on his own authority. Continuing the war, Johnston believed, would inflict needless suffering and privation on North Carolina, which had been spared the war's worst dev-astation. It would also subject the fighting men who remained in his army to greater hardships, and to no good purpose.

On April 25, Johnston wrote to Breckinridge, "I have proposed to General Sherman military negotiations in regard to this army." Johnston and Sherman planned to meet the next day at the Bennett farmhouse.[336]

Grant deliberately kept a low profile, "hoping to see [Sherman] with-out even his army learning of my presence." He wanted to protect his friend from the embarrassment of it becoming known that Grant was in Raleigh to straighten things out. "I did not wish the knowledge of my presence to be known to the army generally; so I left it to Sherman to negotiate the terms of the surrender solely by himself," Grant wrote.

During their private meetings at Sherman's headquarters, where Grant showed him his instructions and orders, Grant neither relieved Sherman of command nor assumed command of his army. He merely directed Sherman to negotiate the same terms with Johnston that Grant had obtained at Appomattox.[337]

Grant reported to Stanton that day that he had apprised Sherman of the agreement's rejection, which Sherman "rather expected." Sherman had notified Johnston. Grant explained that Sherman's actions were guided by his conversations with Lincoln, the terms Grant had given Lee, and the Virginia legislature's authorization to convene, which he did not know had been withdrawn until after the Bennett farmhouse agreement was reached.[338]

Grant's defense of Sherman reflected as much his own changed at-titude toward the now-conquered South as it did his understanding of Sherman's thinking. For both Grant and Sherman the war's end trans-formed their perception of the former Confederacy. Merciless in prose-cuting the war, the North's two most powerful generals were now display-ing compassion toward their former enemy.

In a letter to his wife Julia, Grant described Raleigh's beauty, which remained untouched by the war. "Nothing has been destroyed and the people are anxious to see peace restored so that further devastation need not take place in the country. The suffering that must exist in the South the next year, even with the war ending now, will be beyond conception." Those who had neither fought in the war nor witnessed its annihilat-ing power spoke of "further retaliation and punishment," either from ignorance, or "they are heartless and unfeeling, and wish to stay at home, out of danger, whilst the punishment is inflicted."[339]

Among Sherman's men, rumors abounded. It was now apparent that Sherman's and Johnston's discussions of a week earlier had not resulted in the surrender of Johnston's army. But the news that Sherman was going to meet again with Johnston restoked feverish anticipation for a lasting agreement. "Everybody is in hopes tonight that Johnston will surrender tomorrow, after all. God grant it!" wrote Major Henry Hitchcock of Sherman's staff. "I cannot bear to think of this army marching through the country in a hostile attitude."[340]

Before going to meet with Johnston on the 26th, Sherman wrote Stanton a submissive letter admitting "my folly in embracing in a military convention any civil matters but unfortunately such is the nature of our situation that they seem inextricably united and I understood from you at Savannah that the financial state of the country demanded military success and would warrant a little bending to policy."[341]

That day, Sherman and Johnston signed a second agreement that closely resembled the Appomattox surrender document. General John Schofield, who would soon command this military district, wrote out the terms. Officers were permitted to retain their sidearms, horses, and baggage, and the men their personal property. Brigades were allowed to keep one-seventh of their arms for their march home; the weapons were to be turned in when they reached their state capitals. Sherman ordered the Confederates supplied with 250,000 rations, enough for ten days. In early May in Greensboro, 36,817 of Johnston's men turned in their weapons and battle flags and received their paroles.

Upon learning of Johnston's surrender, diarist Judith McGuire in Richmond wrote, "My native land, good-night!"

Grant approved the agreement as he and Sherman sat at a table in the North Carolina governor's mansion, where they wrote letters and paused occasionally to speak with the other generals in the room: Schofield, John Logan, Montgomery Meigs, and Oliver Howard. Junior officers peered through the windows at the generals, as "a fine brass band" played in the yard. The next morning, Grant left Raleigh to return to Washington.[342]

A couple of days later, a copy of the April 24 *New York Times* reached Sherman, and for the first time he read Stanton's flagellation of him in the press. "To say that I was merely angry at the tone and substance of these published bulletins of the War Department, would hardly express the state of my feelings," Sherman wrote. He particularly resented the insinuation that "I might be bribed by banker's gold to permit Davis to escape. . . . I regarded this bulletin of Mr. Stanton as a personal and official insult, which I afterward publicly resented."[343]

Sherman's violent reaction made an indelible impression on General Carl Schurz. In front of his officers, Sherman paced the governor's mansion in Raleigh "like a caged lion . . . unbosomed himself with an eloquence of furious invective which for a while made us all stare," wrote Schurz. "He lashed the Secretary of War as a mean, scheming, vindictive politician, who made it his business to rob military men of the credit earned by exposing their lives in the service of their country." The press, he said, was "an engine of vilification; which should be bridled by severe laws."[344]

Sherman wrote Grant a letter bristling with anger and hurt feelings. "I did think that my rank (if not past services) entitled me at least to trust that the Secretary of War would keep secret what was communicated for the use of none but the cabinet, until further inquiry could be made." He had never disobeyed orders, but his men "will learn with pain and amazement that I am deemed insubordinate, and wanting in common sense; that I . . . Have brought discredit on our Government."

With acid sarcasm, he continued, "It is true that non-combatants, men who sleep in comfort and security while we watch on the distant lines, are better able to judge than we poor soldiers, who rarely see a newspaper, hardly hear from our families, or stop long enough to draw our pay," he wrote. "I envy not the task of 'reconstruction,' and am delighted that the Secretary of War has relieved me of it." He demanded that his letter be made public as a refutation of Stanton's.[345]

Sherman's men were upset when they read in the newspapers the generous terms their commander had initially given Johnston. "We are very much shocked at Sherman's course," wrote Captain Charles Wills. "I have not heard an officer or soldier who had read them [the initial peace terms], sustain our general." Many officers believed Sherman had succumbed to hubris. "I am very sorry for him, but we have thought for a year, and it has been common talk in the army, that he was ambitious for political honors, etc." The army was taking it hard, Wills said. "We regret his action as much as any calamity of the war, excepting the Washington horror. . . . We all had such confidence in Sherman, and thought it almost impossible for him to make a mistake. The army is very sore over the affair."[346]

Admiral David Porter, who was present when Lincoln and Sherman discussed surrender terms at City Point in March, sympathized with Sherman. "Could the conversation that occurred on board the [*River*] *Queen*, between the President and General Sherman, have been known, Sherman would not, and could not, have been censured. Mr. Lincoln, had he lived, would have acquitted the general of any blame, for he was only carrying out the President's wishes."[347]

∞

The twelve days that had passed since John Wilkes Booth shot President Lincoln in his theater box had been a nightmare for the assassin. Only in the hours immediately following the murder did Booth and coconspirator David Herold enjoy any respite at all from pursuit. At the southern Maryland farmhouse of Dr. Samuel Mudd, the country doctor splinted Booth's broken left leg and allowed the fugitives to rest until nightfall April 15. Since then, though, detectives and Union cavalry had flooded the Maryland countryside, forcing Booth and Herold to hide in pine thickets and wade through swamps. The relentless manhunt had also complicated Booth's plan to quickly cross the Potomac River into Virginia.

On April 20 Stanton offered a $50,000 reward for Booth's capture and $25,000 rewards for the apprehension of his accomplices. The war secretary's proclamation also warned that harboring the killers was punishable by death. "Every man should consider his own conscience charged with this solemn duty, and rest neither night nor day until it is accomplished," Stanton wrote. "Let the stain of innocent blood be removed from the land by the arrest and punishment of the murderers."[348]

That night, Booth and coconspirator David Herold attempted to cross the Potomac River in their rowboat, but the current and the many Union gunboats on the water compelled them to turn back. In his diary, Booth wrote, "After being hunted like a dog through swamps, woods, and last night being chased by gun boats till I was forced to return wet cold and starving, with every mans hand against me, I am here in despair." He had expected some appreciation of his action and was dismayed by the lack of it. "A country groaned beneath this tyranny and prayed for this end. Yet now behold the cold hand they extend me."[349]

The night of April 22, Booth and Herold had better luck on the Potomac and crossed it in their little boat, reaching Virginia's Northern Neck by sunrise. They proceeded to Port Royal, despite the inhospitableness of wary residents.

At Richard Garrett's Locust Hill Farm, Booth was welcomed and given food and lodging after he concocted a story about having been wounded near Petersburg while serving in A. P. Hill's Third Corps. However, Garrett's son John, a former Confederate soldier, grew suspicious of Booth and Herold, who joined Booth at the farm on April 25, and would not permit them to stay in the house that night. He put them up in the tobacco barn, and then quietly padlocked the door as a precaution against the men robbing the Garretts while they slept.[350]

When detectives in Maryland learned that two men had crossed the Potomac in a rowboat, they enlisted twenty-seven volunteers from the 16th New York Cavalry to accompany them across the river on the steamship *John S. Ide*. In Virginia, they showed Northern Neck residents photos and sketches of Booth and Herold and got on the fugitives' trail; it led to the Garrett farm.[351]

Before dawn on April 26, the detectives and troopers surrounded the barn where Booth and Herold were sleeping. The troopers set fire to the barn to flush out the men. Herold surrendered, but Booth refused; he had witnessed John Brown's hanging and preferred to die free.

A cavalry sergeant, Boston Corbett, was eager to oblige him. Corbett was a born-again Christian who grew his hair and beard in the manner that Christ wore his and who, when once tempted by a pair of prostitutes, cut off his own testicles with scissors, literally obeying Christ's injunction to root out the evil in oneself.

Diminutive but fearless, Corbett offered to enter the barn alone and bring out Booth, but his plan was rejected. Watching Booth through the four-inch gaps between the barn's boards, Corbett saw him raise his carbine to fire at the soldiers. Corbett shot Booth in the neck, later claiming, "Providence directed my hand."[352]

Booth was still alive when he was carried from the burning barn to the front porch of the Garrett house. Water was brought to him, but he was unable to swallow it. As life ebbed from his body, he whispered, "My hands." He could not raise them. One of the detectives lifted Booth's hands so he could see them. "Useless! Useless!" Booth said, and died.[353]

MAY 1865

I cannot feel like a beaten man.

—CONFEDERATE PRESIDENT JEFFERSON DAVIS[1]

What a dark picture! What a terrible future our noble old Virginia in chains & governed by Yankees is it not galling & terrible!

—RICHMOND WOMAN[2]

They march like the lords of the world.

—FORMER TREASURY SECRETARY TOM CORWIN,
DESCRIBING SHERMAN'S ARMY DURING THE GRAND REVIEW[3]

May 2, 1865
ABBEVILLE, SOUTH CAROLINA

Jefferson Davis's military advisers stared disbelievingly at the Confederate president. He had summoned them on May 2 to a grand home in Abbeville, South Carolina, where Davis and his entourage had stopped on their southward flight. It quickly became apparent to the attendees that Davis had called them together not to fine tune his escape plan, but for precisely the opposite reason: to ask them how best to continue the war. The question stunned the group, which included War Secretary John Breckinridge, General Braxton Bragg, and a half-dozen second-tier generals and field officers. After all of the catastrophes of the past month, they were astounded that Davis believed victory was still possible.

One hundred miles west of Columbia and virtually untouched by the war, Abbeville had extended a warmer welcome to the Confederate president than any other Southern city along the path of his hegira. Moreover, no place was more appropriate than Abbeville for a discussion of the Confederacy's future. Abbeville was where South Carolina's secession movement began in 1860, and where now, four and a half years later, the Southern cause was completing its round. In Abbeville Davis convened his last war council.[4]

❧

Since abandoning Richmond, Davis may have privately despaired, but publicly he appeared unbowed and at times even cheerful. Never had he acknowledged defeat. Always, he had acted under the presumption that although armies might be compelled by overwhelming numbers to surrender, true Southerners would remain loyal and fight on. Robed in his Southern nationalism, which had progressed from steadfast to fanatical to delusional, Davis believed the battleground of the future would be the Trans-Mississippi states—Texas and Louisiana. He intended to turn west upon reaching Georgia and cross the Deep South, joining General Richard Taylor near Mobile, while drawing to himself others like him who had not given up. After they got over the Mississippi River into Louisiana, Davis and his followers would join General Edmund Kirby Smith's still extant army, Davis believed.[5]

He had defiantly vowed to persevere unto death in his proclamation of April 4, written in Danville, his first stopping place after leaving Richmond. The Union Army's capture of Richmond and Petersburg were no more than "reverses" and, in fact, the opening of "a new phase" of the war, "with an army free to move from point to point and strike in detail the detachments and garrisons of the enemy." If Rebel forces were driven from Virginia or any other state, "again and again will we return, until the baffled and exhausted enemy shall abandon in despair his endless and impossible task of making slaves of a people resolved to be free." He exhorted, "Let us but will it, and we are free; and who, in the light of the past, dare doubt your purpose in the future?"[6]

Davis and his fugitive government had traveled south in a procession of trains from Danville to Greensboro, North Carolina, on April 11. In one slow-moving train were Davis, Secretary of State Judah Benjamin, Navy Secretary Stephen Mallory, Postmaster General John Reagan, Attorney General George Davis, and Treasury Secretary George Trenholm. John Wise, General Henry Wise's son, watched the trains pass by. "I saw a government on wheels. It was the marvelous and incongruous debris of the wreck of the Confederate capital," he wrote. "Among the last in the long procession were trains bearing indiscriminate cargoes of men and things. In one car was a cage with an African parrot, and a box of tame squirrels, and a hunchback!"[7]

While crowds had come out to cheer Davis and his Cabinet at their Virginia stopovers, in North Carolina, with its many Unionists, they encountered outright hostility. North Carolina had lost more young men in the war than any state except Virginia, and Greensboro in 1861 had opposed secession. The dignitaries had difficulty even finding lodgings there. Confederate Army officers cajoled a landlord to give Davis a place in a house near the railroad station, but his department heads had to sleep in a railroad car and eat their meals off tin plates with pocketknives. The heavily guarded Confederate Treasury train, laden with gold and silver, had gotten to Greensboro a few days ahead of Davis and had left about $75,000 for Davis, his Cabinet, and Johnston's army before proceeding on to Charlotte.[8]

In Greensboro Davis received Robert E. Lee's telegram informing him of the surrender of his army, whose immediate cause was the missing food shipment at Amelia Court House that had cost Lee his one-day head start. "I did not see how a surrender could have been avoided,"

Lee wrote. "We had no subsistence for man or horse, and it could not be gathered in the country."[9]

In his final letter to Davis eight days later—it never reached Davis— Lee urged him to abandon the idea of prolonging the war. "I believe an army cannot be organized or supported in Virginia, and as far as I know the condition of affairs, the country east of the Mississippi is morally and physically unable to maintain the contest unaided with any hope of ultimate success." A guerrilla war might be waged, Lee said, "but I see no prospect by that means of achieving a separate independence. . . . I would recommend measures be taken for suspension of hostilities and the restoration of peace."[10]

Before leaving Greensboro, Davis wrote a cheerless note to his wife Varina, who was in Charlotte: "I will come to you if I can—Everything is dark—you should prepare for the worst by dividing your baggage so as to move in wagons. If you can go to Abbeville [South Carolina] it seems best as I am now advised."[11]

The Confederate government, in a dreary caravan of horses and wagons escorted by twenty-five hundred mounted troops, left Greensboro for Charlotte, following the railroad line recently wrecked by General John Stoneman's Union cavalry. It rained heavily the first day, and the wagons stuck fast in the deep mud; the Rebel government's highest officials, soaked to the skin, waded into the muck and pushed them out. It took days to reach Charlotte.[12]

There, Davis learned about Lincoln's assassination. Postmaster General Reagan was with Davis when he received the news. "We felt that his death was most unfortunate for the people of the Confederacy," he wrote. Navy Secretary Mallory reported that Davis appeared to be saddened by Lincoln's death. Davis said, "I certainly have no special regard for Mr. Lincoln; but there are a great many men of whose end I would much rather have heard than his. I fear it will be disastrous to our people, and I regret it deeply." Davis would have preferred the death of Andrew Johnson, whom he intensely disliked and whom hc believed would treat the South more harshly than Lincoln.[13]

Breckinridge brought Davis a copy of the first Sherman-Johnston peace agreement of April 18. Without revealing his opposition to it, Davis solicited written opinions from his Cabinet members; unsurprisingly, they were unanimous in advising Davis to accept the generous terms.

Attorney General Davis's statement concluded, "The chief duty left for you to perform, is to provide as far as possible, for the speedy delivery of the people from the horrors of war and anarchy by approving the convention, issuing a proclamation saying why [the] terms were accepted, disbanding armies, resigning as president, and recommending the states carry the agreement into effect."[14]

Davis telegraphed Johnston his approval of the agreement, but shrewdly guessed that the Johnson administration would reject Sherman's terms. When the agreement was disapproved, Davis immediately sought all of Johnston's troops who could be mounted to join the march to the Southwest. But Johnston sent Davis only a cavalry escort, severed direct communication with the president, and signed the second agreement with Sherman surrendering his army. Davis had never liked Johnston—he had removed him from command in Georgia—and he was undoubtedly feeling wrathful toward him now.

But this was not the time for Davis to indulge in his anger; flight or capture were his choices, and delay meant capture. At what would be the last meeting of Davis's full Cabinet, the decision was made to leave Charlotte immediately. Attorney General Davis resigned so that he could remain in North Carolina and care for his children, whose mother had died. Despite the relentlessly bad news, Jefferson Davis remained unaccountably optimistic. "I *cannot* feel like a beaten man," he was heard to say.[15]

While Davis was holding his last meeting with his military advisers in Abbeville on May 2, coincidentally Andrew Johnson's Cabinet was meeting in Washington to discuss Davis's possible complicity in Lincoln's murder. War Secretary Stanton produced papers from the government's chief prosecutor in the assassination case, Army Judge Advocate General Joseph Holt, implicating Davis and several other Confederate officials. A Kentuckian, Holt had served as postmaster general and then secretary of war under President James Buchanan. When the war broke out, Holt sided with the Union, and in 1862 Lincoln appointed him the Army's judge advocate; he was now a brigadier general. At the April 14 Fort Sumter ceremony, Holt had condemned Confederates as "the Iscariots of the human race. May God in his eternal justice forbid that they should ever be shown mercy or forbearance." It was Holt who also asserted that Davis and the Rebel government possessed between $6 million and $13 million, when the actual amount was about $500,000.[16]

After receiving Holt's assessment—more speculative than factual—of the Confederate government's role in Lincoln's murder, President Johnson issued a proclamation offering a $100,000 reward for Davis's arrest, and another $110,000 for the apprehension of five other men, including the Rebel spymasters who had recruited Booth in Canada to kidnap Lincoln. Although Navy Secretary Welles thought the reward was justified, he acknowledged, "I had no facts."[17]

⧉

At first speechless when Davis sought their advice on how to continue the war, the Confederate generals found their voices. The war was lost, they reluctantly told the Confederate president. They did not believe it was possible to even reach the Mississippi River; their men were ready to quit, and their horses were worn out.

Davis petulantly asked them why they were even in the field. To protect you, they told Davis. This profession of their allegiance seemed to only anger Davis. If "all the friends of the South were prepared to consent to her degradation," he said, there was nothing more that he could do. Thereafter, Davis ceased directing the column's movements and became a passive spectator to his own flight. Breckinridge assumed command of the shrinking party.[18]

They pushed south. At the Savannah River, the South Carolina troops refused to cross into Georgia and demanded payment. Breckinridge obliged them; all of the silver from the Treasury Department wagons was brought into a nearby home, and payrolls from the men's units were produced. Breckinridge paid forty-one hundred men $26.25 apiece—more than $108,000 in all, leaving $179,700 in the wagons. All but a few hundred men took their payment and went home.*

Davis convened a meeting of the few civil and military leaders still traveling with him: Postmaster General Reagan, Quartermaster General A. R. Lawton, and General Bragg. Davis announced that he was temporarily

---

*Later, bandits in Georgia reportedly stole most of the Confederate funds remaining in the wagons. Although some of it was recovered, what happened to the rest of the money remains a mystery that continues to inspire treasure hunters.

disbanding the government. If everything went according to his plan, he said, the government would be reconstituted in the Trans-Mississippi. He was undoubtedly influenced by a recent letter from Varina Davis, who wrote that all of the soldiers from Lee's and Johnston's armies whom she had met on the road had told her they were finished with fighting. "A stand cannot be made in this country; do not be induced to try it," she warned her husband. Better to wait until he crossed the Mississippi River, his wife said.

On May 6, the Davises were reunited in Georgia. Ride ahead to Texas, Varina urged her husband. When Davis expressed remorse over having forced his wife to become a fugitive who might even have to flee the country, she replied, "It is surely not the fate to which you invited me in brighter days, but you must remember that you did not invite me to a great Hero's home, but to that of a plain farmer."[19]

When intelligence reached General James Wilson in Macon that Davis was bivouacked outside of Irwinville, Georgia, about forty miles away, he dispatched two cavalry regiments—the 1st Wisconsin and 4th Michigan—to capture him. Breckinridge learned that the Yankee cavalrymen were on their trail, and he and a few hundred of the remaining men rode north to create a diversion, but it fooled no one.

After riding all night, Wilson's troopers located Davis's camp outside Irwinville. While it was still dark, the 1st Wisconsin and 4th Michigan converged on the Rebel bivouac from different directions. They mistakenly opened fire on one other, each regiment believing that Rebels were shooting at them. Before the fratricidal gun battle ended, two troopers were dead and four others were wounded.

The shooting awakened the sleeping camp. Three figures emerged from a large tent and began walking toward the woods. A trooper called, "Halt!" Davis, who was one of the three, paused momentarily, but then approached a Union trooper who was aiming a carbine at him, intending, he later claimed, to grab the cavalryman's boot and flip him from his horse—a trick he said he had learned in the US Army. Mrs. Davis, believing the trooper was going to shoot her husband, ran to him and, with a cry, flung her arms around his neck. The Confederacy's president was now a prisoner.

Wilson's report said Davis had disguised himself as a woman, wearing "a black mantle wrapped about his head, through the top of which could be seen locks of his hair," and "a lady's waterproof cloak, gathered at the waist." Davis denied that he had attempted to disguise himself as a woman; groping in the darkness of his tent for an outer garment, he said, he had put on Varina's cloak instead of his raincoat. Davis walked off without his hat, and Varina threw her black shawl over her husband's head.

In the North, Davis's attire spawned exaggerated reports in the press, including the myth that he was captured while wearing one of Varina's dresses. *Harper's Weekly* repeated this story in its sensational account of Davis's capture, writing that he "hastily put on one of his wife's dresses and started for the woods, closely followed by our men, who at first thought him a woman, but seeing his boots while he was running, they suspected his sex at once. The race was a short one, and the rebel President was soon brought to bay. He brandished a bowie-knife and showed signs of battle, but yielded promptly to the persuasions of Colt's revolvers." Fabricated though it was, the story was too good to pass up.

The Union troopers looted the Davises' baggage and the belongings of his traveling companions. Of the millions of dollars rumored to be in their possession, the Yankees found just $10,000 in gold coins in the saddlebags of Reagan and some aides.[20]

Breckinridge managed to slip away from the camp. He made his way to Florida and survived a harrowing boat journey to Cuba, arriving on June 11. Secretary of State Benjamin also reached Cuba, and thence proceeded to England, never returning to the United States. Breckinridge lived abroad until 1868, when he went home to Kentucky.[21]

On the day of Davis's capture, May 10, President Johnson, not yet aware that the Confederate president was in custody, proclaimed that "armed resistance to the authority of this Government in the said insurrectionary States may be regarded as virtually at an end."[22]

❧

Robert E. Lee remained near Appomattox Court House until his men surrendered their arms and battle flags on April 12. Then he began the hundred-mile ride to Richmond. He entered the city with his son Rooney on April 15, the morning Lincoln died. In a rainstorm the Lees and the other Confederates who had joined them during their journey rode through the fire-blackened central city, where rubble still lay in the streets and Union soldiers patrolled the neighborhoods. Federal relief agencies distributed food and provisions to people who had neither, and only worthless Confederate money for purchases. A total of 86,555 rations were distributed to about one-third of Richmond's population during the week of Lee's return.

As Lee approached the brick East Franklin Street home that his wife, Mary, and his family had rented for more than a year, he saw that his arrival had been anticipated. Crowds had gathered along Franklin Street to welcome the former general-in-chief, and Union soldiers were even seen cheering Lee. Reaching his home, Lee dismounted and shook many outstretched hands before going in the gate. Bowing to the people, he went inside.[23]

For days Lee, who for the past three years had been "the idol of his soldiers & the Hope of his country," lived as an ordinary citizen, sleeping for long hours in his bedroom or sitting with his family in the back parlor. He seldom went out, but that didn't stop the stream of visitors.

The streets were soon full of men in gray uniforms once more, although without insignia or unit badges, and with brass buttons concealed lest the Union soldiers slice them off. Lee avoided the crowds when needing exercise by going out on foot at night with his daughter Mildred.

One day, two ragged soldiers appeared at Lee's door. Sixty of their comrades were around the corner, they told Lee, but their disreputably tattered clothing made them unfit to enter any decent home. The former Rebel soldiers invited Lee to join them in the mountains on property that they owned. In this remote place, they told him, his loyal men would protect him from the Northern authorities. Although visibly moved by their generous proposition, Lee declined. "You would not have your general run away and hide. He must stay and meet his fate," he said.

Another ragged soldier rang the bell at Lee's home on a day when the general had instructed his family to turn away all callers so that he could concentrate on his backlog of correspondence. Lee's son Custis told the soldier that the general could not see him. The man said he had fought four years under Lee with Hood's Texas Brigade and had wanted to shake his hand before he began the walk home to Texas, but he understood. He turned away. Relenting, Custis called back the soldier, invited him inside, and went upstairs to tell his father. Lee came down, bowed to the soldier, and advanced with outstretched hand. Overcome by emotion, the soldier was unable to speak as he shook Lee's hand. He burst into tears, turned away, and left without saying a word.[24]

First the Confederate soldiers returned, and then the Northern tourists began arriving in the conquered capital, eager to see it firsthand. George Templeton Strong and other members of the US Sanitary Commission board came on a steamer after attending Lincoln's funeral. "Richmondites are cowed and broken in spirit," Strong reported.[25]

One of the Northerners making the pilgrimage to Richmond was Matthew Brady, who persuaded Lee to permit him to photograph him. Outside Lee's home, Brady took four pictures of Lee alone, one with his son Custis, and another photo of Lee with Custis and his former aide, Colonel Walter Taylor.[26]

Two weeks after Appomattox, Lee agreed to an interview with Thomas Cook of the *New York Herald*. Surprisingly, Lee claimed that peace had been achievable in 1863 because the South was then ready to return to the Union if the North would compromise. The abolition of slavery was never a major issue, he told Cook with perfect equanimity, a statement that was patently untrue. He suggested that freeing the slaves, when they were unready for freedom, would do them more harm than good. Lee also warned that if the North adopted a vindictive policy toward the South, there was yet enough "vitality and strength" in the former Confederacy to prolong hostilities indefinitely.[27]

❧

Lee's warning, however, rang as hollow as everything else that he had said to Cook. The South had lost its fighting spirit; Southerners lacked the heart to resume the war. The inhabitants of the formerly rebellious states resigned themselves—if most bitterly—to their new life under occupation.

"The Vulgar Yankee nation exults over our misfortunes, places its foot upon our necks, & extols its own prowess in conquering us," wrote Catherine Edmonston, a North Carolina diarist. "They command all the R Roads & other routes of travel & they have the ability to force their detested oath down the throat of every man amongst us."[28]

"What a dark picture!" lamented a Richmond woman. "What a terrible future our noble old Virginia in chains & governed by Yankees is it not galling & terrible!" She did not so much mind her family losing its slaves, "but to loose [*sic*] my country is to me the most terrible blow that could befall me."[29]

In Chapel Hill, North Carolina, Cornelia Spencer sadly watched the

Stars and Stripes rippling in the breeze over her town for the first time in four years. "Never before had we realized how entirely our hearts had been turned away from what was once our whole country, till we felt the bitterness aroused by the sight of that flag, shaking out its red and white folds over us."[30]

A few days later Spencer saw a squad of unarmed men in gray, "dusty and haggard, walking slowly along the road. A moment's look, a hasty inquiry, and '*Lee's men!*' burst from our lips, and tears from our eyes." The townspeople ran to the road and invited the thin, hungry soldiers into their homes to feed them, "to cry over them, and say again and again, 'God bless you all we are just as proud of you, and thank you just as much as if it had turned out differently.'" The sight of unarmed ex-soldiers trudging to their homes became commonplace. The men passed, "sometimes in twos and threes, sometimes in little companies, making the best of their way toward their distant homes, penniless and dependent on wayside charity for their food, plodding along, while the blue jackets pranced gaily past on the best blood of Southern stables."[31]

The Confederacy's captive president was brought before General Wilson in Macon, and they had a friendly, candid conversation. Davis was certain that he would be charged with treason, but he believed the charge could not stand legal or constitutional scrutiny. Wilson listened in amazement, and when Davis left him, he wrote, "The thought struck me once or twice that Jefferson Davis was a mad man. The indifference with which he seemed to regard the affairs of our day savored of insanity."

Within a few hours, Davis, his wife, their three children, Postmaster General John Reagan, and former Confederate Senator Clement C. Clay—who had had a $25,000 price on his head for allegedly being one of Booth's spymasters in Canada—were on a train headed for the Savannah River. There, they were marched onto a steamer bound for Savannah. Other Confederate prisoners were also on board, Vice President Alexander Stephens and General Joe Wheeler among them. Davis and Stephens met on deck for the first time since February, when Stephens left Richmond for good. Although the two had long disliked one another, Stephens conceded, "I could not but deeply sympathize with [Davis] in his present condition."

They were escorted to the side-wheeler *William P. Clyde* for the trip north. Davis presumed that their destination was Washington, but he was wrong; it was Hampton Roads.

On May 22, under a heavy guard, Davis and Clay were led onto a tug-boat that carried them to Fortress Monroe, the "Gibraltar of the Chesapeake," guarded by thick granite walls and garrisoned by Union troops. Stephens, Wheeler, and Reagan continued on the *Clyde* to prisons in the North.

Inside Fortress Monroe, the Confederate president was ushered into a ten-by-fourteen-foot cell built into the fort's ribbed casement. The *New York Herald* described it as "a living tomb. "No more will Jeff'n Davis be known among the masses of men. He is buried alive," the *Herald*'s sensational report said.

Davis's jailer was General Nelson Miles, an ambitious, capable young field officer who had been wounded four times during the war. His XXIII Corps division had distinguished itself around Petersburg during the war's final days.

Miles escorted Davis to his austere cell, furnished with a desk, chair, and cot. No reading material was permitted. On the desk, a candle burned twenty-four hours a day. Two soldiers stood guard inside the cell, with an officer detailed to peer closely at Davis every fifteen minutes, making it nearly impossible for him to sleep.

The day after Davis was locked up, Assistant Secretary of State Charles Dana hand-delivered an order to Miles instructing him to shackle and manacle Davis and Clay. Miles summoned a blacksmith to chain Davis's ankles together. Davis fought the blacksmith and the guards. Only after several soldiers had pinned Davis down—Davis "showed unnatural strength," a guard captain said—was the blacksmith able to clamp the leg irons on him. He was not manacled. News of Davis's shackling was leaked to the newspapers and, somewhat surprisingly, the descriptions of the Confederate president's harsh treatment began to arouse sympathy for him in the North.

A physician examined Davis days later, and was shocked to find him emaciated and feverish. The doctor told Davis that he should stand up and get exercise. In response, Davis threw off his blanket to show the doctor his chains and the places on his ankles where they had chafed his skin raw.

Miles forwarded the doctor's report to Stanton, who by then was reading the press's censorious coverage of Davis's shackling. The *Springfield (Massachusetts) Republican* warned the government not to make a martyr of Davis. "The wounds inflicted in cold blood are what keep animosities alive," the *Republican* said. If Davis died in prison, it would "perpetuate for a hundred years the sentiment of vengeance."

Stanton ordered the shackles removed. Miles took additional steps to ensure that his celebrity prisoner would not die on his watch. He no longer insisted that a candle perpetually burn in Davis's cell, he granted him reading privileges, and he personally took him for daily walks. Davis's physical condition improved.[32]

As Davis had predicted, the tangled legal and constitutional questions surrounding his case bogged it down for a year. Then, a federal grand jury convened by Judge John Underwood in Norfolk, Virginia, indicted Davis for high treason. The courts struggled to determine whether Davis could be tried in a civil court while in military custody. Two years passed without Davis appearing in court. The Johnson administration, under tremendous pressure to either try Davis or release him, at last had Davis brought before Underwood for a hearing at the old Customs House in Richmond. On May 13, 1867, the judge agreed to set bail; the $100,000 bond was promptly posted by *New York Tribune* editor Horace Greeley and other influential Northerners.

When Davis emerged from the Customs House a free man, a roar, mingled with the keening Rebel yell, rose from the throng gathered outside. A boisterous crowd of about five thousand people was also waiting outside the Spotswood Hotel, where Davis and Varina had booked a room, when Davis's carriage arrived. But when he alighted, a strange hush fell over the crowd and someone called out, "Hats off, Virginians!" Hatless and silent, the spectators watched Davis enter the hotel.[33]

Another Underwood grand jury returned treason indictments against Robert E. Lee, Joseph Johnston, James Longstreet, and other senior Confederate generals. Underwood told the grand jury that the paroles given Lee and the others did not shield them from prosecution. "That was a mere military arrangement, and can have no influence upon civil rights or the status of the persons interested," the judge declared.[34]

A week earlier, on May 29, President Johnson had issued a proclamation giving amnesty to lower-level Confederate military and civil personnel who took a loyalty oath, but denying it to thousands of higher-ranking

Rebel Army, Navy, and government officials. These included officers above the rank of colonel, those educated at West Point, the governors of seceded states, civil and diplomatic officials, former US judges and congressmen, and private citizens owning property whose value exceeded $20,000. Those denied amnesty could apply for a pardon from the president, "and such clemency will be liberally extended as may be consistent with the facts of the case and the peace and dignity of the United States," Johnson's proclamation said.[35]

Lee had decided to seek a pardon to set an example for his men when he learned, to his great surprise, of his treason indictment. Lee was concerned that if his parole did not protect him against prosecution, tens of thousands of his soldiers who received paroles might also be charged. Wondering whether Grant had changed his mind about clemency, Lee sought clarification from the general-in-chief through an intermediary friend, Reverdy Johnson, a US senator from Maryland. Grant unhesitatingly said that he stood by the paroles and would endorse Lee's application for a pardon when he submitted it.[36]

Lee sent Grant his petition for a pardon, and asked him whether the paroles granted at Appomattox trumped the Norfolk indictments. In a letter to War Secretary Stanton accompanying Lee's petition, Grant wrote, "In my opinion the officers and men paroled at Appomattox C.H., and since, upon the same term given to Lee, cannot be tried for treason so long as they observe the terms of their parole. . . . Good faith as well as true policy dictates that we should observe the conditions of that convention." Grant requested that Judge Underwood quash the Norfolk indictments and take no further action against paroled war prisoners.[37]

When the Cabinet failed to act on Lee's request, Grant took it to President Johnson. It quickly became clear to Grant when he met with the president that Johnson was behind the administration's new punitive policy toward Lee and the other Confederate leaders.

"When can they be tried?" Johnson asked Grant.

"Never," Grant replied. "Never, unless they violate their parole." The Appomattox paroles must be honored, he said.

Johnson demanded to know how a military commander could presume "to protect an arch-traitor from the laws."

Grant rarely lost his temper, but he now did. He angrily said that Lee and his men would never have surrendered at Appomattox if they believed that they would be subject to arrest, imprisonment, or execution—and more lives would have been lost.

"So long as General Lee observes his parole, I will never consent to his arrest," Grant declared. He then put his own career on the line, threatening to resign his commission if the Appomattox paroles were violated.

"And I will keep my word," he told the president. "I will not stay in the army if they break the pledges that I made."

Johnson, stubborn and often impetuous, also knew when it was prudent to back down; he could see that Grant was in deadly earnest. Nothing would destroy his presidency quicker than the resignation of the Union's great hero, Grant, in a protest against Johnson.

Two weeks later, Attorney General James Speed ordered the US attorney in Norfolk to stop his prosecution of Lee and his senior generals.[38]

In early May, the victorious Union armies began their long march to Washington for a "Grand Review" on May 23 and 24. The parade through the capital's streets would be the largest in US history. President Johnson decided that it was time to put away the black crepe and end the official mourning for Lincoln, and to now celebrate the momentous victory that culminated four years of death and sacrifice. George Meade's Army of the Potomac would march on the first day, Sherman's Western army on the second. About 150,000 officers and men would converge on Washington for the one and only gathering of the triumphant Union Army. Demobilization would commence immediately afterward.

Scattered over southern Virginia, the Army of the Potomac started for Washington after the official surrender of Lee's army. Just weeks earlier wholly bent on killing and destruction, the Union troops had been quick to adopt a more benevolent role. They were now guardians of the Southern people, who had become prey to lawless bands of former Confederate soldiers who robbed and burned their property, and terrorized their women. The Yankees distributed Confederate commissary food to the people, as well as abandoned wagons, animals, and implements. Union officers presided over ad hoc courts of adjudication, where they heard complaints from civilians and settled disputes.

Peacetime, desolating for the defeated Southerners, also challenged the victors, who worried about the approaching transition to civilian life.

Many resented the relaxation of vigilance. They had grown to love army life and regretted having to leave it.

"Never are we less gay," wrote General Joshua Chamberlain, as he marched north with his V Corps brigades. Chamberlain missed the careful precautions against surprise and the thrilling prospect of imminent combat. "When we took up the long, roundabout march homeward, it was dull to plod along looking only at the muddy road, without scouts and skirmishers about, and reckless of our flanks." Chamberlain was in fact bored. "It was dreary to lie down and sleep at night and think there was no vigilant picket out on the dubious-looking crests around to keep faithful watch and ward."[39]

Captain Charles Wills of the 103rd Illinois took no pleasure in the prospect of "four years of soldiering" soon ending. "I have almost a dread of being a citizen, of trying to be sharp, and trying to make money," he wrote. "I don't think I dread the work. I don't remember of shirking any work I ever attempted, but I am sure that civil life will go sorely against the grain for a time."[40]

V Corps reached Petersburg on May 3. Charles Griffin, the corps commander, notified his predecessor, Gouverneur Warren, awaiting reassignment after his dismissal and brief duty as Petersburg's military commander, that his former corps wished to salute him. Warren and his wife stood on a balcony at the Bollingbrook Hotel as the corps passed them, with bands playing patriotic songs in Warren's honor. The Warrens became emotional when the soldiers raised their caps and cheered their former general.[41]

As the Union divisions marched through Richmond one after the other, the former Confederate capital's citizens marveled at their numbers. "Day after day, we witnessed the passage of the countless, and as they seemed to us, interminable legions of the enemy, against which our comparatively little army had so obstinately . . . held out for four years," wrote Sallie Putnam. She and others wondered how the Confederate armies had done it. "Our pride, our glory in our countrymen was heightened, and we felt indeed 'the South' is the land for soldiers."[42]

North of Richmond, Chamberlain's brigade bivouacked on a battlefield where it had fought during Grant's 1864 Overland Campaign. A sentinel awakened Chamberlain around midnight. Chamberlain's horse was behaving strangely, the sentinel said; the general went to investigate.

While pawing the ground, the horse had become upset when it un-earthed two skulls and some bones, Chamberlain discovered. After the general collected the human remains, the animal calmed down. "It was a weird, uncanny scene," wrote Chamberlain, "the straggling, uncompanionable pines; the night brooding still and chill; black lowering clouds . . . the white skulls mocking life."

The next morning, his men canvassed the area for more shallow graves, looking for evidence of old friends who had disappeared in combat. By initials cut into the breastplates or other marks, they found fragmentary remnants of comrades long ago listed as missing in action. They packed the bones and personal items into empty cracker boxes to send to the dead soldiers' friends and relatives. "And so the strange column set forth bearing in its train that burden of unlost belongings," wrote Chamberlain, "as Moses coming up out of Egypt through the wilderness of the Red Sea, bearing with him the bones of Joseph the well-beloved."[43]

As the Union Army continued its journey through northern Virginia, Edwin Houghton of the 17th Maine was sobered by what he saw in Fredericksburg, which had been both battleground and Union hospital. "The buildings were riddled with shot and shell, and an air of decay and desolation hung over the once beautiful and prosperous city," he wrote.[44]

William Sherman sailed from Morehead City to Fortress Monroe and then up the James River to City Point. After writing his final campaign report there, he rode the train to his army's encampment in Manchester, across the James from Richmond; his men had marched there from North Carolina. On their way to Manchester, Sherman's troops had passed Fort Stedman, the objective of General John Gordon's failed breakout on March 25, and saw the partially exposed remains of forty Union soldiers as well as the Rebel burial ground—"quite a large and thickly settled village. Poor fellows," wrote Captain Charles Wills.

The day before Sherman's arrival in Manchester, during a nighttime thunderstorm, lightning struck a XV Corps tent, killing four soldiers. "The boys think it is pretty hard for anyone to be killed now after all we have gone through," remarked Theodore Upson of the 100th Indiana.[45]

Sherman still seethed over the abuse heaped upon him by War Secretary Stanton and Army Chief of Staff Henry Halleck. Stanton had practically called him a traitor; Halleck had countermanded Sherman's orders to his subordinate generals, and had insinuated that he might take a bribe from Jefferson Davis so that Davis could escape. Halleck's countermanding order had even appeared in the *New York Times.*

At Fortress Monroe, Sherman had received a telegram from Halleck professing friendship and admiration. "When you arrive here [in Richmond] come directly to my headquarters," wrote Halleck. "I have a room for you, and will have rooms elsewhere for your staff."

Sherman declined Halleck's invitation. "After your dispatch to the Secretary of War of April 26 I cannot have any friendly intercourse with you," Sherman wrote. "I will come to City Point to morrow and march with my troops, and I prefer we should not meet."

Halleck replied that he regretted having upset Sherman, but claimed that he was only acting on the War Department's wishes. If "I used language which has given you offense, it was unintentional, and I deeply regret it," Halleck wrote. "You have not had during this war nor have you now a warmer friend and admirer than myself."

Sherman was unappeased. "I cannot possibly reconcile the friendly expressions of the former with the deadly malignity of the latter, and cannot consent to the renewal of a friendship I had prized so highly til I can see deeper into the diabolical plot than I now do," he wrote. "I will march my army through Richmond quietly and in good order, without attracting attention, and I beg you to keep slightly perdu [out of sight], for if noticed by some of my old comrades, I cannot undertake to maintain a model behavior, for their feelings have become aroused by what the world adjudges an insult to at least an honest commander."

Halleck intensified Sherman's hostility toward him by refusing to allow his men to visit Richmond as sightseers. Army of the Potomac troops blocked the bridges into the city from Manchester. When they were turned away, soldiers from XV Corps threw stones at the Eastern troops and pitched an officer into the James River.

Then Halleck ordered XIV Corps to pass in review before him when Sherman's men resumed their march north. "I never before saw [Sherman] in such a towering passion," wrote Lieutenant Colonel Andrew Hickenlooper, "and never believed that he was capable of using such scathing and denunciatory language as he did in reference to General Halleck." It was now the turn of Sherman, furious over the treatment of his soldiers, to countermand one of Halleck's orders. There would be no review; if he were to "tamely submit," Sherman said, his men would think less of him.

From the portico of the home that was Halleck's headquarters, the general, evidently believing that the men might yet salute him, watched Sherman's army file through Richmond on May 11. The Western troops marched past Halleck with their eyes fixed ahead of them and did not acknowledge his presence. One of Sherman's ragged men briefly stepped out of the column to expel a stream of tobacco juice onto the blacked boots of a crisply uniformed guard outside Halleck's door.[46]

Still fuming over Halleck's refusal to allow his men to tour Richmond, Sherman told General John Logan, the XV Corps commander, that the army's hostile reception "was a part of a grand game to insult us—us who had marched a thousand miles through a hostile country in mid-winter to help them. We did help them, and what has been our reward? Your men were denied admission to the city, when Halleck had invited all citizens (rebels, of course) to come and go without passes. . . . If such be the welcome the East gives to the West, we can but let them make war and fight it out themselves."[47]

Near Alexandria on May 20, Sherman's army bivouacked on the Potomac River's south bank, downriver from where the Army of the Potomac was camped. A city of white tents soon sprawled along the riverbank for miles. Rather than foster a fraternal spirit, the proximity of the two armies and the Western men's treatment in Richmond only aggravated the already tense relationship between the Western troops and the Eastern army. Sherman's men mocked the Army of the Potomac as "babies and hospital cats" that had to be taught how to fight by Western men such as Grant and Phil Sheridan. George Meade's troops nicknamed the Western men "Sherman's greasers" because their prolonged exposure to pine smoke had darkened their skin.

Matters escalated to threats of physical violence, and the Army of the Potomac doubled its camp guards and created special reserve forces to react quickly if Sherman's men attacked them. On some nights, the Eastern men slept in their boots, with their swords and pistols by their sides, in case their brother soldiers should strike. "This was a serious condition of things," Joshua Chamberlain understatedly said. Sherman later moved his army over to the river's north bank, claiming that the campgrounds on the south bank had been fouled by previous overuse.[48]

❧❧

The Cavalry Corps, excluded from the surrender ceremony at Appomattox Court House on April 12, was going to play a prominent role in the review of the Army of the Potomac, but without its hard-driving commander, Phil Sheridan. He was on his way to the Southwest, and General Wesley Merritt, Sheridan's senior division commander, was going to lead the corps during the parade.

Grant had appointed Sheridan commander of all US troops west of the Mississippi River. "Your duty is to restore Texas, and that part of Louisiana held by the enemy, to the Union in the shortest practicable time," Grant's order read. "You will proceed without delay." Realizing that "without delay" meant being unable to accompany his elite Cavalry Corps for the last time, before its demobilization, Sheridan appealed to Grant to first let him lead his corps in the Grand Review. Grant refused.

The reason for Sheridan's urgent departure was not the one stated in his orders—to obtain the surrender of Confederate General Edmund Kirby Smith and his nearly forty-thousand-man Trans-Mississippi command. It was something else altogether: to help drive from Mexico the European monarchy that now ruled that country; the Emperor Maximilian's regime had aided the Confederacy during the war. Grant wanted Sheridan to assist the insurgency of Benito Juarez in casting out the Europeans and Maximilian, and to stop armed ex-Confederates from entering Mexico.

Sheridan's new command was unusually large—more than fifty thousand troops—bespeaking Grant's seemingly boundless faith in Sheridan. Sylvanus Cadwallader, the newspaper correspondent, said Grant had told him, "No army would ever be raised on this continent so large that Sheridan could not competently command it."[49]

While on a steamboat en route to New Orleans, Sheridan learned that Smith had surrendered his isolated Rebel army to General Edward Canby. Two weeks earlier, the last battle of the war had been fought near Brownsville, Texas, at Palmito Ranch. Ironically, it was a Confederate victory: three hundred Rebel cavalrymen drove two Union regiments for seven miles.[50]

❧❧

They had come to see the Union Army, at the pinnacle of its might, parade victoriously through the nation's capital in celebration of having crushed the Rebellion. From all over the North people had poured into Washington by every available conveyance. Trains alone brought an estimated seventy-five thousand passengers into the city. "Every available nook and corner" in every boarding house and hotel was taken. Many people slept on park benches or walked the streets all night. "Never in the history of Washington had there been such an enormous influx of visitors," wrote Noah Brooks of the *Sacramento Daily Union*. Indeed, an estimated three hundred thousand people would watch the parade. All public offices were closed May 23 and 24. The night before the parade, Mary Lincoln, "somewhat unhinged" since her husband's death, vacated the White House. She would not watch the triumphal procession.

The crowds began gathering on the sidewalks along Pennsylvania Avenue at sunrise on Tuesday, May 23, until every foot was occupied, as were the rooftops, windows, and trees. So were the grandstands built by federal, city, and private crews, and decorated in red, white, and blue. They stretched in unbroken ranks along the mile-and-a-half long parade route between the Capitol and the White House.

Rain had fallen during the previous two days, settling the dust, but this day was a bright, pellucid one. Flags and bunting were everywhere. A large gilded eagle adorned the front door of the Capitol.

At 8 a.m., schoolgirls dressed in white and schoolboys in blue jackets and white trousers marched in a procession to the Capitol. They spread out over the Capitol steps and much of Capitol Hill, holding wreaths and bouquets to present to the soldiers. All along the parade route were banners: "Welcome, Brave Soldiers, "Honor to the Brave," "The Only National Debt We Can Never Pay Is The Debt We Owe To The Victorious Union Soldiers."[51]

At 9 a.m., a signal gun barked and General George Meade cried, "Forward!" to his Army of the Potomac, whose 180 infantry regiments, 29 cavalry regiments, and 33 artillery batteries had formed ranks on the Capitol's north side. The Eastern army, following its purple silk battle flag, marched toward Pennsylvania Avenue as bands launched into "When Johnnie Comes Marching Home," followed by other wartime favorites, including "Battle Cry of Freedom" and "Rally Round the Flag."[52]

At 9:15 a.m., a carriage drove up to the large reviewing stand in front of the White House, and out of it stepped President Johnson, War Secretary Stanton, and some staff generals. Grant arrived on foot from the War Department and was joined on the platform by Sherman, Supreme Court justices, Cabinet members, senators and congressmen, and state governors.

The onlookers roared "Gettysburg! Gettysburg!" when Meade's army appeared, and the people in the grandstands stood and cheered loudly. They sang along with the bands. Some people wept, some smiled broadly, and others darted from the crowd to kiss the weather-beaten, bullet-riddled regimental flags inscribed with the battles they had seen. Only regiments that had been in combat were permitted to march in the parade.[53]

The crowds cheered Meade every step of the way. They strewed his path with flowers, and garlanded the general and his mount with wreaths. After passing the reviewing stand, Meade dismounted and joined the dignitaries there.

The Cavalry Corps came first, followed by the artillery batteries, whose cannons had been polished until they gleamed. The engineers, with their pioneer implements and "huge dromedary caravans"—the pontoons—were followed by the infantry corps: IX, V, and II. VI Corps was in southern Virginia; Horatio Wright's men would be reviewed separately two weeks later.

The Army of the Potomac might have marched with "machine-like precision," as the *Philadelphia Inquirer* reported the next day, but it was also an army of young men basking in their nation's gratitude. They "turned their eyes around like country gawks to look at the big people on the stand," Sherman observed from the grandstand. His army would not rubberneck when it paraded the next day.[54]

From the ranks of the Cavalry Corps burst a rider on a madly plunging, galloping horse. The hatless man, his long yellow curls and red necktie flowing behind him, managed to hold his saber at a salute as his horse careered past the reviewing stand like "a tornado." It was General George Custer, the personification of the dashing cavalryman. As Custer flew by, the crowd shrieked with delight. His charger had spooked when someone tossed a wreath of flowers over its head. At last he gained mastery of his horse and rode back to his division, saluting once more as he passed the reviewing stand. He was "a beautiful figure, lithe, graceful, and every inch a soldier," wrote Noah Brooks.[55]

During a thirty-minute interval between the passing of V and IX Corps, about two thousand people left their places to stand before the review stand and cheer the dignitaries. Johnson, Grant, and Stanton bowed to them, each in turn. At 3:30 p.m., the last units of the Army of the Potomac marched by, and some people wondered aloud where the army's black units were. They were in fact at City Point, preparing to board ships and join Sheridan in the Southwest.[56]

The crowd evinced intensive curiosity about Sherman's army, which would march the following day. Few people in Washington had ever actually seen the Army of the Mississippi. During the Army of the Potomac's parade, Sherman had turned to Meade and said, "I'm afraid my poor tatterdemalion corps will make a poor appearance tomorrow when contrasted with yours." Meade patronizingly replied, "The people in Washington are so fond of the army that they will make allowances."[57]

The Grand Review interrupted the trial of the Lincoln assassination conspirators, which had begun May 10 at the Old Arsenal Grounds. Because witnesses were unable to cross Pennsylvania Avenue to reach the military court near the Potomac River, General Joseph Holt postponed the proceedings until May 25. Eight defendants were on trial before a nine-officer military tribunal. The officers would ultimately send four to prison in the Dry Tortugas, and condemn four to die: Lewis Powell, who invaded William Seward's home and severely injured the secretary of state and his son; George Azterodt, who was supposed to murder Andrew Johnson but lost his nerve; and David Herold, John Wilkes Booth's cofugitive. Mary Surratt, whose boarding house was a meeting place for the conspirators, would become the first woman executed in the United States. It was General Winfield Scott Hancock, Gettysburg hero and arguably the Union's best infantry corps commander, who signaled the hangman to carry out the sentences on July 7 at Washington's Old Arsenal Prison. Until the last instant, Hancock hoped for a presidential reprieve for Surratt, admitting that he would rather be in a battle "ten thousand times over" than hang a woman.[58]

Sherman did not want anyone to have to make allowances for his men; he intended for his far-marching army to step smartly down Pennsylvania

Avenue in new uniforms. He ordered his officers to maintain proper intervals and to not permit their men to look around—there would be plenty of time later for sightseeing. But some of the "Western men," proud of their ragged attire, spurned the new uniforms; for their first and last parade through Washington, they wished to appear as their authentic selves. There were not enough new uniforms available anyway to clothe seventy thousand men.[59]

It was another bright, clear day. At 9 a.m. on March 24, four of Sherman's six army corps—X and XXIII Corps of the Army of the Ohio remained in North Carolina—stepped onto the densely crowded avenue connecting the Capitol and the White House. New welcoming banners were everywhere: "Hail to the Western Heroes" and "Hail, Champions of Belmont, Donelson, Shiloh, Vicksburg, Chattanooga, Atlanta, Savannah, Bentonville—Pride of the Nation." Wearing a new uniform, Sherman rode at the head of his army. Beside him was one-armed General Oliver Howard, the Army of the Tennessee's commander and destined to soon become the new Freedman Bureau's first commissioner. As Sherman passed each grandstand, doffing his slouch hat, the crowds, just as large as those who witnessed the Army of the Potomac's passage, stood and cheered him.

Most of the people had never seen the red-haired general before, and they were eager to judge whether his demeanor matched his reputation for ruthlessness. "His tall, spare figure, war-worn face, and martial bearing made him all that the people had pictured him," one observer wrote.

Upon reaching the US Treasury building, Sherman could not resist looking back at the army—the very thing he had forbidden his men to do—that he had led from Vicksburg to Chattanooga, and thence to Atlanta, Savannah, Columbia, and Raleigh. "The sight was simply magnificent," Sherman wrote. "The column was compact, and the glittering muskets looked like a solid mass of steel, moving with the regularity of a pendulum."[60]

Three of Sherman's corps had bivouacked the previous night around the Capitol, simplifying their preparations that morning. Many of the soldiers wore the prescribed uniform of loose blue blouses and felt hats, a striking contrast to the Army of the Potomac's tight-fitting uniforms and kepis.[61]

But then there were those who either eschewed or could not obtain new clothing. Many wore mismatched blouses and trousers. Others marched barefoot, with torn trousers tied around their legs and with their hair billowing from their crownless hats. An onlooker called them "Sherman's wolves . . . all looking lean and hungry."[62]

Sherman's men displayed their iconoclasm like badges of honor. Black pioneers, carrying picks and shovels and marching in step in dressed ranks, preceded each corps. Ambulances passed by with bloodstained stretchers fastened to their sides; that sight silenced the crowds. Bummers trailed each brigade, with their grunting pigs, dogs, oxen, milk cows, goats, and pack mules loaded with crowing cocks, hams, camp gear, and poultry. One displayed a half-dozen live raccoons, others had brought cats and birds of prey. Families of liberated slaves marched with them. One of the mules, it was reported, came from Jefferson Davis's plantation in Mississippi. "The good-humored crowds laughed and cheered" the bummers and their motley entourages, a newspaper reporter wrote.[63]

"Many good people . . . had looked upon our Western army as a sort of mob," wrote Sherman, "but the world then saw, and recognized the fact, that it was an army in the proper sense, well organized, well commanded and disciplined; and there was no wonder that it had swept through the South like a tornado."[64]

"Down the avenue poured the shining river of steel," wrote General Joshua Chamberlain. An Iowa soldier saw "a moving wall of bright blue tipped with glittering steel, every man keeping step, the whole looking like one connected body." "They displayed a fine physique," the *Baltimore Sun* reported. "Their faces were finely bronzed, and they marched with a firm, elastic step." Each corps prominently displayed its banners and badges: XV Corps's split cartridge box with the legend "Forty Rounds," XVII Corps's arrow, the star signifying XX Corps, and the acorn of XIV Corps. The onlookers pressed bouquets on the marching men, draped wreaths over their horses, and sang along when the bands played "Battle Hymn of the Republic."[65]

"They march like the lords of the world," remarked former treasury secretary Tom Corwin.[66]

Passing William Seward's home, Sherman raised his hat in a salute to the recovering secretary of state, who was watching from his window, his head covered in bands of steel and rubber as a result of his many wounds. Seward returned Sherman's salute with a raised hand.

The onlookers noted that Sherman's men marched with a longer, springier stride. They were taller and leaner than the Army of the

Potomac's soldiers; their beards were longer and shaggier. When XV Corps passed, the German ambassador said to Bishop Edward R. Ames of the Methodist Episcopal Church, "An army like that could whip all Europe," and when XX Corps passed, he said, "An army like that could whip the world." After XIV Corps went by, the ambassador told Ames, "An army like that could whip the devil."[67]

The head of the procession neared the reviewing stand, and a band struck up "Marching Through Georgia," which was met by thunderous applause. Sherman raised his sword in a salute to President Johnson, and "the whole assemblage raised up and waved and shouted as if he had been the personal friend of each and every one of them," wrote a *New York World* reporter. "Sherman was the idol of the day."

He and Howard dismounted at the reviewing stand and joined the president, Grant, and the dozens of other dignitaries crowding the large platform. Noah Brooks, the *Sacramento Daily Union* correspondent, got his first good look at Sherman through field glasses from the grandstand across the avenue. He was highly impressed. "In the group of notable men on the grand stand, Sherman was certainly the most notable in appearance," Brooks wrote. "His head was high and narrow, his hair and whiskers were sandy in hue, his moustache stiff and bristling, and his eyes keen and piercing. He was very tall, walked with an immense stride, talked rapidly and nervously, and would be picked out in any assemblage as a man of distinction."[68]

While testifying two days earlier before the Committee on the Conduct of the War, Sherman had denounced the condemnatory statements made by Stanton and Halleck about his peace terms with Joseph Johnston. Questioned by the committee's Radical Republicans about whether Lincoln had proposed the terms at their meeting at City Point, Sherman became inexplicably vague, evincing an unwillingness to cast blame on the murdered president.

Grant had offered to reconcile Sherman and Stanton, but Sherman refused. "On the contrary, [I] resolved to resent what I considered an insult, as publicly as it was made." He could not forget Stanton's published statements insinuating that he was "a common traitor and public enemy."

Now, as he mounted the reviewing stand, Sherman shook hands with President Johnson; Grant; his father-in-law, Thomas Ewing; and every member of the Cabinet—until he came to Stanton. "He offered me his hand, but I declined it publicly, and the fact was universally noted," Sherman wrote. Whispers rippled through the reviewing stand dignitaries.[69]

Brooks witnessed the snub through his binoculars. "We could see that Sherman, declining Stanton's greet [*sic*], firmly placed his right hand by his side with a slight gesture." Stanton's expression did not change, but as Sherman turned to the passing troops, he "looked grimmer than ever, and a dark-red scar, the mark of a recent slight accident, imparted to his visage a certain sinister expression." For the next six hours, Sherman proudly watched his men pass by, returning every salute.[70]

Sherman's wife, Ellen, and his brother, Senator John Sherman, tried to smooth things over with the Stantons, who were John Sherman's neighbors. Mrs. Sherman and Mrs. Stanton were friends, and she sent the Stantons a bouquet of flowers the next day, and later called on the secretary of state. John Sherman told the general that the assassination conspiracy had badly frightened Stanton, causing him to overreact. Sherman, however, was unrepentant. Noting the "strong military guards" at the homes of Stanton and other high government officials, Sherman was unimpressed by the "sense of insecurity [that] pervaded Washington, for which no reason existed." Sherman nursed his grudge against Stanton for years.[71]

⁂

Mustering out the million Union troops in uniform began as soon as the last mule in Sherman's army passed the White House reviewing stand. Unlike the defeated Rebel Army, which had simply melted away after paroles were issued, the Union demobilization required diligent record keeping and took longer. Nonetheless, it proceeded with surprising speed. By August 7, a total of 640,806 soldiers were mustered out; complete demobilization took longer, until November 1866.[72]

Sherman bade farewell to his army on May 30 in Special Field Order No. 76. "The time has come for us to part. Our work is done, and armed Enemies no longer defy us. Some of you will go to your homes and others will be retained in service till further orders. . . . To such as go home he will only say, that our favored country is so grand, so extensive, so diversified in climate, soil, and productions, that every man may find a home and occupation suited to his taste, and none should yield to the natural impatience sure to result from our past life of excitement and adventure.

... Your general now bids you all farewell, with the full belief that as in war you have been good soldiers so in peace you will make good citizens."[73]

In later speeches to his veterans Sherman would habitually refer to their shared bond, and he would urge them to be proud of their accomplishments, and unrepentant about the trail of ruin that they had left in their wake in Georgia and the Carolinas. The Confederates had "ventured their all in their efforts to destroy our Government. . . . So, soldiers, when we marched through and conquered the country of the rebels, we became owners of all they had, and I don't want you to be troubled in your consciences for taking, while on our great march, the property of conquered rebels. They forfeited their rights to it."[74]

Meade's prosaic good-bye to the Army of the Potomac dwelled on the successes of his two years as the army's commander, from Gettysburg, "the turning point of the war," to Lee's surrender at Appomattox. "Soldiers! Having accomplished the work set before us, having vindicated the honor and integrity of our Government and flag . . . let us earnestly pray for strength and light to discharge our duties as citizens, as we have endeavored to discharge them as soldiers."

Separation from the Union Army was bittersweet for many soldiers. "None of us were fond of war, but there had grown up between the boys an attachment for each other they never had nor ever will have for any other body of men," wrote an Indiana infantryman. In West Virginia, General Rutherford Hayes wrote to his wife as his discharged men departed, "I have no idea that many of them will ever see as happy times as they have had in the army."

Grant's General Orders No. 35 of June 28 was masterfully concise, as befitted its famously succinct author: "By virtue of Special Orders, No. 339, current series, from the Adjutant-General's Office, this army, as an organization, ceases to exist."[75]

When General Joshua Chamberlain read this, he was moved to write, "What wonder that a strange thrill went through our hearts."[76]

EPILOGUE

Furl that Banner, for 'tis weary

Round its staff 'tis drooping dreary;

Furl it, fold it—it is best;

For there's not a man to wave it,

And there's not a sword to save it,

And there's no one left to lave it

In the blood which heroes gave it;

And its foes now scorn and brave it;

Furl it, hide it—let it rest!

—"THE CONQUERED BANNER,"
WRITTEN BY CONFEDERATE CHAPLAIN ABRAHAM JOSEPH RYAN,
AFTER LEARNING OF ROBERT E. LEE'S SURRENDER

Few Southerners were more committed to the Confederacy than Edmund Ruffin, born into Virginia's planter class in 1794. For most of his adult life, however, Ruffin was renowned for his contributions to agriculture. Experimenting on his own land in Prince George County, east of Petersburg, he discovered that the application of lime, along with fertilizer, could revive worn-out, acidic soil, whose productivity could then be sustained with crop rotation. Ruffin wrote articles and an influential book about his theories.

A wealthy slave owner and prolific diarist, Ruffin also ardently promoted states rights and slavery, and he was one of the first Virginians to propose secession. Disappointed when Virginia did not become the first state to secede, Ruffin went to South Carolina and joined the Charleston Palmetto Guard. At the age of sixty-six Ruffin, his white hair brushing his shoulders, pulled the lanyard on a coastal battery as the bombardment of Fort Sumter began. He later claimed that he fired the first shot of the war.[1]

The collapse of Petersburg on April 2 prompted him to despair. "I am without any resource left, either of property or escape," he wrote in his diary.[2]

On June 17, Ruffin made his last diary entry:

I hereby declare my unmitigated hatred to Yankee rule—to all political, social, & business connections with the Yankees—& to the Yankee race . . . the now far-distant day shall arrive for just retribution for Yankee usurpation, oppression, & atrocious outrages—& for deliverance & vengeance for the now ruined, subjugated, & enslaved Southern States! . . . And now with my last writing & utterance, & with what will be near my latest breath, I hereby repeat & would willingly proclaim my unmitigated hatred to Yankee rule.

Ruffin then set down his pen, placed the muzzle of his gun in his mouth, and pressed the trigger with a forked stick.[3]

Defeat was calamitous for all Confederates, especially for those who had sacrificed loved ones, property, and health in the cause of Southern sovereignty. Few, though, were willing to follow Ruffin in a defiant, Masada-like gesture of mass self-immolation. Instead, they privately nursed their bitterness toward their conquerors as they struggled to resume their lives.

A North Carolinian who lost two sons in the war, as well as his slaves and his home—burned by Union troops—told a Northern journalist, "They've left me one inestimable privilege, to hate 'em. I git up at half-past four in the morning, and sit up till twelve at night, to hate 'em!"

"I have vowed that if I have children," said an embittered planter, "the first ingredient of the first principle of their education shall be uncompromising hatred & contempt of the Yankee."[4]

Hatred was practically all that remained for many former Confederates. Southern industry lay in the blackened ruins of factories and in the harbors now clogged with Union warships and Northern merchantmen. In the countryside, millions of acres of farmland lay fallow and scorched, and farmers with tillable acreage often lacked animals for plowing and planting. In the cities, there was desolation and dejection.

Although Confederate General Edmund Kirby Smith had surrendered his Trans-Mississippi army to General Edward Canby, not all of the Confederate soldiers in the Southwest had given up. Jo Shelby, the Confederate cavalry general, chose Mexico over being paroled. While riding across Texas. he attracted a following of former soldiers and Confederate civilian officials that grew to brigade size and included former Generals John Magruder, Sterling Price, and even General Smith. Upon reaching the Rio Grande River, Shelby weighted his battle flag with stones and sank it to the river bottom before entering Mexico. The Emperor Maximilian politely declined the ex-Confederates' offer to help shore up his shaky regime; he knew that accepting the aid of other outsiders would only antagonize Mexicans further. But the emperor offered the Confederate exiles some land near Vera Cruz to colonize. A few settled there, but the others either drifted on to other countries, or returned to the South.[5]

Even after Lee's surrender, the Confederate raider *Shenandoah* continued to plunder, burn, and sink New England whaling ships in the Pacific. In late June, the captain of a seized ship showed the *Shenandoah*'s captain, James Waddell, an April newspaper reporting both Lee's surrender and Abraham Lincoln's assassination. But the newspaper article also said that other Rebel units remained in the field, and it included excerpts from Jefferson Davis's Danville proclamation, in which he vowed to fight on. Waddell took this to mean that he should continue raiding; he captured six whalers off St. Lawrence's Island and eleven more two days later at the Bering Strait. In August, the *Shenandoah* met an English bark that had newspapers aboard reporting Davis's capture, General Smith's surrender, and the death of the Confederacy. Waddell knew that his raiding days were over; he was no pirate. But rather than surrender at a US port and risk imprisonment, Waddell and his crew remained at sea. They passed Cape Horn, entered the Atlantic, and traveled to England, where they turned themselves in to port authorities in Liverpool. In thirteen months the *Shenandoah* had sailed fifty-eight thousand miles, and had captured more ships than any Confederate raider except the *Alabama*.[6]

❧

A tragedy unfolded on the Mississippi River during the predawn hours of April 27. At 2 a.m. that day, the sidewheel steamer *Sultana*, dangerously overloaded with up to twenty-four hundred recently liberated Union war prisoners, was laboring in the strong Mississippi current eight miles north of Memphis. The vessel's capacity was four hundred passengers, but the master had taken on as many prisoners as the *Sultana* could hold after hastily repairing the vessel's cracked boiler. Paid by the government $5 for every enlisted man and $10 per officer that he transported, the master expected to reap a big profit. But the overloaded vessel's cracked boiler couldn't withstand the strain put on it, and it exploded. Between fifteen and eighteen hundred men drowned or died in the fire.

A month later, an explosion at a Mobile ordnance warehouse killed two to three hundred people. Investigators speculated that Union soldiers mishandled shells in the warehouse, causing the explosion. But no one knew for certain because there was nothing left of the warehouse or its occupants except a massive ten-foot-deep hole. The blast razed buildings in an eight-square-block area, trapping civilians and soldiers in the burning rubble. Some of them were roasted alive.[7]

Navy Secretary Gideon Welles toured Charleston, South Carolina, in late May. "There was both sadness and gratification in witnessing the devastation of the city and the deplorable condition of the seat of the Rebellion," he wrote. "Luxury, refinement, happiness have fled from Charleston; poverty is enthroned here. Having sown error, she has reaped sorrow. She has been, and is, punished. I rejoice that it is so."[8]

General Carl Schurz, one of Sherman's generals, wrote about the devastation that he observed while revisiting South Carolina three months after the war ended. "The track of Sherman's march . . . looked for many miles like a broad, black streak of ruin and desolation . . . the fences all gone; lonesome smoke stacks, surrounded by dark heaps of ashes and cinders, marking the spots where human habitation had stood. . . . No part of the South I then visited had indeed suffered as much from the ravages of the war as South Carolina."[9]

Sarah Hines of Georgia summarized the South's plight in a letter to a friend: "Bankrupt in men, in money, & in provisions, the wail of the bereaved & the cry of hunger rising all over the land, Our cities burned with fire and our pleasant things laid waste, the best & bravest of our sons in captivity, and the entire resources of our country exhausted—what else could we do but give up. . . . I am sure you echo the sentiments of every heart in this land when you say 'I detest the United States.'"[10]

Yet the South was quickly restored to its former position in the US government, at least initially. President Andrew Johnson implemented Abraham Lincoln's lenient Reconstruction policy, and he generously granted pardons to high-ranking Confederates who had been ineligible for amnesty. By the end of 1865, every Southern state except Texas had established a provisional government controlled by pardoned former Rebels. The new state governments quickly enacted so-called Black Codes, which transformed the freedmen into de facto slaves by keeping them out of the cities, under white control, and working in the fields.

General Phil Sheridan, whose military district compassed Louisiana and Texas, deplored the abrogation of blacks' newly established civil rights, and Johnson's failure to curb it. The blacks were left "at the mercy of a people who, recently their masters, now seemed to look upon them as the authors of all the misfortunes that had come upon the land." In Texas, a Freedman's Bureau official reported that blacks "are frequently beaten unmercifully, and shot down like wild beasts, without any provocation." White mobs in Memphis and New Orleans, abetted by police, slaughtered blacks and burned churches and schools.[11]

There was a backlash against the rapid return to power of former Confederates among congressional Republicans, who created a joint House-Senate committee to investigate. Congress repudiated the state governments approved by Johnson, and refused to seat recently elected Southern senators and representatives, setting the stage for a titanic power struggle with the president. In February 1868, the House voted to impeach Johnson on eleven counts, but in May the Senate fell one vote shy of the two-thirds needed to convict him and remove him from office.[12]

Besides abusing and murdering the new freedmen, the former Confederates also directed their hatred at Southern Republicans and Unionists who supported the North during the war. They shunned Elizabeth Van Lew, the wealthy Richmond spinster whose spy ring gave intelligence to Generals Benjamin Butler and Ulysses Grant. If Van Lew's sympathies had remained necessarily opaque during the war, there was nothing mysterious about them in its aftermath.

When Grant and his wife Julia visited Richmond, they called on Van Lew and drank tea with her on the veranda. "You have sent me the most valuable information received from Richmond during the war," Grant told her in a letter. After Grant's inauguration as president in 1869, he appointed Van Lew to be Richmond postmistress.

But Van Lew had few visitors and fewer friends; acquaintances avoided her on Richmond's streets. "[I am] held in contempt & scorn by the narrow minded men and women of my city for my loyalty," she wrote. "We are held so utterly as outcasts here." She became impoverished, but was sustained in her last years by friends in Boston. When Van Lew died in 1900, they sent a granite boulder from Boston's Capitol Hill to Richmond to serve as her gravestone at Shockoe Cemetery.[13]

Those who spurned Van Lew belonged to the legion of former Confederates who persisted in believing that their lost cause was righteous and that God someday would reward them. The Confederacy, they insisted, represented the ideals of the American Revolution. "We were engaged in a just and holy war," wrote James A. Scott of the 3rd Virginia Cavalry. "It's hard to think that our glorious old Confederate banner—which we have borne aloft unconquered so long—must now be furled—but I doubt not—in his own good time God will give us a new & more beautiful one which shall float proudly and wide over all of our foes. Let us put our trust in him."[14]

※

There were seventy-six full-scale battles and more than six thousand skirmishes and engagements during the Civil War. The cost in soldier's lives was shockingly high—roughly 750,000, according to recent estimates, vastly higher than the American losses in any other war, and at a time when the US population was just 34 million, one-tenth of today's total. Two-thirds of the deaths were due to disease and noncombat injuries. In dollars and cents, the war cost the US government $3.4 billion, plus another $8.2 billion in pensions, for a total of $11.6 billion—the equivalent of $173 billion today.[15]

For 150 years historians have postulated reasons why the North won and the South lost. The Confederacy's military leaders were superior to the Union's during the war's early stages, and so were their troops—Southern country boys who had grown up on horseback and with firearms in their hands. Moreover, they were inspired by the belief, religious in its intensity, that their country was under attack, and that Southern culture—code for slavery—must be preserved at all costs.

The North's daunting advantages in manpower and resources, clumsily wielded at the war's start, were decisive over the course of a war that most people had believed would last months, but that instead spanned four years. Northern might, finally applied competently by Ulysses Grant and William Sherman, ground down the Rebel armies, as Robert E. Lee predicted would happen from the beginning—and as Abraham Lincoln had fervently hoped. During their desolating campaigns, Sherman and Phil Sheridan thrust the horror of war onto the doorsteps of the Southern people, undermining public support for Jefferson Davis and the Confederacy.

Had Lee's army fought a defensive strategy from the beginning—and Robert E. Lee was a brilliant defensive strategist—while waging a robust guerrilla war, the South might have won the sovereignty that it craved. Thwarted by entrenched Rebel forces and bloodied by partisans, the Union Army would have lost public support, and there might have been a negotiated peace. But Lee and his commanders, being conventional, offensive-minded generals, eschewed such an unorthodox strategy, as did the Southern people. They repeatedly attempted to take the war into enemy country. But rather than demoralizing the Union, each of these Confederate incursions acted as a fire bell in the North, where life went on largely as though there were no war; the Union, it has been said, fought the South one-handed. The Confederate campaigns in Maryland and Pennsylvania awakened the North to the threat to their homeland, rousing it to greater efforts to crush the Rebellion.

The war radically changed the tools for fighting and the strategies employed by generals. Ironclads replaced wooden ships on the waters, and the advent of breech-loaded repeating weapons rang down the end of the musket era. Clothing and weapons were mass produced for the first time.

Other changes were less visible but nonetheless paradigm-shifting: the use of complex entrenchments, introduced during the Overland Campaign of May and June 1864, and afterward ubiquitous outside Petersburg and Richmond; the strategy of continuous operations, inaugurated by Grant during the same campaign, a feature of which was constant contact between the two armies; and the Union's destruction not only of the Confederate Army, but also the South's farmlands, factories, barns, and livestock—a "strategy of exhaustion," or "total war," designed to sap manpower, resources, and public support.

Lincoln's able Cabinet and the support of the US Congress gave the North a distinct advantage over the Confederacy, which became riven by ideological disagreements over states' rights and the central government's role. Moreover, the Confederacy's civilian administration, with a few exceptions, was second rate; in Davis's defense, he had to form an entire government from scratch in a matter of weeks. Davis was not the administrator that Lincoln was; he micromanaged, whereas Lincoln appointed competent people and allowed them to manage their departments.

The war changed the ideologically pure Confederacy in ways that it could not have imagined in 1861. To raise men to beat back the Northern onslaught, the Confederacy began a military draft, something it had deplored in 1861 as a violation of Southern states' rights when Lincoln issued his call for men after Fort Sumter. The Union's policy soon became the Confederacy's, along with a strong central government, taxes, a war industry, and food requisitions for the army. When the Union recruited and trained 180,000 black troops, it compelled the Confederacy, with the greatest reluctance, to arm its slaves and promise them emancipation in exchange for their service. Thus, the Confederacy gave up two of the principles that had propelled the South into rebellion in the first place—states' rights and slavery—in order to secure its independence from the Union. Ironically, if the Rebellion had succeeded, the postwar South would have resembled the North more than the antebellum South.

The war also changed the North. The federal government became more powerful than ever before, at the expense of the states. Besides drafting men into military service, it levied taxes on individuals and created an "internal revenue bureau" to collect those taxes; it also established a national currency and a banking system. With the war, productivity increased exponentially, and when the fighting ended, the United States had become a global economic power. With the increase of federal authority came a shift in power to the North both in Congress and the presidency that would last for many decades. A Harvard professor remarked, "It does not seem to me as if I were living in the country in which I was born."[16]

General Richard Taylor, the son of President Zachary Taylor and a Louisiana sugar planter, commanded the Confederate Department of Alabama and Mississippi when the war ended. After surrendering his troops, Taylor returned to New Orleans and learned that he was destitute. "My estate had been confiscated and sold, and I was without a penny," he wrote.

As Taylor looked around at the war's aftermath, he realized that the abolishment of slavery had destroyed an institution that had existed in the South since the earliest colonial days, and that "was interwoven with the thoughts, habits, and daily lives of both races, and both suffered by the sudden disruption of the accustomed tie." Taylor continued, "The [French] revolution of '89 did not produce a greater change in the 'Ancien Regime' than [the Civil War] has in our social life."

The Southern landscape, financial and actual, was a shipwreck. "Bank stocks, bonds, all personal property, all accumulated wealth had disappeared," wrote Taylor. "Thousands of houses, farm-buildings, work-animals, flocks and herds, had been wantonly burned, killed or carried off. The land was filled with widows and orphans crying for aid."[17]

While Jefferson Davis brooded in his prison cell over the Southern nation that might have been, Robert E. Lee, Ulysses Grant, William Sherman, Phil Sheridan, James Longstreet, John Gordon, and Joseph Johnston were going forward with their lives.

After returning to his family in Richmond, Lee passed up a number of business opportunities before agreeing to become president of Washington College in Lexington, Virginia (now Washington & Lee University) for an annual salary of $1,500. The trustees hoped that Lee's name would pull the college back from the brink of bankruptcy. Although surrounded by the Blue Ridge Mountains and 140 miles from Richmond, Lexington did not afford Lee sanctuary from wartime memories. Stonewall Jackson was buried there, and the adjacent Virginia Military Institute was struggling to recover from having been shelled and burned in 1864.[18]

When Lee died in 1870 after suffering a stroke, he was the living symbol of the nascent "Lost Cause" movement spreading across the South. More than any wartime figure, Lee embodied the chivalric ideals that by 1865 already seemed to belong to a distant, quaintly romantic era.

By contrast, Grant represented the future. In 1868, Republicans nominated the general of the Army as their candidate for president. He was elected by a comfortable margin, and he was reelected in 1872. Tarnished by scandals, Grant's administration reflected the president's political in-experience, his weakness for appointing friends to high places, and his failure to cajole Radical Republicans in Congress into supporting his re-forms. "It was my fortune, or misfortune, to be called to the office of Chief Executive without any previous political training," he later wrote.

After leaving the White House, the Grants went on a two-and-a-half-year trip around the world, accompanied by a *New York Herald* reporter, John Russell Young. Young's regular reports of the warm, enthusiastic re-ceptions that Grant received wherever he went appeared in newspapers across America. The trip reminded Americans of Grant's enduring pop-ularity, and helped them forget the scandals that had plagued his admin-istration. Grant made it known that he might be induced to seek another term as president, but the Republican nomination went to James Garfield in 1880, and there was no third term for Grant.

Failing to secure the presidential nomination in 1880, Grant set out to amass a fortune, but in this he was unlucky, going bankrupt in 1884 after a brokerage partner bilked him in a Ponzi scheme. Broke, Grant set out to recover his financial footing by writing—first, magazine articles about the war and, then, his memoirs. While writing his memoirs, Grant was diagnosed with terminal throat cancer.

Battling constant pain, Grant raced against death to complete his *Personal Memoirs of Ulysses S. Grant*, which he hoped would provide Julia with an income after he died. Grant won the race, completing his mem-oirs five days before his death on July 23, 1885. A Grant friend, Samuel Clemens, who had founded Webster and Company to publish his *The Adventures of Huckleberry Finn*, took on Grant's *Memoirs* too. Clem-ens sent veterans dressed in their old uniforms to canvass the North for customers. The sales strategy worked: the book's royalties brought Julia Grant nearly half a million dollars.[19]

Longstreet settled in New Orleans and served as US minister to Turkey, and later as commissioner of Pacific railroads under William McKinley and Theodore Roosevelt, from 1897 to 1904.

John Gordon returned to Georgia a war hero and went into poli-tics. He served three terms in the US Senate and one term as Georgia governor. Gordon was the first commander-in-chief of the United Confederate Veterans.

Sherman became general of the Army after Grant's election as president. His relationship with War Secretaries John Rawlins and William Belknap, however, became so strained—Sherman said they usurped his authority—that he moved his headquarters from Washington to St. Louis for two years, thereby abdicating whatever authority remained to him. Sherman declined overtures to run for president, famously saying, "I will not accept if nominated and will not serve if elected." After Sherman retired from the Army in 1884, Phil Sheridan succeeded him as general of the Army, serving until his death in 1888.[20]

After he was released from prison on bail, Jefferson Davis became president of Carolina Life Insurance Company in Memphis. The company failed during the financial panic of 1873, and Davis lost the only private-sector job that he ever had, along with his last $15,000. Then he began writing his epic justification and history of the war, *The Rise and Fall of the Confederate Government*. Because Davis had no permanent residence at the time, a wealthy widow and novelist, Sarah Anne Ellis Dorsey, invited him to stay at her estate, Belvoir, near Biloxi. Before Dorsey died in 1879, she bequeathed Belvoir to him, and there he finished *Rise and Fall* in 1881.

Davis's book was rambling and disjointed. In it, he attempted to settle old scores with P. G. T. Beauregard and Joseph Johnston, while glossing over the flaws of Braxton Bragg and other favorites. It was alternately anecdotal and dull, with long verbatim quotes from documents. At fifteen hundred pages, *Rise and Fall* lost money.

Davis died in December 1889. At first entombed in New Orleans, his remains were reinterred in Hollywood Cemetery in Richmond at his widow Varina's insistence.[21]

⁂

They came from every state in the South and many Northern states too—an estimated one hundred thousand people—to pay tribute to Robert E. Lee, dead now twenty years, and to the "Lost Cause," a concatenation of myth and memory made from the ashes of the Confederacy's defeat, and abetted by returning prosperity and the aging of the war's veterans.

The occasion on this clear, balmy day was the unveiling of a sixty-foot-tall equestrian statue dedicated to Lee. The passage of twenty-five years had thinned the Confederate ranks, but Generals Longstreet, Johnston, Jubal Early, and Fitzhugh Lee were there, as were Wade Hampton, Beauregard, and Henry Heth. Fittingly, Fitz Lee, the deceased honoree's nephew and a former Virginia governor, was the event's chief marshal.

The idea of a statue in Richmond honoring Lee was conceived in the months following his death in 1870. Jubal Early summoned surviving officers of the Army of Northern Virginia to a meeting in Richmond on November 3, 1870. Fund-raising began, land was purchased at the edge of one of Richmond's principal downtown residential streets, and a plan was made to build not only a statue honoring Lee, but also a grand boulevard extending beyond it, lined with trees and with a grassy median.

On this day, May 29, 1890, Confederate flags rippled in the light breeze alongside the Stars and Stripes. Fitz Lee had encouraged everyone to display the Rebel colors, while explaining that they were now "only a sentiment. The Confederation decorations mean that we honor those who led us and therefore shed their blood for us—nothing more."

More than anyone present, Early, the irascible combat general and Lynchburg lawyer, was responsible not only for this event. but also for cultivating the nearly mythical belief in the "Lost Cause" accepted throughout the South. As the first president of the Southern Historical Association, Early had written and solicited numerous articles extolling Confederate principles and arguing that the war was lost not because of them, but because the Union possessed "overwhelming numbers and resources," as Robert E. Lee had said in his farewell address to his army in 1865.

The parade began at noon in downtown Richmond, and soon the procession of bands, carriages, fire engines, and Confederate veterans on foot and horseback stretched for miles; news accounts said it was easily the largest parade in the South since the end of the war. Hampton commanded the cavalry, and Heth led the infantry along the parade route, densely crowded with spectators, many of them in Confederate gray. When their former commanders rode by, the veterans in the crowd erupted in their familiar keening foxhunters' cry.

At the monument, the Reverend Charles Minnigerode, the rector of St. Paul's Episcopal Church in Richmond and the pastor of Lee, Davis, and their families, offered a prayer. Jubal Early gave a short address.

Then Joseph Johnston, Lee's friend from their days at West Point, pulled a halyard that removed the shroud covering the statue. The crowd cheered loudly. Cannons heaved and barked. The audience sang, "How Firm a Foundation, Ye Saints of the Lord," which was a favorite of Lee's and was sung at his funeral. It had since become the unofficial Confederate hymn.[22]

Johnston also figured prominently in Ulysses Grant's funeral in August 1885, proof that former enemies might reconcile while still revering the antipodean causes for which they fought.

The "most imposing funeral that ever took place in America" until that time was Grant's in New York City; the crowds were even more massive than those that watched Lincoln's remains paraded through that city twenty years earlier. A million and a half people clogged the sidewalks and streets to witness the passing of Grant's casket and sixty thousand soldiers and civilians, all led by General Winfield Scott Hancock, Grant's best infantry corps commander during the war. For six and a half hours, New York's streets rang with the tread of marching troops and the clatter of horses' hooves as the procession advanced at a stately pace from City Hall to a temporary vault in Riverside Park. There Grant's casket would rest for twelve years, until being transferred to the neoclassical monument yet to be built nearby, Grant's Tomb.

The pallbearers included Johnston and former Confederate General Simon Buckner—who surrendered Fort Donelson to Grant in February 1862, launching him on the path to fame—along with former Union Generals William Sherman and Phil Sheridan, and Admiral David Porter. Before the funeral procession, Grant's remains were displayed publicly at City Hall, and Johnston and Buckner clasped hands with Sherman and Sheridan across the blue-covered coffin, "and together they looked down upon the dead face of the soldier of the Union," a newspaperman wrote.

If this signified a beginning of reconciliation, there were other signs, too. In Chicago, fifty ex-Confederate soldiers marched in a procession honoring the late general, and Confederate veterans' groups paid homage to Grant during meetings and parades at Dallas; Jacksonville, Florida; and Norfolk, Virginia. "The death of the beloved, lamented soldier will be one more link that draws together in amity and kindliness the northern and southern sections of this Union," declared the *New York Herald*.

The graying veterans had first met on a hundred flaming, blood-drenched battlefields, bound by a fiery commitment to give their last full measure either to preserve the Union or to wrest a new Southern nation from it. But in now coming together to mourn a great warrior's passing, they shared something entirely different: peace's annealing grace.[23]

NOTES

Prologue

1 US War Department, *The War of the Rebellion: A Compilation of the Official Records of the Union and Confederate Navies*, 2 series, 30 vols, I:11:261–262, Washington, DC: US Government Printing Office, 1894–1922, available online through the Cornell Library website at http://ebooks.library.cornell.edu/m/moawar/ofre.html (henceforth "O.R., Naval Operations," series I, unless otherwise indicated).

2 US War Department, *The War of the Rebellion: A Compilation of the Official Records of the Union and Confederate Armies*, 4 series, 128 vols, I:46:1045, Washington, DC: US Government Printing Office, 1880–1901, available online through the Cornell Library website at http://ebooks.library.cornell.edu/m/moawar/waro.html (henceforth "O.R.," series 1, unless otherwise indicated); Lamb, "The Defense of Fort Fisher," 646–647; Warner, *Generals in Gray*, 30; Wheelan, *Terrible Swift Sword*, 45; Foote, *Civil War*, III, 741–742.

3 Lamb, "The Defense of Fort Fisher," 646.

4 J. B. Jones, *War Diary*, 2:374–375.

5 Welles, *Diary of Gideon Welles*, II:127.

6 Barrett, *Civil War*, 266.

7 Ibid., 271–272, 262–263.

8 Ibid., 262–267; McPherson, *War on the Waters*, 214; O.R., *Naval Operations*, 11:209–210.

9 McPherson, *War on Waters*, 214–215; Barrett, *Civil War*, 267; O.R., *Naval Operations*, 11:245.

10 O.R., *Naval Operations*, 11:363.

11 Carr, *Gray Phantoms*, 50; O.R., III:42:1075–1076.

12 Grant, *Memoirs*, 509; Welles, *Diary of Gideon Welles*, II:213.

13 O.R., *Naval Operations*, 11:261–262.

14 Grant, *Papers*, 13:223–224, 207; O.R., II:46:60; Warner, *Generals in Blue*, 497–498; Welles, *Diary of Gideon Welles*, II:215.

Chapter 1: January 1865

1 Chesnut, *Mary Chesnut's Civil War*, 694.

2 O.R., 44:798–799.

3 Lincoln, *Collected Works*, 8:254–255.

4 Catton, *Grant Takes Command*, 404; O.R., III:42:1110.

347

5 Greene, *Civil War Petersburg*, 228; Furgurson, *Ashes of Glory*, 386.

6 Freeman, *Lee's Lieutenants*, 3:617–618.

7 Trudeau, *Last Citadel*, 416–417.

8 Hess, *In the Trenches*, xiii, xiv; Stern, *End to Valor*, 65–66; Trudeau, *Last Citadel*, 286–289.

9 Hess, *In the Trenches*, 204–205, 235–237; Wadsworth, *13th South Carolina Volunteer Infantry*, 70–71.

10 Stern, *End to Valor*, 66; Hess, *In the Trenches*, 209–211, 217–218; Wadsworth, *13th South Carolina Volunteer Infantry*, 71; Trudeau, *Last Citadel*, 297, 289–290.

11 Hess, *In the Trenches*, 216, 209–211; Stern, *End to Valor*, 1–2.

12 Furgurson, *Ashes of Glory*, 286–287; Pollard, *Lost Cause*, 647.

13 Greene, *Civil War Petersburg*, 230.

14 Ibid., 227, 233–234.

15 Trudeau, *Last Citadel*, 298–299, 290–291.

16 Strong, *Diary*, 3:535–536.

17 Mark Wilson, *Business of Civil War*, 1–2; Gallman, *Northerners at War*, 104, 108; Fite, *Social and Industrial Conditions*, 1, 5, 24, 27, 43–44, 67, 85–87, 105, 213, 263, 232; Stern, *End to Valor*, 355.

18 Greene, *Civil War Petersburg*, 228–229.

19 Coxe, "Last Struggles and Successes of Lee," 359.

20 J. B. Jones, *War Diary*, II:101, 400, 453, 381; McGuire, "Diary," 327–328; Conolly, *Irishman in Dixie*, 61; Wheelan, *Libby Prison*, 134; Putnam, *Richmond During the War*, 341.

21 Blackford, *Memoirs*, 2:223–224.

22 McGuire, "Diary," 329; Putnam, *Richmond During the War*, 342; DeLeon, *Four Years*, 352–353.

23 Conolly, *Irishman in Dixie*, 37–38; J. B. Jones, *War Diary*, II:458; Bill, *Beleaguered City*, 262–264.

24 Lee, *Wartime Papers*, 907.

25 McGuire, "Diary," 332, 356; Beringer et al., *Why the South Lost*, 433; Pollard, *Lost Cause*, 649–652; Wheelan, *Libby Prison*, 134; Greene, *Civil War Petersburg*, 221–222, 231fn.

26 Putnam, *Richmond During the War*, 340.

27 J. B. Jones, *War Diary*, II:154, 397.

28 Glatthaar, *Lee's Army*, 442.

29 Gallagher, *Confederate War*, 77.

30 Chesnut, *Mary Chesnut's Civil War*, 694, 702, 678; Gallagher, *Confederate War*, 5.

31 J. B. Jones, *War Diary*, II:373.

32 Grant, *Memoirs*, 501–506; Foote, *Civil War*, III:757–759; Warner, *Generals in Gray*, 143 (Hood never held another command).

33 Lee, *Wartime Papers*, 868.

34 Walter Taylor, *Four Years*, 146.

35 Foote, *Civil War*, III:756; Lonn, *Desertion*, 27–28; O.R., II:46:1258; Hardy, *Thirty-seventh North Carolina Troops*, 220.

36 O.R., I:46:1143.

37 Freeman, *Lee's Lieutenants*, 3:615, 619.

38 Glatthaar, *Lee's Army*, 440; Battle, *Forget-Me-Nots*, 125; Hess, *In the Trenches*, 222.

39 Osborn, *Fiery Trail*, 80; Sherman, *Memoirs*, II:231.

40 Lincoln, *Collected Works*, 8:182.

41 Sherman, *Memoirs*, II:254; Hitchcock, *Marching with Sherman*, 205.

42 Welles, *Diary*, II:208.

43 Burke Davis, *Sherman's March*, 130; O.R., 44:809.

44 Foote, *Civil War*, III:737–738; Horace Porter, *Campaigning with Grant*, abridged, 261–262; Catton, *Grant Takes Command*, 405–407.

45 Grant, *Papers*, 13:72–73, 75–77.

46 Ibid., 129–130.

47 O.R., 44:797, 741.

48 Ibid., 798–799.

49 O.R., II:17:288, 260.

50 Marszalek, *Sherman*, 253–254.

51 Horace Porter, *Campaigning with Grant*, unabridged, 374–375.

52 Marszalek, *Sherman*, 114, 178–180; Smith, *Grant*, 200–201.

53 Grant, *Papers*, 10:187–188fn. (Sherman's family had a history of mental illness; his maternal grandmother and an uncle spent time in asylums. Flood, *Grant and Sherman*, 22.)

54 Flood, *Grant and Sherman*, 284; Grant, *Papers*, 13:154.

55 Marszalek, *Sherman*, 192; Flood, *Grant and Sherman*, 33–34.

56 Kerr, "From Atlanta to Raleigh," 215–216; Connolly, *Three Years in the Army of the Cumberland*, 354; *Washington Evening Star*, January 27, 1865, genealogybank .com.

57 Marszalek, *Sherman*, 312–313.

58 O.R., II.47.16.

59 Marszalek, *Sherman*, 271; Burke Davis, *Sherman's March*, 132.

60 O.R., 44:836–837.

61 O.R., II:47:36–37.

62 Burke Davis, *Sherman's March*, 133–138.

63 Marszalek, *Sherman*, 314; Sherman, *Memoirs*, II:250–252. (The plan was never fully implemented because lenient early Reconstruction policies enabled Southerners to reclaim their confiscated low-country lands. Burke Davis, *Sherman's March*, 138; McPherson, *Ordeal*, 508.)

64 Sherman, *Sherman's Civil War*, 797–798.

65 Welles, *Diary*, II:222.

66 Nicolay and Hay, *Abraham Lincoln*, 10:74; Lincoln, *Collected Works*, 8:149; *The Constitution*, 66–67.

67 Goodwin, *Team of Rivals*, 687; Donald, *Lincoln*, 554; Oates, *With Malice Toward None*, 405; Nicolay and Hay, *Abraham Lincoln*, 10:74; Sandburg, *Abraham Lincoln*, 8.

68 Vorenberg, *Final Freedom*, 187–188; *Reconstruction Amendment Debates*, 82–83, 86, 84.

69 Alley, *Reminiscences*, 585–586.

70 McPherson, *Battle Cry*, 839; Sandburg, *Abraham Lincoln*, 11–14; Nicolay and Hay, *Abraham Lincoln*, 10:86; Strong, *Diary*, III:549; Vorenberg, *Final Freedom*, 208, 211; Brooks, *Washington in Lincoln's Time*, 206–207; Oates, *With Malice Toward None*, 406.

71 Lincoln, *Collected Works*, 8:254; McPherson, *Battle Cry*, 841.

72 Lincoln, *Collected Works*, 8:254–255.

73 O.R., *Naval Operations*, 11:434; O.R., II:46:1045, 1053, 1057; Foote, *Civil War*, III: 741–742.

74 O.R., *Naval Operations*, 11:434; Gragg, *Confederate Goliath*, 141, 190.

75 O.R., *Naval Operations*, 11:261; Lamb, "The Defense of Fort Fisher," 647.

76 Barrett, *Civil War*, 274; Foote, *Civil War*, III:743; Gragg, *Confederate Goliath*, 140.

77 O.R., *Naval Operations*, 11:439; Carr, *Gray Phantoms*, 191–196; Lamb, "The Defense of Fort Fisher," 643.

78 Lamb, "The Defense of Fort Fisher," 647.

79 Ibid., 649.

80 Lee, *Wartime Papers*, 882.

81 Gragg, *Confederate Goliath*, 145–146.

82 Evans, *Sailor's Log*, 88–92; Selfridge, "The Navy at Fort Fisher," 655.

83 Little, *Seventh Regiment*, 391–393.

84 O.R., *Naval Operations*, 11:434; O.R., I:46:1064; Lamb, "The Defense of Fort Fisher," 653–654, Gragg, *Confederate Goliath*, 191–205. (Whiting died of his wounds on March 10 while a prisoner of war at Fort Columbus in New York Harbor; Lamb recovered. Warner, *Generals in Gray*, 335.)

85 O.R., II:46:1071; Carr, *Gray Phantoms*, 197.

86 Foote, *Civil War*, III:745–746; Gragg, *Confederate Goliath*, 214.

87 O.R., *Naval Operations*, 11:433; Gragg, *Confederate Goliath*, 235, 244; Foote, *Civil War*, III:746.

88 Gragg, *Confederate Goliath*, 231.

89 Foote, *Civil War*, III:747; Gragg, *Confederate Goliath*, 235; O.R., I:46:431.

90 O.R., *Naval Operations*, 11:445–446.

91 Grant, *Memoirs*, 512.

92 Strong, *Diary*, III:546; Welles, *Diary*, II:226.

93 Foote, *Civil War*, III:740.

94 J. B. Jones, *War Diary*, II:380.

95 O.R., II:46:1061.

96 Lee, *Lee's Dispatches*, 318–321.

97 Stephens, *Constitutional View*, 619–620.

98 Foote, *Civil War*, III:768–769; Calkins, "Land Operations," 1; Gallagher, *Confederate War*, 88–89; J. B. Jones, *War Diary*, II:395; Bill, *Beleaguered City*, 260.

99 William C. Davis, *Jefferson Davis*, 582; Foote, *Civil War*, III:766–767; William C. Davis, *Breckinridge*, 480–485, 490; William C. Davis, *Honorable Defeat*, 22–23, 28, 5–8.

100 Wheelan, *Bloody Spring*, 33.

101 Richmond *Examiner*, genealogybank.com; Conolly, *Irishman in Dixie*, 47–48;

Freeman, *Lee's Lieutenants*, I:4; Foote, *Civil War*, III:767-768; J. B. Jones, *War Diary*, II:372; Lee, *Wartime Papers*, 884, 888; Warner, *Generals in Gray*, 62-63.

102 Goodwin, *Team of Rivals*, 690.

103 Trudeau, *Last Citadel*, 300-303; Sandburg, *Abraham Lincoln*, 28-42.

104 Lincoln, *Collected Works*, 8:221; Trudeau, *Last Citadel*, 305.

105 William C. Davis, *Jefferson Davis*, 590; Trudeau, *Last Citadel*, 305-307.

Chapter 2: February 1865

1   Foote, *Civil War*, III:764.

2   Marszalek, *Sherman*, 320.

3   Stokes, *South Carolina Civilians*, 60.

4   Meade, *Life and Letters*, II:260; Catton, *A Stillness*, 331-333.

5   Stephens, *Constitutional View*, II:597; Grant, *Memoirs*, 522.

6   Lincoln, *Collected Works*, 8:248.

7   Grant, *Papers*, 13:345-346.

8   Lincoln, *Collected Works*, 8:249-250; Goodwin, *Team of Rivals*, 692; Welles, *Diary*, II:235.

9   Stephens, *Constitutional View*, II:618-619; Seward and Seward, *Seward at Washington*, 260.

10   Foote, *Civil War*, III:775-776; Grant, *Memoirs*, 524; Sandburg, *Abraham Lincoln*, 43-44.

11   Stephens, *Constitutional View*, II:602; Seward and Seward, *Seward at Washington*, 260.

12   Stephens, *Constitutional View*, II:613.

13   Ibid., 614.

14   Ibid., 617; Coates, "The Case for Reparations," 63.

15   Sandburg, *Abraham Lincoln*, 27, 46, 51; Catton, *A Stillness*, 333.

16   Welles, *Diary*, II:235-237; Sandburg, *Abraham Lincoln*, 48.

17   Walter Taylor, *Lee's Adjutant*, 221; J. B. Jones, *War Diary*, II:411; Strong, *Diary*, III:552; *Boston Evening Transcript*, genealogybank.com.

18   Putnam, *Richmond During the War*, 351.

19   Sandburg, *Abraham Lincoln*, 58.

20   Stephens, *Constitutional View*, II:619, 622-623.

21   Sandburg, *Abraham Lincoln*, 49-50; William C. Davis, *Jefferson Davis*, 593-594; Durden, *Gray and the Black*, 188-189; Pollard, *Lost Cause*, 684-685.

22   Stephens, *Constitutional View*, 625-626; William C. Davis, *Jefferson Davis*, 594.

23   *Richmond Examiner*, February 7, 1865, genealogybank.com; www.marshall.edu/library/speccoll/virtual_museum/hampton_roads/pdf/ConfederatePeace Resolutions-1.pdf.

24   O.R., 52:589; Beringer et al., *Why the South Lost*, 370-371; Risley, *Civil War*, 269.

25   Durden, *Gray and the Black*, 102-106; Risley, *Civil War*, 269.

26   Durden, *Gray and the Black*, 139-140.

27   Risley, *Civil War*, 274, 276, 279-280; Durden, *Gray and the Black*, 183, 110.

28 McPherson, *Battle Cry*, 836; J. B. Jones, *War Diary*, II:416–417, 431; Risley, *Civil War*, 280.

29 O.R., II:51:1063; Glatthaar, *Soldiering*, 154–155; Durden, *Gray and the Black*, 202–203, 206–207.

30 O.R., IV:3:1012–1013.

31 James Richardson, *Compilation*, 2:705–716; J. B. Jones, *War Diary*, II:449.

32 Beringer et al., *Why the South Lost*, 374–375; Durden, *Gray and the Black*, 240; Foote, *Civil War*, III:756; Jefferson Davis, *Rise*, I:518.

33 Durden, *Gray and the Black*, 250, 268–269.

34 Furgurson, *Ashes of Glory*, 308–309; Durden, *Gray and the Black*, 272–274; Jefferson Davis, *Rise*, I:519.

35 Strong, *Diary*, III:564.

36 Lincoln, *Collected Works*, 8:362.

37 William C. Davis, *Breckinridge*, 496; Lee, *Wartime Papers*, 906; Freeman, *Lee*, III:534.

38 O.R. II:46:1210.

39 Foote, *Civil War*, III:761; Bill, *Beleaguered City*, 265.

40 Lee, *Wartime Papers*, 892; Trudeau, *Last Citadel*, 294–295.

41 Lonn, *Desertion*, 29.

42 Freeman, *Lee's Lieutenants*, III:623–624; O.R., II:46:1254, 1265; Hess, *In the Trenches*, 225–226.

43 Lonn, *Desertion*, 19, 231.

44 O.R. II:46:1254; Freeman, *Lee*, III:542.

45 O.R., II:47:1270–1271.

46 Glatthaar, *Lee's Army*, 438.

47 Lonn, *Desertion*, 18; Burke Davis, *To Appomattox*, 49.

48 Foote, *Civil War*, III:764.

49 Lee, *Wartime Dispatches*, 837, 847, 907; Trudeau, *Last Citadel*, 421.

50 Lee, *Lee's Dispatches*, 329–330; Catton, *Grant Takes Command*, 410–411; Freeman, *Lee*, 4:6.

51 Hitchcock, *Marching with Sherman*, 217, 219.

52 Burke Davis, *Sherman's March*, 145; Sherman, *Memoirs*, II:255.

53 Sherman, *Memoirs*, II:272.

54 Upson, *With Sherman to the Sea*, 46.

55 Nichols, *Story of the Great March*, 179.

56 Osborn, *Fiery Trail*, 84.

57 Barrett, *Sherman's March*, 47; Sandburg, *Abraham Lincoln*, 81.

58 Sandburg, *Abraham Lincoln*, 81.

59 Strong, *Diary*, III:556.

60 Hitchcock, *Marching with Sherman*, 253.

61 Barrett, *Sherman's March*, 47.

62 Sherman, *Sherman's Civil War*, 797.

63 O.R., 44:1011.

64 Freeman, *Lee's Lieutenants*, III:639, 615–616; Foote, *Civil War*, III:762; Lee, *Lee's Dispatches*, 316–317.

65 Barrett, *Sherman's March*, 42–43.

66 Ibid., 41.

67 Nichols, *Story of the Great March*, 131–132.

68 Conyngham, *Sherman's March*, 310–311.

69 Sherman, *Memoirs*, II:254; Nichols, *Story of the Great March*, 132.

70 Sherman, *Memoirs*, II:254.

71 Marszalek, *Sherman*, 320.

72 Conyngham, *Sherman's March*, 311.

73 Sandburg, *Abraham Lincoln*, 83; Sherman, *Memoirs*, II:249.

74 Burke Davis, *Sherman's March*, 146; Warner, *Generals in Gray*, 124–125.

75 Burke Davis, *Sherman's March*, 146–147.

76 Sherman, *Memoirs*, II:273–274; Osborn, *Fiery Trail*, 99; Burke Davis, *Sherman's March*, 146–147.

77 Nichols, *Story of the Great March*, 141; Sherman, *Memoirs*, II:273–277; Burke Davis, *Sherman's March*, 146–147.

78 Lewis, *Sherman*, 490.

79 Burke Davis, *Sherman's March*, 146–147.

80 Osborn, *Fiery Trail*, 102, 113.

81 Charles Wills, *Army Life*, 343.

82 Sherman, *Memoirs*, II:271; Walter A. Clark, *Under the Stars and Bars*, 182–183; Trudeau, *Out of the Storm*, 211.

83 Sherman, *Memoirs*, II:273–274; Barrett, *Sherman's March*, 51.

84 Burke Davis, *Sherman's March*, 145; Hitchcock, *Marching with Sherman*, 260.

85 Charles Wills, *Army Life*, 345.

86 Walter Clark, *North Carolina Regiments*, 3:191.

87 Stokes, *South Carolina Civilians*, 19.

88 Hitchcock, *Marching with Sherman*, 261.

89 Lewis, *Sherman*, 493.

90 Osborn, *Fiery Trail*, 117–118; Barrett, *Sherman's March*, 589.

91 Fleharty, *Our Regiment*, 132.

92 Aldrich, "In the Track of Sherman's Army," 198–204; Burke Davis, *Sherman's March*, 149; Barrett, *Sherman's March*, 52–53.

93 Hitchcock, *Marching with Sherman*, 242.

94 Osborn, *Fiery Trail*, 119; Nichols, *Story of the Great March*, 153–154; Conyngham, *Sherman's March*, 310–312.

95 Barrett, *Sherman's March*, 56.

96 Stokes, *South Carolina Civilians*, 27, 33; Walter Clark, *North Carolina Regiments*, 3:191.

97 Burke Davis, *Sherman's March*, 150–151; Barrett, *Sherman's March*, 56–57.

98 Upson, *With Sherman to the Sea*, 150; Hitchcock, *Marching with Sherman*, 66.

99 Marszalek, *Sherman*, 321; Osborn, *Fiery Trail*, 109fn2.

100 Osborn, *Fiery Trail*, 107; Lewis, *Sherman*, 495.

101 Barrett, *Sherman's March*, 96–97.

102 Charles Wills, *Army Life*, 355.

103 Walter Clark, *North Carolina Regiments*, 3:192.

104 Barrett, *Sherman's March*, 63–64.

105 Furgurson, *Ashes of Glory*, 303.

106 Burke Davis, *Sherman's March*, 160.

107 Barrett, *Sherman's March*, 67–68; Osborn, *Fiery Trail*, 125–126; Sherman, *Memoirs*, II:279.

108 Sherman, *Memoirs*, II:277–278.

109 Burke Davis, *Sherman's March*, 160; Sherman, *Memoirs*, II:279–280. (Later, in his memoirs, Sherman downplayed Columbia's significance, writing that he regarded it "as simply one point on our general route of march, and not as an important conquest." Sherman, *Memoirs*, II:278.)

110 Byers, *With Fire and Sword*, 144–153.

111 Conyngham, *Sherman's March*, 326.

112 Sherman, *Memoirs*, II:279–280.

113 Marszalek, *Sherman*, 44; Sherman, *Memoirs*, II:284–285.

114 Byers, *With Fire and Sword*, 153–163.

115 Ibid.

116 Ibid., 168, 174–176; Sherman, *Memoirs*, II:282–283; Burke Davis, *Sherman's March*, 156. (Byers later served as US consul at Zurich.)

117 Trezevant, *Burning of Columbia*, 6; Barrett, *Sherman's March*, 72–74; Osborn, *Fiery Trail*, 127–128.

118 Barrett, *Sherman's March*, 75.

119 Stokes, *South Carolina Civilians*, 45, 51, 60.

120 Osborn, *Fiery Trail*, 110–111; Burke Davis, *Sherman's March*, 167–168; Simms, *Sack and Destruction*, 17–18.

121 Sarah Richardson, "The Burning," 302; "The Burning of Columbia," 288–297.

122 LeConte, *When the World Ended*, 44–45.

123 Simms, *Sack and Destruction*, 18–19.

124 LeConte, *When the World Ended*, 44–45.

125 Conyngham, *Sherman's March*, 330–333.

126 Simms, *Sack and Destruction*, 19.

127 Sherman, *Memoirs*, II:285–287; Osborn, *Fiery Trail*, 128–129, 131; Charles Wills, *Army Life*, 351.

128 Barrett, *Sherman's March*, 87–89; Osborn, *Fiery Trail*, 134; Conyngham, *Sherman's March*, 333.

129 O.R., II:47:475.

130 "The Burning of Columbia," 297–298; Sarah Richardson, "The Burning," 304–306.

131 Osborn, *Fiery Trail*, 130–132.

132 Hitchcock, *Marching with Sherman*, 268.

133 O.R., I:46:22; Sherman, *Memoirs*, II:287.

134 Sherman, *Memoirs*, II:288.

135 Ibid., 287; Burke Davis, *Sherman's March*, 183; Osborn, *Fiery Trail*, 136fn5.

136 Chesnut, *Mary Chesnut's Civil War*, 734.

137 O.R., II:47:533; Charles Wills, *Army Life*, 352.

138 Sherman, *Sherman's Civil War*, 818–819; Conyngham, *Sherman's March*, 311.

139 O.R., II:47:546.

140 Ibid., 596–597.

141 Burke Davis, *Sherman's March*, 187.

142 O.R., II:47:1238; J. B. Jones, *War Diary*, 428; Osborn, *Fiery Trail*, 200, 150–155; Barrett, *Sherman's March*, 95.

143 Osborn, *Fiery Trail*, 148; Conyngham, *Sherman's March*, 343.

144 Thomas, *Confederate Nation*, 282; Barrett, *Civil War*, 281–284; J. B. Jones, *War Diary*, 433fn.

145 Chesnut, *Mary Chesnut's Civil War*, 708.

146 J. B. Jones, *War Diary*, 425; Chesnut, *Mary Chesnut's Civil War*, 725–728, 744; Strong, *Diary*, III:556.

147 O.R., V:38:885; II:47:1303; Symonds, *Joseph E. Johnston*, 341–344.

148 Freeman, *Lee's Lieutenants*, I:260–262.

149 Warner, *Generals in Gray*, 161–162.

150 Symonds, *Joseph E. Johnston*, 320–328, 333, 347; Chesnut, *Mary Chesnut's Civil War*, 700, 725, 729–730; Bradley, *This Astounding Close*, 17; Johnston, *Narrative*, 372; O.R., II:47:1247, 1297.

151 O.R., II:47:1298–1299.

152 O.R., II:47:1297–1298, 1372.

153 Chesnut, *Mary Chesnut's Civil War*, 738.

154 Hitchcock, *Marching with Sherman*, 263 266.

155 Sherman, *Sherman's Civil War*, 823–824.

156 Cheraw Visitors Bureau, www.cheraw.com; Osborn, *Fiery Trail*, 162–163; Stokes, *South Carolina Civilians*, 80; Barrett, *Sherman's March*, 109; Charles Wills, *Army Life*, 353.

157 Foote, *Civil War*, III:784–785; Caldwell, *History of a Brigade*, 201.

158 Bill, *Beleaguered City*, 266 (Dr. Charles Minnigerode, the rector of St. Paul's Episcopal Church in Richmond, had married Pegram and his bride, Hetty Cary of Baltimore, on January 19 before a distinguished gathering that included the Jefferson Davises, who had lent Pegram and his bride their carriage for the ride to the church. Minnigerode also presided at Pegram's funeral.); Douglas, *I Rode with Stonewall*, 311–312; Furgurson, *Ashes of Glory*, 298.

159 Trudeau, *Last Citadel*, 318–320; Hess, *In the Trenches*, 230–232; Wainwright, *Diary of Battle*, 497.

160 Gordon, *Reminiscences*, 382; Glatthaar, *Lee's Army*, 443–447.

161 Hunter, "The Peace Commission," 308–309.

162 O.R., I:47:1044; Lee, *Wartime Papers*, 906.

163 Greene, *Civil War Petersburg*, 235.

164 William C. Davis, *Breckinridge*, 33–34; William C. Davis, *Jefferson Davis*, 600.

165 Glatthaar, *Lee's Army*, 435; Lee, *Wartime Papers*, 908.

166 Grant, *Memoirs*, 524–525.

167 O.R., II:7:62–63, 615; Strong, *Diary*, III:570.

168 Catton, *Grant Takes Command*, 411–412; Stern, *End to Valor*, 32–39; Varon, *Southern Lady*, 188.

169 Catton, *Grant Takes Command*, 409; Meade, *Life and Letters*, 2:246.

Chapter 3: March 1865

1   Lincoln, *Collected Works*, 8:333.
2   Freeman, *Lee*, 3:538.
3   Freeman, *Lee's Lieutenants*, 3:643.
4   Lee, *Wartime Papers*, 911.
5   O.R., II:46:824.
6   Horace Porter, *Campaigning with Grant*, abridged, 264–265.
7   O.R., II:46:825.
8   Greene, *Civil War Petersburg*, 225–226; Warner, *Generals in Gray*, 111.
9   Freeman, *Lee*, 4:7–10; Gordon, *Reminiscences*, 385–393.
10   William C. Davis, *An Honorable Defeat*, 45–46; William C. Davis, *Breckinridge*, 497.
11   O.R., II:46:1295–1296.
12   Freeman, *Lee*, 3:537.
13   Ibid., 537–538.
14   Gordon, *Reminiscences*, 403; Catton, *A Stillness*, 335–336; Hess, *In the Trenches*, 246–249; Walker, "Gordon's Assault," 20–23; Trudeau, *Last Citadel*, 334–335.
15   Stern, *End to Valor*, 72–73.
16   Sandburg, *Abraham Lincoln*, 86–89.
17   Lincoln, *Collected Works*, 8:236.
18   Stern, *End to Valor*, 7–8; Brooks, *Lincoln Observed*, 166; Sandburg, *Abraham Lincoln*, 90; Donald, *Lincoln*, 565.
19   Sandburg, *Abraham Lincoln*, 91–94; Brooks, *Washington in Lincoln's Time*, 238.
20   Stern, *End to Valor*, 16, 42.
21   Brooks, *Washington in Lincoln's Time*, 239.
22   Ibid., 239–240; Lincoln, *Collected Works*, 8:333.
23   Brooks, *Washington in Lincoln's Time*, 240–241; *Holy Bible*, King James Version, 628.
24   Sandburg, *Abraham Lincoln*, 95–96; Stern, *End to Valor*, 19–20.
25   Strong, *Diary*, III:560.
26   Lincoln, *Collected Works*, 8:356.
27   Sandburg, *Abraham Lincoln*, 96–97; McPherson, *Battle Cry*, 840; Kendrick and Kendrick, *Douglass and Lincoln*, 230–231.
28   Stern, *End to Valor*, 23.
29   Donald, *Lincoln*, 568; Sandburg, *Abraham Lincoln*, 134.
30   Brooks, *Lincoln Observed*, 175–176.
31   Welles, *Diary*, II:257.
32   Brooks, *Lincoln Observed*, 176; Hill, "The First Burial," 3:320.
33   Mitchell, *Edmund Ruffin*, 249–250.
34   James D. Richardson, *Compilation*, 1:544–547.
35   Sandburg, *Abraham Lincoln*, 137.
36   Conyngham, *Sherman's March*, 357; Sherman, *Memoirs*, II:294–295; O.R., 47:719; Sherman, *Sherman's Civil War*, 825.
37   O.R., 47:719, 721, 760.

38 Byers, *With Fire and Sword*, 184.

39 Barrett, *Sherman's March*, 114, 121.

40 Osborn, *Fiery Trail*, 184–186; Barrett, *Sherman's March*, 135–138; Sherman, *Memoirs*, II:288, 292, 297; Sherman, *Sherman's Civil War*, 826.

41 Charles Wills, *Army Life*, 358–362; Upson, *With Sherman to the Sea*, 157; Osborn, *Fiery Trail*, 179.

42 Conyngham, *Sherman's March*, 356; Johnston, *Narrative*, 380; Burke Davis, *Sherman's March*, 212–214.

43 Burke Davis, *Sherman's March*, 219.

44 Sherman, *Memoirs*, II:294–195; Burke Davis, *Sherman's March*, 220–221; Barrett, *Sherman's March*, 140.

45 O.R., II:47:1338; Warner, *Generals in Gray*, 137.

46 Johnston, *Narrative*, 372; O.R., II:47:1347, 1372, 1380.

47 O.R., I:49:1042; II:47:1373–1374.

48 Chesnut, *Mary Chesnut's Civil War*, 768, 737.

49 Symonds, *Joseph E. Johnston*, 347–348; Johnston, *Narrative*, 379; Broadwater, *Battle of Despair*, 33.

50 O.R., II:47:857.

51 Symonds, *Joseph E. Johnston*, 347–348; O.R., I:47:23.

52 Burke Davis, *Sherman's March*, 225–227; Johnston, *Narrative*, 382–383; Barrett, *Sherman's March*, 152–156, 158; Hitchcock, *Marching with Sherman*, 248; Averasboro battle site online at www.cr.nps.gov/hps/abpp/battles/nc019.htm; O.R., II:47:1400, 1403–1404; Symonds, *Joseph E. Johnston*, 348; Broadwater, *Battle of Despair*, 60.

53 Trudeau, *Out of the Storm*, 211; Johnston, *Narrative*, 384–385; Barrett, *Sherman's March*, 159–163.

54 Barrett, *Sherman's March*, 163–166; O.R., I:47:25.

55 Hampton, "The Battle of Bentonville," 702–703; Barrett, *Civil War*, 327; Walter Clark, *North Carolina Regiments*, 3:194; Howard, *Autobiography*, II:148.

56 O.R., II:47:910.

57 Barrett, *Sherman's March*, 167.

58 Walter A. Clark, *Under the Stars and Bars*, 192–195; Bradley, *This Astounding Close*, 21; Burke Davis, *Sherman's March*, 235–236.

59 Burke Davis, *Sherman's March*, 236–237.

60 Broadwater, *Battle of Despair*, 113; Burke Davis, *Sherman's March*, 237; O.R., II:47:918.

61 Barrett, *Sherman's March*, 179–180; Hampton, "The Battle of Bentonville," 704; O.R., II:47:919–920; Sherman, *Memoirs*, II:304.

62 O.R., II:47:920.

63 Sherman, *Memoirs*, II:299; Warner, *Generals in Blue*, 338–339.

64 Hampton, "The Battle of Bentonville," 704–705; Sherman, *Memoirs*, II:304; Barrett, *Sherman's March*, 180–181; Walter Clark, *North Carolina Regiments*, 3:198; Howard, *Autobiography*, II:150–151; Hughes, *Bentonville*, 187–192, 204, 206; Broadwater, *Battle of Despair*, 147.

65 Symonds, *Joseph E. Johnston*, 351; Hitchcock, *Marching with Sherman*, 282–283; Hughes, *Bentonville*, 206–207, 209; Broadwater, *Battle of Despair*, 138–143.

66 Sherman, *Memoirs*, II:304.

67 Hitchcock, *Marching with Sherman*, 274; Osborn, *Fiery Trail*, 200.

68 Barrett, *Sherman's March*, 183.

69 Andrews, *North Reports*, 626; Sandburg, *Abraham Lincoln*, 138–139; Barrett, *Sherman's March*, 186–187; Bradley, *This Astounding Close*, 28–29; Burke Davis, *Sherman's March*, 241–242; Kerr, "From Atlanta to Raleigh," 222.

70 Barrett, *Sherman's March*, 188–189, 194; Osborn, *Fiery Trail*, 203–205; Burke Davis, *Sherman's March*, 284; Sherman, *Memoirs*, II:306, 334.

71 O.R., II;47:1055; Lee, *Lee's Dispatches*, 339.

72 Trudeau, *Last Citadel*, 330; Gordon, *Reminiscences*, 407.

73 Gordon, *Reminiscences*, 401–405.

74 Ibid., 407–408; Walker, "Gordon's Assault," 25–26.

75 Walker, "Gordon's Assault," 26; Stern, *End to Valor*, 74–75.

76 Gordon, *Reminiscences*, 408–409.

77 Hess, *In the Trenches*, 251–253; Trudeau, *Last Citadel*, 347; Stern, *End to Valor*, 77–81; Walker, "Gordon's Assault," 29.

78 Gordon, *Reminiscences*, 408; Strong, *Diary*, III:572.

79 O.R., I:46:319; Freeman, *Lee's Lieutenants*, 3:651.

80 Trudeau, *Last Citadel*, 351; Hess, *In the Trenches*, 253.

81 Douglas, *I Rode with Stonewall*, 329.

82 Lyman, *Meade's Headquarters*, 324.

83 Freeman, *Lee's Lieutenants*, 3:652–653.

84 Lee, *Wartime Papers*, 917–918.

85 Pfanz, *Abraham Lincoln*, 7–10.

86 Ibid., 1–2.

87 Welles, *Diary*, II:264.

88 Pfanz, *Abraham Lincoln*, 11.

89 Bates, *Lincoln in the Telegraph Office*, 378.

90 Sandburg, *Abraham Lincoln*, 137, 99.

91 Lyman, *Meade's Headquarters*, 325.

92 David Porter, *Incidents*, 283.

93 Sherman, *Memoirs*, II:324; Parker, *Story of the Thirty-Second*, 229.

94 Sherman, *Memoirs,* II:324; Foote, *Civil War*, III:13; Horace Porter, *Campaigning with Grant*, abridged, 276; Lyman, *Meade's Headquarters*, 327.

95 Horace Porter, *Campaigning with Grant*, unabridged, 418–420; Lyman, *Meade's Headquarters*, 327.

96 Stern, *End to Valor*, 87; Sandburg, *Abraham Lincoln*, 147; Badeau, *Grant in Peace*, 356–360; Pfanz, *Abraham Lincoln*, 15, 17–18.

97 Horace Porter, *Campaigning with Grant*, unabridged, 410.

98 Stern, *End to Valor*, 107–108; Horace Porter, *Campaigning with Grant*, unabridged, 422–424; Grant, *Memoirs*, 524–525; Sherman, *Memoirs*, II:326.

99 Sherman, *Memoirs*, II:325; David Porter, *Incidents*, 315.

100 Trudeau, *Out of the Storm*, 5, 11–13; Brian Wills, *Battle from the Start*, 300–304.

101 David Porter, *Incidents*, 314; Sherman, *Memoirs*, II:326–327.

102 Sherman, *Memoirs*, II:327.

103 Pfanz, *Abraham Lincoln*, 28; Catton, *A Stillness*, 340.

104 David Porter, *Incidents*, 285–287.

105 Burke Davis, *To Appomattox*, 15–17.

106 Furgurson, *Ashes of Glory*, 309–310; Blackford, *Memoirs*, 2:225; Putnam, *Richmond During the War*, 359.

107 Beringer et al., *Why the South Lost*, 362.

108 Blackford, *Memoirs*, 2:227; J. B. Jones, *War Diary*, II:441.

109 Hotchkiss, *Make Me a Map*, 259; Wheelan, *Terrible Swift Sword*, 166–168; Starr, *Union Cavalry*, 2:371–374; Sheridan, *Memoirs*, 2:117–119; Drake, *Little Phil*, 356; Urwin, *Custer Victorious*, 233.

110 Horace Porter, *Campaigning with Grant*, abridged, 273; Grant, *Papers*, 13:457–458.

111 Foote, *Civil War*, III:853.

112 Starr, *Union Cavalry*, 2:425–428; Horace Porter, *Campaigning with Grant*, unabridged, 422; Wheelan, *Terrible Swift Sword*, 170; Foote, *Civil War*, III:853; Simson, *Crisis of Command*, 10; Wittenberg, *Little Phil*, 150.

113 Horace Porter, *Campaigning with Grant*, unabridged, 422; Starr, *Union Cavalry*, 2:425–426; Wheelan, *Terrible Swift Sword*, 170–171.

114 Starr, *Union Cavalry*, 2:425–426; Grant, *Memoirs*, 527; Barrett, *Sherman's March*, 196–197; Wheelan, *Terrible Swift Sword*, 171; Badeau, *Military History*, 3:451.

115 Sheridan, *Memoirs*, II:132–133.

116 Horace Porter, *Campaigning with Grant*, unabridged, 426.

117 Lincoln, *Collected Works*, 8:378–379.

118 O.R., III:46:266.

119 Starr, *Union Cavalry*, 2:432–433; Horace Porter, *Campaigning with Grant*, unabridged, 426–427.

120 Sheridan, *Memoirs*, 2:140–141; Newhall, *With General Sheridan*, 56, 61–62.

121 Sheridan, *Papers*, reel 50, box 55; Sheridan, *Memoirs*, 2:143–144.

122 Horace Porter, *Campaigning with Grant*, unabridged, 428–429; Grant, *Memoirs*, 531; Sheridan, *Memoirs*, II:145–148.

123 Lee, *Wartime Papers*, 917–918.

124 Gordon, *Reminiscences*, 416.

125 Lee, *Wartime Papers*, 918.

126 Freeman, *Lee*, 4:24.

127 Freeman, *Lee's Lieutenants*, 3:656–659; Freeman, *Lee*, 4:33.

128 Conolly, *Irishman in Dixie*, 76–77.

129 Freeman, *Lee*, 4:34–35; Lee, *Wartime Papers*, 918–920.

130 Bearss and Calkins, *Battle of Five Forks*, 59–66; Wadsworth, *13th South Carolina Volunteer Infantry*, 74–75; O.R., III:46:306, Sheridan, *Papers*, reel 94; Sheridan, *Memoirs*, II:149; Simson, *Crisis of Command*, 122–124; Warner, *Generals in Blue*, 541–542.

131 Wert, *Custer*, 214–215.

132 Tremain, *Last Hours*, 50–56; Newhall, *With General Sheridan*, 70–72; Sheridan, *Memoirs*, II:152–153.

133 O.R., III:46:381; Sheridan, *Papers*, reel 94; Starr, *Union Cavalry*, 2:443–444; Horace Porter, *Campaigning with Grant*, unabridged, 432.

Chapter 4, April 1865

1   Pendleton, *Memoirs*, 400.
2   Longstreet, *Manassas to Appomattox*, 614–615.
3   O.R., III:46:610; Sheridan, *Memoirs*, II:187.
4   Sheridan, *Papers*, reel 94; Hergesheimer, *Sheridan*, 307–309.
5   Horace Porter, *Campaigning with Grant*, unabridged, 435–436.
6   Ibid., 435–436.
7   Newhall, *With General Sheridan*, 98–99; O.R., I:46:1105.
8   Foote, *Civil War*, III:869–870; Newhall, *With General Sheridan*, 103–104; Bearss and Calkins, *Battle of Five Forks*, 89–91; Horace Porter, *Campaigning with Grant*, unabridged, 437–441.
9   Bearss and Calkins, *Battle of Five Forks*, 69–70; Drake, *Little Phil*, 387–388; Horace Porter, *Campaigning with Grant*, unabridged, 437–444.
10 Chamberlain, *Passing of the Armies*, 99–100.
11 Starr, *Union Cavalry*, 2:448–449; Harrell, *2nd North Carolina Cavalry*, 363.
12 Freeman, *Lee's Lieutenants*, 3:661–665.
13 Longacre, *Cavalry at Appomattox*, 88–89; Calkins, *History and Tour Guide*, 180.
14 Warner, *Generals in Gray*, 239; Freeman, *Lee's Lieutenants*, 3:658.
15 Longacre, *Cavalry at Appomattox*, 88–89; Calkins, *History and Tour Guide*, 180–181.
16 Freeman, *Lee's Lieutenants*, 3:669–670; Douglas, *I Rode with Stonewall*, 326; Furgurson, *Ashes of Glory*, 298; McGuire, "Diary," 341; Harrell, *2nd North Carolina Cavalry*, 365–366; Chamberlayne, *Ham Chamberlayne*, 318.
17 Calkins, *History and Tour Guide*, 98.
18 O'Connor, *Sheridan the Inevitable*, 254.
19 Wainwright, *Diary of Battle*, 510.
20 Catton, *A Stillness*, 357; Trudeau, *Last Citadel*, 410; Pfanz, *Abraham Lincoln*, 39.
21 Grant, *Memoirs*, 533–534; Sheridan, *Memoirs*, II:163; Starr, *Union Cavalry*, 2:449.
22 Chamberlain, *Passing of the Armies*, 108.
23 Horace Porter, *Campaigning with Grant*, unabridged, 441.
24 O'Connor, *Sheridan the Inevitable*, 253; Horace Porter, *Campaigning with Grant*, unabridged, 442; Morris, *Sheridan*, 250–252; O.R., III:46:420; Hill, "The First Burial," 809.
25 Chamberlain, *Passing of the Armies*, 114–116.
26 Grant, *Memoirs*, 534–535.
27 Horace Porter, *Campaigning with Grant*, unabridged, 442–443.
28 Newhall, *With General Sheridan*, 123–126.
29 James Wilson, *John Rawlins*, 316.
30 Lee, *Wartime Papers*, 922.

31   O.R., III:46:1374–1375, 1377; Alexander, *Military Memoirs*, 590.

32   Trudeau, *Last Citadel*, 378; Grant, *Memoirs*, 535–536.

33   Greene, *Final Battles*, 200–202; Catton, *A Stillness*, 361; Trudeau, *Last Citadel*, 367.

34   Hyde, *Following the Greek Cross*, 251; Greene, *Final Battles*, 190, 199.

35   Parsons, *Put the Vermonters Ahead*, 144; Trudeau, *Last Citadel*, 371–375; Hyde, *Following the Greek Cross*, 253–254; Wilkeson, *Turned Inside Out*, 187; Walter Clark, *North Carolina Regiments*, 2:576; Beyer and Keydel, *Deeds of Valor*, 508.

36   Hess, *In the Trenches*, 273–274; Trudeau, *Last Citadel*, 376.

37   Trudeau, *Last Citadel*, 381; Freeman, *Lee's Lieutenants*, 3:682; Greene, *Final Battles*, 281–285; Freeman, *Lee*, 4:51–52.

38   Hess, *In the Trenches*, 274–275; Hardy, *Thirty-seventh North Carolina Troops*, 228; Greene, *Final Battles*, 303–304; Foote, *Civil War*, III:882–883.

39   Greene, *Final Battles*, 307; Trudeau, *Last Citadel*, 383–388; Freeman, *Lee's Lieutenants*, 3:682.

40   Trudeau, *Last Citadel*, 388–389; Freeman, *Lee's Lieutenants*, 3:682–683.

41   Greene, *Final Battles*, 241–242.

42   Robertson, *General A. P. Hill*, 11–12, 310–313.

43   Freeman, *Lee's Lieutenants*, 3:676–677.

44   Tucker, "Death of General A. P. Hill," 565; Burke Davis, *To Appomattox*, 52.

45   Freeman, *Lee*, 4:51.

46   Robertson, *General A. P. Hill*, 312.

47   Tucker, "Death of General A. P. Hill," 564–569; Matthews, "How General A. P. Hill Met His Fate," 26–38; Freeman, *Lee*, 4:46–47.

48   Hyde, *Following the Greek Cross*, 256–258; Greene, *Civil War Petersburg*, 247; Freeman, *Lee*, 4:51.

49   Gorman, *Lee's Last Campaign*, 13–14.

50   Greene, *Final Battles*, 332–333, 336–340; Foote, *Civil War*, III:878; Trudeau, *Last Citadel*, 356–365; Hess, *In the Trenches*, 365–370; Walter Clark, *North Carolina Regiments*, 3:57–58.

51   Stern, *End to Valor*, 165; Greene, *Final Battles*, 242; Walter Taylor, *Lee's Adjutant*, 241–243.

52   Badeau, *Military History*, 3:517; Horace Porter, *Campaigning with Grant*, abridged, 304.

53   O.R., III:46:447, 449; Hess, *In the Trenches*, 279.

54   Caldwell, *History of a Brigade*, 220–225; Hess, *In the Trenches*, 277–278; Greene, *Final Battles*, 329–330; O.R., III:46:490.

55   O.R., III:46:447–449; Horace Porter, *Campaigning with Grant*, abridged, 303.

56   Horace Porter, *Campaigning with Grant*, abridged, 307.

57   Lyman, *Meade's Headquarters*, 339.

58   O.R., III:46:1378; Freeman, *Lee's Lieutenants*, III:681–682.

59   Furgurson, *Ashes of Glory*, 319–320; Putnam, *Richmond During the War*, 362–363; Burke Davis, *To Appomattox*, 95–96; J. B. Jones, *War Diary*, II:440–441; Conolly, *Irishman in Dixie*, 82.

60   Furgurson, *Ashes of Glory*, 320.

61   O.R., III:46:1378; Freeman, *Lee*, 4:55.

62   Blackford, *Memoirs*, II:235–237; Putnam, *Richmond During the War*, 363.

63   Greene, *Final Battles*, 341, 343; Greene, *Civil War Petersburg*, 246, 248, 250.

64   O.R. III:46:1379–1380; Walter Taylor, *General Lee*, 275; Logan, *My Confederate Girlhood*, 70–71; Freeman, *Lee*, 4:54; Freeman, *Lee's Lieutenants*, III:684–685.

65   William C. Davis, *Jefferson Davis*, 601–602.

66   Bill, *Beleaguered City*, 270–272; Pollard, *Lost Cause*, 694.

67   Burke Davis, *To Appomattox*, 116–117, 106.

68   Bill, *Beleaguered City*, 271; Sulivane, "The Fall of Richmond," 726; Wheelan, *Libby Prison*, 220; Putnam, *Richmond During the War*, 366–367.

69   Boykin, *Falling Flag*, 12–14.

70   Bill, *Beleaguered City*, 251.

71   Semmes, *Memoirs*, 809–812; Putnam, *Richmond During the War*, 365; Furgurson, *Ashes of Glory*, 330–331.

72   Wheelan, *Libby Prison*, 220; Stern, *End to Valor*, 175.

73   Furgurson, *Ashes of Glory*, 328, 333–334; Stern, *End to Valor*, 177.

74   Foote, *Civil War*, III:888; Boykin, *Falling Flag*, 12–14; Sulivane, "The Fall of Richmond," 725–726.

75   Boykin, *Falling Flag*, 15.

76   Putnam, *Richmond During the War*, 368; J. B. Jones, *War Diary*, 468; Pollard, *Lost Cause*, 697.

77   Wheelan, *Libby Prison*, 219, 221, 213.

78   Van Lew, *Yankee Spy*, 105, 110; Varon, *Southern Lady*, 193; Wheelan, *Libby Prison*, 220.

79   Foote, *Civil War*, III:890; Bill, *Beleaguered City*, 27.

80   Bruce, *Capture and Occupation*, 12.

81   Ibid., 10; Furgurson, *Ashes of Glory*, 336–337; Burke Davis, *To Appomattox*, 130.

82   Pollard, *Lost Cause*, 696.

83   Bruce, *Capture and Occupation*, 17; Haynes, *History of the Tenth Regiment*, 342.

84   Bruce, *Capture and Occupation*, 17–18.

85   Ibid., 19–21; Furgurson, *Ashes of Glory*, 337; Bill, *Beleaguered City*, 276–279.

86   Furgurson, *Ashes of Glory*, 338.

87   Bill, *Beleaguered City*, 281; J. B. Jones, *War Diary*, II:470fn1.

88   David Bates, *Lincoln in the Telegraph Office*, 360; O.R., III:46:509; Stern, *End to Valor*, 189.

89   Welles, *Diary*, II:272–273.

90   Strong, *Diary*, III:574–575.

91   Mulholland, *Story of the 116th Regiment*, 339.

92   Chesnut, *Mary Chesnut's Civil War*, 782.

93   Stern, *End to Valor*, 166; Gordon, *Reminiscences*, 388; Greene, *Civil War Petersburg*, 249–252; Trudeau, *Last Citadel*, 390.

94   Freeman, *Lee*, 4:57.

95   Caldwell, *History of a Brigade*, 225.

96   Grant, *Memoirs*, 539.

97   Greene, *Final Battles*, 345; Kimbrough, "From Petersburg to Hart's Island Prison," 498–500.

98   Catton, *A Stillness*, 364; Greene, *Final Battles*, 351–353; Trudeau, *Last Citadel*, 405.

99   Haynes, *History of the Tenth Regiment*, 339–340; Lyman, *Meade's Headquarters*, 340; NY *Herald*, April 5, 1865, genealogybank.com; Greene, *Civil War Petersburg*, 221, 261.

100 Burke Davis, *To Appomattox.*, 153.

101 Lyman, *Meade's Headquarters*, 341.

102 Greene, *Civil War Petersburg*, 256; Trudeau, *Last Citadel*, 416.

103 Grant, *Memoirs*, 539.

104 O.R., III:46:509.

105 David Porter, *Incidents*, 284–285.

106 Ibid., 292–293.

107 Ibid., 288–289.

108 Ibid., *Incidents*, 290–291.

109 Grant, *Memoirs*, 541–542; Horace Porter, *Campaigning with Grant*, unabridged, 450–451.

110 O.R. III:47:129.

111 Ibid., III:46:510.

112 Harrell, *2nd North Carolina Cavalry*, 370–371; O.R., III:46:529.

113 Freeman, *Lee*, 4:58–59; Alexander, *Military Memoirs*, 594; Douglas, *I Rode with Stonewall*, 331; Wheeler, *Witness to Appomattox*, 147.

114 Polley, *Hood's Texas Brigade*, 275; Douglas, *I Rode with Stonewall*, 331; Wheeler, *Witness to Appomattox*, 147.

115 Freeman, *Lee*, 4:66–67, 71; Longacre, *Cavalry at Appomattox,* 125–128; Thomas, *Lee*, 356.

116 Longacre, *Cavalry at Appomattox*, 128–129; Freeman, *Lee's Lieutenants*, 3:693–694; Freeman, *Lee*, 4:75–77.

117 Starr, *Union Cavalry*, 2:464; Sheridan, *Memoirs*, II:175.

118 Harrell, *2nd North Carolina Cavalry*, 376.

119 Stern, *End to Valor*, 214; Burke Davis, *To Appomattox*, 215–216; Freeman, *Lee's Lieutenants*, 3:696; Marvel, *Lee's Last Retreat*, 60–62, 72; Stiles, *Four Years*, 326; Krick, *14th South Carolina Infantry Regiment*, 27; Stern, *End to Valor*, 215; Pendleton, *Memoirs*, 400.

120 Freeman, *Lee*, 4:80–81.

121 Owen, *In Camp and Battle*, 375–376; Brown, *Campbell Brown's Civil War*, 279.

122 Marvel, *Lee's Last Retreat*, 45–46; Catton, *A Stillness*, 373.

123 Tremain, *Last Hours*, 98–100.

124 O.R., III:46:576–578.

125 Sheridan, *Memoirs*, II:177.

126 O.R., III:46:582.

127 Ibid., 449.

128 Cadwallader, *Three Years with Grant*, 312.

129 Grant, *Memoirs*, 546, 548; Sheridan, *Memoirs*, II:178–179.

130 Chamberlain, *Passing of the Armies*, 208.

131 Newhall, *With General Sheridan*, 146.

132 Chamberlain, *Passing of the Armies*, 157–158, 160.

133 Crook, *Through Five Administrations*, 53; Sandburg, *Abraham Lincoln*, 242.

134 Stern, *End to Valor*, 193, 196–197; David Porter, *Incidents*, 294–295; Sandburg, *Abraham Lincoln*, 176; Pfanz, *Abraham Lincoln*, 58–60.

135 David Porter, *Incidents*, 295–296; Sandburg, *Abraham Lincoln*, 176–178; Furgurson, *Ashes of Glory*, 342–343; Bruce, *Capture and Occupation*, 24; Pfanz, *Abraham Lincoln*, 66.

136 Crook, *Through Five Administrations*, 53–54.

137 Sandburg, *Abraham Lincoln*, 178–180; Putnam, *Richmond During the War*, 372; Furgurson, *Ashes of Glory*, 347.

138 Lincoln, *Collected Works*, 8:387, 389.

139 Stern, *End to Valor*, 290–291; Welles, *Diary*, II:275; Lincoln, *Collected Works*, 8:388–389.

140 McGuire, "Diary," 350.

141 J. B. Jones, *War Diary*, II:470.

142 Pember, *Southern Woman's Story*, 135–136.

143 Ibid., 136.

144 Bill, *Beleaguered City*, 285; Beecher, *History of the First Light Battery*, 2:682.

145 Starr, *Union Cavalry*, 2:468–469.

146 Pendleton, *Memoirs*, 400; O.R., III:46:609.

147 Drake, *Little Phil*, 408–412.

148 Freeman, *Lee's Lieutenants*, 3:701–702.

149 Foote, *Civil War*, III:918. (Lieutenant Tom Custer was awarded the Medal of Honor for his feat. Beyer and Keydel, *Deeds of Valor*, 517.)

150 Freeman, *Lee's Lieutenants*, 3:706.

151 Stiles, *Four Years*, 330–322; Newhall, *With General Sheridan*, 174–175; Marvel, *Lee's Last Retreat*, 85–86.

152 Sheridan, *Memoirs*, II:183; Stiles, *Four Years*, 333; Schaff, *Sunset of the Confederacy*, 107–108; Eanes, *Black Day of the Army*, 107; Catton, *A Stillness*, 371; Gerrish, *Army Life*, 249; Major Evan Jones, *Four Years in the Army of the Potomac*, 199.

153 Freeman, *Lee's Lieutenants*, 3:685, 706; Marvel, *Lee's Last Retreat*, 22–25; Hergesheimer, *Sheridan*, 350; Urwin, *Custer Victorious*, 246.

154 Stern, *End to Valor*, 227.

155 Freeman, *Lee's Lieutenants*, 3:698, 710; Starr, *Union Cavalry*, 2:473; Eanes, *Black Day of the Army*, 149–150; Muffly, *Story of Our Regiment*, 353–354.

156 Longstreet, *Manassas to Appomattox*, 614–615; Marvel, *Lee's Last Retreat*, 91.

157 Starr, *Union Cavalry*, 2:473; Longstreet, *Manassas to Appomattox*, 612.

158 Freeman, *Lee's Lieutenants*, 3:708–709; Marvel, *Lee's Last Retreat*, 75–77; Owen, *In Camp and Battle*, 376; Burke Davis, *To Appomattox*, 264.

159 Freeman, *Lee's Lieutenants*, 3:714; Wheeler, *Witness to Appomattox*, 191–192; O.R., III: 46:622.

160 Trudeau, *Out of the Storm*, 115.

161 Lyman, *Meade's Headquarters*, 351–352; Owen, *In Camp and Battle*, 379.

162 O.R., III:46:610; Sheridan, *Memoirs*, II:187.

163 Newhall, *With General Sheridan*, 188; Eanes, *Black Day of the Army*, 161; Hergesheimer, *Sheridan*, 350.

164 John Wise, *End of an Era*, 429.

165 Beach, *First New York (Lincoln) Cavalry*, 504.

166 Henry Wise, "The Career of Wise's Brigade," 18–19; Gordon, *Reminiscences*, 434.

167 Alexander, *Military Memoirs*, 598–599.

168 Freeman, *Lee*, 4:99.

169 Stern, *End to Valor*, 230; Caldwell, *History of a Brigade*, 231–232; Freeman, *Lee*, 4: 95–101.

170 Horace Porter, *Campaigning with Grant*, abridged, 313–315; Chamberlain, *Passing of the Armies*, 166.

171 Marvel, *Lee's Last Retreat*, 128.

172 Ibid., 137; Sheridan, *Memoirs*, II:187–188.

173 Stern, *End to Valor*, 230–231; Catton, *Grant Takes Command*, 456; Wheeler, *Witness to Appomattox*, 148, 160.

174 Wheeler, *Witness to Appomattox*, 153; Freeman, *Lee*, 4:106; Wiatt, *Confederate Chaplain*, 236; Burke Davis, *To Appomattox*, 290; Tobie, *History of the First Maine Cavalry*, 418.

175 Freeman, *Lee's Lieutenants*, 3:718.

176 O.R., III:46:619.

177 Burke Davis, *To Appomattox.*, 291–292.

178 Longstreet, *Manassas to Appomattox*, 619.

179 O.R., III:46:619.

180 Armistead Long, *Memoirs*, 416–417.

181 Pendleton, *Memoirs*, 402.

182 Freeman, *Lee*, 4:111–112.

183 Bernard, *War Talks*, 256; Grant, *Memoirs*, 551.

184 Sheridan, *Papers*, reel 50, box 55.

185 Marvel, *Lee's Last Retreat*, 144–146.

186 Newhall, *With General Sheridan*, 192–194.

187 Ibid., 191–192.

188 Starr, *Union Cavalry*, 2:477–478.

189 Hergesheimer, *Sheridan*, 359; Longacre, *Cavalry at Appomattox*, 171; Starr, *Union Cavalry*, 2:480; Burke Davis, *To Appomattox*, 331–332; Sheridan, *Memoirs*, II:189–190; O.R., I:46:1120–1121.

190 Starr, *Union Cavalry*, 2:480; Longstreet, *Manassas to Appomattox*, 622; O.R., III:46:654; Sheridan, *Memoirs*, II:190; Pendleton, *Memoirs*, 403; Marvel, *Lee's Last Retreat*, 147–151; www.nps.gov/apco/final-battles.htm.

191 Freeman, *Lee's Lieutenants*, 3:723.

192 Grant, *Memoirs*, 551; Stern, *End to Valor*, 244–245; O.R., III:46:654.

193 O.R., I:46:57–58.

194 Stern, *End to Valor*, 240.

195 Gordon, *Reminiscences*, 434–436; O.R., I:46:1266–1267; Freeman, *Lee's Lieutenants*, 3:724–725.

196 Pendleton, *Memoirs*, 404; Badeau, *Grant in Peace*, 20; Freeman, *Lee*, 4:118; Colonel Charles Marshall, 259–260.

197 Wiatt, *Confederate Chaplain*, 236–237.

198 Sheridan, *Memoirs*, II:191; Military Order of the Loyal Legion of the United States, Illinois, 1:433; Longacre, *Cavalry at Appomattox*, 180; Chamberlain, *Passing of the Armies*, 172–173.

199 Horace Porter, *Campaigning with Grant*, abridged, 317–318; Varon, *Appomattox*, 38; O.R., I:46:57.

200 Grant, *Memoirs*, 553; Burke Davis, *To Appomattox*, 335; O.R., III:46:653.

201 Sheridan, *Memoirs*, II:191.

202 Caldwell, *History of a Brigade*, 234–235.

203 Longstreet, *Manassas to Appomattox*, 623; Sheridan, *Memoirs*, II:192; Gordon, *Reminiscences*, 436–437; Walter Clark, *North Carolina Regiments*, 3:59; Burke Davis, *To Appomattox*, 347–348.

204 Sheridan, *Memoirs*, II:192.

205 Gordon, *Reminiscences*, 437; Longstreet, *Manassas to Appomattox*, 624; Newhall, *With General Sheridan*, 211; Longacre, *Cavalry at Appomattox*, 193; Foote, *Civil War*, III:941.

206 Chamberlain, *Passing of the Armies*, 175–177.

207 Sheridan, *Memoirs*, II:193; Gordon, *Reminiscences*, 436–438; Polley, *Hood's Texas Brigade*, 277.

208 Gordon, *Reminiscences*, 437–438; Longstreet, *Manassas to Appomattox*, 624; Freeman, *Lee's Lieutenants*, 3:726.

209 Armistead Long, *Memories of Robert E. Lee*, 421–422.

210 Freeman, *Lee*, 4:121.

211 Longstreet, *Manassas to Appomattox*, 624–625; Foote, *Civil War*, III:942; Sorrel, *Recollections*, 276–277.

212 Freeman, *Lee*, 4:118; Alexander, *Military Memoirs*, 603-605.

213 Grant, *Memoirs*, 554; O.R., III:46:664–665; Catton, *Grant Takes Command*, 461–463.

214 Newhall, *With General Sheridan*, 210–211.

215 O.R., I:46:1303–1304.

216 Chamberlain, *Passing of the Armies*, 182–183; Catton, *Grant Takes Command*, 462.

217 Sheridan, *Memoirs*, II:195–197; Starr, *Union Cavalry*, 2:485; Blackford, *Memoirs*, 2:ii–iii appendix.

218 Gordon, *Reminiscences*, 441–442; O'Connor, *Sheridan the Inevitable*, 270.

219 Freeman, *Lee's Lieutenants*, 3:733–734.

220 Ibid., 736.

221 Varon, *Appomattox*, 53; Freeman, *Lee*, 4:133–134; *Century Magazine*, 60:156–157.

222 Horace Porter, *Campaigning with Grant*, abridged, 324; Forsyth, *Thrilling Days*, 184–186.

223 Varon, *Appomattox*, 56–57.

224 Winik, *April 1865*, 183; Horace Porter, *Campaigning with Grant*, abridged, 329–330; Freeman, *Lee*, 4:135–136.

225 Horace Porter, *Campaigning with Grant*, abridged, 331–332; O.R., III:46:665.

226 Horace Porter, *Campaigning with Grant*, abridged, 333–334.

227 Ibid., 334–335; O.R., III:46:666.

228 Varon, *Appomattox*, 55; Burke Davis, *To Appomattox*, 369, 385–386.

229 Horace Porter, *Campaigning with Grant*, abridged, 336–337.

230 Sheridan, *Memoirs*, II:201–202.

231 Forsyth, *Thrilling Days*, 191–196; Andrews, *North Reports*, 636; Sheridan, *Memoirs*, II:202.

232 Newhall, *With General Sheridan*, 221.

233 Grant, *Memoirs*, 555–556.

234 Ibid., 559; Horace Porter, "The Surrender," 744.

235 Horace Porter, *Campaigning with Grant*, abridged, 340; *History of the 121st Pennsylvania*, 100; Melcher, *With a Flash of the Sword*, 217; Rhodes, *All for the Union*, 222; Houghton, *Campaigns of the Seventeenth Maine*, 271.

236 Merington, *Custer Story*, 159; Wert, *Custer*, 167; Horace Porter, *Campaigning with Grant*, unabridged, 487; Horace Porter, "The Surrender," 743–744; Cadwallader, *Three Years with Grant*, 330.

237 Blackford, *Memoirs*, 2:appendix iii–iv; Varon, *Appomattox*, 90.

238 Freeman, *Lee*, 4:144–146; Blackford, *Memoirs*, 2:appendix, v.

239 Caldwell, *History of a Brigade*, 237.

240 Burke Davis, *To Appomattox*, 391; Wiatt, *Confederate Chaplain*, 237.

241 McGuire, "Diary," 351; J. B. Jones, *War Diary*, II:474; Putnam, *Richmond During the War*, 375; Furgurson, *Ashes of Glory*, 354–355.

242 Eppes, *Through Some Eventful Years*, 270.

243 Chesnut, *Mary Chesnut's Civil War*, 814, 773.

244 O.R., I:46:1265–1267.

245 Chamberlain, *Passing of the Armies*, 188.

246 Starr, *Union Cavalry*, 2:430.

247 Sheridan, *Memoirs*, II:202–203.

248 Starr, *Union Cavalry*, 2:489–490.

249 O.R., I:46:58.

250 Grant, *Memoirs*, 559; Gordon, *Reminiscences*, 392; Marshall, *Lee's Aide-de-Camp*, 275; Freeman, *Lee*, 4:150–151. (Their meeting was on May 1, 1869, when Lee stopped to see Grant while returning from a trip to Baltimore.)

251 Marshall, "General Lee's Farewell," 747.

252 O.R., 46:1267.

253 O.R., III46:666–667.

254 Chamberlain, *Passing of the Armies*, xii–xiii, 186–187, 195–196, 199–200; Freeman, *Lee's Lieutenants*, 746, 813; Gordon, *Reminiscences*, 444.

255 Chamberlain, *Passing of the Armies*, 268–269.

256 Grant, *Memoirs*, 561; Varon, *Appomattox*, 111–112; O.R., III:46:667.

257 Ford, *Adams Letters*, II:263–264.

258 Brooks, *Lincoln Observed*, 181–183; Lincoln, *Collected Works*, 8:395.

259 Pfanz, *Abraham Lincoln*, 88; Sandburg, *Abraham Lincoln*, 194.

260 Greene, *Civil War Petersburg*, 263; Sandburg, *Abraham Lincoln*, 171–172, 186; Pfanz, *Abraham Lincoln*, 84–85.

261 Chambrun, *Impressions*, 83; Burke Davis, *To Appomattox*, 408; Sandburg, *Abraham Lincoln*, 393.

262 Sandburg, *Abraham Lincoln*, 244–245.

263 Ibid., 194–196; Crook, *Through Five Administrations*, 58.

264 Lincoln, *Collected Works*, 8:399.

265 Ibid., 388–389; O.R., III:46:619.

266 Welles, *Diary*, II:279–280; Lincoln, *Collected Works*, 8:407.

267 Varon, *Appomattox*, 117, 120; Oates, *With Malice Toward None*, 406–407; Sandburg, *Abraham Lincoln*, 67–71; Lincoln, *Collected Works*, 8:400–405.

268 Sandburg, *Abraham Lincoln*, 224–225, 256–257; genealogybank.com.

269 O.R., III:46:619, 677, 696–697, 711.

270 Lincoln, *Collected Works*, 8:406.

271 Furgurson, *Ashes of Glory*, 353; McGuire, "Diary," 355.

272 Whitman, *Complete Poetry*, 240.

273 Donald, *Lincoln*, 590–592; Stern, *End to Valor*, 308–309, 313; O.R., III:46:744; Welles, *Diary*, II:280, 282–283; Sandburg, *Abraham Lincoln*, 264–265.

274 Donald, *Lincoln*, 549–550.

275 Crook, *Through Five Administrations*, 66.

276 Donald, *Lincoln*, 593.

277 Titone, *My Thoughts Be Bloody*, 355; Stern, *End to Valor*, 314; Donald, *Lincoln*, 594.

278 William C. Davis, *Jefferson Davis*, 595; Richmond *Whig*, genealogybank.com; Titone, *My Thoughts Be Bloody*, 332; Booth, *Writings*, 130.

279 Kauffman, *American Brutus*, 160–162.

280 Swanson, *Manhunt*, 24; Kauffman, *American Brutus*, 205, 210–212.

281 Kauffman, *American Brutus*, 212.

282 Booth, *Writings*, 147–150.

283 Sandburg, *Abraham Lincoln*, 272, 278.

284 Ibid., 278.

285 Ibid., 281.

286 Kauffman, *American Brutus*, 226; Titone, *My Thoughts Be Bloody*, 360–363; Pitch, *"They Have Killed Papa Dead!"*, 114–115; Sandburg, *Abraham Lincoln*, 281.

287 Goodrich, *Darkest Dawn*, 99.

288 Titone, *My Thoughts Be Bloody*, 360–363; Pitch, *"They Have Killed Papa Dead!"*, 119–120.

289 Pitch, *"They Have Killed Papa Dead!"*, 123–127.

290 Welles, *Diary*, II:283–288; Goodrich, *Darkest Dawn*, 111, 119, 121–122, 126; O.R., III:47:220–221; Pitch, *"They Have Killed Papa Dead!"*, 129–130, 136, 158.

291 Goodrich, *Darkest Dawn*, 115–116.

292 Brooks, *Washington in Lincoln's Time*, 260.

293 Kendrick and Kendrick, *Douglass and Lincoln*, 235; Brooks, *Lincoln Observed*, 194; Goodrich, *Darkest Dawn*, 132–133.

294 Strong, *Diary*, III:583, 587.

295 Hartwell, *To My Beloved Wife*, 351.

296 Chamberlain, *Passing of the Armies*, 210–213.

297 John Wise, *End of an Era*, 454–455.

298 Lowry, "Not Everybody Mourned," 96, 107; Kauffman, *American Brutus*, 237.

299 Stern, *End to Valor*, 329; Fowler, *Character and Death*, 4, 15.

300 Chamberlain, *Passing of the Armies*, 214.

301 Brooks, *Washington in Lincoln's Time*, 261–263; Goodrich, *Darkest Dawn*, 187–188; *Philadelphia Age*, genealogybank.com; Sandburg, *Abraham Lincoln*, 391.

302 Sandburg, *Abraham Lincoln*, 391; Brooks, *Washington in Lincoln's Time*, 265; Sloan, "Abraham Lincoln's New York City Funeral," 56; Goodrich, *Darkest Dawn*, 188; Brooks, *Lincoln Observed*, 197.

303 Sandburg, *Abraham Lincoln*, 394; Swanson, *Bloody Crimes*, 229; Goodrich, *Darkest Dawn*, 189, 213; Sloan, "Abraham Lincoln's New York City Funeral," 79.

304 Swanson, *Bloody Crimes*, 281–283; McPherson, *Battle Cry*, 853; Ohio *Statesman*, genealogybank.com.

305 Sherman, *Memoirs*, II:346–347; Johnston, *Narrative of Military Operations*, 396–401.

306 Sherman, *Memoirs*, II:347–348; O.R., III:47:220–221.

307 Sherman, *Memoirs*, II:343–344; Barrett, *Sherman's March*, 203–204.

308 Hitchcock, *Marching with Sherman*, 296; Upson, *With Sherman to the Sea*, 164–165; Burke Davis, *Sherman's March*, 248–249; O.R., III:47:180.

309 O.R., III:47:177.

310 Sherman, *Home Letters*, 340.

311 Sherman, *Memoirs*, II:333–334.

312 Charles Wills, *Army Life*, 368.

313 Ward, *Last Flag of Truce*, 16; Barrett, *Sherman's March*, 215; Burke Davis, *Sherman's March*, 254–255; Spencer, *Last Ninety Days*, 160–162; Bradley, *This Astounding Close*, 116–117, 123.

314 Sherman, *Memoirs*, II:347–349; Johnston, *Narrative of Military Operations*, 401–404; Burke Davis, *Sherman's March*, 260–262.

315 Sherman, *Memoirs*, II:352–354; O.R., III:47:243–244.

316 Foote, *Civil War*, III:992–994.

317 Nichols, *Story of the Great March*, 311; Hitchcock, *Marching with Sherman*, 313; Bradley, *This Astounding Close*, 162.

318 Thomas, *Confederate Nation*, 301; O.R., III:47:813–814.

319 Burke Davis, *Sherman's March*, 266.

320 Ibid., 266.

321 Grant, *Papers*, 14:423.

322 Sherman, *Sherman's Civil War*, 878fn1.

323 Flood, *Grant and Sherman*, 339.

324 Welles, *Diary*, II:294–295; O.R., III:47:276–277; Sherman, *Memoirs*, II:372.

325 *Hartford Daily Courant*, genealogybank.com.

326 *Philadelphia North American*, genealogybank.com.

327 Welles, *Diary*, II:295–297.

328 Barrett, *Sherman's March*, 245–246; Sherman, *Memoirs*, II:368.

329 Brian Wills, *Battle from the Start*, 309–310; Foote, *Civil War*, III:904–905, 967.

330 O.R., II:49:1289–1290.

331   Sherman, *Sherman's Civil War*, 874–875.

332   Sherman, *Memoirs*, II:358; Burke Davis, *Sherman's March*, 273.

333   Catton, *Grant Takes Command*, 486; Grant, *Papers*, 14:424–425.

334   O.R., III:47:294.

335   Barrett, *Sherman's March*, 269.

336   O.R., V:47, 835–836.

337   Grant, *Memoirs*, 570.

338   O.R., III:47:293.

339   Grant, *Papers*, 14:433.

340   Hitchcock, *Marching with Sherman*, 315.

341   Sherman, *Memoirs*, II:362.

342   Ibid., 363, 370; McGuire, "Diary," 360; Hitchcock, *Marching with Sherman*, 316.

343   Sheridan, *Memoirs*, II:365.

344   Schurz, *Reminiscences*, 3:116.

345   Sherman, *Memoirs*, II:366–367.

346   Charles Wills, *Army Life*, 374, 377–378.

347   Sherman, *Memoirs*, II:329–330.

348   Swanson, *Manhunt*, 129–130, 155; Kauffman, *American Brutus*, 285–286.

349   Booth, *Writings*, 154.

350   Swanson, *Manhunt*, 287, 292, 306–312.

351   Kauffman, *American Brutus*, 310–311, Pitch, *"They Have Killed Papa Dead!"*, 272, 275.

352   Kauffman, *American Brutus*, 310; Goodrich, *Darkest Dawn*, 222; Swanson, *Manhunt*, 340.

353   Kauffman, *American Brutus*, 315–320; Swanson, *Manhunt*, 328, 332, 334, 337, 342; Pitch, *"They Have Killed Papa Dead!"*, 288–290.

Chapter 5: May 1865

1   Foote, *Civil War*, III:1004.

2   Conolly, *Irishman in Dixie*, 116–117.

3   Burke Davis, *Sherman's March*, 294–295.

4   William C. Davis, *Jefferson Davis*, 628–630.

5   Ibid., 621.

6   James D. Richardson, *Compilation*, 1:568–570.

7   John Wise, *End of an Era*, 415.

8   Burke Davis, *Sherman's March*, 256–257.

9   Lee, *Wartime Papers*, 935–938.

10   Ibid., 939; Swanson, *Bloody Crimes*, 206.

11   Jefferson Davis, *Essential Writings*, 367.

12   Clint Johnson, *Pursuit*, 124–126.

13   Swanson, *Bloody Crimes*, 196.

14   Clint Johnson, *Pursuit*, 141.

15   William C, Davis, *Jefferson Davis*, 622–626; Foote, *Civil War*, III:1004.

16   Clint Johnson, *Pursuit*, 157–158; O.R., III:46:954.

17 Andrew Johnson, The American Presidency Project, www.presidency.ucsb.edu/ws/ ?pid=72356; Welles, *Diary*, II:299–300.

18 Clint Johnson, *Pursuit*, 156–157.

19 William C. Davis, *Jefferson Davis*, 633–634; William C. Davis, *Breckinridge*, 248–252, 271; Foote, *Civil War*, III:1005.

20 William C. Davis, *Jefferson Davis*, 636–637; Foote, *Civil War*, III:1009–1010; O.R., 49: 378; Clint Johnson, *Pursuit*, 181; *Harper's Weekly*, May 27, 1865.

21 Clint Johnson, *Pursuit*, 186.

22 Andrew Johnson, American Presidency Project.

23 Thomas, *Lee*, 368–369; McGuire, "Diary," 347–349; Putnam, *Richmond During the War*, 373; Freeman, *Lee*, 4:163–164, 188–189.

24 Bill, *Beleaguered City*, 285; Freeman, *Lee*, 4:191–193.

25 Strong, *Diary*, III:598.

26 Varon, *Appomattox*, 184.

27 *New York Herald*, genealogybank.com.

28 Gallagher, *Confederate War*, 158.

29 Conolly, *Irishman in Dixie*, 116–117.

30 Spencer, *Last Ninety Days*, 171.

31 Ibid., 188–189.

32 Clint Johnson, *Pursuit*, 192, 212–214; *Providence Evening Press*, *New York Herald*, *Springfield Republican*, genealogybank.com; Swanson, *Bloody Crimes*, 340; Foote, *Civil War*, III:1013, 1034–1035; Welles, *Diary*, II:308–309; William C. Davis, *Jefferson Davis*, 641–645.

33 *New York Times* archives; www.jeffersondavis.rice.edu; Foote, *Civil War*, III:1038–1039.

34 Grant, *Papers*, 15:150.

35 O.R., II:8:578–580.

36 Freeman, *Lee*, 4:202–203; Greene, *Civil War Petersburg*, 268.

37 Grant, *Papers*, 15:210–211.

38 Badeau, *Grant in Peace*, 26; Smith, *Grant*, 417–418. (Lee recited and signed the amnesty oath in October 1865, but the document disappeared until 1970, when it turned up in the National Archives. In 1975 President Gerald Ford formally pardoned Robert E. Lee. Varon, *Appomattox*, 203.)

39 Chamberlain, *Passing of the Armies*, 217–219, 206.

40 Charles Wills, *Army Life*, 370.

41 Greene, *Civil War Petersburg*, 266.

42 Putnam, *Richmond During the War*, 386.

43 Chamberlain, *Passing of the Armies*, 233–234.

44 Houghton, *Campaigns of the Seventeenth Maine*, 283.

45 Charles Wills, *Army Life*, 379–380; Upson, *With Sherman to the Sea*, 168.

46 Sherman, *Memoirs*, II:374; O.R., III:47:435, 446, 454–455; Flood, *Grant and Sherman*, 355; Bradley, *This Astounding Close*, 248–249; Lewis, *Sherman*, 564–566.

47 O.R., III:47:478.

48 Chamberlain, *Passing of the Armies*, 283–284; Sherman, *Memoirs*, II:376; Trudeau, *Out of the Storm*, 316.

49   Sheridan, *Memoirs*, II:208–209; Cadwallader, *Three Years with Grant*, 306.

50   Sheridan, *Memoirs*, II:211; Warner, *Generals in Gray*, 280; Trudeau, *Out of the Storm*, 310.

51   Flood, *Grant and Sherman*, 379–380; Brooks, *Washington in Lincoln's Time*, 308–310; Welles, *Diary*, II:310; Stern, *End to Valor*, 342; Swanson, *Bloody Crimes*, 335; *New York Herald*, May 24, 1865, and *Philadelphia Inquirer*, May 24, 1865, genealogy bank.com.

52   *New York Herald*, genealogybank.com; Brooks, *Washington in Lincoln's Time*, 317.

53   *Philadelphia Inquirer*, genealogybank.com; Horace Porter, *Campaigning with Grant*, abridged, 353; Flood, *Grant and Sherman*, 380–384; Stern, *End to Valor*, 344–345.

54   Burke Davis, *Sherman's March*, 288.

55   Horace Porter, *Campaigning with Grant*, abridged, 354–355; Chamberlain, *Passing of the Armies*, 252; Brooks, *Washington in Lincoln's Time*, 311–313.

56   *Philadelphia Inquirer*, genealogybank.com; Brooks, *Washington in Lincoln's Time*, 315.

57   Burke Davis, *Sherman's March*, 288.

58   Stern, *End to Valor*, 330–331, 346; Trudeau, *Out of the Storm*, 374–375.

59   Flood, *Grant and Sherman*, 377; Burke Davis, *Sherman's March*, 288.

60   Horace Porter, *Campaigning with Grant*, unabridged, 509; Sherman, *Memoirs*, II:376–377.

61   Stern, *End to Valor*, 346–348.

62   Burke Davis, *Sherman's March*, 289.

63   Sherman, *Memoirs*, II:378; *Philadelphia Inquirer*, *Baltimore Sun*, genealogybank. com; Brooks, *Washington in Lincoln's Time*, 320.

64   Sherman, *Memoirs*, II:378.

65   Chamberlain, *Passing of the Armies*, 276; *Baltimore Sun*, genealogybank.com; Brooks, *Washington in Lincoln's Time*, 321; Burke Davis, *Sherman's March*, 290.

66   Burke Davis, *Sherman's March*, 294–295.

67   Sherman, *Memoirs*, II:376; Lewis, *Sherman*, 575–576.

68   Brooks, *Washington in Lincoln's Time*, 316–318.

69   Lewis, *Sherman*, 568–569, 575; Sherman, *Memoirs*, II:371–377.

70   Brooks, *Washington in Lincoln's Time*, 316; McAllister, *Ellen Ewing*, 306.

71   Marszalek, *Sherman*, 357; Sherman, *Memoirs*, II:375–376.

72   Trudeau, *Out of the Storm*, 378.

73   O.R., I:47:44.

74   Pollard, *Lost Cause*, 717–718.

75   Foote, *Civil War*, III:3, 1041; O.R., III:46:1301–1302.

76   Chamberlain, *Passing of the Armies*, 294.

Epilogue

1   *Concise Dictionary*, 878.

2   Greene, *Civil War Petersburg*, 250.

3   Ibid., 250; Mitchell, *Edmund Ruffin*, 255, 256; Thomas, *Confederate Nation*, 305–306.

4   McPherson, *Ordeal*, 494.

5   Warner, *Generals in Gray*, 274; Foote, *Civil War*, III:1022–1023.

6   Stern, *End to Valor*, 352; Foote, *Civil War*, III:1029–1031.

7   Foote, *Civil War*, III:1026–1027; Trudeau, *Out of the Storm*, 265–270, 275.

8   Welles, *Diary*, II:312–313.

9   Schurz, *Reminiscences*, 3:167.

10 Joslyn, *Charlotte's Boys*, 310.

11 Sheridan, *Memoirs*, 2:261; Wheelan, *Terrible Swift Sword*, 217.

12 Whitney and Whitney, *American Presidents*, 148.

13 Wheelan, *Libby Prison*, 221, 226–227; Furgurson, *Ashes of Glory*, 361.

14 Gallagher, *Confederate War*, 163–164.

15 Foote, *Civil War*, III:1040; Stern, *End to Valor*, 355.

16 McPherson, *Ordeal*, 859–861.

17 Richard Taylor, *Destruction and Reconstruction*, 228, 236; McPherson, *Ordeal*, 859–861.

18 Foote, *Civil War*, III:1050.

19 McFeely, *Grant*, 490–494, 504–517; Foote, *Civil War*, III:1055–1056.

20 Warner, *Generals in Gray*, 182–183, 193, 111; Whitney and Whitney, *American Presidents*, 154–155.

21 William C. Davis, *Jefferson Davis*, 664, 670–678, 705; Foote, *Civil War*, III:1050, 1054.

22 *Trenton Evening News*, and *Cleveland Plain Dealer*, genealogybank.com; Goldfield, *Still Fighting*, 54–55.

23 Brands, *The Man Who Saved the Union*, 633–634; *New York Herald*, *Boston Herald*, *Charleston Weekly News* and *Courier*, all August 9, 1885, genealogybank.com.

BIBLIOGRAPHY

Aldrich, Mrs. Alfred P. "In the Track of Sherman's Army." In Weekly News and Courier, *Our Women in the War: The Lives They Lived; the Deaths They Died*, 197–211.

Alexander, General Edward Porter. *Fighting for the Confederacy: The Personal Recollections of General Edward Porter Alexander*. Edited by Gary W. Gallagher. Chapel Hill: University of North Carolina Press, 1989.

———. *Military Memoirs of a Confederate: A Critical Narrative*. New York: Charles Scribner's Sons, 1907.

Alley, John B. In Rice, *Reminiscences of Abraham Lincoln by Distinguished Men of His Time*, 573–591.

Andrews, J. Cutler. *The North Reports the Civil War*. Pittsburgh, PA: University of Pittsburgh Press, 1955.

The Atlantic. Washington, DC: Atlantic Monthly Group, June 2014.

Badeau, Adam. *Grant in Peace: From Appomattox to Mount McGregor, A Personal Memoir*. Hartford, CT: S. S. Scranton & Company, 1887.

———. *Military History of Ulysses S. Grant, from April 1861 to April 1865*. 3 vols. New York: D. Appleton and Company, 1882.

Barrett, John G. *The Civil War in North Carolina*. Chapel Hill: University of North Carolina Press, 1963.

———. *Sherman's March Through the Carolinas*. Chapel Hill: University of North Carolina Press, 1956

Bates, David Homer. *Lincoln in the Telegraph Office: Recollections of the United States Military Telegraph Corps during the Civil War*. New York: Century, 1907.

Bates, Edward. *The Diary of Edward Bates, 1859–1866*, vol. 4, edited by Howard K. Beale. Washington, DC: US Government Printing Office, 1933.

Battle, Laura Elizabeth Lee. *Forget-Me-Nots of the Civil War: A Romance, Containing Reminiscences and Original Letters of Two Confederate Soldiers*. St. Louis: A. R. Fleming Printing, 1909.

Beach, William Harrison. *The First New York (Lincoln) Cavalry from April 19, 1861, to July 7, 1865*. New York: Lincoln Cavalry Association, 1902.

Bearss, Edwin, and Chris Calkins. *Battle of Five Forks*. Lynchburg, VA: H. E. Howard, 1985.

Beecher, Herbert W. *History of the First Light Battery Connecticut Volunteers, 1861–1865*. 2 vols. New York: A. T. De La Mare Printing, 1901.

Beringer, Richard E., Herman Hattaway, Archer Jones, William N. Still Jr. *Why the South Lost the Civil War*. Athens, GA, and London: University of Georgia Press, 1986.

Bernard, George S. *War Talks of Confederate Veterans*. Petersburg, VA: Fenn & Owen. 1892.

Beyer, W. F., and O. F. Keydel, eds. *Deeds of Valor: How America's Civil War Heroes Won the Congressional Medal of Honor*. Stamford, CT: Longmeadow Press, 1992.

Bill, Alfred Hoyt. *The Beleaguered City: Richmond, 1861–1865*. New York: Alfred A. Knopf, 1946.

Blackford, Susan Leigh, ed. *Memoirs of Life In and Out of the Army in Virginia During the War Between the States*. 2 vols. Lynchburg, VA: Warwick House Publishing, 1996.

Booth, John Wilkes. *"Right or Wrong, God Judge Me." The Writings of John Wilkes Booth*, edited by John Rhodehamel and Louise Taper. Urbana, IL, and Chicago: University of Illinois Press, 1997.

Boykin, Edward M. *The Falling Flag: Evacuation of Richmond, Retreat and Surrender at Appomattox*. New York: E. J. Hale, 1874.

Bradley, Mark L. *This Astounding Close: The Road to Bennett Place*. Chapel Hill: University of North Carolina Press, 2000.

Brands, H. W. *The Man Who Saved the Union: Ulysses Grant in War and Peace*. New York: Doubleday, 2012.

Broadwater, Robert P. *Battle of Despair: Bentonville and the North Carolina Campaign*. Macon, GA: Mercer University Press, 2004.

Brooks, Noah. *Lincoln Observed: Civil War Dispatches of Noah Brooks*, edited by Michael Burlingame. Baltimore, MD: Johns Hopkins University Press, 1998.

——. *Washington in Lincoln's Time*. New York: Rinehart, 1958.

Brown, Campbell. *Campbell Brown's Civil War: With Ewell and the Army of Northern Virginia*. Baton Rouge: Louisiana State University Press, 2001.

Bruce, George. *The Capture and Occupation of Richmond*. Self-published, 1927.

Burne, Alfred H. *Lee, Grant and Sherman: A Study in Leadership in the 1864–1865 Campaign*. Lawrence: University of Kansas Press, 2000.

"The Burning of Columbia," an extract from a circular letter by the Ursuline sisters. In Smythe, Poppenheim, and Taylor, *South Carolina Women in the Confederacy*, 288–298. Columbia, SC: State Company, 1903.

Byers, Major Samuel Hawkins. *With Fire and Sword*. New York: Neale Publishing, 1911.

Cadwallader, Sylvanus. *Three Years with Grant*, edited by Benjamin P. Thomas. Lincoln: University of Nebraska Press, 1996.

Caldwell, J. F. J. *The History of a Brigade of South Carolinians*. Philadelphia, PA: King & Baird, 1866.

Calkins, Chris M. *The Appomattox Campaign, March 29–April 9, 1865*. Conshohocken, PA: Combined Books, 1997.

——. *History and Tour Guide of the Battle of Five Forks*. Columbus, OH: Blue and Gray Magazine, 2003.

——. "Land Operations in Virginia in 1865: Time Catches Up with Lee at Last." In Davis and Robertson, *Virginia at War 1865*, 1–14.

Carr, Dawson. *Gray Phantoms of the Cape Fear: Running the Civil War Blockade*. Winston-Salem, NC: John F. Blair, 1998.

Carruth, Gorton. *What Happened When: A Chronology of Life & Events in America.* New York: Signet, 1991.

Casler, John O. *Four Years in the Stonewall Brigade.* Girard, KS: Appeal Publishing Company, 1906.

Catton, Bruce. *The Army of the Potomac: A Stillness at Appomattox.* Garden City, NY: Doubleday, 1953.

———. *The Army of the Potomac: Grant Takes Command.* Boston: Little, Brown and Company, 1968.

The Century Illustrated Monthly Magazine. 120 vols. New York: Scribner & Co.; The Century Co., 1881–1906.

Chamberlain, Joshua Lawrence. *The Passing of the Armies.* New York: Bantam Books, 1993. Originally published in 1913.

Chamberlayne, John Hampden. *Ham Chamberlayne, Virginian Letters and Papers of an Artillery Officer in the War for Southern Independence, 1861–1865.* Richmond, VA: Press of the Dietz Printing, 1932.

Chambrun, Adolphe de Pineton, marquis de. *Impressions of Lincoln and the Civil War.* New York: Random House, 1952.

Chesnut, Mary. *Mary Chesnut's Civil War*, edited by C. Vann Woodward. New Haven, CT, London: Yale University Press, 1981.

Claiborne, Dr. John H. "Last Days of Lee and his Paladins." In Bernard, *War Talks of Confederate Veterans*, 237–277.

Clark, James C. *Last Train South. The Flight of the Confederate Government from Richmond.* Jefferson, NC: McFarland & Company, 1984.

Clark, Walter, ed. *Histories of the Several Regiments and Battalions From North Carolina in the Great War, 1861–1865.* Raleigh, NC: E. M. Uzzell, 1901.

Clark, Walter A. *Under the Stars and Bars, or Memories of Four Years Service with the Oglethorpes, of Augusta, Georgia.* Jonesboro, GA: Freedom Hill Press, 1987.

Coates, Ta-Nehisi. "The Case for Reparations." In *The Atlantic*, June 2014, 55–71.

Concise Dictionary of American Biography. New York: Charles Scribner's Sons, 1977.

Confederate Southern Memorial Association, ed. *Confederate Veteran* magazine. Nashville, TN: S. A. Cunningham, 1893–1932.

Connolly, Major James A. *Three Years in the Army of the Cumberland: The Letters and Diary of Major James A. Connolly.* Bloomington: Indiana University Press, 1996.

Conolly, Thomas. *An Irishman in Dixie: Thomas Conolly's Diary of the Fall of the Confederacy*, edited by Nelson D. Lankford. Columbia: University of South Carolina Press, 1988.

The Constitution of the United States with the Declaration of Independence and the Articles of Confederation. New York: Barnes & Noble Books, 2002.

Conyngham, David Power. *Sherman's March Through the South.* New York: Sheldon and Company, 1865.

Coxe, John. "Last Struggles and Successes of Lee." In *Confederate Veteran*, vol. 22, 356–359.

Crook, Colonel William H. *Through Five Administrations: Reminiscences of Colonel*

William H. Crook, Body-Guard to President Lincoln, edited by Margarita Spalding Gerry. New York: Harper & Brothers, 1910.

Dana, Charles A., and James Wilson. *The Life of Ulysses S. Grant, General of the Armies of the United States*. Springfield, MA: Gordon Bill & Company, 1868.

Davis, Burke. *Sherman's March*. New York: Vintage Books, 1988.

———. *To Appomattox: Nine April Days, 1865*. New York, Toronto: Rinehart & Company, 1959.

Davis, Jefferson. *Jefferson Davis: The Essential Writings*, edited by William F. Cooper Jr. New York: Modern Library, 2003.

———. *The Papers of Jefferson Davis*, edited by Haskell M. Monroe Jr. and James T. McIntosh. 13 vols. Baton Rouge: Louisiana State University Press, 1971–2012.

———. *The Rise and Fall of the Confederate Government*. 2 vols. New York: D. Appleton and Co., 1881.

Davis, William C. *An Honorable Defeat. The Last Days of the Confederate Government*. New York: Harcourt, 2001.

———. *Breckinridge: Statesman, Soldier, Symbol*. Baton Rouge: Louisiana State University Press, 1974.

———. *Jefferson Davis: The Man and His Hour*. New York: Harper Collins, 1991.

Davis, William C., and James I. Robertson Jr., eds. *Virginia at War 1865*. Lexington: University Press of Kentucky, 2012.

De Leon T. C. *Four Years in Rebel Capitals: An Inside View of Life in the Southern Confederacy*. Mobile, AL: Gossip Printing, 1892.

Donald, David Herbert. *Lincoln*. New York: Simon & Schuster, 1995.

Douglas, Henry Kyd. *I Rode with Stonewall*. Chapel Hill: University of North Carolina Press, 1940.

Douglass, Frederick. *Narrative of the Life of Frederick Douglass, an American Slave, Written by Himself*, edited by William L. Andrews and William S. McFeely. New York: W. W. Norton & Company, 1997.

Drake, William F. *Little Phil: The Story of General Philip Henry Sheridan*. Prospect, CT: Biographical Publishing Company, 2005.

Dunkelman, Mark H. *Marching with Sherman, Through Georgia and the Carolinas with the 154th New York*. Baton Rouge: Louisiana State University Press, 2012.

Durden, Robert F. *The Gray and the Black. The Confederate Debate on Emancipation*. Baton Rouge: Louisiana State University Press, 2000.

Eanes, Greg. *Black Day of the Army, April 6, 1865. The Battles of Sailor's Creek*. Burkeville, VA: E & H Publishing, 2001.

Eppes, Susan Bradford. *Through Some Eventful Years*. Macon, GA: J. W. Burke Company, 1926.

Evans, Robley Dunglison. *A Sailor's Log: Recollections of Forty Years of Naval Life*. New York: D. Appleton, 1908.

Fite, Emerson David. *Social and Industrial Conditions in the North during the Civil War*. New York: MacMillan, 1910.

Fleharty, Stephen F. *Our Regiment: A History of the 102nd Illinois Infantry Volunteers*. Bedford, MA: Applewood Books, 2008.

Flood, Charles Bracelen. *Grant and Sherman: The Friendship That Won the Civil War.* New York: Farrar, Strauss and Giroux, 2005.

———. *Grant's Final Victory: Ulysses S. Grant's Heroic Last Year.* Boston: DaCapo Press, 2011.

Foote, Shelby. *The Civil War: A Narrative. Volume 3: Red River to Appomattox.* New York: Vintage Books, 1986. First published 1974.

Forsyth, George. *Thrilling Days in Army Life.* New York, London: Harper & Brothers, 1900.

Ford, Worthington Chauncey, ed. *A Cycle of Adams Letters, 1861–1865,* 2 vols. Boston, New York: Houghton Mifflin, 1920.

Fowler, Reverend Henry. *Character and Death of Abraham Lincoln. A Discourse Preached at Auburn, N.Y., April 23, 1865.* New York: William J. Moses' Steam Press Establishment, 1865.

Freeman, Douglas Southall, ed. *Lee's Dispatches: Unpublished Letters of General Robert E. Lee, C.S.A., to Jefferson Davis and the War Department of the Confederate States of America, 1862–1865.* New York, London: C. P. Putnam's Sons, 1915.

———. *Lee's Lieutenants: A Study in Command.* 3 vols. New York: Charles Scribner's Sons, 1943–1944.

———. *R. E. Lee: A Biography.* 4 vols. New York, London: Charles Scribner's Sons, 1934–1935.

Furgurson, Ernest B. *Ashes of Glory: Richmond at War.* New York: Alfred A. Knopf, 1996.

Gallagher, Gary W. *The Confederate War.* Cambridge, MA: Harvard University Press, 1997.

Gallman, J. Matthew. *Northerners at War: Reflections on the Civil War Home Front.* Kent, OH: Kent State University Press, 2010.

Genealogybank.com. Northern, Southern newspapers from 1864–1865.

Gerrish, Theodore. *Army Life: A Private's Reminiscences of the Civil War.* Portland, ME: Hoyt, Fogg & Donham, 1882.

Glatthaar, Joseph T. *Lee's Army: From Victory to Collapse.* New York: Free Press, 2008.

———. *Soldiering in the Army of Northern Virginia. A Statistical Portrait of the Troops Who Served under Robert E. Lee.* Chapel Hill: University of North Carolina Press, 2011.

Goldfield, David. *Still Fighting the Civil War: The American South and Southern History.* Baton Rouge: Louisiana State University Press, 2002.

Goodrich, Thomas: *The Darkest Dawn: Lincoln, Booth, and the Great American Tragedy.* Bloomington, Indianapolis: Indiana University Press, 2005.

Goodwin, Doris Kearns. *Team of Rivals: The Political Genius of Abraham Lincoln.* New York: Simon & Schuster, 2005.

Gordon, General John B. *Reminiscences of the Civil War.* Baton Rouge: Louisiana State University Press, 1993. First published 1903.

Gorman, Captain J. C. *Lee's Last Campaign.* Raleigh, NC: William B. Smith & Company, 1866.

Gragg, Rod. *Confederate Goliath: The Battle of Fort Fisher*. Baton Rouge: Louisiana State University Press, 2006.

Grant, Ulysses S. *The Papers of Ulysses S. Grant*, edited by John Y. Simon. 31 vols. Carbondale: Southern Illinois University Press, 1967–2008.

———. *Personal Memoirs of U.S. Grant*, edited by E. B. Long. New York: Da Capo Press, 1982.

Green, Virginia. "Reminiscences of Sherman's Raid." In Smythe, Poppenheim, and Taylor, *South Carolina Women in the Confederacy*, 351–356. Columbia, SC: State Company, 1903.

Greene, A. Wilson. *Civil War Petersburg. Confederate City in the Crucible of War*. Charlottesville and London: University of Virginia Press, 2006.

———. *The Final Battles of the Petersburg Campaign: Breaking the Backbone of the Rebellion*. Knoxville: University of Tennessee Press, 2008.

Hampton, Lieutenant General Wade. "The Battle of Bentonville." In Johnson and Buel, *Battles and Leaders*, vol. 4, 700.

Hardy, Michael C. *The Thirty-seventh North Carolina Troops: Tar Heels in the Army of Northern Virginia*. Jefferson, NC: McFarland & Company, 2003.

Harper's Weekly magazine. Serial. New York: Harper & Brothers, 1857–1916.

Harrell, Roger H. *The 2nd North Carolina Cavalry*. Jefferson, NC: McFarland & Company, 2004.

Hartwell, John F. L. *To My Beloved Wife and Boy at Home: The Letters and Diaries of Orderly Sergeant John F. L. Hartwell*, edited by Ann Hartwell Britton and Thomas J. Reed. Cranbury, NJ: Associated University Presses, 1997.

Hattaway, Herman, and Archer Jones. *How the North Won: A Military History of the Civil War*. Urbana: University of Illinois Press, 1983.

Haynes, Edwin Mortimer. *A History of the Tenth Regiment, Vermont Volunteers*. Rutland, VT: The Tuttle Company, 1894.

Hergesheimer, Joseph. *Sheridan: A Military Narrative*. Boston, New York: Houghton Mifflin, 1931.

Hess, Earl J. *In the Trenches at Petersburg: Field Fortifications & Confederate Defeat*. Chapel Hill: University of North Carolina Press, 2009.

Hesseltine, William B. *Ulysses S. Grant, Politician*. New York: Dodd, Mead & Company, 1935.

Heth, General Henry. *The Memoirs of Henry Heth*, edited by James L. Morrison Jr. Westport, CT: Greenwood Press, 1974.

Hill, G. Powell. "The First Burial of General Hill's Remains." In *Southern Historical Society Papers*, vol. 19, 183–186.

History of the 121st Regiment of Pennsylvania Volunteers: "An Account from the Ranks," edited by US Army. Philadelphia, PA: Press of the Catholic Standard and Times, 1906.

Hitchcock, Henry. *Marching with Sherman*. Lincoln: University of Nebraska Press, 1995.

The Holy Bible, Containing the Old and New Testaments. King James Version. New York: American Bible Society, 1980.

Holzer, Harold, Craig L. Symonds, and Frank J. Williams, eds. *The Lincoln Assassination: Crime and Punishment, Myth and Memory*. New York: Fordham University Press, 2010.

Hotchkiss, Jedediah. *Make Me a Map of the Valley: The Civil War Journal of Stonewall Jackson's Topographer*, edited by Archie P. McDonald. Dallas, TX: Southern Methodist University Press, 1973.

Houghton, Edwin B. *The Campaigns of the Seventeenth Maine*. Portland, ME: Short & Loring, 1866.

Howard, Oliver O. *Autobiography of Oliver Otis Howard, Major General United States Army*. 2 vols. New York: Baker & Taylor, 1908.

Hughes, Nathaniel Cheairs Jr. *Bentonville: The Final Battle of Sherman and Johnston*. Chapel Hill: University of North Carolina Press, 1996.

Hunter, R. M. T. "The Peace Commission—Hon. R. M. T. Hunter's Reply to Jefferson Davis' Letter." In *Southern Historical Society Papers*, vol. 4, 303–316.

Hyde, Thomas Worcester. *Following the Greek Cross, or, Memories of the Sixth Army Corps*. Boston, New York: Houghton, Mifflin, 1894.

Johnson, Andrew. *Papers of Andrew Johnson*. At The American Presidency Project, www.presidency.ucsb.edu/andrew_johnson.php.

Johnson, Clint. *Pursuit: The Chase, Capture, Persecution, and Surprising Release of Confederate President Jefferson Davis*. New York: Citadel Press, 2008.

Johnson, Robert Underwood, and Clarence Clough Buel, eds. *Battles and Leaders of the Civil War*. 4 vols. New York: Century, 1884–1888.

Johnston, Joseph. *Narrative of Military Operations, Directed During the Late War Between the States*. New York: D. Appleton and Company, 1874.

Jones, Major Evan Rowland. *Four Years in the Army of the Potomac: A Soldier's Recollections*. London: Tyne Publishing, 1881.

Jones, J. B. *A Rebel War Clerk's Diary at the Confederate States Capital*. New York: Old Hickory Bookshop, 1935.

Jones, John William. *Christ in the Camp: Or, Religion in Lee's Army*. Richmond, VA: B. F. Johnson & Co., 1888.

Joslyn, Mauriel Phillips. *Charlotte's Boys: Civil War Letters of the Branch Family of Savannah*. Gretna, Louisiana: Pelican Publishing Company, 1996.

Journal of the Congress of the Confederate States of America, 1861–1865. 7 vols. Washington, DC: US Government Printing Office, 1905.

Kauffman, Michael W. *American Brutus: John Wilkes Booth and the Lincoln Conspiracies*. New York: Random House, 2004.

Kean, Robert Garlick Hill. *Inside the Confederate Government. The Diary of Robert Garlick Hill Kean, Head of the Bureau of War*, edited by Edward Younger. New York: Oxford University Press, 1957.

Kendrick, Paul, and Stephen Kendrick. *Douglass and Lincoln: How a Revolutionary Black Leader and a Reluctant Liberator Struggled to End Slavery and Save the Union*. New York: Walker & Company, 2008.

Kerr, Colonel Charles D. "From Atlanta to Raleigh." In *Military Order of the Loyal Legion of the United States*, Minnesota Commandery, vol. 1, 202–223.

Kimbrough, J. S. "From Petersburg to Hart's Island Prison." In *Confederate Veteran*, vol. 22 (1914), 498–500.

Kreiser, Lawrence A., Jr. *Defeating Lee: A History of the Second Corps, Army of the Potomac*. Bloomington: Indiana University Press, 2011.

Krick, Robert. *The 14th South Carolina Infantry Regiment of the Gregg-McGowan Brigade, Army of Northern Virginia*. Wilmington, NC: Broadfoot Publishing, 2008.

Lamb, Col. William. "The Defense of Fort Fisher." In Johnson and Buel, *Battles and Leaders*, vol. 4, 642–654.

LeConte, Emma. *When the World Ended*. Lincoln: University of Nebraska Press, 1987.

Lee, Robert E. *Lee's Dispatches: Unpublished Letters of General Robert E. Lee, C.S.A., to Jefferson Davis and the War Department. From the Private Collection of Wymberley Jones De Renne*. New York: G. P. Putnam's Sons, 1915.

———. *The Wartime Papers of Robert E. Lee*, edited by Clifford Dowdey and Louis H. Manarin. New York: Bramhall House, 1961.

Lewis, Lloyd. *Sherman, Fighting Prophet*. New York: Harcourt, Brace and Company, 1932.

Lincoln, Abraham. *Collected Works of Abraham Lincoln*, 8 vols, edited by Roy P. Basler. New Brunswick, NJ: Rutgers University Press, 1953.

Little, Henry F. W. *The Seventh Regiment New Hampshire Volunteers in the War of the Rebellion*. Concord, NH: Ira C. Evans, 1896.

Logan, Kate Virginia Cox. *My Confederate Girlhood: The Memoirs of Kate Virginia Cox Logan*. Richmond, VA: Garrett & Massie, 1932.

Long, Armistead Lindsay. *Memoirs of Robert E. Lee, His Military and Personal History*, edited by Marcus J. Wright. London: Sampson Low, Marston, Searle, and Rivington, 1886.

Long, E. B., and Barbara Long. *The Civil War Day by Day: An Almanac, 1861–1865*. Garden City, NY: Doubleday & Company, 1971.

Longacre, Edward G. *The Cavalry at Appomattox*. Mechanicsburg, PA: Stackpole Books, 2003.

———. *Custer and His Wolverines. The Michigan Cavalry Brigade, 1861–1865*. Conshohocken, PA: Combined Publishing, 1997.

Longstreet, James. *From Manassas to Appomattox: Memoirs of the Civil War in America*. Philadelphia, PA: J. B. Lippincott Company, 1908.

Lonn, Ella. *Desertion During the Civil War*. Lincoln, NE, and London: University of Nebraska Press, 1998. First published in 1928.

Lowry, Thomas P. "Not Everybody Mourned Lincoln's Death." In Holzer, Symonds, and Williams, *The Lincoln Assassination: Crime and Punishment, Myth and Memory*, 95–114.

Lyman, Theodore. *Meade's Army: The Private Notebooks of Lt. Col. Theodore Lyman*, edited by David W. Lowe. Kent, OH: Kent State University Press, 2007.

———. *Meade's Headquarters, 1863–1865: Letters of Colonel Theodore Lyman from the Wilderness to Appomattox*, edited by George R. Agassiz. Boston: Atlantic Monthly Press, 1922.

Marshall, Colonel Charles. "General Lee's Farewell Address to his Army." In Johnson and Buel, *Battles and Leaders*, vol. 4, 747.

———. *Lee's Aide-de-Camp*, edited by Frederick Maurice. Lincoln: University of Nebraska Press, 2000.

Marszalek, John F. *Sherman: A Soldier's Passion for Order*. New York: Free Press, 1993.

Marvel, William. *Lee's Last Retreat: The Flight to Appomattox*. Chapel Hill: University of North Carolina Press, 2002.

Matthews, James P. "How General A. P. Hill Met His Fate." In *Southern Historical Society Papers*, vol. 27, 26–38.

McAllister, Anna Shannon. *Ellen Ewing, Wife of General Sherman*. New York: Benziger Brothers, 1936.

McFeely, William S. *Grant: A Biography*. New York, London: W. W. Norton & company, 1982.

McGuire, Judith Brockenbrough. "Diary of a Southern Refugee during the War, June 1863–July 1864," edited by James I. Robertson Jr. in *Virginia at War, 1864*, edited by Robertson and William C. Davis, 159–224. Lexington: University of Kentucky Press, 2009.

McKim, Randolph H. *A Soldier's Recollections. Leaves from the Diary of a Young Confederate*. New York: Longmans, Green, and Co., 1911.

McPherson, James M. *Battle Cry of Freedom. The Civil War Era*. New York, Oxford: Oxford University Press, 1988.

———. *Ordeal by Fire: The Civil War and Reconstruction*. New York: Alfred A. Knopf, 1982.

———. *Tried by War: Abraham Lincoln as Commander in Chief*. New York: Penguin Press, 2008.

———. *War on the Waters: The Union & Confederate Navies, 1861–1865*. Chapel Hill: University of North Carolina Press, 2012.

Meade, George. *The Life and Letters of George Gordon Meade, Major-General United States Army*. 2 vols. New York: Charles Scribner's Sons, 1913.

Melcher, Major Holman S. *With a Flash of the Sword: The Writings of Major Holman S. Melcher, 20th Maine Infantry*, edited by William B. Styple. Kearny, NJ: Belle Grove Publishing, 1994.

Merington, Marguerite, ed. *The Custer Story: The Life and Intimate Letters of General George A. Custer and His Wife Elizabeth*. New York: Devin-Adair, 1950. Reprinted by Bison Books, 1987.

Miers, Earl Schenck, ed. *Lincoln Day by Day, a Chronology, 1809–1865*. 3 vols. Washington, DC: Lincoln Sesquicentennial Commission, 1960.

Military Order of the Loyal Legion of the United States. *War Papers*. 70 vols. Wilmington, NC: Broadfoot Publishing, 1991–1997.

Mitchell, Betty L. *Edmund Ruffin: A Biography*. Bloomington: Indiana University Press, 1981.

Morris, Roy Jr. *Sheridan: The Life and Wars of General Phil Sheridan*. New York: Crown Publishers, 1992.

Muffly, Joseph Wendel, ed. *The Story of Our Regiment: A History of the 148th Pennsylvania Volunteers, "Written by the Comrades."* Des Moines, IA: Kenyon Printing & Mfg., 1904.

Mulholland, Colonel St. Clair A. *The Story of the 116th Regiment Pennsylvania Volunteers in the War of the Rebellion*. New York: Fordham University Press, 1996.

Newhall, F. C. *With General Sheridan in Lee's Last Campaign*. Philadelphia, PA: J. B. Lippincott & Co., 1866.

Newsome, Hampton. *Richmond Must Fall: The Richmond-Petersburg Campaign, October 1864*. Kent, OH: Kent State University Press, 2013.

Nichols, Brevet Major George Ward. *The Story of the Great March, from the Diary of a Staff Officer*. New York: Harper & Brothers, 1865.

Nicolay, John G., and John Hay. *Abraham Lincoln, A History*. 10 vols. New York: Century, 1890.

Oates, Stephen B. *With Malice Toward None: A Life of Abraham Lincoln*. New York: HarperCollins, 1994.

O'Connor, Richard. *Sheridan the Inevitable*. Indianapolis, New York: Bobbs-Merrill, 1953.

Osborn, Thomas. *The Fiery Trail: A Union Officer's Account of Sherman's Last Campaigns*. Knoxville: University of Tennessee Press, 1986.

Owen, William Miller. *In Camp and Battle with the Washington Artillery of New Orleans*. Gretna, LA: Pelican Publishing, 1998. Originally published in 1885.

Parker, Francis Jewett. *The Story of the Thirty-Second Regiment, Massachusetts Infantry*. Boston: C. W. Calkins & Co., 1880.

Parsons, George W. *Put the Vermonters Ahead: The First Vermont Brigade in the Civil War*. Shippensburg, PA: White Mane Publishing, 1996.

Pember, Phoebe Yates. *A Southern Woman's Story: Life in Confederate Richmond*, edited by Bell Irvin Wiley. Jackson, TN: McCowat-Mercer Press, 1959. Originally published in 1879.

Pendleton, William Nelson. *Memoirs of William Nelson Pendleton, D.D.: Rector of Latimer Parish*, edited by Susan Pendleton Lee. Philadelphia, PA: J. B. Lippincott, 1893.

Pfanz, Donald C. *Abraham Lincoln at City Point, March 20–April 9, 1865*. Lynchburg, VA: H. E. Howard, 1989.

Pitch, Anthony S. *"They Have Killed Papa Dead!" The Road to Ford's Theatre, Abraham Lincoln's Murder, and the Rage for Vengeance*. Hanover, NH: Steerforth Press, 2008.

Pollard, Edward A. *The Lost Cause: A New Southern History of the War of the Confederates*. New York: E. B. Treat & Co., 1868.

Polley, Joseph Benjamin. *Hood's Texas Brigade: Its Marches, Its Battles, Its Achievements*. Dayton, OH: Press of Morningside Bookshop, 1988.

Porter, Admiral David Dixon. *Incidents and Anecdotes of the Civil War*. New York: D. Appleton and Co., 1885.

Porter, General Horace. *Campaigning with Grant*. Abridged. New York, Toronto, London: Bantam Books, 1991.

——. *Campaigning with Grant*. Unabridged. New York: Century, 1907.

——. "The Surrender at Appomattox Court House." In Johnson and Buel, *Battles and Leaders*, vol. 4, 729–746.

Powell, William Henry. *The Fifth Army Corps (Army of the Potomac)*. New York: G. P. Putnam's, 1896.

Power, J. Tracy. *Lee's Miserables: Life in the Army of Northern Virginia from the Wilderness to Appomattox*. Chapel Hill: University of North Carolina Press, 1998.

Putnam, Sallie Brock. *Richmond During the War: Four Years of Personal Observation*. Lincoln: University of Nebraska Press, 1996. Originally published in 1867.

Ratchford, James Wylie. *Memoirs of a Confederate Staff Officer: From Bethel to Bentonville,* edited by Evelyn Ratchford Sieburg. Shippensburg, PA: White Mane Books, 1998.

The Reconstruction Amendment Debates. The Legislative History and Contemporary Debates in Congress on the 13th, 14th and 15th Amendments. Richmond: Virginia Commission on Constitutional Government, 1987.

Rhodes, Elisha Hunt. *All for the Union: The Civil War Diary and Letters of Elisha Hunt Rhodes*. New York: Vintage Books, 1992.

Rice, Allen Thorndike, ed. *Reminiscences of Abraham Lincoln by Distinguished Men of His Time*. New York: North American Review, 1888.

Richardson, James D., ed. *A Compilation of the Messages and Papers of the Confederacy, including the Diplomatic Correspondence, 1861–1865*. 2 vols. Nashville, TN: US Publishing Company, 1906.

Richardson, Sarah Aldrich. "The Burning of the Ursuline Convent by Sherman." In Smythe, Poppenheim, and Taylor, *South Carolina Women in the Confederacy*, 298–319. Columbia, SC: State Company, 1903.

Risley, Ford, ed. *The Civil War: Primary Documents on Events from 1860 to 1865*. Westport, CT: Greenwood Press, 2004.

Robertson, James I., Jr. *General A. P. Hill: The Story of a Confederate Warrior*. New York: Random House, 1987.

Sandburg, Carl. *Abraham Lincoln: The War Years*, vol. 4. New York: Harcourt, Brace & World, 1939.

Schaff, Morris. *The Sunset of the Confederacy*. Boston: J. W. Luce and Co., 1912.

Schurz, Carl. *The Reminiscences of Carl Schurz, 1829–1869*. 3 vols. New York: McClure, 1907–1908.

Selfridge, Captain Thomas O., Jr. "The Navy at Fort Fisher." In Johnson and Buel, *Battles and Leaders*, vol. 4, 655–661.

Semmes, Admiral Raphael. *Memoirs of Service Afloat, During the War Between the States*. Baltimore, MD: Kelly, Piet & Co., 1869.

Seward, William, and Frederick Seward. *Seward at Washington, 1861–1872*. New York: Derby and Miller, 1891.

Sheridan, Philip H. *Papers of Philip Henry Sheridan*. Washington, DC: Library of Congress. 104 microfilm reels, 1985.

———. *Personal Memoirs of P. H. Sheridan, General, United States Army*. 2 vols. New York: Charles L. Webster & Company, 1888.

Sherman, William Tecumseh. *Home Letters of General Sherman*, edited by M. A. DeWolfe Howe. New York: Charles Scribner's Sons, 1909.

———. *Memoirs of General William T. Sherman*. 2 vols. New York: D. Appleton and Company, 1875.

———. *Sherman's Civil War: Selected Correspondence of William T. Sherman, 1860–1865*, edited by Brooks D. Simpson and Jean V. Berlin. Chapel Hill: University of North Carolina Press, 1999.

Simms, William Gilmore. *Sack and Destruction of the City of Columbia, S.C.* Columbia, SC: Power Press of Daily Phoenix, 1865.

Simson, Jay W. *Crisis of Command in the Army of the Potomac: Sheridan's Search for an Effective General*. Jefferson, NC, and London: McFarland & Company, 2008.

Sloan, Richard E. "Abraham Lincoln's New York City Funeral." In Holzer, Symonds, and Williams, *The Lincoln Assassination: Crime and Punishment, Myth and Memory*, 55–93.

Smith, Jean Edward. *Grant*. New York: Simon & Schuster, 2006.

Smythe, Mrs. A. T., Miss M. B. Poppenheim, and Mrs. Thomas Taylor, eds. *South Carolina Women in the Confederacy*. Columbia, SC: State Company, 1903.

Sorrel, Gilbert Moxley. *Recollections of a Confederate Staff Officer*. New York: Neale Publishing, 1905.

Southern Historical Society Papers, 52 vols. Richmond, VA: Southern Historical Society, 1876–1959.

Spencer, Cornelia Phillips. *The Last Ninety Days of the War in North Carolina*. New York: Watchman Publishing, 1866.

Starr, Stephen Z. *The Union Cavalry in the Civil War: Vol. 2: The War in the East from Gettysburg to Appomattox, 1863–1865*. Baton Rouge: Louisiana State University Press, 1979.

Stephens, Alexander Hamilton. *A Constitutional View of the Late War Between the States*. 2 vols. Philadelphia, PA: National Publishing, 1870.

Stern, Philip Van Doren. *An End to Valor: The Last Days of the Civil War*. Boston: Houghton Mifflin, 1958.

Stevens, George Thomas. *Three Years in the Sixth Corps*. Albany, New York: S. R. Gray, 1866.

Stiles, Robert. *Four Years Under Marse Robert*. New York: Neale Publishing, 1904.

Stokes, Karen. *South Carolina Civilians in Sherman's Path*. Charleston, SC, and London: History Press, 2012.

Stone, DeWitt Boyd, ed. *Wandering to Glory: Confederate Veterans Remember Evans' Brigade*. Columbia: University of South Carolina Press, 2002.

Strong, George Templeton. *The Diary of George Templeton Strong: The Civil War, 1860–1865*, vol. 3, edited by Allan Nevins and Milton Halsey Thomas. New York: MacMillan, 1952.

Sulivane, Captain Clement. "The Fall of Richmond." In Johnson and Buel, *Battles and Leaders*, vol. 4, 725–726.

Swanson, James L. *Bloody Crimes: The Chase for Jefferson Davis and the Death Pageant for Lincoln's Corpse*. New York: William Morrow, 2010.

———. *Manhunt: The 12-Day Chase for Lincoln's Killer*. New York: Harper Perennial, 2006.

Symonds, Craig L. *Joseph E. Johnston: A Civil War Biography*. New York: W. W. Norton & Company, 1992.

Taylor, Lieutenant General Richard. *Destruction and Reconstruction: Personal Experiences of the Late War*. New York: D. Appleton and Company, 1879.

Taylor, Walter H. *Four Years with General Lee*. Bloomington: Indiana University Press, 1996. First published in 1878.

———. *General Lee: His Campaigns in Virginia, 1861–1865*. Brooklyn, New York: Braunworth & Co., 1906.

———. *Lee's Adjutant: The Wartime Letters of Colonel Walter Herron Taylor, 1862–1865*. Columbia: University of South Carolina Press, 1995.

Thomas, Emory. *The Confederate Nation, 1861–1865*. New York: Harper & Row, Publishers, 1979.

———. *Robert E. Lee: A Biography*. New York, London: W. W. Norton & Company, 1995.

Titone, Nora. *My Thoughts Be Bloody: The Bitter Rivalry Between Edwin and John Wilkes Booth That Led to an American Tragedy*. New York: Free Press, 2010.

Tobie, Edward P. *History of the First Maine Cavalry, 1861–1865*. Boston: Emery & Hughes, 1887.

Tremain, Henry Edwin. *Last Hours of Sheridan's Cavalry*. New York: Bonnell, Silver & Bowers, 1904.

Trezevant, Daniel Heyward. *The Burning of Columbia, S.C.* Columbia: South Carolinian Power Press, 1866.

Trudeau, Noah Andre. *The Last Citadel: Petersburg, Virginia, June 1864–April 1865*. Boston: Little, Brown and Company, 1991.

———. *Out of the Storm. The End of the Civil War, April–June 1865*. Boston, New York: Little, Brown and Company, 1994.

———. *Southern Storm: Sherman's March to the Sea*. New York: HarperCollins, 2008.

Tucker, G. W. "Death of General A. P. Hill." In *Southern Historical Society Papers*, vol. 11, 564–569.

United States Naval War Records Office. *Official Records of the Union and Confederate Navies in the War of the Rebellion*. Washington, DC: US Government Printing Office. 30 vols, 1894–1922. Available online through the Cornell Library website at http://ebooks.library.cornell.edu/m/moawar/ofre.html.

United States War Department. *The War of the Rebellion: a Compilation of the Official Records of the Union and Confederate Armies*. 128 vols. Washington, DC: US Government Printing Office, 1880–1901. Available online through the Cornell Library website at http://ebooks.library.cornell.edu/m/moawar/waro.html.

Upson, Theodore. *With Sherman to the Sea: The Civil War Letters, Diaries & Reminiscences of Theodore F. Upson*. Baton Rouge: Louisiana State University Press, 1943.

Urwin, Gregory J. W. *Custer Victorious: The Civil War Battles of General George Armstrong Custer*. Rutherford, NJ: Fairleigh Dickinson University Press, 1983.

Van Lew, Elizabeth. *A Yankee Spy in Richmond: The Civil War Diary of "Crazy Bet" Van Lew*, edited by David Ryan. Mechanicsburg, PA: Stackpole Books, 1996.

Varon, Elizabeth R. *Appomattox: Victory, Defeat, and Freedom at the End of the Civil War*. New York: Oxford University Press, 2014.

———. *Southern Lady, Yankee Spy: The True Story of Elizabeth Van Lew, a Union Agent in the Heart of the Confederacy*. New York: Oxford University Press, 2003.

Venable, Colonel Charles S. *Papers*. Chapel Hill: Southern Historical Collection, University of North Carolina-Chapel Hill.

Vorenberg, Michael. *Final Freedom: The Civil War, the Abolition of Slavery, and the Thirteenth Amendment*. Cambridge: Cambridge University Press, 2001.

Wadsworth, Mike. *The 13th South Carolina Volunteer Infantry, C.S.A.* Wilmington, NC: Broadfoot Publishing, 2008.

Wainwright, Charles S. *A Diary of Battle: The Personal Journals of Colonel Charles S. Wainwright, 1861–1865*, edited by Allan Nevins. New York: Da Capo Press, 1998. Originally published in 1962.

Walker, James. "Gordon's Assault on Fort Stedman." In *Southern Historical Society Papers*, vol. 31, 19–30.

Ward, Dallas T. *The Last Flag of Truce*. Franklinton, NC: private printing, 1915.

Warner, Ezra J. *Generals in Blue. Lives of the Union Commanders*. Baton Rouge: Louisiana State University Press, 2006. Originally published in 1964.

———. *Generals in Gray. Lives of the Confederate Commanders*. Baton Rouge: Louisiana State University Press, 2000. Originally published in 1959.

Weekly News and Courier, Charleston, SC. *Our Women in the War: The Lives They Lived; the Deaths They Died*. Charleston, SC: The News and Courier Book Presses, 1885.

Welles, Gideon. *Diary of Gideon Welles, Secretary of the Navy under Lincoln and Johnson*. 3 vols. Boston, New York: Houghton Mifflin, 1909–1911.

Wert, Jeffry D. *Custer: The Controversial Life of George Armstrong Custer*. New York: Simon & Schuster, 1996.

Wheelan, Joseph. *Bloody Spring: Forty Days That Sealed the Confederacy's Fate*. Boston: Da Capo Press, 2014.

———. *Libby Prison Breakout: The Daring Escape from the Notorious Civil War Prison*. New York: PublicAffairs, 2010.

———. *Terrible Swift Sword: The Life of General Philip A. Sheridan*. Cambridge, MA: Da Capo Press, 2012.

Wheeler, Richard. *Witness to Appomattox*. New York: Harper & Row, 1989.

Whitman, Walt. *Complete Poetry and Selected Prose*, edited by James E. Miller Jr. Boston: Houghton Mifflin, 1959.

Whitney, David C., and Robin Vaughn Whitney. *The American Presidents*. New York: Prentice Hall, 1993.

Wiatt, William Edward. *Confederate Chaplain William Edward Wiatt: An Annotated Diary*. Lynchburg, VA: H. E. Howard, 1994.

Wilkeson, Frank. *Turned Inside Out: Recollections of a Private Soldier in the Army of the Potomac*. Lincoln: University of Nebraska Press, 1997.

Williams, T. Harry. *Lincoln and the Radicals*. Madison: University of Wisconsin Press, 1941.

Williamson, James J. *Mosby's Rangers: A Record of the Operations of the Forty-Third Battalion of Virginia Cavalry*. New York: Ralph B. Kenyon, 1896.

Wills, Brian Steel. *A Battle from the Start: The Life of Nathan Bedford Forrest*. New York: HarperCollins, 1992.

Wills, Charles W. *Army Life of an Illinois Soldier*. Carbondale: Southern Illinois University Press, 1996. Originally published in 1906.

Wilson, James Harrison. *The Life of John A. Rawlins, Lawyer, Assistant Adjutant-General, Chief of Staff, Major General of Volunteers, and Secretary of War*. New York: Neale Publishing, 1916.

Wilson, Mark R. *The Business of Civil War: Military Mobilization and the State, 1861–1865*. Baltimore, MD: Johns Hopkins University Press, 2006.

Winik, Jay. *April 1865: The Month That Saved America*. New York: HarperCollins, 2001.

Wise, Henry. "The Career of Wise's Brigade." In *Southern Historical Society Papers*, vol. 25, 1–22.

Wise, John S. *The End of an Era*. Boston: Houghton, Mifflin, 1899.

Wittenberg, Eric J. *Little Phil: A Reassessment of the Civil War Leadership of General Philip H. Sheridan*. Washington, DC: Brassey's, 2002.

INDEX